CW01308721

Camden House History of German Literature

Volume 5

*German Literature of the Eighteenth Century:
The Enlightenment and Sensibility*

The Camden House History of German Literature

Volume 5

The Camden House History of German Literature

Edited by James Hardin

Vol. 1: Early Germanic Literature and Culture
Edited by Brian Murdoch and Malcolm Read,
University of Stirling, UK

Vol. 2: German Literature of the Early Middle Ages
Edited by Brian Murdoch, University of Stirling, UK

Vol. 3: German Literature of the High Middle Ages
Edited by Will Hasty, University of Florida

Vol. 4: Early Modern German Literature
Edited by Max Reinhart, University of Georgia

*Vol. 5: German Literature of the Eighteenth Century:
The Enlightenment and Sensibility*
Edited by Barbara Becker-Cantarino, Ohio State University

Vol. 6: Literature of the Sturm und Drang
Edited by David Hill, University of Birmingham, UK

Vol. 7: The Literature of Weimar Classicism
Edited by Simon Richter, University of Pennsylvania

Vol. 8: The Literature of German Romanticism
Edited by Dennis Mahoney, University of Vermont

Vol. 9: German Literature of the Nineteenth Century, 1832–1899
Edited by Clayton Koelb and Eric Downing,
University of North Carolina

*Vol. 10: German Literature of the Twentieth Century:
From Aestheticism to Postmodernism*
Ingo R. Stoehr, Kilgore College, Texas

German Literature of the Eighteenth Century

The Enlightenment and Sensibility

Edited by
Barbara Becker-Cantarino

CAMDEN HOUSE

Copyright © 2005 by the Editor and Contributors

All Rights Reserved. Except as permitted under current legislation, no part of this work may be photocopied, stored in a retrieval system, published, performed in public, adapted, broadcast, transmitted, recorded, or reproduced in any form or by any means, without the prior permission of the copyright owner.

First published 2005
by Camden House

Camden House is an imprint of Boydell & Brewer Inc.
668 Mt. Hope Avenue, Rochester, NY 14620, USA
www.camden-house.com
and of Boydell & Brewer Limited
PO Box 9, Woodbridge, Suffolk IP12 3DF, UK
www.boydellandbrewer.com

ISBN: 1–57113–246–5

Library of Congress Cataloging-in-Publication Data

German literature of the eighteenth century: the enlightenment and sensibility / edited by Barbara Becker-Cantarino
  p. cm. — (Camden House history of German literature; v. 5)
Includes bibliographical references and index.
ISBN 1–57113–246–5 (hardcover: alk. paper)
  1. German literature — 18th century — History and criticism.
2. Enlightenment — Germany. 3. Enlightenment — Influence.
I. Becker-Cantarino, Barbara. II. Title. III. Series.

PT289.G45 2005
830.9'006—dc22

2004019948

A catalogue record for this title is available from the British Library.

This publication is printed on acid-free paper.
Printed in the United States of America.

Contents

Illustrations · vii

Preface and Acknowledgments · ix

Introduction: German Literature in the Era of Enlightenment and Sensibility · 1
Barbara Becker-Cantarino

Enlightenment Thought and Natural Law from Leibniz to Kant and its Influence on German Literature · 33
Kai Hammermeister

Gottsched's Literary Reforms: The Beginning of Modern German Literature · 55
Katherine Goodman

The Literary Marketplace and the Journal, Medium of the Enlightenment · 79
Helga Brandes

Religious and Secular Poetry and Epic (1700–1780) · 105
Kevin Hilliard

Literary Developments in Switzerland from Bodmer, Breitinger, and Haller to Gessner, Rousseau, and Pestalozzi · 131
Rosmarie Zeller

Lessing, Bourgeois Drama, and the National Theater · 155
Francis Lamport

Musical Culture and Thought · 185
Sarah Colvin

The Era of Sensibility and the Novel of Self-Fashioning   223
Anna Richards

Enlightenment in Austria: 245
Cultural Identity and a National Literature
Franz M. Eybl

Eighteenth-Century Germany in its Historical Context   265
W. Daniel Wilson

The Legacy of the Enlightenment: Critique from   285
Hamann and Herder to the Frankfurt School
Robert Holub

Bibliography	309
Primary Literature	309
Secondary Literature	317
Contributors	329
Index	331

Illustrations

"Family Entertainment." Painting by Daniel Chodowiecki, 1757 — xii

Immanuel Kant. Etching by F. W. Bollinger, 1781 — 32

Johann Christoph Gottsched and Luise Adelgunde Victorie, anonymous painting, ca. 1740 — 54

First issue of the moral weekly *Die vernünftigen Tadlerinnen* — 78

Title page spread, Anna Louisa Karsch, *Auserlesene Gedichte* — 104

Alpine landscape, copperplate after painting by Caspar Wolf — 130

Illustrations to Lessing's *Minna von Barnhelm*, by Daniel Chodowiecki — 154

Flute concert at Sanssouci, painting by Adolf Menzel — 184

Sophie La Roche, ca. 1772. Drawing by anonymous artist — 222

Josef Anton Stranitzky as Hanswurst — 244

"Tolerance." Allegorical engraving by Daniel Chodowiecki — 264

Johann Gottfried Herder, painting by Anton Graff — 284

Preface and Acknowledgments

COMPRISING THE ERA OF ENLIGHTENMENT AND SENSIBILITY, this volume serves as a major new reference work providing a fresh look at major literary figures, works, and cultural developments from around 1700 up to the literature of the late Enlightenment (*Spätaufklärung*) in up-to-date scholarly essays. These trace literary developments in eighteenth-century German-speaking countries from occasional and learned literature under the influence of French Neoclassicism to the establishment of a new German drama, religious epic, and secular poetry, and the sentimentalist novel of self-fashioning. The volume gives due attention to the newly recognized, stimulating works of women, and contains a chapter on music and literature, chapters on literary developments in Switzerland and in Austria, and concludes with a chapter on changing philosophical attitudes toward the Enlightenment up to the present. The recent re-evaluation of cultural and social phenomena affecting literary works informs the presentations in the individual chapters and allows for the inclusion of hitherto neglected but important texts not considered in older literary histories, works such as essays, travelogues, philosophical texts, and letters.

Thanks are due to the distinguished contributors to this volume who brought their expertise in the diverse aspects of eighteenth-century studies to their chapters and situated them within the framework of the overall design of the Camden House History of German Literature. I owe a sincere debt to the editor of the Camden House History of German Literature, James Hardin, for his indispensable advice and assistance in the preparation of this volume and to Camden House editor Jim Walker for his technical advice. For their thoughtful suggestions, I am indebted to the participants of the Roundtable "Writing a Literary History of the Enlightenment in Germany for an English-Speaking Audience" at the XI. Congress on the Enlightenment held at the University of California, Los Angeles in August 2003. The essays in this volume benefited from colleagues' responses to earlier drafts.

Ohio State University provided research support over many years, in particular by granting a sabbatical leave for work on this volume. My special thanks go to the Alexander von Humboldt Foundation, whose Research Award has made possible numerous research trips to Germany and other locations in Europe during the past decade to conduct my research into early modern and eighteenth-century German literature and culture. This support was instrumental in allowing me to attend specialized workshops and conferences, give lectures, and meet with colleagues in Germany, England, and Poland. In particular I thank Hans-Gert Roloff (Berlin), Wilfried Barner (Göttingen), Klaus Garber (Osnabrück), Wolfram Mauser and Axel Aurnhammer (Freiburg), and Wolfgang Sauder (Saarbrücken) for their advice and interest in my research. Last but not least, in early 2003 a Director's Invitation from the Herzog August Bibliothek in Wolfenbüttel enabled me to work in the peaceful and studious environment of the fabulous collection of that library. I am indebted to Helwig Schmidt-Glintzer and Gillian Bepler for enabling my work there.

Barbara Becker-Cantarino
Columbus, Ohio, 2004

Note on Translations

On first occurrence, titles of German works are followed by a translation and the date of first publication in parentheses. When an English translation exists, that title has been used, but in most cases titles have been translated anew, following closely the original German wording for the information of the reader. The same applies to original German quotations; all are followed by a close English translation by the author of the respective chapter, unless an existing translation is credited.

*"Family Entertainment." A daughter reads aloud for the family.
Painting by Daniel Chodowiecki, 1757.*

Introduction:
German Literature in the Era of Enlightenment and Sensibility

Barbara Becker-Cantarino

The Scope of German Literature in the Eighteenth Century

RICHARD RORTY HAS REMARKED about the Enlightenment, the cultural and philosophical movement most associated with the eighteenth century: "It is sometimes said that the Enlightenment project has failed. But there were two Enlightenment projects — one political and one philosophical. One was to create heaven on earth: a world without caste, class, or cruelty. The other was to find a new, comprehensive, worldview which would replace God with Nature and Reason. The political project has not failed, although it is proceeding very slowly [. . .]. The second, philosophical project is being pursued . . ."[1] However we assess the success or failure of the Enlightenment, the eighteenth century stands out for its important and decisive cultural developments, the effects of which are still felt today.[2] Within a span of about a hundred years, the Age of Enlightenment, as the eighteenth century is usually referred to, brought intellectual and social changes based on the use of reason, common sense, and natural law. These were paralleled by an emphasis on morality, feelings, and the emotions in religious, especially Pietist circles. Progressive thinkers in England, France, and later in Germany began assailing the orthodoxy and authority of the Church and the absolutism of rulers; in Germany the line led from Thomasius, Leibniz, and Wolff to Lessing and Kant, to the advocacy of religious tolerance, the demand for emancipation of the bourgeois individual, and the rise of an educated bourgeois middle class. Literary developments encompassed the emergence of a shared literary language, a bourgeois, secular literature and a national (German-language) theater. This was made possible by advances in literacy and education, especially among bourgeois women, and the reorganization of book production and the book market.

Although often identified solely with the Enlightenment, its most prominent philosophical movement, "the eighteenth century is plural," and has many faces.[3] There is no singular literary work or phase that might signal a clear-cut beginning or distinct ending on which scholars of German literature could nowadays easily agree. Strict periodization and dividing lines appear more problematic today than ever before. Literary periods do not live by dates, and in selecting works or authors whose spirit or works would embody a specific period or set of literary characteristics, we encounter anomalies and anachronisms. Were the poets Johann Christian Günther (1695–1723) and Anna Luisa Karsch (1722–1791) such anomalies, since their poetry can hardly be regarded as enlightened? Was Klopstock's epic *Der Messias,* whose first cantos appeared in 1748, really *the* beginning of modern German literature? Or is the literary classification of "Empfindsamkeit" (sensibility) more appropriate here, and are we to dwell on a dichotomy between Enlightenment and Sensibility? And what about Kant's famous essay "Was ist Aufklärung?" (What is Enlightenment?, 1784) and the intense discussion of Enlightenment during the 1780s that coincided with what is usually called the Storm and Stress movement. Which "story" are we to tell about eighteenth-century German literature when we are aware that every selection of works and authors and every developmental thread or connectivity is but a subjective story, albeit one transmitted by tradition. Differing from older literary historians, we are today especially careful in making claims about historical truth. Moreover, literary and cultural phenomena are now being read as "texts," and the distinction between literary and non-literary texts has largely disappeared or become less important. Avoiding teleological views of literary history, we can no longer reiterate the formerly progressive view according to which all things lead up to the present moment, or in terms of the eighteenth century, lead up to what was for a long time *the* Age of Goethe, the presumed peak of genuine, "deep" German culture: German Classicism and Romanticism (more about this below).

Any literary history serves a pragmatic goal, that of codification, transmission, and teaching in the humanities, and must consider and address its readers' expectations. Thus, it requires pragmatic decisions about periodization, setting a beginning and end, selecting representative topics and materials, and presenting a cohesive, reasoned narrative. Given the vast store of texts, data, and scholarship, it requires as much selectivity and deliberate omission as it begs for justification of the material chosen and how it is represented.[4] The Camden House History of German Literature decided to include in each multi-authored volume a collection of essays offering the expertise of a number of specialists. The diversity of perspectives represented here decreases the chance of exclusion, and brings out the significance of a subject and era.

Following the most convenient and by now established timeline, the present volume begins with the eighteenth century as distinct from the previous century's "baroque era" or the "early modern" period (now the more common term in German literary scholarship).[5] But it is important to remember that eighteenth-century German literature developed in what might be seen as gradual transformation from the learned literature on one hand and the religious, devotional texts of the seventeenth century on the other. With the publications of the legal scholars Samuel Pufendorf (1632–1694) and Christian Thomasius (1655–1728), a new fashion in philosophy, the theories of natural law (a body of law held to be derived from nature and from man's reason, not from God, and binding for human society in addition to divine law) ushered in the early stages of the Enlightenment.[6] Thomasius was the instigator of Enlightenment in Germany who did not hesitate to criticize the weaknesses of monarchy, argued for limitations, and held reason to be necessarily social and sociable ("gesellig"); rulers should listen to reason and the state should become subject to natural law.[7]

Important works were published at this threshold of a new era in German intellectual history, as Klaus Garber has recently reminded us:[8] on Church history (Gottfried Arnold's *Unpartheyische Kirchen- und Ketzer-Historie,* Impartial History of the Church and Heretics, 1688–99), on national education and culture (Leibniz's *Ermahnung an die Teutschen, ihren Verstand und Sprache besser zu üben,* Exhortations to the Germans to Make Better Use of Their Reason and Language, 1697), and on the Christian egalitarian state (Thomasius's *Das Recht Evangelischer Fürsten in theologischen Streitigkeiten,* The Right of Protestant Princes in Theological Disputes, 1697). The traditions of radical religious renewal, of Humanism and the movement of learned societies merged with early modern political theory in the writings of a new community of enlightened citizens—a significant, albeit small group of intellectuals. Thus, it seems appropriate to open the present literary history of German-speaking countries in the eighteenth century with a presentation of the Enlightenment as a cultural and philosophical movement from Thomasius and Leibniz to Kant in the essay by Kai Hammermeister, which reveals the transformations and lasting impact of the period.

As important as the intellectual traditions around 1700 were, they were transmitted and elaborated in philosophical and religious texts, not in major fictional or poetic works. The German *literary* canon rarely recognized them and excludes the flood of popular, gallant novels, poetry, operas, school plays, and a large body of devotional literature from about 1680 to 1720.[9] It was Johann Christoph Gottsched (1700–1760) who effectively proclaimed and worked for a "new" beginning in German literature patterned on French neo-classical models and enlightened principles, while conveniently negating, devaluing, and forgetting what had preceded him.[10] In many respects, his amazing career as innovator, editor, critic, author, reformer, and, last but not least, Leipzig university professor signaled a new beginning, as Katherine Goodman elaborates in her essay. A "self-made" man, Gottsched exemplified the rise of an educated, bourgeois class in eighteenth-century Germany. As the story goes, the exceptionally tall "Magister" left his hometown Königsberg (East Prussia) to escape Prussian recruiters who were drafting recruits for the "Soldier King's" (Friedrich Wilhelm I) tall palace guard. In 1724 Gottsched appeared in Leipzig, the commercial and cultural center of Saxony with its thriving book fair and university, where Gottsched — with his unusual learning, talent for lecturing, writing, and sense of organization — rose to professor of rhetoric and poetry at a leading German university. His prolific publications and efforts on behalf of German-language literature — including women readers in his literary program — had a lasting influence on eighteenth-century German literary culture of the rising bourgeois class that lies at the heart of this volume's presentation of German eighteenth-century literature.[11]

By analyzing bourgeois literary culture, we leave aside the elaborate festival culture at the larger and smaller courts — the tournaments, processions, opera, drama, ballet, fireworks, horse ballet, masquerade, and musical performances especially in Vienna, Dresden, Munich, Stuttgart and other residential cities.[12] However, Sarah Colvin's essay on musical culture in eighteenth-century Germany presents what was the most prominent, lasting, and outstanding artistic aspect of court culture: music. The study and performance of music, usually singing and playing an instrument (the clavichord and early forms of the piano, flute, and the violin) became a favorite cultural activity among the educated bourgeois. Upper-middle-class women sang and performed in private settings only — as professional singers they shared the bad reputation of actors. Some, like patrician Christiane Mariane von Ziegler in Leipzig in the 1720s and 1730s, had music salons of their own. At the same time, festive, dramatic, and artistic entertainment for the nobility continued to flourish throughout the eighteenth century, activities, of course, to which only persons admitted to court had access. Non-aristocrats — like Gottsched or Lessing — were naturally excluded, and they then fostered a bourgeois literary culture quite independently and for a different reading public.[13] The rift between court and bourgeois literary culture can be seen in Lessing's inability in the 1750s to establish himself in Berlin as head of the Royal Library and in Friedrich's disdain for Lessing and German literature in his *De la Littérature Allemande* (1780).[14]

But then bourgeois literary culture, characterized by its enlightened, distinctively middle-class values — gradually infiltrated the courts and replaced the (mostly French and Italian) festival culture by the end of the eighteenth century. The court of the tiny principality of Sachsen-Weimar-Eisenach (largely due to the efforts of Duchess Anna Amalia, a niece of Friedrich II's) became the best known cultural center, as it attracted and employed Wieland, Goethe, Herder, and later Schiller. Lessing's most acclaimed bourgeois drama *Emilia Galotti* (1772) was first performed in homage to his employer's wife — the Duchess of Braunschweig-Wolfenbüttel, sister of Friedrich II — on her birthday, but *Emilia Galotti* was hard pressed to compete with the Duke's preference for French and Italian ballerinas and opera divas. Lessing was not pleased by the circumstances surrounding its staging and did not attend the performance.[15] This drama subsequently enjoyed tremendous success on the stage of the Hamburg Nationaltheater with a bourgeois audience. Its presentation of the Galotti family embodies the new bourgeois, enlightened values, while the figures of the Prince and his secretary Marinelli show an implicit criticism of the aristocracy's lack of humanity and morality, even though the play by no means advocates revolution. Francis Lamport's essay deals with Lessing and the development of the rich tradition of bourgeois drama from the 1730s to the 1770s.

The rise of a bourgeois literature and with it the shift away from court culture and from learned and devotional literature would not have been possible without the creation of a large, new reading public, the proliferation of journals, and a reorganization of the book trade. Helga Brandes takes up that topic in her essay. Kevin Hilliard's essay on religious and secular poetry and epic analyzes the second major cultural strand in eighteenth-century German literature: the fashion of "Empfindsamkeit" (Sensibility) with its predilection for sensitivity, human sentiments, pathos, and virtue. Already in the first half of the eighteenth century, there existed a rich body of verse, some by young (would-be) lovers on the seemingly eternal "wine, women, and song" themes, and some by women. The religious tradition was still strong and was instrumental in helping Klopstock's *Messias* (1748) to unprecedented success. There was also religious poetry in the Lutheran song tradition of Paul Gerhardt (1607–1676) as well as more learned poetry like the Swiss Albrecht von Haller's (1708–1777). Rosmarie Zeller's essay addresses Haller's poetry theses along with other original developments in Switzerland, like Johann Jakob Bodmer's (1698–1783) poetological reflections, and the emergence of the myth of Switzerland celebrating freedom and nature, in which Enlightenment ideas seem to blend effortlessly with the new Sensibility.

In the heterogeneous picture of eighteenth-century German literature, the rise of an Austrian national literature, running parallel with the Prussian-Austrian military conflicts and enduring rivalry, is the subject of Franz M. Eybl's essay. Although "Josephinism," the liberal, productive phase under the rule of Joseph II (1780–1790) came late in the century and has more often that not been excluded from accounts of German literary history, its seminal importance has since been acknowledged. It encompassed the high point of the "Catholic Enlightenment," a variant of the northern German

Protestant scene with colorful anti-clerical and patriotic works and the development of a popular theater. While already in the 1770s the generation of young Goethe (born in 1749) rebelled against their (literary) fathers in what has been called Storm and Stress, other authors continued to experiment with fiction, biography, and letters, often eclectically using enlightened and sentimental features.[16] Anna Richards's essay deals with the development of the sentimental, self-fashioning novel, including Wieland, Moritz, and two major women writers, Sophie La Roche and Friederike Helene Unger. Dan Wilson's essay assesses cultural developments leading up to the French Revolution and the end of the century.

There was no clearly discernable "end" to Enlightenment and Sensibility, nor to eighteenth-century German literature as such, just as there had been no easily definable beginning. Variously, the French Revolution in 1789, Napoleon's dissolution of the Holy Roman Empire in 1806, and (in more literary terms) the appearance of the Friedrich Schlegel's *Athenäum* in 1798 and his proclamations of Romanticism as a new literary school could be seen to mark "the end" of the eighteenth century. Yet much of Romanticism — its subjectivity and individualism; its fascination with friendship, love, and sexuality; its obsession with fantasy and imagination; its concept of the poet as genius and priest; its exploration of femininity and masculinity — had begun or been anticipated in works of Sensibility. Moral values and ethical concepts of the Enlightenment lived on in German Classicism and Romanticism. The Enlightenment, already in its day highly contested as a cultural and philosophical movement, had its critics (and enemies and detractors) throughout the eighteenth century. The controversy has lingered on into our times. Thus it is only fitting to conclude the volume with Robert Holub's essay on the various forms of critique of the Enlightenment over the past two centuries.

The Enlightenment as a Cultural and Literary Period

A history of eighteenth-century German literature must look at the origin, usage, and meaning of the two traditional classifications, Enlightenment and Sensibility, and consider their points of convergence and divergence. Although the penchant for strict classifications, lists of characteristics, unequivocal judgments, and standard interpretations in earlier histories has given way to today's literary scholars' preference for crossing boundaries, unstable margins, ambiguities, and subversive readings, these earlier classifications have left their stamp on standard reference works, editions, handbooks and on many of our — often unconscious — notions and valuations of literary texts and periods. The origin and history of the terms Enlightenment and Sensibility are part of the shifting, unstable views on eighteenth-century German literature.

Enlightenment refers to the dominant philosophical movement of the eighteenth century *and* to the cultural (including the literary) production at large that is influenced by this body of thought. Enlightenment as a cultural and literary period is of interest here in what then-contemporary writers called "the philosophical century."[17] Based on a light metaphor, the German word "aufklären" closely parallels the English "enlighten." Christoph Martin Wieland explained to the readers of his *Teutscher Merkur* in 1789 that everyone knew the meaning of the word "Aufklärung," who "vermittelst eines Paars sehender Augen erkennen gelernt hat, worin der Unterschied zwischen Hell und Dunkel, Licht und Finsternis besteht. Im Dunkeln sieht man entweder gar nichts oder wenigstens nicht so klar, daß man die Gegenstände recht erkennen und voneinander unterscheiden kann: sobald Licht gebracht wird, klaren sich die Sachen auf, werden sichtbar und können voneinander unterschieden werden"[18] (by means of a pair of eyes that see has learned to recognize the difference between brightness and dark, light and darkness. In the dark one either sees not at all or at least not clearly enough so that one can recognize objects and can distinguish them from one another). Light was considered the sphere of cognition and reason, night the realm of irrational fantasies, when already Gottsched in his *Critische Dichtkunst* (Critical Poetics, 1730) declared that magic and fairy tale figures no longer belonged in his enlightened century. Light was to be spread through the print media.

The Enlightenment was an ongoing project. It was based on the free use of reason and empiricism and aimed at fostering scholarship and the sciences. The age was marked by an inherent optimism and an intense questioning of religious ritual and doctrine. This new skepticism led gradually to secularization, the separation of the individual from the dogma and authority of the Church. It generated a belief in universal human progress and in the essentially good, and thus educable nature of the human being. The new worldview was thought capable of ushering in an age of self-fashioning and of education (*Bildung*). Kant's emphasis on man's critical faculties gave rise to dubbing the Enlightenment "Zeitalter der Kritik" (the age of criticism),[19] whose "most characteristic mode of expression was witty, informed, and didactic."[20] In Germany the term "Aufklärung" established itself as a period designation as a result of Hegel's Berlin lectures on the history of philosophy and religion in the 1820s.[21]

Romantic authors rebelled against what they perceived as sheer rationalism and the anti-religious attitudes of the Enlightenment. They considered themselves the true, original poets, the beginning of German literature.[22] But early on Heinrich Heine took a broader cultural view emphasizing "Geistesfreihheit und Protestantismus" (freedom of thought and Protestantism) that belonged together like "Mutter und Tochter" (mother and daughter).[23] Lessing became a symbolic figure, as did Kant when German literature and German national identity were linked by the Young Germans of the 1840s, the liberal, patriotic writers who strove for a united and democratic German nation. For one of the first great literary historians, Georg Gottfried Gervinus (1805–1873), who wrote the enduring *Geschichte der poetischen National-Literatur der Deutschen* (History of the Poetic National Literature of the German People), the eighteenth century was the rebirth of German literature under the influence of religiosity, ethics, and criticism.[24] The Storm and Stress became the German revolution as it sought vigorously to compare and equal German and French intellectual and literary achievements.[25] Gervinus's patriotic history grew out of the intense German-French rivalry of the nineteenth century and out of the longing for a strong, unified, democratic German national state. For such a vision, the classical age of Kant, Goethe, and Schiller appeared as the pinnacle and fulfillment of a true German humanity that was ready for such a new state.

Later nineteenth-century German literary historians like Hermann Hettner (1821–1882)[26] and Wilhelm Scherer (1841–1886)[27] applauded reunification under Bismarck in the German Empire under Prussian leadership and elevated the Age of Goethe and German Classicism to the peak of German literature. Nietzsche criticized this patriotic, optimistic, liberal concept of German literature; he called Gervinus "eine dumme Gans" (a stupid goose) and abhorred the contemporary historicism of philologists like Hettner and Scherer, describing them as "das ganze historische Gesindelpack" (the rabble pack of historians).[28] Nevertheless, the patriotic view of German literature as ascending from its nadir in the seventeenth century to its zenith in the Age of Goethe with the eighteenth-century as its anti-chamber has dominated German literary history throughout most of the twentieth century. The English translation of Scherer's work published by Scribner's in 1887 and its several reprints until 1971 have helped entrench this view also in Anglo-American students of German.[29]

With the neo-Romantic movement at the turn of the century and Wilhelm Dilthey's influential *Das Erlebnis und die Dichtung*[30] (Poetry and Experience, 1907), Romanticism was reevaluated and included as a major, "deep" and characteristically German literary period, the ultimate fulfillment of a process that began with the *German* Enlightenment. For decades to come, Dilthey's teleological view, according to which all German literary and cultural developments lead up to the great Age of Goethe, to classicism, Romanticism, and German idealism, reigned supreme.[31] His insistence on a hermeneutic approach to the study of literature made "Geisteswissenschaft" (search for the spirit, for ideas) the fashionable literary theory in Germany.[32] Dilthey's category "Erlebnis" (personal experience, intuition, inwardness) became the standard for valorizing poetic texts and individual authors as an expression of genuine human experience. Thus, Goethe's poetry was characterized as "Erlebnisdichtung," the poetry of experience, and set up as a model by which more formalistic and less subjective verses that were considered poetic and beautiful in baroque and eighteenth-century literature before Goethe, came to be judged as stale, artificial, and uninteresting.

Alongside this view, dismissive attitudes toward eighteenth-century literature and Enlightenment culture were common around 1900, attitudes that considered the eighteenth century an imperfect, "alien" stepping stone toward classicism and Romanticism. Critics pointed to the supposedly "un-German" French rationalism of German eighteenth-century literature, and detected in it shallow and superficial English empiricism. In short, the valuation of periods began to take a nationalistic turn. The cultural philosopher Hermann Nohl (1879–1960) spoke of three generations of German "Geistesgeschichte" from 1770 to 1830 as the "Deutsche Bewegung" (German movement) comprising the era of Storm and Stress, Classicism, and Romanticism when the "genuine" German spirit manifested itself and set German literature apart from the "foreign" Enlightenment under the influence of France and England.[33] Already in the 1920s the prolific German scholar Heinz Kindermann (1896–1978) had diagnosed a "Durchbruch der deutschen Seele" (a breakthrough of the German soul) in Pietism and Storm and Stress.[34] Soon thereafter Hermann August Korff's initial two volumes of his influential *Geist der Goethezeit* (Spirit of the Age of Goethe, 1923 and 1930) toned down the rhetoric of a genuine Germanic culture and nation that would feed right into National Socialist ideology, and instead propagated an ideal beauty as "die ganze Formel für den Weg, auf dem die deutsche Klassik emporgestiegen ist: Freiheit, Gesetz, Schönheit und Entwicklung!"[35] (the very formula for the path by which German classicism rose up high: freedom, lawfulness, beauty and development!). The trajectory of such idealization remained a comforting interpretation in post-war Germany and beyond.

Periodization in terms of national characteristics has become obsolete; nevertheless the valorization of classicism and Romanticism as the model, the most creative, aesthetic period of what has been termed "the invention of aesthetic autonomy" persists.[36] Since the 1960s there have been trends to historicize and politicize literary investigation and to apply sociology and social history to the study of literature,[37] yet more recent scholarship on eighteenth-century German literature shows a renewed interest in the works themselves,[38] in literary sociability and reading,[39] in mentality and anthropology,[40] gender questions,[41] institutions,[42] and everyday history.[43] Major developments during the Enlightenment have been recognized and investigated: the reliance on reason; the importance and development of education; the role of scholarship, science, and investigation; the process of secularization, the diminishing authority of the Church and of religious writings, anti-clericalism, the fight against superstition.[44] New forms of religious thinking are being analyzed: the subjectivist form of Christian devotion, Pietism, Physico-Theology, Neology, Deism, and Pantheism;[45] and exploration continues apace in new, optimistic concepts of a moral human being; new freedoms for the individual; changes in the public sphere; and new forms of organization, political theory, and statehood. All aspects and effects of man's faculty of reason, a search for ultimate truth, and virtue and morality came to characterize German literature of the Enlightenment. Literature was to teach virtue in a pleasing way; it was as much subject to rules and laws (Gottsched's program of neoclassicism) as the role of the imagination and the marvelous was recovered and aesthetics established (Breitinger's *Critische Dichtkunst*, Lessing, Kant). Poetry was often mimetic, didactic (Haller), but also religious, enthusiastic (Klopstock), entertaining and occasional (Karsch), patriotic, fervent (Gleim), and entertaining, witty, erotic (Wieland). Verse forms popular with readers were the religious epic (Klopstock), the comic epic (Wieland), the fable (Gellert) and the epigram (Lessing). Tragedy developed from the models proposed in Gottsched's *Deutsche Schaubühne* to the bourgeois tragedy showing the new, enlightened, middle-class values and family settings (even though the protagonists were often minor aristocrats, the plot derived from classical literature, and sentimental feeling dominated). With Luise Gottsched's comedies to Gellert's, Wieland's, and Lessing's plays, virtue, moral standards, a certain didacticism, but also compassion, wit, and humor prevailed. Prose forms such as moral tales, essays, travel narratives, idylls, fairy tales, and biographical stories filled the moral weeklies, journals, and almanacs. The novel, including translations from English and French, gained in popularity with readers and became more respectable as a literary genre in the eyes of critics.[46] The genre took on increasingly bourgeois, subjective, autobiographical traits and themes, such as the family, marriage, gender relations, father-son and father-daughter conflicts, and education. Integration problems of young intellectual men were reflected in literary texts from Lessing's *Der junge Gelehrte* (The Young Scholar, 1748) to Moritz's *Anton Reiser* (1785), while women authors took up socialization problems of young women from an insider's perspective as reflected in one of the first popular woman's novels, Friderike Helene Unger's *Julchen Grünthal: Eine Pensionsgeschichte* (A Boarding School Story, 1784).

There is no clearly drawn boundary between Enlightenment and Sensibility, though the latter gained increasing influence in fictional and poetic texts by the 1760s. Enlightenment dominated more in philosophy and the public sphere, Sensibility became the trademark for literature and domestic culture.

"Empfindsamkeit": An Era of Sensibility[47]

"Empfindsam" (sentimental, sensible) became a popular phrase in Lessing's age (mid-eighteenth century) — its coinage in German was even (wrongly) attributed to him.[48] "Empfindsam" denoted the penchant for both morality and emotion, a conflation of reason and an emotional impulse or feeling leading to an opinion or principle. A person might be called an "empfindsame Seele" (a sensitive soul), a literary work "eine empfindsame Lektüre" (a sensible read), and letters "empfindsame Briefe" (sentimental letters). In 1757 Louise Adelgunde Victorie Gotttsched (1713–1762) wrote to her friend Dorothea Henriette von Runckel (1724–1800):

> Ein empfindsames Herz gehört unter die geheimen Beschwerlichkeiten dieses Lebens, es leydet bei allen leidenden Gegenständen, wenn es sich außer Stand siehet, allen zu helfen. Und doch möchte ich dieser Leiden ohngeachtet, und die kein Arzt helfen kann, kein gleichgültig Gemüth haben. Wie viel wahres Vergnügen entbehren die kalten unempfindlichen Seelen.[49]

> [A sensitive heart belongs to the hidden discomforts of our life, it suffers with all suffering objects when unable to help everywhere. And yet, even considering these sufferings that no doctor can cure, I do not wish to be indifferent. The cold and unfeeling souls, how much true pleasure do they miss out on!]

Considered the model of a "gelehrte Frau" (learned lady) and an enlightened woman in her day, even the "Gottschedin" used the conventional metaphor of the heart to describe sensible feelings as an essential complement to reason. "Empfindsam" became the fashionable term and attitude in the latter half of the eighteenth century when *Yoricks empfindsame Reise durch Frankreich und Italien* (translated by Johann Joachim Christoph Bode in 1769) popularized Laurence Sterne's *Sentimental Journey* (1768) in Germany. "Empfindsam" denoted a delicate emotional and physical susceptibility, refined, tender feelings (whose expression was termed "Zärtlichkeit," tenderness), and an immediate, emotional display of sympathy for suffering. Sensibility was in alliance with true virtue, was man's moral sense; a sympathetic heart showed the genuine human quality of empathy and stood for the belief that mankind was not innately self-serving, but benevolent. With sensibility, a human being could perceive and respond to the beautiful and better appreciate art and literature.

Sensibility also denoted a person's special sensuous quality, an "innate sensitiveness or susceptibility revealing itself in a variety of spontaneous activities such as crying, swooning and kneeling."[50] This form of sensibility was thought to be physically based, to affect the organization of the nervous system, and to turn easily into "Empfindelei" (sentimentality), a fashionable illness as the educational author and professor Joachim Heinrich Campe (1746–1818) explained in his essay *Ueber Empfindsamkeit und Empfindelei in pädagogischer Hinsicht* (Concerning Sensibility and Sentimentality in Pedagogy, 1779). Too much sentiment would detract from the faculty of reasoning; sensibility was not only complimentary to, but in excess could also conflict with and be detrimental to sound, enlightened judgment if feelings were merely cultivated for their own sake and enjoyment ("Empfindelei"). Enlightened educators like Campe preached the use of reason, pointing out the destructive and debilitating consequences of the emotions, and deriding such public display of feeling as tears and swooning, often called womanish and associated with women, though by no means exclusively so. Yet women were considered more prone to crying, blushing, fainting, and hysteria, the "female disease": "The entire female body is riddled by obscure but strangely direct paths of sympathy [. . .] from one extremity of its organic space to the other, it encloses a perpetual possibility of hysteria. The sympathetic sensibility of her organism [. . .] condemns woman to [. . .] diseases of the nerves," as Michel Foucault described the eighteenth-century concept of hysteria.[51] Early in the century English moral weeklies already stressed the special female association with sensibility: "Women were formed to temper Mankind, and sooth them into Tenderness and Compassion."[52] Female virtues were the superior ones, but they were to be used for the benefit of men. The probings into female sensibility and moral sense in Richardson's *Pamela* and *Clarissa* and in Rousseau's *La Nouvelle Héloïse* constructed the fashionable female sensibility; Rousseau especially insisted on the sentimental gender distinction, a seemingly biological absolute that separated, according to Rousseau, female from male physically, mentally, and emotionally.

"Empfindsamkeit" became also the designation for the literary period from about 1730 to 1800 with its heyday from about 1740 to 1780. The literary circles around Martin Bodmer in Zurich, the messianic poet Klopstock in Hamburg and northern Germany, the young Wieland from his days in Biberach to Erfurt (both Klopstock and Wieland visited and paid homage to Bodmer in Zurich). The poet Gleim and his friendship circle in Halberstadt wrote often in the fashionable style of Sensibility. Gellert's "rührende" (moving) comedies, which brought audiences to tears (like the French *comédie larmoyante*) and Lessing's play *Miß Sara Sampson* (1755) in which the wayward daughter, faithless lover, and the deserted father are all motivated by feelings and passions and all find, understand, and forgive each other in the end (though they do not live happily ever after) were fine examples of the sentimental genre. Bestsellers in their time included such sentimental novels as Sophie La Roche's *Geschichte des Fräuleins von Sternheim* (The History of Lady Sophia Sternheim, 1771) and, of course, Goethe's *Die Leiden des jungen Werther* (1774), the first German-language novel of international (European) acclaim in the eighteenth century *after* the moving, sentimental epic *Der Tod Abels: In fünf Gesängen* (The Death of Abel in Five Cantos, 1758) by the Swiss Salomon Gessner (1730–1788) whose pathos and religiosity were a sign of the religious, Pietist heritage of "Empfindsamkeit."[53] Parodies of the sentimental fashion soon appeared; best known of the parodies is Friedrich Nicolai's (1733–1811) novel *Freuden des jungen Werthers* (1775, The Pleasures of Young Werther) and Goethe's own playful *Der Triumph der Empfindsamkeit* (1777, revised 1786). The cult of feelings ushered in modern psychology, as Karl Philip Moritz (1757–1793) pioneered in his *Magazin der Erfahrungsseelenkunde* (Magazine for Knowing the Soul, 1783–93).[54]

As a cultural and literary movement, "Empfindsamkeit" has not enjoyed the same degree of attention and discussion in traditional histories as the Enlightenment (the era of Gottsched and especially Lessing and the Berlin enlighteners Mendelssohn and Nicolai) has. The philosophical underpinnings of "Empfindsamkeit" appear less prominent, though the susceptibility to tender feelings, to the beautiful, and the notion that man had a moral sense, near reason but also close to intuition, had been the subject of the Earl of Shaftesbury's (1621–1683) rhapsodic, immensely influential writings and English moral-sense philosophy. The literature that followed in its wake, like the moralistic novels of Samuel Richardson — *Pamela* (1740–41), *Clarissa* (1747–48), and *Sir Charles Grandison* (1753–54) — were also influential in Germany. Lessing published a translation of the Scottish Francis Hutcheson's *A System of Moral Philosophy* (1755) as early as 1756. Lessing's interpretation of Aristotle's notion of *katharsis* as outlined in his *Hamburgische Dramaturgie* (1767–68) may well have been influenced by moral-sense philosophy.[55] Lessing maintained that the effect of tragedy was to arouse in the spectator pity for others and fear for ourselves; the tragic effect was not so much cathartic, purging emotions, as educative, cultivating the abilities of the audience to feel. Pity and compassion for others was a hotly debated topic in the 1750s when Rousseau's *Discours sur l'inégalité* (1755) conceived it as a natural human sentiment, an instinctive emotional compassion for other people's misery, an emotion that the "savage" still knew and applied, but that modern man had lost in the civilization process. Rousseau became the dominant influence on popular sentimental thought focusing on sensibility as special and refined susceptibility — a complex, refined character trait and intuitive capacity that especially women protagonists in his novels exemplified and popularized.

Until recently, historians of German literature expressed relatively little interest in Pietism, the other source of "Empfindsamkeit," nor in religion and religious literature in general. Because of the nationalistic misreading of Pietism as an expression of the "German soul" and because of Marxist leanings, social historians of the generation of the student revolt (the so-called "68ers") neglected the religious aspects of the eighteenth century and stressed its social and secular components. Their literary histories, like Rolf Grimminger's *Deutsche Aufklärung bis zur Französischen Revolution 1680–1780* (The German Enlightenment up to the French Revolution)[56] or the one-volume *Deutsche Literaturgeschichte* (1989)[57] (*A History of German Literature from the Beginnings to the Present Day,* 1992)[58] omitted a period designation of "Empfindsamkeit" altogether and replaced it by a revalued, "liberal" Storm and Stress. In the meantime new research and discussions have taken up the role and nature of "Empfindsamkeit," its relationship to the Enlightenment, and its significance in eighteenth-century literature including Pietism and the substantial body of devotional and autobiographical literature it produced.[59] In its heyday from about 1690 to about 1750, the subjective, mystical, emotional religiosity of "the heart" that defied dogmatic orthodoxy spread (in Protestant areas) far beyond the organized Pietist groups like Nikolaus Ludwig von Zinzendorf's Moravian Brethren in Herrnhut and Herrnhag or August Hermann Francke's schools in Halle. Jacob Spener's call to reforms, *Pia desideria* (Pious Wishes, 1655), Johann Heinrich Reitz's *Historie der Wiedergebohrnen* (History of the Reborn, 1698), among others, and Pietist hymns were read widely and left their mark on the German language and on literary texts.[60]

Gerhard Sauder's study and text collection entitled *Empfindsamkeit* (1974) has had a lasting effect because he presented a coherent, historical development close to actual texts and because he consulted and published a large selection of (mostly little known) poetic and theoretical texts in conjunction with his history.[61] Sauder saw a close connection between the rise and social emancipation of the bourgeois (Bürgertum) and the culture of Sensibility.[62] He stressed their goal of achieving an equilibrium between "head and heart," of fostering the development of a reasonable, empathetic, and virtuous individual and the attendant moral values, sociability, and friendship in family and society. For Sauder, Enlightenment culture (not philosophy) and Sensibility were two sides of the same coin: Sensibility was Enlightenment's turn to the inner human being. Sensibility was a logical reaction, an outgrowth, or parallel development to Enlightenment as far as the literary culture of the newly prominent, educated, urban middle class was concerned. Sauder acknowledged the influence of English moral-sense philosophy and downplayed the influence of Pietism. He dismissed the view that the process of secularization of Pietism resulted in a secular emotionalism that celebrated the senses and the sensual.

There have been few major modifications of Sauder's work on Sensibility.[63] Lothar Pikulik's *Leistungsethik contra Gefühlskult* (Ethics of Achievement Versus the Cult of Feelings, 1984) diagnosed an exaggerated, confining turn to the inner man and an estranged, unworldly egocentricity in the era of Sensibility that could *not* serve as a potentially emancipatory cultural trajectory.[64] Pikulik saw the return of feelings and emotions as a counter-effect against an already civilized aristocracy and bourgeoisie, the cultivation of sentimentality an end in itself: feelings for the sake of feelings. Pikulik presented a narrow view of Sensibility in which the one extreme type of the sensitive individual was seen mostly through the eyes of contemporary criticism of the excesses. In a recent essay Pikulik has modified his position, or rather shifted his focus to the ongoing debate about the emotions.[65] He explains Sensibility's movement toward emancipation and autonomy not as a function of Enlightenment, but rather as a way for sensitivity to emancipate itself from reason and become autonomous by posing the emotional sphere as an alternative to reason. In this evolutionary, cultural process, Moses Mendelssohn's *Briefe über die Empfindungen* (Letters on the Emotions, 1755) with its concept of "vermischte Empfindung" (mixed feelings) provided a new insight: the parallelism of "Lust und Leid" (joy and sorrow) and "Lust *am* Leid" (joy *of* sorrow) produced "Rührung" (sympathy), the enjoyment of a tragic subject as in watching a tragedy. Sensibility then is the self-experience of feeling, distinct from both reason and sensuality. The eighteenth century distinguished not only between spheres of values, but also between the spheres of the mind, a plausible conclusion that will surely have to be refined with a broader basis of texts.

In a detailed presentation and interpretation of poetry from the sixteenth century to the end of the eighteenth, Hans-Georg Kemper devoted one volume to *Empfindsamkeit,* showing the close interrelationship of Pietism and Sensibility.[66] Kemper makes an excellent case for the enduring, symbiotic relationship between religion and German lyrical poetry throughout much of the eighteenth century, citing for instance the emotionalism in Pietist verses such as Nikolaus Ludwig von Zinzendorf's *Teutsche Gedichte* (1735) and their echo in the collection by Immanuel Jakob Pyra (1715–1744) and Samuel Gotthold Lange (1711–1781) *Thirsis und Damons freundschaftliche Lieder* (Thirsis's and Damon's Friendship Songs, 1745) and in Klopstock's *Geistliche Lieder* (Spiritual Songs, 1758).[67] Adaptations, intertextuality, and transformations of Pietist hymns establish the close relationship between the often mystic, emotional language with its body, love, and sexuality metaphors and their transference into verses by Klopstock, Gellert, the young Wieland, and other poets of the same generation.

The recent interest in anthropology has found fertile historical ground in the eighteenth century. Using discourse analysis, communication theory, literary anthropology, and sexuality studies, Albrecht Koschorke rereads "Empfindsamkeit" in his monumental *Körperströme und Schriftverkehr: Mediologie des 18. Jahrhunderts* (Body Currents and Script Traffic: Mediology of the Eighteenth Century, 1999) as a shift in the circulation of social energies.[68] Koschorke first describes (well-known) changes in social interaction in the nobility and the bourgeois with regard to conversation, gallantry, and love that lead to a closure of the body. This type of closure strengthened the body and enabled self-control as seen in the new, enlightened bourgeois concept of virtue.[69] Tears became substitutes for other bodily effusions, a form of sublimation in a culture of empathy and compassion. The rise of literacy and the bourgeois reading culture produced a turn away from bodily fluids to sensations of the soul, from desire and passion to sensibility and sociability. Writing belonged to the process of substitutions, and no longer competed with orality, but rather created new forms of communication. The debate about reading signaled the split of self-consciousness of enlightened literary culture, according to Koschorke a duality like that of nature and culture (with reference to Julie's garden in Rousseau's *Julie*). In other words, Koschorke first constructs a development of bodies closing themselves off from one another, then conceptualizes them as a closed, self-referenced system, and in a third step shows a substitution of the exchange of bodies by the medium of writing; the body is replaced by the written text. Koschorke's study may have linked his reading of the eighteenth century to modern media studies, but it has not produced any startling new, nor coherent interpretation as its abstraction clouds historic specificity and textual detail. By the same token, it nevertheless shows the richness of that literature and its possibilities for subjective, novel, creative readings and associations using the gamut of currently fashionable theories. This will surely find students and followers.

Eighteenth-Century Literary Culture, Gender, and the Rise of "Schöne Literatur" (*Belles Lettres*)

Recent research and reevaluations of eighteenth-century German literature have established the importance of the development of a bourgeois literary culture with the rise of literacy (especially among women), changes in the book market and in the public sphere, the importance of letters and letter writing and of friendship, the beginnings of modern authorship, the shift from devotional to secular literature: the development of "Schöne Literatur" that became *the* entertaining and formative (even educational) pastime (together with music). Since it has also been called a "feminization of literary culture" by some, it seems important to address the new role of women.[70] They were instrumental in the rise of *belles lettres* and by the same token literature became a stepping stone and a medium for women's beginning cultural (not political) emancipation in eighteenth-century Germany. The interdependence of the rise of a young, mostly female reading public coupled with an increase in women writing and the flourishing of *belles lettres*—poetry and songs, bourgeois drama and comedy for the professional stage, experimental dramatic forms for lay groups, stories, essays, novels, and letters — comprised the literary culture of Sensibility.

Friedrich Gottlieb Klopstock's (1724–1803) readings were legendary in his day. He was "von liebenswürdigen Leserinnen zugleich liebkost und verehrt" (at the same time beloved and venerated by amiable women readers) as evidenced in his detailed description of one such reading in the garden of a wealthy Magdeburg merchant "in einem Ringe von Mädchen, die entfernter von Männern umschlossen waren.[. . .] Wie man dann mit Händeklatschen, mit Entzückungen und mit Tränen Fanny lobte, so sah ich auf schwimmende Augen um mich herum, wie auf Elysäer Felder"[71] (in a circle of young women who were surrounded by young men at some distance.[. . .] When they applauded and praised Fanny [Klopstock's beloved], I was looking at teary eyes around me as if in the Elysian fields). It was a social occasion, a garden party with entertainment for a select group of educated, upper middle class friends — a typical setting for literary culture in mid-eighteenth-century Germany. In a theatrical self-stylization the poet Klopstock saw himself as the center of attention; his audience was a mixed one, young, and emotionally aroused by his poetry.[72] For Klopstock, religion became poetry and poetry became religion, a religion for a lay, especially a female audience. The emotional reaction, the mixed audience of young women and men who enjoyed Klopstock signaled the shift away from learned theologians (who had little use for Klopstock's theology and effusions) to a secular audience. Klopstock's inventive, original vocabulary, his pathos, his enthusiastic and mystic, dark language, his exalted and often contrived images without a specific dogmatic content appealed to a young lay audience with a Pietist upbringing who were equally leery of the theologian's dogmatic fights and the clergy's moralistic preaching. With his poetry and the epic *Messias,* Klopstock spoke the "language of the heart,"[73] and he polished his *Oden und Elegien* (1771) to fit the emotional needs and tastes of the new reading public.[74] Like his fellow authors Wieland, Herder, Voss, Spalding or Lavater, Klopstock used his poetic works to communicate and socialize with women; in 1771 he founded one of the very first reading societies for young women, who had been excluded from the numerous, flourishing reading societies in eighteenth-century Germany established by and for men alone, with statutory exclusion of women, students, and Jews. Reading and recitation of literature became a pastime in private social gatherings of mixed gender (scholars and theologians were exclusively male), literary sociability ("Geselligkeit") a new phenomenon in well-to-do bourgeois circles by the mid-eighteenth century.

The new literary sociability was due to a large extent to the spread of literacy among women, especially in the middle-class, that took place from about the 1730s on. In the seventeenth century, for the most part, only women of the nobility could read well, could patronize authors or write themselves, but with few exceptions only devotional verses and diary type chronicles.[75] There were no novels, dramas, or major *secular* poetry published by women in German before Luise Gottsched (born in 1713) and the generation of the somewhat younger Sophie von La Roche (born in 1730).[76] Both owed their unusual education and learning to ambitious, well-to-do and well-meaning fathers with a professional occupation. By about 1700, the religious instruction (catechism schools) required of all children except the very poor had provided most girls with some rudimentary literacy which included memorization of biblical passages and church songs, but this training was insufficient for sustained reading, let alone writing. When the enlighteners advocated women's education and emphasized the importance of literacy and reading — printing, for instance, suggestions for a lady's personal library such as the Hamburg moral weekly *Der Patriot* did in 1724 — well-to do bourgeois girls began receiving private tutoring (often together with their brothers). The general interest in education during the Enlightenment coincided with the Pietists' desire to read scriptures and devotional texts and fostered a reading ability that went beyond mere spelling. Changes in household chores and improved living conditions for upper middle-class women allowed reading to develop as a pastime, and eventually fostered a writing ability that far surpassed the rudimentary literacy skills still evident in the first third of the century in the older generation. For instance, mothers' letters to their famous sons, such as Justina Salome Lessing's (ca. 1700–1775) letters to Gotthold Ephraim (1729–1781), were still ungrammatical and riddled with spelling errors in the early 1700s.[77] But by 1783, literacy had become an essential skill and quality for middle class women and even reading quietly alone was considered an entertaining, useful pastime, not a learned, critical occupation;[78] or, as Sophie von La Roche explained to her women readers in "Ueber das Lesen" (On reading) in her journal *Pomona,* it was seen as a "stilles Lesen zur Erweiterung des Verstandes" (a quiet reading to widen the intellectual horizon).[79]

Reading ability was usually acquired first with religious literature and through reading aloud for others, as Friderika Baldinger (1739–1786), a parson's daughter from Langensalza, later married to a prominent professor of medicine in Marburg and Göttingen, elaborated in her "Versuch über meine Verstandeserziehung" (1791, Essay on My Intellectual Education). Baldinger described the time around 1750:

> Ich wünschte so gar gelehrt zu werden, und ärgerte mich, dass mich mein Geschlecht davon ausschloss. Je so willst du wenigstens klug werden, dachte ich, und dies wird man aus Büchern, du willst brav lesen. — Aber woher nun die Bücher, die mich klug machen sollten? Denn in einer Handelsstadt gabs keine. — Ich konnte überaus fertig lesen und konnte lesen eh ich sollte, ich glaube in meinem dritten Jahr

schon! Das von meiner Mutter immer für ein Wunder erkannt wurde. — Bei ihr wurde immer viel in der Bibel gelesen, und gebetet. Dies war mein Amt, weil ich mich auszeichnete und mit Empfindung las.[80]

[I wanted to become very learned and was annoyed that my sex was excluded from it. At least, you want to become sensible, I thought, and that one becomes through books. — But how could I get books that would make me sensible? In our industrial town there were none. — I was able to read extremely well, could read before I was supposed to, I believe when I was only three! My mother thought of this as a miracle. — There was much Bible reading with her and praying. That was my part, because I excelled and read with sentiment.]

Baldinger's statement demonstrates the shift from the older, enlightened concept of education for women as a way of becoming learned to the newer one as a way of acquiring sensibility or common sense. Books were a means of self-education, but around 1750 young girls obviously were no longer interested in religious books as their mother's generation which had read from the Bible and spent much time in prayer. Reading with "Empfindung" was appreciated and rewarded by Baldinger's Pietist uncle (he stood in for the deceased father as head of the household), who required the girl and her siblings to read a certain number of chapters from the Bible each day:

Dafür kriegte jedes von jedem Kapitel einen Pfennig. Die Mägde und meine Schwester schliefen gemeiniglich schon bei dem dritten Capitel fest, ich aber, durch den Beifall des Vetters und durch die vielen Pfennige aufgemuntert, las so lange, bis mich der Vetter selbst schweigen hies, und eben dadurch wurde meine Fertigkeit im lesen so sehr vergrössert. Ich las nun bei dem andern Vetter alles mit, was man mir vorlegte, und wurde nicht wenig bewundert, wenn ich die schweren Namen der alten Kayser, so ohne Anstand weg las.[81]

[Each one of us received for each chapter a penny. The maids and my sisters usually were fast asleep by the third chapter, but encouraged by my uncle's applause and the many pennies I read on until my uncle made me stop. This increased my reading ability very much. Then I read at another relative's house everything that was put in front of me, and I was admired for the way I read the difficult names of the ancient emperors without blinking an eye.]

This scene reflects the enduring importance of reading aloud from the Bible in the family circle. Until well into the eighteenth century, reading began with the Bible and religious literature, these formed the basis for literacy and writing. But history, stories, and fictional literature soon followed and became the preferred reading matter by the second half of the century. Baldinger's shift from the "gelehrt" (learned) to "klug" (sensible) also illustrates the typical orientation of German women's education in the course of the eighteenth century. Women had not received professional education nor advanced schooling, had not trained their minds with the study of classical literature, rhetoric, and sciences; instead, they had relied much more on instinct, common sense, emotions, introspection, compassion — qualities that religious practice and especially Pietism taught and required of them.

Unlike the growing class of "professional men," bourgeois women were not to become professionals (tutors, professors, lawyers, doctors, public officials, theologians), and by 1750 "learning" had become the exclusive province of men. A generation earlier, Louise Gottsched and a few selected, scholarly women were praised for their learning. But by mid-century the ideal shifted to the "schöne Seele" (beautiful soul), to the emotional qualities of woman, sensibility was considered the foremost and finest quality of woman.[82] In 1770 the then young theologian and aspiring author Johann Gottfried Herder wrote to Caroline Flachsland (1750–1809), who would later become his wife:

> So abscheulich in meinen Augen ein gelehrtes Frauenzimmer ist; so schön, dünkt mich, ists für eine zarte Seele, wie Sie, so feine Empfindungen nachfühlen zu können. Sie veredeln u. verfeinern die Seele, u. wenn sie Roman sind [...] so sind sie der geistigste und zärtlichste Roman den eine menschliche Seele nur in der schönsten Blüte ihrer Zeit, ihrer Kräfte, und ihres Lebens durchwandern kann.[83]

> [As despicable as a learned woman appears to me, so beautiful is, I believe, a tender soul like you who can sympathize with such tender emotions. They ennoble and refine the soul, and if they are a fiction, they are the most spiritual fiction that a human soul can traverse in the most beautiful flowering of its time, its energy, and its life.]

Not so much reason, but sensibility and sensitivity were considered woman's foremost natural and most desirable qualities. The cultural myth of equating women with feelings became a generally accepted notion during the second half of the eighteenth century. It was used to limit woman to the realm of feelings when Fichte posited in 1796: "In das Innere über die Grenze ihres Gefühls eindringen, kann [das Weib] nicht"[84] (woman cannot enter into the innermost being, cannot go beyond the limitations of her emotions). Feelings were assigned to women and implicitly here the lesser cognitive capabilities of woman. The more rigid gender dichotomy that assigned intellect and learning to men, feelings and passion to women as their "natural character" developed towards the end of the century, when "Empfindsamkeit" became mostly associated with excessive, sickly emotions and trivial literature that had fallen out of fashion. It was a good enough argument to keep women from professional knowledge and (higher, university) education, and it showed them their place in the ever more competitive literary marketplace around 1800 as well.

But earlier in the eighteenth century, authors from Gottsched to Klopstock's generation had responded to their new, young, and increasingly female audience accordingly, providing "schöne Literatur" for the "schöne Geschlecht" (the "fair" sex). As Kant suggested in 1764:

> Das schöne Geschlecht hat eben so wohl Verstand als das männliche, nur ist es ein schöner Verstand, der unsrige soll ein tiefer sein [. . .]. Gefühl vor Schildereien von Ausdruck, und vor die Tonkunst, nicht in so ferne sie Kunst sondern Empfindung äussert, alles dieses verfeinert oder erhebt den Geschmack dieses Geschlechts, und hat jederzeit einige Verknüpfungen mit sittlichen Regungen.[85]

> [The fair sex has intelligence no less high than we do, but it is beautiful, ours is to be profound and approaching the sublime [. . .] An interest in fiction of some expressiveness and in music, not as an expression of art but of sentiment, all this refines and elevates the taste of this sex, and is always somewhat related to moral sensations.]

Beauty, sentiments, and women were considered interrelated, and the "schöne Geschlecht" was served with "schöne Literatur." The authors wrote about a then-contemporary utopian world of sensibility and morality in mostly middle class, contemporary settings presenting, for instance, the trials of loyal and broken friendships and familial relations that were played out in ever new variations on and against plots of romantic love and passionate attachment. The presentation of friendship and love was set in allegorical, historical and often contemporary modes made for spirited entertainment and moral lessons on the perils of love, the power and rewards of friendship and honor, as in Christian Fürchtegott Gellert's *Die zärtlichen Schwestern* (The Tenderhearted Sisters, 1747). Women protagonists abounded showing a women's world, albeit from a curious male perspective, as in Gellert's popular novel *Das Leben der Schwedischen Gräfin von G**** (The Life of the Swedish Countess of G***, 1747) in an improbable plot: when the countess's husband is believed to have died in war, she marries his best friend who gives his marital place back to his friend after the friend's unexpected return. With his sentimental friendship ethos, the bachelor professor Gellert shunned all complications of gender and passion in the heyday of the friendship cult in Germany in the 1750s and 1760s. It seems that he merely revived a traditional literary motif, the male friendship tradition of antiquity, and created a utopia of male friendship.

The epistolary novel became a favorite narrative form in the eighteenth century when personal and literary correspondence was the mainstay for carrying out friendly exchanges and establishing friendships. A model was Samuel Richardson, who corresponded with a large number of educated and literary women about his own relationship and about his writing, portrayed sentimental female friendship in his immensely popular and influential epistolary fiction. Friendship served as a close emotional bond and support in a patriarchal world, a negotiation of feelings, desires, and identity, as did the correspondence and friendship of Clarissa and Anna in *Clarissa or, the History of a Young Lady* (1747–48) with an intimate portrayal of female protagonists.

In her first and most successful novel *Geschichte des Fräuleins von Sternheim* (1771), the prolific German writer Sophie von La Roche (1730–1807) portrayed the life of a young contemporary woman who eludes passionate suitors and attains a certain autonomy as a single woman through friendships, founding a school, charity, and compassion. Lady Sternheim encounters and accepts friendship, and finds her higher calling by befriending other women, being sociable and working for disadvantaged women before returning to the fold of patriarchal society in a seemingly ideal and egalitarian marriage set in an idyllic country estate in England. La Roche decisively expanded and changed the structure of the traditional romance novel by allowing her heroine to elude male tutelage and develop as an autonomous, but nevertheless sociable individual through the emotional support of friends and the heroine's active support and exercise of friendship.

How responsive such sentimental fiction was to contemporary readers' taste can be seen in young Caroline Flachsland's (born in 1750) reaction in a 1771 letter to Herder:

> Ich habe indeßen auch [die] Geschichte der Fräulein von Sternheim gelesen. mein ganzes Ideal von einem Frauenzimmer! sanft, zärtlich, wohlthätig, stolz und tugendhaft. und betrogen. Ich habe köstliche, herrliche Stunden beym Durchlesen gehabt. ach, wie weit bin ich noch von meinem Ideal von mir selbst weg! welche Berge stehn gethürmt vor mir! ach! ach, ich werde im Staub und in der Asche bleiben![86]

> [In the meantime I have also read *The History of Lady Sophia Sternheim*. My very ideal of a woman! Humble, tender, compassionate, proud, and virtuous. And deceived. I have had wonderful, delicious hours in reading it. Alas, how far away I am from my own ideal! What mountains are towering ahead of me. Alas, alas, I shall remain in ashes and dust.]

Like Klopstock, La Roche wrote for the new sensible reading public, young men and women, and touched her readers' hearts. The sentimental narrative occupied a central place in the development of a new and innovative *belles letters* in eighteenth-century Germany. Reason and sentiment were no longer posited as contradictory polarities, the "head" was set in relationship to "the heart." The new *belles lettres* spoke to both and were closely linked to the inner and the outer life of the new readership; they were central to and mirrored literary sociability and social relationships. But this phenomenon still awaits full critical appreciation, as "Empfindsamkeit" comes increasingly into view as a project marked by its innovations rather than its disabling moments.

What "Empfindsamkeit" achieved for "schöne Literatur," the Enlightenment did for criticism as we know it.[87] The modern concept of literature and of literary criticism was closely tied to the rise of the new, educated, bourgeois reading public and authors. Literature, journals, literary feuds, publishing, and reading served the emancipation movement of the middle class, including in a more restricted way the cultural emancipation of middle class women, as an instrument to gain self-esteem and articulate human demands. A powerful convention had come into being: the convention that ideas and humanity were equally accessible to educated men and women and that human beings were judged by their intellectual and humane qualities, not by birth or social rank (to be sure: the intellectual was considered more man's domain, the moral or humane side more woman's realm). The literature of the eighteenth century in Germany that ends with an avalanche of new publications—novels, stories, journals, dramatic works of all kinds, and poetry—should be presented along its own historical and cultural terms and aspirations *and* with critical analysis, as the essays in this volume have attempted to do. Eighteenth-century German literature thus evolves as a lively tapestry of readable, sometimes sophisticated, sometimes sensible texts about the century's human condition.

Notes

[1] Richard Rorty, "The Continuity between the Enlightenment and 'Postmodernism,'" in *What's Left of Enlightenment: A Postmodern Question*, ed. Keith Michael Baker and Peter Hanns Reill (Stanford: Stanford UP, 2001), 19.

[2] For an excellent discussion of the Enlightenment in Germany and an exploration of its significance for the present, see the essays in James Schmidt, ed., *What is Enlightenment? Eighteenth-Century Answers and Twentieth-Century Questions*, Philosophical Traditions, vol. 7 (Berkeley: U of California P, 1996).

[3] Lawrence Lipkin, "Inventing the Eighteenth Centuries: A Long View," in *The Profession of Eighteenth-Century Literature*, ed. Leo Damrosch (Madison: U of Wisconsin P, 1992), 7. While speaking, of course, of English literature, the same applies to German.

[4] "The old historicist ideal of value-free scholarship seems increasingly a delusion even in the case of works like catalogs, much less editions and biographies. Choices grounded in various interests and assumptions must be made in simple listings and

topologies," writes John Bender, "A New History of the Enlightenment?," in *The Profession of Eighteenth-Century Literature,* 63. Bender voices the present "discipline in crisis" with a hope for "sustained critical discourse yielding genuine knowledge" (77).

[5] "Barock," originally a designation for art, architecture, and music and here extending deep into the eighteenth century (Bach died in 1750), was the period designation of choice for German handbooks, older literary histories, and scholarship of the seventeenth century, see Wilfried Barner, ed., *Der literarische Barockbegriff,* Wege der Forschung, vol. 358 (Darmstadt: Wissenschaftliche Buchgesellschaft, 1975). Historians now use "early modern" for the period of roughly 1450 through 1750, avoiding earlier period designations such as Renaissance, Humanism, Reformation, Baroque; most literary scholars in German have followed suit; see Helen Watanabe-O'Kelly, "The Early Modern Period (1450–1720)," in *The Cambridge History of German Literature* (Cambridge: Cambridge UP, 1997), 92–147.

[6] See T. J. Hochstrasser, *Natural Law Theories in the Early Enlightenment* (Cambridge: Cambridge UP, 1999).

[7] Recent research has pointed to the importance of natural law theory in Germany as liberal, albeit monarchist, political theory; see Frank Grunert, *Normbegründung und politische Legitimität: Zur Rechts- und Staatsphilosophie der deutschen Frühaufklärung* (Tübingen: Niemeyer, 2000).

[8] Klaus Garber, "Begin with Goethe? Forgotten Traditions at the Threshold of the Modern Age," in *Imperiled Heritage: Tradition, History, and Utopia in Early Modern German Literature: Selected Essays by Klaus Garber,* ed. Max Reinhart. Studies in European Cultural Transition, vol. 5 (Aldershot: Ashgate, 2000), 209–51.

[9] An exception is Richard Newald's literary history, *Vom Späthumanismus zur Empfindsamkeit, 1570–1750. Geschichte der deutschen Literatur von den Anfängen bis zur Gegenwart,* vol. 5 (Munich: Beck, 1951), with chapters on devotional literature (417–46) and on the early Enlightenment (447–60). Alt, *Aufklärung* 65 points to changing literary norms and imagery (for instance Christian Weise's, 1642–1708) novels and plays. away from the convoluted style ("Schwulst") of the baroque era. Olaf Simons, *Marteaus Europa oder der Roman, bevor er Literatur wurde: Eine Untersuchung des deutschen und englischen Buchangebots der Jahre 1710 bis 1720.* Internationale Forschungen zur Allgemeinen und Vergleichenden Literaturwissenschaft, vol. 52 (Amsterdam: Rodopi, 2001) is one of few recent studies to deal with fictional texts in the early eighteenth century, while there are countless studies on the latter half of the century and quite a few on the canonical works by Schnabel and Gellert.

[10] The history of German literature is a history of new beginnings, belatedness, and forgetfulness, as Wilfried Barner has succinctly discussed in "Über das Negieren von Tradition: Zur Typologie literaturprogrammatischer Epochenschwellen in Deutschland," in *Epochenschwelle und Epochenbewußtsein,* ed. Reinhart Herzog and Reinhart Koselleck (Munich: Fink, 1987), 3–51.

[11] I prefer the translation "bourgeois" for the ubiquitous "bürgerlich" used in German texts of the eighteenth century to denote an urban, educated class of mostly

what we now call professionals and administrators; this leaves out artisans, merchants and their households, a large group within the middle class. The translation "middle class" used in some historical texts is too broad and undifferentiated; it has by no means been generally accepted.

[12] Helen Watanabe O'Kelly has demonstrated how important and lavish court culture was still in the eighteenth century, much of it using or performing literary texts; see her *Court Culture in Dresden: From Renaissance to Baroque* (New York: Palgrave, 2002), and *Spectaculum Europaeum: Theatre and Spectacle in Europe (1580–1750)*, ed. Pierre Béhar and Helen Watanabe (Wiesbaden: Harrassowitz, 1999).

[13] There were numerous points of mutual influence — for instance some of the frivolous, erotic Rococo poetry of young Lessing and his generation followed French, Italian or classical models and were equally popular at court.

[14] Lessing's altercation with Voltaire, who resided in Berlin upon Friedrich's invitation and whose *Siècle de Louis XIV* Lessing had translated, ultimately prevented his appointment. Lessing did receive appointment as librarian to the Ducal Library in Wolfenbüttel in 1770 and held it to his death in 1781, but the court had moved to Braunschweig leaving a huge empty palace and the entire, famous baroque library behind in the small town of Wolfenbüttel.

[15] In a letter to his fiancée Eva König, Lessing also mentioned a terrible toothache and cold weather, and that he was indeed invited. — For legends surrounding the famous drama see Reinhart Meyer, *Hamburgische Dramaturgie und Emilia Galotti* (Wiesbaden: Humanitas Verlag, 1973), 243 and 258. Meyer's study of the drama's reception also conveniently summarizes various interpretations, especially the political reading as an anti-feudal, revolutionary play.

[16] See volume 6 in the Camden House History of German Literature, edited by David Hill. It was the decision of the general editor to separate out Storm and Stress for a single volume and to assign one to Classicism and one to Romanticism. Vol. 8 on Romanticism, edited by Dennis Mahoney, appeared in 2003.

[17] It was used for instance as a subtitle in Johann Pezzl's *Faustin oder das philosophische Jahrhundert* (1783–85).

[18] Quoted from *Was ist Aufklärung? Thesen und Definitionen*, ed. Erhard Bahr (Stuttgart: Reclam, 1977), 23.

[19] Immanuel Kant. *Gesammelte Schriften*. Akademieausgabe (Berlin: G. Reimer, 1911), 4:9.

[20] Peter Gay, *The Enlightenment: An Interpretation. The Rise of Modern Paganism* (New York: Random House, 1968), 197; Peter-André Alt, *Aufklärung: Lehrbuch Germanistik* (Stuttgart: Metzler, 1996), 7–11 suggests "Kritizismus" for the late phase of 1780–95.

[21] See Alt, *Aufklärung* 5–7. The lectures were published posthumously as *Über die Geschichte der Philosophie and Geschichte der Religion*. Hegel spoke of a "deutsche Aufklärung" from the beginning of Friedrich II's reign in 1740 to the French Revolution in 1789; Peter Pütz, ed., *Die deutsche Aufklärung*, Neue wissenschaftliche Bibliothek, vol. 94 (Königsheim, Ts.: Verlagsgruppe Athenäum, 1980), 48–50.

[22] See Joseph von Eichendorff, *Geschichte der poetischen Literatur Deutschlands* (1857) in *Werke und Schriften,* ed. Gerhart Baumann and Siegfried Grosse (Stuttgart: Cotta, 1958), 4:9–424.

[23] See Rainer Rosenberg, "'Aufklärung' in der deutschen Literaturgeschichtsschreibung des 19. Jahrhunderts," in *Aufklärungsforschung in Deutschland,* ed. Holger Dainat and Wilhelm Vosskamp (Heidelberg: Winter, 1999), 10.

[24] (Leipzig: W. Engelmann, 1842); Gervinus's handbook comprised five volumes in the second edition of 1842–46, was later renamed *Geschichte der Deutschen Dichtung* and was in its fifth, totally revised edition in 1771–74 at the time of Gervinus's death. Gervinus was tried for treason in the Grand Duchy of Baden for his liberal stand and activities during the 1848 revolution. He disdained Bismarck for his anti-democratic, military politics of unification.

[25] Gervinus, *Geschichte der deutschen Dichtung.* 4th ed.(Leipzig: W. Engelmann, 1853), 4: 9.

[26] *Geschichte der deutschen Literatur im 18. Jahrhundert* (Braunschweig: F. Vieweg, 1862–70) 3 vols. See the introduction to vol. 2: "Der Kampf gegen die Schranken der Aufklärung" (The Fight against the Constraints of Enlightenment).

[27] *Geschichte der deutschen Literatur* (Berlin: Weidmann, 1883), 272–73.

[28] Rosenberg, "'*Aufklärung*'" 17.

[29] *A History of German Literature by W. Scherer,* translated from the third German edition by Mrs. F. C. Conybeare, edited by F. Max Müller (New York: Scribner's Sons, 1887) was reprinted in 1890, 1912, and 1971.

[30] The (rarely mentioned) subtitle reads: *Lessing, Goethe, Novalis, Hölderlin: Vier Aufsätze.* In spite of its immense influence on German literary scholarship, a translation into English appeared only in 1985: *Poetry and Experience,* ed. by Rudolf A. Makkreel and Frithjof Rodi (Princeton: Princeton UP, 1985).

[31] See Holger Dainat, "Die wichtigste aller Epochen: Geistesgeschichtliche Aufklärungsforschung," in *Aufklärungsforschung in Deutschland* 29–31.

[32] The current meaning of "Geisteswissenschaft*en*" is, of course: the Humanities.

[33] Hermann Nohl, *Die deutsche Bewegung: Vorlesungen und Aufsätze zur Geistesgeschichte von 1770–1830,* ed. O. F. Bollnow and F. Rodi (Göttingen: Vandenhoeck & Ruprecht, 1970), 10–11, 91.

[34] Heinz Kindermann, *Durchbruch der Seele: Literarhistorische Studien über die Anfänge der "Deutschen Bewegung" vom Pietismus zur Romantik* (Danzig: A. W. Kafemann, 1928), 12–13.

[35] H. A. Korff, *Geist der Goethezeit,* vol. 2: *Klassik* (Leipzig: J. J. Weber, 1930), 7. Classicism meant for Korff that the spirit of a nation has reached the zenith of its self (vol. 1, 4), also called "flowering." The entire work (4 volumes plus an index volume) was not completed until 1964; it was in its eighth printing in 1966.

[36] See Jonathan M. Hess, *Reconstituting the Body Politic: Enlightenment, Public Culture and the Invention of Aesthetic Autonomy* (Detroit: Wayne State UP, 1999), esp. 155–80.

[37] Jürgen Habermas's classic study *Strukturwandel der Öffentlichkeit* (1962) with its revised English version *The Structural Transformation of the Public Sphere: An Inquiry into the Category of Bourgeois Society* (Cambridge, MA: MIT Press, 1989) continues to be discussed, see Benjamin W. Redekop, *Enlightenment and Community: Lessing, Abbt, Herder, and the Quest for a German Public* (Montreal: McGill-Queens UP, 2000), 1–29. Equally influential was Reinhart Koselleck, *Kritik und Krise* (1959), *Critique and Crisis: Enlightenment and the Pathogenesis of Modern Society* (Cambridge, MA: MIT P, 1988). Typical for socio-historical studies was Heinz Schlaffer, *Der Bürger als Held: Sozialgeschichtliche Auflösungen literarischer Widersprüche* (Frankfurt a. M.: Suhrkamp, 1973).

[38] Several reprint series have produced a large number of reprints; new editions of collected works and letters appeared for Gottsched, Gellert, Klopstock, Wieland, Lessing, Mendelssohn, Nicolai, Lichtenberg, Herder, and Moritz.

[39] See for instance, Detlef Gaus, *Geselligkeit und Gesellige: Bildung, Bürgertum und bildungsbürgerliche Kultur um 1800* (Stuttgart: Metzler, 1998); Erich Schön, *Der Verlust der Sinnlichkeit oder die Verwandlung des Lesers: Mentalitätswandel um 1800* (Stuttgart: Klett, 1987); Rolf Engelsing, "Perioden der Lesergeschichte in der Neuzeit. Das statistische Ausmaß und die soziokulturelle Bedeutung der Lektüre," in *Archiv für Geschichte des Buchwesens,* 10 (1970): col. 945–1002.

[40] Hans-Jürgen Schings, ed., *Der ganze Mensch: Anthropologie und Literatur im 18. Jahrhundert* (Stuttgart: Metzler, 1994); John H. Zammito, *Kant, Herder and the Birth of Anthropology* (Chicago: U of Chicago P, 2002).

[41] See for instance, Silvia Bovenschen, *Die imaginierte Weiblichkeit: Exemplarische Untersuchungen zu kulturgeschichtlichen und literarischen Präsentationsformen des Weiblichen* (Frankfurt: Suhrkamp, 1979); Ulrike Weckel, *Zwischen Häuslichkeit und Öffentlichkeit: Die ersten deutschen Frauenzeitschriften im 18. Jahrhundert und ihr Publikum,* Studien und Texte zur Sozialgeschichte der Literatur, vol. 61(Tübingen: Niemeyer, 1998) brings an extensive bibliography of gender studies on eighteenth-century German literature, 645–73.

[42] See for instance, Richard van Dülmen, *Die Gesellschaft der Aufklärer* (1986), trans. Anthony Williams (New York: St. Martin's Press, 1992).

[43] Rebekka Habermas, *Frauen und Männer des Bürgertums: Eine Familiengeschichte (1750–1850).* Bürgertum, Beiträge zur europäischen Gesellschaftsgeschichte, vol. 14 (Göttingen: Vandenhoeck & Ruprecht, 2002).

[44] See Martin Pott, *Aufklärung und Aberglaube: die deutsche Frühaufklärung im Spiegel ihrer Aberglaubenskritik,* Studien zur deutschen Literatur, vol. 119 (Tübingen: Niemeyer, 1992).

[45] Theology or divinity illustrated or enforced by physics and natural law was first discussed in England in John Ray's popular *Wisdom of God Manifested in the Works of the Creation* (1691) and William Denham's *Physico-Theology* (1713) and *Astro-Theology* (1715) and influenced especially the early Enlightenment in northern Germany where a flood of conservative theological works tried to align the findings of the new empirical sciences with the Bible and God's wisdom. Neology was a theological position between the orthodox Physico-Theology and the rationalist

Deism that did not gain acceptance in Germany. Based on Leibniz's position of assuming an identity between the truth of reason and of revelation, Neologists considered human reason the tool with which to understand and elucidate the Bible; among its adherents were Gottsched and the prominent theologians Friedrich Wilhelm Jerusalem in Braunschweig and Johann Joachim Spalding in Berlin.

[46] On translations from English, see Michael Maurer, *Aufklärung und Anglophilie in Deutschland*, Veröffentlichungen des Deutschen Historischen Instituts in London, vol. 19 (Göttingen: Vandenhoeck & Ruprecht, 1987).

[47] I prefer the term "sensibility" over "sentimentality" (in the 1770s a pejorative term in England) or "sentimentalism," as "sensibility" lacks the negative connotation of the latter two and since "sensibility" is now commonly used for English literature; see Janet Todd, *Sensibility: An Introduction* (London: Methuen, 1986), 6–9. It was T. S. Eliot who insisted on "sensibility," as it represented for him also the creative faculty and quality of temperament in a poet.

[48] See the discussion in Georg Jäger, *Empfindsamkeit und Roman: Wortgeschichte, Theorie und Kritik im 18. und frühen 19. Jahrhundert,* Studien zur Poetik und Geschichte der Literatur, vol. 11 (Stuttgart: Kohlhammer, 1969), 11–26.

[49] Jäger, *Empfindsamkeit,* 13. Louise Gottsched — *"mit der Feder in der Hand": Briefe aus den Jahren 1730–1762,* ed. Inka Kording (Darmstadt: Wissenschaftliche Buchgesellschaft, 1999), 271. The wording in this letter to Dorothea Henriette von Runckel of 4 September 1757 and published in 1776 could well have been introduced by the original editor, Von Runckel, who took many liberties with the texts. The present edition has not consulted the actual manuscripts preserved in the University Library of Leipzig.

[50] Todd, *Sensibility* 7.

[51] Michael Foucault, *Madness and Civilization* (London: Travistock, 1967), 153–54.

[52] *Selections from the Tatler and the Spectator of Steele and Addison,* ed. Angus Ross (Harmondsworth: Penguin, 1982), 252; quoted from Todd, *Sensibility* 20.

[53] Goethe's *Werther* and much of the drama and poetry by the young generation of the 1770s has also been claimed for the era of Storm and Stress; in English literary history, *Werther* is more often than not seen as the beginning of German Romanticism, Goethe as a Romantic author. Though forgotten today, Gessner's epic was very popular in his day, translated into English several times and reprinted continuously until the early nineteenth century.

[54] See Doris Kaufmann, *Aufklärung, bürgerliche Selbsterfahrung und die "Erfindung" der Psychiatrie in Deutschland 1770–1850,* Veröffentlichungen des Max-Planck-Instituts für Geschichte, vol. 122 (Göttingen: Vandenhoeck & Ruprecht, 1995).

[55] Lessing's use of "Mitleid" (empathy, compassion) must be seen within the contemporary moral-sense debate. There are conflicting scholarly views on Lessing's actual sources for his theory of tragedy, see Hans-Jürgen Schings, *Der mitleidigste Mensch ist der beste Mensch: Poetik des Mitleids von Lessing bis Büchner* (Munich: Beck 1980), 22–30, and Peter Michelsen, *Der unruhige Bürger: Studien zu Lessing und zur Literatur des 18. Jahrhunderts* (Würzburg: Königshausen & Neumann, 1990), 111–15.

[56] Vol. 3 of *Sozialgeschichte der deutschen Literatur,* ed. Rolf Grimminger (Munich: Hanser, 1980).

[57] *Von den Anfängen bis zur Gegenwart,* ed. Wolfgang Beutin et al. (Stuttgart: Metzler, 1979). The fourth edition (1992) now includes a discussion of sensibility as the dialectic of enlightened rationalism.

[58] *A History of German Literature from the Beginnings to the Present Day,* trans. Clare Krojzl (London: Routledge, 1993).

[59] See the annual bibliography in the yearbook *Pietismus und Neuzeit* (1973–), Martin Brecht, *Geschichte des Pietismus,* 4 vols. (Göttingen: Vandenhoeck & Ruprecht, 1993–98), and Hans-Jürgen Schrader, *Literaturproduktion und Büchermarkt: Johann Heinrich Reitz' "Historie der Wiedergebohrnen" und ihr geschichtlicher Kontext,* Palaestra, vol. 283 (Göttingen: Vandenhoeck & Ruprecht, 1989).

[60] See August Langen, *Der Wortschatz des deutschen Pietismus,* 2nd ed. (Tübingen: Niemeyer, 1968).

[61] Vol. 1: *Voraussetzungen und Elemente* (Metzler: Stuttgart, 1974); and *Empfindsamkeit: theoretische und kritische Texte,* ed. Wolfgang Doktor and Gerhard Sauder (Stuttgart: Reclam, 1976); vol. 3: *Quellen und Dokumente* (Stuttgart: Metzler, 1980).

[62] See Sauder's recent remarks on his earlier work and research survey "Empfindsamkeit — Tendenzen der Forschung," in *Aufklärung: Interdisziplinäres Jahrbuch zur Erforschung des 18. Jahrhunderts und seiner Wirkungsgeschichte* 13 (2001): 307–40, here 308.

[63] Using discourse analysis and systems theory, Nikolaus Wegmann, *Diskurse der Empfindsamkeit: Zur Geschichte eine Gefühls* (Stuttgart: Metzler, 1988) has not really been able to bring new insights or new materials to light.

[64] "Wende nach innen" and "dem Objekt entfremdete wirklichkeitsarme Egozentrik." Lothar Pikulik, *Leistungsethik contra Gefühlskult: Über das Verhältnis von Bürgerlichkeit und Empfindsamkeit in Deutschland* (Göttingen: Vandenhoeck & Ruprecht, 1984), 212. Pikulik wrote against the dominant fashion of literary sociology and Marxist criticism of the 1970s.

[65] Lothar Pikulik, "Die Mündigkeit des Herzens. Über die Empfindsamkeit als Emanzipations- und Autonomiebewegung," in *Aufklärung* 9–32.

[66] (Tübingen: Niemeyer, 1997). It is vol. 6, 1 of Hans-Georg Kemper, *Deutsche Lyrik der frühen Neuzeit,* begun in 1986.

[67] See also Wolfgang Martens, *Literatur und Frömmigkeit in der Zeit der frühen Aufklärung* (Tübingen: Niemeyer, 1991),

[68] (Munich: Fink, 1999), 15. The cryptic title plays with the interaction of the body (nature) and the print medium (technology); "Schriftverkehr" also means simply correspondence, and "Verkehr" connotes the range from traffic to intercourse; "mediology" seeks to elucidate cultural transmissions, the system through which an idea or visual representation becomes a material force.

[69] *Körperströme,* 54. The effusive, often associative study suffers from the presentation of too much heterogeneous material, thoughts, and observations that the author tries

to pin together with theoretical excursions. Koschorke's extensive use of some of his earlier essays forces him to digressions. The study is more challenging and suggestive than informative or cohesive.

[70] Erich Schön, "Weibliches Lesen: Romanleserinnen im späten 18. Jahrhundert," in *Romane von Frauen um 1800,* ed. Helga Gallas and Magdalene Heuser (Tübingen: Niemeyer, 1990), 22; Helga Brandes, "Die Entstehung eines weiblichen Lesepublikums im 18. Jahrhundert. Von den Frauenzimmerbibliotheken zu den literarischen Damengesellschaften," in *Lesen und Schreiben im 18. Jahrhundert: Studien zu ihrer Bewertung in Deutschland, England und Frankreich,* ed. Paul Goetsch. ScriptOralia, vol. 65 (Tübingen: Niemeyer, 1994), 125–34.

[71] See Richard Alewyn, "Klopstocks Leser," in *Festschrift für Rainer Gruenter,* ed. Bernhard Fabian (Heidelberg: Carl Winter, 1978), 100–21, here 114–15.

[72] See Klaus Hurlebusch, *Klopstock, Hamann und Herder als Wegbereiter autorzentrischen Schreibens: Ein philologischer Beitrag zur Charakterisierung der literarischen Moderne,* Studien und Texte zur Sozialgeschichte der Literatur, vol. 86 (Tübingen: Niemeyer, 2001), 7–35.

[73] Helmut Pape, *Klopstock: Die "Sprache des Herzens" neu entdeckt. Die Befreieung des Lesers aus seiner emotionalen Unmündigkeit. Idee und Wirklichkeit dichterischer Existenz um 1750* (Frankfurt a. M.: Lang, 1998).

[74] Erich Schön, *Der Verlust der Sinnlichkeit,* 303–06, could establish that the readership for the new "Schöne Literatur" consisted mostly of young women and men, mostly students, and professional literati.

[75] See Helga Meise, *Das archivierte Ich: Schreibkalender und höfische Repräsentation in Hessen-Darmstadt 1624–1790* (Darmstadt: Hessische Historische Kommission, 2002).

[76] Only the volume *Deutsche Poetische Gedichte* (1650) by Sibylle Schwarz (1621–1638) contains some secular poems and sonnets. The volume was put together by a Greifswald Magister, since Schwarz died at the age of 17. For the beginnings of secular poetry in German by women see Katherine Goodman, *Amazons and Apprentices: Women and the German Parnassus in the Early Enlightenment* (Rochester, NY: Camden House, 1999). As to secular prose, Duke Anton Ulrich of Braunschweig-Lüneburg's sister Sibylle Ursula may have drafted (or simply copied?) part of the novel *Aramena* (1669) — a section of part one is in her handwriting. Also, Margarethe Stockfleth probably wrote much and completed part 2 of her husband's novel *Die Kunst- und Tugend-gezierte Macarie* (1669–1673), but no woman published secular literature under her own name in Germany in the seventeenth century.

[77] See Barbara Becker-Cantarino, *Der lange Weg zur Mündigkeit: Frau und Literatur in Deutschland von 1500 bis 1800* (Stuttgart: Metzler, 1987), 182–84.

[78] Until the late eighteenth century, reading usually meant "vorlesen" (reading aloud) when a text was read to a group (often of illiterates) or by a companion or governess to an aristocratic woman. Solitary readers would read aloud until "silent reading" became the norm around 1800; Erich Schön, *Der Verlust der Sinnlichkeit,* 99–107.

[79] *Pomona. Für Teutschlands Töchter,* ed. Jürgen Vorderstemann (Rpt. 1783, Munich: Saur, 1987), 2: 845.

[80] "*Ich wünschte so gar gelehrt zu werden*": *Drei Autobiographien von Frauen,* ed. Magdalene Heuser et al. (Göttingen: Wallstein-Verlag, 1994), 16. The *Versuch* was published in 1791 as *Lebensbeschreibung von Friderika Baldinger, von ihr selbst verfasst* by Sophie von La Roche, who had received from E. G. Baldinger the manuscript of his wife, who died in 1786, with a request for publication.

[81] "*Ich wünschte so gar gelehrt zu werden,*" 17.

[82] Silvia Bovenschen, *Die imaginierte Weiblichkeit,* 158–80.

[83] Letter of 12 September 1770; Johann Gottfried Herder, *Briefe. April 1763–April 1771,* ed. Karl-Heinz Hahn (Weimar: Herrmann Böhlaus Nachfolger, 1977), 1:214 (no. 92).

[84] Johann Gottlieb Fichte, *Grundlage des Naturrechts* (Foundations of Natural Law, 1796), quoted from Gesa Stedman, "Gefühl und Geschlecht — Stimmen von der Antike bis zur Gegenwart," in *Querelles: Jahrbuch für Frauenforschung* 7 (2002): 269.

[85] Immanuel Kant, "Beobachtungen über das Gefühl des Schönen und Erhabenen," in *Werke,* ed. Wilhelm Weischedel (Darmstadt: Insel, 1960), 1:851, 854.

[86] *Herders Briefwechsel mit Caroline Flachsland: Nach den Handschriften des Goethe- und Schiller-Archivs,* ed. Hans Schauer. Schriften der Goethe-Gesellschaft, vol. 39 (Weimar: Verlag der Goethe-Gesellschaft, 1926), 2:238–39.

[87] Peter Hohendahl, speaking from the Frankfurt School tradition, affirms the importance of the Enlightenment; see his *The Institution of Criticism* (Ithaca: Cornell UP, 1982), 52–53.

Immanuel Kant. Etching by F. W. Bollinger, 1781.

Enlightenment Thought and Natural Law from Leibniz to Kant and its Influence on German Literature

Kai Hammermeister

Enlightenment in Europe

ENLIGHTENMENT IS A RECURRENT MOVEMENT within the history of thought that demands justification of all current values, customs, and beliefs *vis-à-vis* the faculty of reason.[1] As such, it neither advances its own set of philosophical doctrines nor can it be reduced to being the primary characteristic of eighteenth-century thought. Rather, it is a periodic event in the intellectual history of the West and in recent years also of non-Western cultures, in which reason becomes more concerned with its own operations than with specific contents.[2] In the history of philosophical thought, Enlightenment has a cleansing function that often provides a new freedom and sense of discovery for the spirit of inquiry. Yet, although it generally claims to proceed both in the analytic *and* the synthetic mode, more often than not it focuses its energies on dismantling previous systems without advancing to new concrete and coherent contents.[3] Thus, Enlightenment periods tend to give rise to subsequent philosophical movements that aim to work out specific contents without relinquishing the critical use of reason achieved by Enlightenment efforts and, hence, to make good on the unfulfilled Enlightenment promise to unite analytic and synthetic functions of reason.

In a narrower sense, Enlightenment refers to the dominant, albeit not exclusive, philosophical movement of the eighteenth century in Europe and North America as well as the literary and cultural production at large that is influenced by this thinking. As is the case with almost every historical period, the Enlightenment cannot be dated with precision. Moreover, its beginning and duration differ in different countries. And because the Enlightenment was also adopted as a certain style of government, it had social and political ramifications that did not always coincide precisely with purely intellectual events and, hence, must be dated separately without entirely divorcing them from the intellectual currents. *Intellectually,* one could let the Enlightenment in England begin in 1689, the year of the publication of Locke's (1632–1728) *Letters on Toleration*. In Germany, 1687 was suggested for a starting date, the year in which Christian Thomasius (1655–1728) first announced and held a university lecture in German instead of Latin, the standard language of discourse in universities. In France, the Enlightenment is often stated to begin with Montesquieu's (1689–1755) *Lettres Persanes* of 1721, although it certainly has roots reaching as far back as the work of Pierre Bayle's (1647–1706) *Dictionnaire historique et critique* of 1697 which had argued that religion and truth are irreconcilable. This dictionary was translated into German in the 1740s under the supervision of Johann Christoph Gottsched (1700–1766), and it exerted an influence on Gotthold Ephraim Lessing (1729–1781), Johann Joachim Winckelmann (1717–1768), on French philosophers and the Americans Benjamin Franklin (1706–1790) and Thomas Jefferson (1743–1826).[4] *Politically,* 1688 stands as the date for both England (The Glorious Revolution) and France (The revocation of the Edict of Nantes). For Germany, Enlightenment scholars often suggest the ascension of Frederick the Great of Prussia to the throne in 1740 as the beginning date.

The *end* of the Enlightenment is probably easier to date politically than intellectually. In France, one could point to 1804, when Napoleon crowned himself emperor. In Germany, 1806 is a usable date, marking as it does the end of the Holy Roman Empire of the German Nation. In the rest of Europe the beginning of the Vienna Congress and the period of Restoration in 1815 might be set as an ending date. Although publications written in the spirit of Enlightenment continued to be published throughout at least the first two decades of the nineteenth century (only to mention Heinrich von Kleist's [1777–1811] essay "Über die Aufklärung des Weibes" [On the Enlightenment of women] of 1800), one could set 1796 as a date for the end of this intellectual movement in Germany. It was in this year that the journal *Berlinische Monatsschrift,* which had become the leading forum for German Enlightenment authors, ceased publication. Ultimately, these dates are only of minor importance, and it suffices to remember that the Enlightenment began in the late seventeenth century, gained momentum and peaked first in England in the first third of the eighteenth century, in France around mid-century and in Germany probably in the 1770s and 1780s.

In Great Britain, John Locke initiated the critical philosophy of the eighteenth century by examining the means and limitations of thought itself. David Hume (1711–1776) continued this investigation through his critique of the concepts of substance and causality, and arrived at the conclusion that knowledge should be conceptualized as probability rather than certainty. Like Pierre Bayle he argues that morality does not need religion, but is based on a feeling of sympathy. The same idea was developed by the Earl of Shaftesbury (1671–1713) and Adam Smith (1723–1790), both of whom argue for a moral and communal sense as the basis of moral conduct. In France; Montesquieu elaborated on Locke's theory of checks and balances; Voltaire popularized the French Enlightenment through his essayistic and fictional works; Diderot (1713–1784) and d'Alembert (1717–1783) compiled and edited the most successful encyclopedia of the eighteenth century—based on a British model; Lamettrie (1709–1751), d'Holbach (1723–1789) and Helvétius (1715–1771) propagated a kind of materialism intended to answer the theoretical impasses of the metaphysical systems of Spinoza (1632–1677), Descartes (1569–1650), and Leibniz (1646–1716); and Rousseau (1712–1778) advanced a theory of civilization that viewed it as a process of decline. In Italy, Cesare Beccaria's (1738–1794) work *Dei delitti e delle pene* (On Crimes and Punishment, 1764) had a significant impact on the European legal system and in several countries led to the abolishment of torture in the juridical process and to the end of the death penalty. In the Unites States, thinkers and statesmen like Jefferson, Franklin, and Thomas Paine (1737–1809) wedded Enlightenment thought with political praxis and based a newly founded nation on Enlightenment principles.

The following overview focuses on the main characteristics of the German Enlightenment within its European context; on the response to the metaphysical systems of Descartes, Spinoza and Leibniz; on the theory of natural law and its decline; on the self-definition of the Enlightenment movement; on the challenges to religion and the unique German way to address this criticism; on the emergence of the philosophies of history and art; and, finally, on the significant challenges to reason as the primary principle reflected in the skeptical voices that coexisted with Enlightenment's optimistic rationalism throughout the eighteenth century.

Rational Metaphysics and Natural Law

Enlightenment thought in Europe developed within the context of seventeenth-century rational metaphysics, that is, the systems of Descartes, Spinoza and Leibniz. While all three philosophers were considered forerunners by Enlightenment thinkers in some respects, the Enlightenment also directly opposed other aspects of their complex metaphysical systems. The least influential of the three seems to have been Descartes, lauded for his methodological rigor, but simultaneously criticized for the attempt to extend his mathematical method to all areas of inquiry.[5] In Germany, eighteenth-century thought is largely dominated by the influence of Leibniz, mediated by his student Christian Wolff (1679–1754),[6] and less by Descartes and Spinoza.[7] Spinoza's works, however, exerted significant influence in the

1780s and beyond, so that one can speak of a strong Spinozian current in late Enlightenment, classical, and Romantic thought in Germany.

Descartes's system developed from his questioning of Scholastic philosophy, which, in his view, did not arrive at absolute certainties but ultimately demanded an act of faith. As Thomas Aquinas (1224/25–1274) had taught, revelation and philosophical inquiry were two separate modes of knowledge. Descartes's search for a *fundamentum inconcussum,* an unshakable foundation of knowledge, led him to the *cogito,* the certainty of the questioning self. A consequence of this finding, however, was the separation of cognition and matter, *res cogitans* and *res extensa,* as two different substances. Descartes oriented himself at the theological discussion of the scholastics with this concept of substance, yet the notion of two different substances caused a number of problems that he could not convincingly solve. Hence, both Spinoza and Leibniz opposed Descartes's concept of duality of substance in order to solve differently the three problems of the movement of matter, the lawfulness of such movement, and the body-soul-interaction that had emerged from the Cartesian doubling of substances.

Spinoza suggests a collapse of creation and created substances, of God and nature, as well as of God and mind into one substance. God, nature, and the mind should be considered all of the same substance. Movement of matter could be explained as *energeia,* an inner drive; the lawfulness of movement as God's thinking; and the interaction of body and soul as the unity of matter and mind in God. Body and soul are not two different substances, merely two attributes of the same substance. This God, however, is not the Jewish God who reveals himself to Moses as the *I Am* nor the Christian God of the Gospels. He is no longer the transcendent cause of the world, nor is his freedom unlimited; rather, he is bound to the necessity of natural laws. But on the other hand, the universe as a whole becomes deified, and matter loses its status as a lesser substance. The reception of Spinoza's philosophy in Germany led to the *Pantheismusstreit* of 1785, the argument about pantheism. Moses Mendelssohn (1729–1786), by pointing to his friend Lessing, argued that an enlightened pantheism is neither damaging for religion nor for morality. Friedrich Heinrich Jacobi (1743–1819) likewise suggested that Lessing had confessed to being a follower of Spinoza's pantheism, but for him Spinozism was all but harmless. While arguing that Spinoza's thought was philosophically the most rigorous and coherent, Jacobi nevertheless claimed that it ultimately led to nihilism. This controversy stirred up a significant reaction among contemporary German intellectuals and writers. Johann Gottfried Herder suggested a theistic re-interpretation of Spinoza's *Ethica* in his *Gott, einige Gespräche* (God, Some Conversations, 1787). He took up Spinoza's notion of substance to overcome the Kantian dualism of nature and reason, but he amended this concept with Leibniz's notion of *Kraft* (*potestas,* energy, might). Herder defined God as the *Urkraft,* the teleologic cause of all things.[8] Goethe, on the other hand, took recourse to Spinoza's *Ethica* in order to support his own non-Christian pantheism. And the philosopher Johann Gottlieb Fichte (1762–1814) found support in Spinoza's notion of the one substance with two attributes for his conception of the identity of I and Non-I. Further, Spinoza was applauded by Enlightenment thinkers for his courageous support of freedom of speech and tolerance in the state.

Leibniz agreed with Descartes, Spinoza, and their scholastic precursors that all metaphysics rests on the concept of substance.[9] For Leibniz, the world is not made up merely of atoms and the void, as Democritus (ca. 460–370) and Epicurus (341–271) had suggested, but something is needed in addition to the atoms to turn them from a mere conglomerate into a continuum. Hence, he insists that all substances have an inherent potential to act, namely *Kraft*. These "substantial atoms" are conceived in analogy to the soul; they were created by God when he created the world and are without end in time. Yet these substances, of which an endless number exists, cannot be influenced from the outside. Therefore, the sensualist solution to the problem of the interaction between matter and mind suggested by English philosophers was not convincing for Leibniz. Instead, he postulated "une parfaite *conformité*"[10] between soul and external world, thus arguing for a complete coherence of mind and matter that he would soon call *"Harmonie preétablie,"*[11] pre-established harmony. It follows that the soul cannot be subject to causality, hence is free. Leibniz also suggested that this harmony serves as indirect proof of God and as such perfect conformity must by necessity have a perfect cause.[12]

Leibniz's notion of the substantial atom, the monad, undercuts the strict opposition of reason and sensuality that are considered to be gradations of cognition rather than radically different spheres. With this theory, Leibniz helps to prepare the rise of autonomous aesthetics — Herder's aesthetics and his "Vom Erkennen und Empfinden der menschlichen Seele" (About the Cognition and Sensation of the Human Soul) owe much to Leibniz[13] — as well as for a more benevolent view of human affections which are no longer considered to be a mere interference with reason.[14]

Leibniz directly championed the cause of Enlightenment when he argued "daß nichts mehr zur Glückseligkeit diene, als die Erleuchtung des Verstandes und Übung des Willens"[15] (That nothing will further happiness more than the illumination of reason and the coercion of the will). Leibniz also exerted an influence on the legal debates of the eighteenth century and became one of the pathbreaking thinkers of modern international law with his edition of documents from the history of international law, the *Codex iuris gentium diplomaticus* of 1693.

The eighteenth century was also the age in which the theory of natural law spread throughout Europe and was imported to North America by Jefferson and others. Natural law generally refers to the postulation of a law that precedes all existing legal systems deemed to be positive law. As such, natural law is considered to be based on cosmological, divine or anthropological facts that allow both a prescriptive relation to positive law as well as its critique. Obviously, the defense of natural law changed over time so that — in an oversimplified manner — we can detect a cosmological rationale in antiquity (Plato, Aristotle) which gives way to a theistic interpretation in the Middle Ages (Thomas Aquinas) and is in turn supplanted by an anthropological reading in the modern era. In fact, it was during the age of absolutism that natural law was newly conceived from the perspective of social anthropology. Hobbes's model of the natural state of man as one of enmity against his fellow human beings was opposed by Hugo Grotius (1583–1645) and Samuel Pufendorf (1632–1694).[16] Both of these thinkers argued that man has an inborn tendency toward communality upon which all positive law within the state and between states can be based. Pufendorf argues that because man depends on society, natural law obliges him to be social and to serve his community. To comprehend these basic principles of natural law, no divine revelation is necessary; instead, man's natural reason suffices. Thomasius agrees with Pufendorf in this respect; for him, too, religion and law can be separated. Ultimately, law is again defined as positive law: only that which can be enforced by means of political power must be deemed legal. Hence, natural law remains an ethical principle, but no longer possesses legally binding force. Thomasius was also one of the first scholars to attack both the use of torture in legal proceedings and the prosecution of witches. In the latter, he was preceded by the Jesuit Friedrich von Spee, although Spee did not attack the belief in witches so much as their unfair treatment by the legal system.[17]

In Germany, natural law theory underwent a process of individualization in the hands of Leibniz. He argued that the individual possesses certain inborn and inalienable rights. This pronouncement was read by subsequent generations of Enlightenment philosophers to mean that all citizens have irrevocable rights which no state may withhold from them. Obviously, this position not only influenced the theoretical underpinnings of the French Revolution, but also of the American *Declaration of Independence* and a number of European legal reforms, among them the *Preußisches Landrecht* (The Prussian General Code, 1794), the French *Code Civil* (1804), and the German *Allgemeines Bürgerliches Gesetzbuch* (Common Code of Civil Law, 1811). In the early nineteenth century, natural law theories exerted a certain influence on political and economic liberalism as well as on early socialist thinkers, but soon after a decline set in. In Germany, however, interest in natural law was rekindled and it regained influence after the defeat of Hitler's regime and its legal abuses, as is particularly evident in the constitution of the Federal Republic of Germany, the *Grundgesetz* (Basic Law), which clearly demonstrates traces of natural law theory (for example, *Die Würde des Menschen ist unantastbar;* The dignity of man is inalienable).

What is Enlightenment?

The 1780s in Germany are characterized by the attempts of its leading thinkers to come to an understanding about the nature of Enlightenment. Although the very term "Aufklärung" quickly became an overused catchword and the site of struggle between opposing factions, all of which claimed the exclusive right to the term, the debate regarding the Enlightenment in the *Berlinische Monatsschrift* in the 1780s is characteristic of the German situation.

In the decades between 1740 and 1780, the so-called popular philosophy had gained more and more ground.[18] Its main representative was Moses Mendelssohn (1729–1786), who answered the question regarding the nature of this disputed and somewhat vague term by arguing that Enlightenment is the theoretical aspect of *Bildung*, a concept referring to the formation of man in intellectual, moral, social, and aesthetic respects. While practical *Bildung*, that is, culture, aims at the improvement of the trades, arts, and mores in its objective form, *Bildung* strives to better man's drives and habits in its subjective form. As the theoretical manifestation of *Bildung*, Enlightenment champions rational cognition and the ability to deliberate rationally. As a social being, man needs culture; when viewed as a human being outside the social sphere, Enlightenment suffices for him. Here Mendelssohn allows for the possibility of a conflict between "Menschenaufklärung" (Enlightenment of man) and "Bürgeraufklärung" (Enlightenment of the citizen). The former can actually be detrimental to the social life, which ranks as the superior value. When religion and morality are endangered by Enlightenment critique, one ought to privilege prejudice over damaging inquiry.[19]

In the same year Kant published what would become the best-known text of the German Enlightenment, although it was neither its most coherent nor its most typical.[20] The essay's opening statement ranks among the most oft quoted philosophical sentences ever written and has almost become a canonical definition of Enlightenment: "Aufklärung ist der Ausgang des Menschen aus seiner selbst verschuldeten Unmündigkeit"[21] (Enlightenment is man's exit from his self-caused tutelage). Kant argues that laziness and cowardice are the reasons for the self-inflicted immaturity, and that the process of individual Enlightenment can only be initialized by an act of daring. In light of this, Kant modifies the Horacian imperative *Sapere aude!* — Dare to be wise! — and calls for the independent use of reason, "Habe Mut, dich deines eigenen Verstandes zu bedienen"[22] (Have the courage to make use of your own reason). Enlightenment for Kant is a long and slow process; revolutions do not lead to a reform of thought, but merely to new prejudices (*A* 484). The only precondition for societal Enlightenment is the freedom for the public use of reason. This freedom, however, is primarily the freedom of inquiry for the purpose of research. When it comes to the sphere of civil government, it will often be required that the individual pursuit of truth be harnessed by the obligation to guarantee effective government. Here, "man muß gehorchen" (*A* 485; one must obey). Enlightenment is not a state to be reached, but a continuous process. It is the natural development of the human race, and therefore it can only be stopped by means of force. Yet interference with the process of Enlightenment must ultimately be considered a violation of human rights (*A* 490).

Kant's essay was probably meant to be more a journalistic piece than a coherent scholarly inquiry. Hence, his definition of Enlightenment remains strictly formal on the one hand, and on the other it suffers from vagueness and a shifting of the content of the term's definition referring alternately to Enlightenment as an anthropological tendency, a phase in the development of the species, a specific use of reason, and an *hexis,* that is, an attitude of character acquired by training. No wonder that shortly after the essay's first appearance Kant was criticized for it. One clear-sighted criticism was voiced by Johann Georg Hamann (1730–1788) in a 1784 letter to his Königsberg friend and colleague Christian Jacob Kraus. He argued against Kant that one's incapacity ("Unvermögen") to use one's own reason cannot be considered to be one's own fault. Man is only at fault if he is unwilling to emancipate himself from false authority.[23]

A different criticism was voiced about a decade later by Friedrich Schiller in his *Über die ästhetische Erziehung des Menschen in einer Reihe von Briefen* (Letters on the Aesthetic Education of Man in a Series of Letters). Schiller challenged Kant's equation of Enlightenment with the natural development of the human race toward more intellectual independence and hence a higher state of development. For him, the age was enlightened indeed, yet it was still barbaric. In fact, contemporary overemphasis on reason had furthered modern man's self-alienation. Rather than to advance the rule of reason, the "Ausbildung des Empfindungsvermögens ist also das dringendere Bedürfnis der Zeit"[24] (the development of sensibility is the more urgent need of the time).

The German *Sonderweg* Regarding Religion

In Germany, Enlightenment criticism of religion lacked the radicalism of anti-theological and anti-clerical thought that could be witnessed in England and France. While England's Enlightenment thinkers generally moved toward a non-confessional deism that still allowed for a creator god,[25] France's intellectuals radicalized this tendency and steadily moved toward materialism and atheism. However, most European philosophers were united by one aspect of the discussion of religious faith, namely their support for confessional and general tolerance. Although several Enlightenment authors also cautioned that tolerance *tout court* can have harmful effects, Bayle, Locke, Spinoza, Voltaire, Lessing, and many others agreed that tolerance was a desirable character trait and the duty of ecclesiastic and political rulers. This call was taken to heart by enlightened monarchs like Joseph II of Austria and Friedrich II of Prussia, the latter of whom famously stated in his edict of 1740: "Die Religionen müssen alle toleriert werden, und muß der Fiscal nur das Auge darauf heben, daß keine der anderen Abbruch tue; denn hier muß ein jeder nach seiner Façon selig werden" (All religions must be tolerated, and the state must merely ensure that none interferes with the other, because in this realm everyone must achieve salvation in his own fashion). However the most influential and important document of support for religious tolerance in Germany was not philosophical or political, but literary, namely Lessing's drama *Nathan der Weise* (1779). Borrowing Boccaccio's parable of the ring, Lessing — motivated to write this play by his theological arguments with the Hamburg pastor Goeze — concludes that all religions should feel free to regard theirs as the true one, as long as this fosters a loving competition between the religions to outdo each other in kindness and devotion without ever seeking to abolish other religions.[26]

A general tendency in the theological debates of the eighteenth century was to emphasize questions of ethics over those of dogmatics, hence to underscore the practical dimension of faith. One of the prime targets of philosophical criticism was the doctrine of original sin that seemed to limit man's perfectibility. Theologically, this criticism involved a paradigm shift away from the Augustinian-Thomasian tradition and toward the teachings of Pelagius who taught that man can overcome the evil aspect of his nature through and owing to the existence of his free will. Although it was decried as heretical by the Catholic Church, this ethics based on individual effort still possessed a strong appeal for a century intent on human betterment.

Much of the critique of orthodox religion in Germany and elsewhere centered on the relation of reason and revelation. Leibniz, and even more his student Wolff, insisted that reason and revelation are not mutually exclusive, but complementary. Leibniz's attempt to avoid Spinoza's pantheism had allowed him to retain the idea of God as the transcendent creator of the universe, yet his doctrine of pre-established harmony might be seen as calling into question the need for redemption. If this world is already as perfect as it can be imagined, one is hard pressed to see how it could be improved without revoking that feature which accounts for the existence of a certain amount of evil, namely the freedom of the will. The assumption of the most perfect of all possible worlds, however, would soon be ridiculed by Voltaire in his *Candide* as well as in Johann Carl Wezel's 1776 novel *Belphegor*. Wezel argues both against the freedom of the will by claiming that man is "eine Maschine des Neides und der Vorzugssucht" (a machine of envy and addiction to preferential treatment), thus resorting to the machine metaphor of Descartes and the French materialists, as well as against Leibniz's optimism in general: "In allen Ständen der Gesellschaft und der Menschheit ist der Mensch Krieger, Unterdrücker, Räuber, Mörder gewesen"[27] (In all estates of society and of mankind man has been warrior, oppressor, robber, murderer).

Much like Leibniz and Wolff, the enlightened branch of eighteenth-century theology, the so-called neologists, similarly stressed the coexistence of reason and revelation by emphasizing the reconcilability of the modern scientific worldview with Biblical teachings. The Bible itself, however, became the object of renewed critical attention and was increasingly studied from the standpoint of historical-critical textual scholarship. Although most German theologians and philosophers retained the possibility of revelation, some thinkers — albeit a minority — went as far as to deny the possibility of all revealed religion. Hermann Samuel Reimarus (1694–1768) was the best known author to argue against the possibility of all trans-rational forms of knowledge and insisted on a purely ethical religion.

Lessing, too, imagined a "Vernunftreligion," a religion of reason that coincides with the religion of Christ. But this religion that was to develop some time in the future had to be clearly distinguished from Christianity as a dogmatic and confessional faith. Humankind is called upon to transform Christianity into a universal moral religion of reason, a new, eternal Gospel.[28] Still, this stance did not lead Lessing to a denial of revelation. For him, though, revelation did not provide man with a type of knowledge that is different from that attained by reason. "Also gibt auch die Offenbarung dem Menschengeschlechte nichts, worauf die menschliche Vernunft, sich selbst überlassen, nicht auch kommen würde: sondern sie gab und gibt ihm die wichtigsten dieser Dinge nur früher"[29] (Hence revelation does not give the human race anything that human reason, left to its own devices, would not also find: rather it gave and gives the most important of these things merely sooner).

Kant, too, criticizes the theology of revelation without falling into agnosticism or atheism. In his 1781 *Kritik der reinen Vernunft*, he argues that God, freedom, and immortality cannot become objects of knowledge as they do not fall within the categories of our cognition.[30] However, the concept of God still turns out to be a necessity within Kantian philosophy, not as the result of metaphysical exploration, but as the requirement for moral conduct. Virtuous living does not necessarily make man happy, as we all know that good deeds can go without reward in this life and evil often triumphs; yet virtue renders man worthy of happiness. In order to be duly rewarded, however, we must assume the immortality of the soul as well as the existence of God.[31] "Es ist moralisch notwendig, das Dasein Gottes anzunehmen"[32] (It is morally necessary to assume the existence of God). God is removed from the sphere of cognition and at the same time turned into a postulate necessary for the grounding of practical philosophy.

Philosophy of History

Except for a few thinkers like Rousseau who viewed the history of civilization as a process of decline, most Enlightenment philosophers regarded history with great hope and a large dose of optimism.[33] While the past might have been bleak, there certainly was hope enough that the efforts of this age of Enlightenment would usher in a brighter future. In Germany, the most interesting debate — if one can call it such, as there was no back and forth between positions — was that between historical cosmopolitanism and historical nationalism. Kant was the most prominent and eloquent supporter of the first stance; the second position was advanced by Herder.

Kant argued that the natural potentials of the human race would unfold in the realm of history. Since man is characterized by rationality, history too must be a rational process that leads to an ever richer employment of this and all other human faculties. One must note, though, that Kant envisions perfection — or at least an approximation to it — not for the individual, but for the human race. The individual would have to live an eternal life in order to develop completely all his potential. Hence, perfection can only be achieved by the species that Kant considers to be eternal. In fact, it might even be that the individual has to suffer a loss of contentment in the interest of promoting collective happiness. Politically, attaining the goal of humanity's development does not equal man's peaceful cooperation without authority or hierarchies. Rather, "der Mensch ist ein Tier, das, wenn es unter andern seiner Gattung lebt, einen Herrn nötig hat. Denn er mißbraucht gewiß seine Freiheit in Ansehung anderer seinesgleichen"[34] (Man is an animal who, when he lives among his species, requires a master. Because he surely abuses his liberty in respect to others).

The means that nature uses to further historical development are primarily those of antagonism, struggle, revolution, and war. In this respect, Kant agrees with the Greek developmental theory that was based on the *agon* as the means for both individual and societal advancement. The ultimate goal will be a "Völkerbund," a community of peoples, that can guarantee the rights of all states and that will have overcome all internal and external opposition so that it can run like an automaton until eternity. All nation-states will adhere to the same "bürgerliche Verfassung," a republican constitution.

In other words, the politically, socially, and ethically most advanced ideas of Western civilization will steadily permeate the rest of the world; that is, the Western world will "wahrscheinlicher Weise dereinst allen anderen dereinst Gesetze geben"[35] (will probably prescribe its laws eventually for all others), and in due time bring about a politically uniform world society. In this developmental scheme, the individual epochs within the history of the West as well as the non-Western cultures cannot claim any inherent value apart from their contribution to the ultimate aim of progress.

Herder developed exactly the opposite vision of history. He agrees with Kant that history is the continuation of natural evolution. But for him, cosmopolitanism is only one side of the historical coin. Certainly, the awareness of planetary cultural developments is a worthy and necessary project, yet it must not lead to the construction of an overarching process of cosmopolitan maturation that ultimately negates the right of existence of individual cultures. History, Herder argues, always brings forth new and unique forms of social life that cannot be reduced to a universal, generic form. Rather, these individual expressions of human communality resist all efforts to construct a totalizing view of history. "Ist nicht das Gute auf der Erde ausgestreut? Weil eine Gestalt der Menschheit und ein Erdstrich es nicht fassen konnte, wards verteilt in tausend Gestalten, wandelt — ein ewiger Proteus! — durch alle Weltteile und Jahrhunderte hin"[36] (Is not the good strewn out all over the world? Because one form of humanity and one region could not contain it, it was split up into a thousand expressions, and wanders about — an eternal Proteus! — through all continents and centuries). For Herder, world history is a process of palingenesis, an eternal rebirth that is nevertheless not circular, but adheres to an upward movement. This developmental scheme breaks with the principle of identity and emphasizes the insubsumable difference of all cultures. To the late twentieth and early twenty-first century, this intellectual position seems strikingly familiar. In Herder's days, it was an entirely new concept. Yet both Kant's and Herder's position remain paradigmatic today; their ultimate persuasiveness will have to be determined by the process of history itself.

Anti-Rationalist Tendencies

To equate the eighteenth century with the age of reason would be an unwarranted simplification and, hence, a falsification. In fact, the eighteenth century witnessed many strong anti-rationalist currents within its thinking that took up a variety of traditions skeptical of reason's supremacy in all matters human and divine. One of the staunchest forces to oppose reason was that movement within Protestantism called Pietism. It arose in the seventeenth century in the Netherlands and was introduced to Germany by

Johann Arndt (1555–1621), a mystic forerunner of the movement, and Johann Jacob Spener (1635–1705). Pietism reached the apex of its development in the first half of the eighteenth century under the influence of August Hermann Francke (1663–1727), the founder of an orphanage and educational institutions in Halle, and Count Zinzendorf (1739–1813), the founder of the Herrnhut in Saxony, other Pietist colonies, and of the Church of Brethren. While Pietism championed the founding of local communities of believers (*Brüdergemeinden*) with differing customs and teachings, Pietist Christians shared a number of beliefs that set them apart from the official Protestant church which the Pietists opposed because of its overemphasis on dogma. Rather than right teaching (orthodoxy), Pietism emphasized the practical moment of faith, the *praxis pietatis*. This practical faith placed substantial emphasis on humility, defended the necessity of a spiritual crisis that precedes conversion, advocated withdrawal from the world and the subsequent integration into a community of believers following the severing of previous social bonds, and elevated religious sentiment over all cognitive aspects of faith.

One of the strongest links between the religious movement of Pietism and the philosophical and literary circles of eighteenth century Germany was Johann Georg Hamann (1730–1788), who was raised as a Pietist.[37] Hamann argued that reason cannot prove the existence of our selves and our reality, but these must be believed before they can be examined. "Unser eigen Daseyn und die Existenz aller Dinge ausser uns muß geglaubt und kann auf keine andere Art ausgemacht werden" (We must believe in our own existence and in the existence of all things around us and cannot know this in any other way). It follows that faith, too, is not a matter of reason, and can neither be logically demonstrated nor refuted, as faith does not rest on reason. "Der Glaube ist kein Werk der Vernunft und kann daher auch keinem Angriff derselben unterliegen; weil *Glauben* so wenig durch Gründe geschieht als *Schmecken* und *Sehen*"[38] (Faith is not a product of reason and can therefore also not be attacked by the latter, as faith rests as little on reasons as tasting and seeing). In his *Aesthetica in nuce* (Aesthetics in a Nutshell), Hamann subsequently delivered a religious defense of the poetic genius (a position echoed in the poetic works of Klopstock, 1724–1803) by claiming that "Poesie ist die Muttersprache des menschlichen Geschlechts"[39] (poetry is the mother tongue of the human race). Not the language of scientific inquiry or of rational exegesis provides us with ultimate insights, but poetry and love.

Much like Hamann, Jacobi was also influenced by Pietist religiosity. In his two novels, *Aus Eduard Allwills Papieren* (1775–76) and *Woldemar* (1779), he aimed to demonstrate the superiority of immediate sensations over abstract rationality. In his critique of Spinoza, Jacobi developed this position philosophically by arguing that all rational cognition is based on deductions, chains of logical steps. But this procedure necessarily leads to an infinite regress that moves from argument to argument without ever arriving at something absolutely certain. Hence, this mode of thinking is doomed to proceed without reaching a knowledge that is no longer contingent upon other facts. It is like a chain that is not anchored, it dangles within nothingness. Therefore, Jacobi charged that rationalism led to nihilism (a term that Jacobi introduces into the philosophical debate), the advocacy of nothingness. What man is looking for, however, namely the certainty of the absolute, will only reveal itself to him in religious sentiment. Yet in order to arrive at faith, a person must first free himself from the limitations of the rational method that blocks the access to the absolute. With these ideas, Jacobi influenced especially the early Romantics Novalis (1772–1801), Schleiermacher (1768–1834), and Schelling (1775–1854), among others. Novalis for example argued in his critique of Enlightenment that the hostility against organized religion eventually had to turn into hatred of all imagination and art.[40]

Aesthetics[41]

Enlightenment thought does not have an inherent preference for one style of art over another or a coherent view of the usefulness of art for the Enlightenment project. During the eighteenth century, the baroque styles turned rococo, France's art developed the splendors of classicism, England began exploring neo-classical expressions in the visual and decorative arts, and Germany developed its own forms of rococo poetry and architecture that emerged now as *Empfindsamkeit* (sensibility), now as *Anakreontik*. None of these artistic articulations found more genuine support by Enlightenment philosophy than any other. In fact, while some Enlightenment philosophers were also the authors of works of fiction — Diderot, Voltaire, Lessing, and Wieland readily come to mind — others were suspicious of the poetic imagination in general. They argued that the fancy of the writers of fiction stems from the same source as the religious imagination, and both are equally prone to muddying the clear waters of reason. Hence, critical philosophy must keep poetry from contaminating Enlightenment thought.[42] By and large, however, Enlightenment thinkers supported freedom of artistic expression and did not seem to concern themselves with the stylistic form this expression took.

One aspect of eighteenth-century thought, however, was meant to have a large impact on the intellectual history of the following time, and that is the emergence of philosophical aesthetics. Naturally, artists and thinkers have always reflected on the nature of art and beauty, but these two topics were not necessarily seen as interrelated. Nor has art been seen as an autonomous expression of man, but rather as one aspect of an overarching social or theological structure. But the eighteenth century brought forth an independent philosophical discipline under the name of aesthetics that aimed to investigate questions of art's epistemological and practical value. The term 'aesthetics' shifted its meaning from a theory of sense perception to a theory of art and the beautiful; shortly thereafter, in the Romantic era, it would also include phenomena like the ugly, the grotesque, and the obscene.

Alexander Gottlieb Baumgarten (1714–1762) introduced aesthetics as a separate philosophical discipline with the intention to strengthen the rationalist metaphysics of Leibniz and Wolff by emphasizing the epistemological relevance of sensual perception. He argues that sensuality is not merely a hindrance or a truncated form of rational cognition, but rather its precondition. Furthermore, aesthetics has its own truth claim that retains the richness and multifacetedness of sensual material, an immediacy that gets lost in rational cognition. Baumgarten defines beauty as the perfection of sensual cognition, and hence art as the manifestation of the beautiful aims to represent the purposeful unity and harmony of the world. True art, however, depends on the correct application of rules which aesthetics as the science of art and beauty is to develop. With this proposition, Baumgarten exerted some influence on the *Regelpoetiken* (normative poetics) of the eighteenth century that continued the baroque tradition of Opitz and others.

While Baumgarten strove to gain acceptance for the cognitive relevance of the sensual and of art, Mendelssohn emphasized the pleasurable sensation induced by the perfection of art and beauty. His aesthetics constitute the link between the rationalism of Leibniz and Wolff and the aesthetics of the classicists Goethe, Schiller, Wilhelm von Humboldt, and others. With this emphasis on art's emotional elements, Mendelssohn introduced a paradigmatic shift away from the aesthetics of production and normative poetics to the aesthetics of reception and a general psychological aesthetics that reached its epitome in the writings of Karl Philipp Moritz (1756–1793) and was further developed by the romantic generation.

Yet it was Kant's 1790 *Kritik der Urteilskraft* (Critique of Judgment) that was to become the single most influential text in the history of philosophical aesthetics. This Third Critique is Kant's attempt to bridge the rift between theory and practice by advancing judgment as a faculty that mediates between sensuality and cognition on the one hand and between sensuality and moral action on the other. A judgment of taste, Kant argues, does not refer to any qualities of the object, but merely to the feeling of pleasure or displeasure experienced by the subject. It has no connection to our rational judgments, and hence beauty as the object of the judgment of taste does not relate to insight and cognition. Beauty grants us pleasure because the richness of the aesthetic material can never be subsumed under a concept. Yet this pleasure is not merely private, but we expect others to share our judgment even in the absence of rational arguments for it. This universality of the aesthetic judgment, however, also provides the ground for art's important communal function, namely that of integrating the isolated individual into a community of recipients of art. Art for Kant is the product of a genius, who is able to make a manmade product look as if it were created by nature. Art's non-cognitive nature, though, does not mean that it has severed all ties to morality. Rather, the beautiful in art and nature functions as a symbol of the good.

Especially this effort to unite art and morality is what drew Schiller to Kant's aesthetics. Yet for him, a stronger historical and anthropological grounding was necessary in order to convincingly establish aesthetics. Schiller in his *Über die ästhetische Erziehung des Menschen in einer Reihe von Briefen* (On the Aesthetic Education of Man in a Series of Letters, 1795) claimed that the achievement of a moral community transcends the individual and becomes political, but such community cannot be established by means of political education or revolution. Rather, the only way to create a republic of free and equal members is by detour through an aesthetic education that mediates between the natural state of man and the utopian vision of humanity.

Before philosophical aesthetics united systematic analysis with historical interpretations of art, especially in the works of Schelling and Hegel, two thinkers of the eighteenth century already combined detailed analyses of artworks with theoretical speculation: Johann Joachim Winckelmann and Lessing. Winckelmann's *Gedanken über die Nachahmung der griechischen Werke in der Malerey und Bildhauerkunst* (Thoughts on the Imitation of Greek Works in Painting and Sculpture, 1755) granted ancient Greek art normative status for all artistic production. To be successful, even to be original — as paradoxical as that may sound — mimesis was not to take nature as its origin, but rather the works of antiquity. Although Winckelmann later insisted more strongly on the uniqueness of classical art and hence on the impossibility of repeating this period, he continued to uphold ancient art as normative instances for all artistic beauty. This beauty cannot be defined by means of philosophical inquiry resting on abstract operations of thought, rather it must be experienced sensually vis-à-vis the concrete object of art. Such insistence on the sensual nature of beauty further strengthened the anti-rationalist tendencies of philosophical aesthetics as developed by Baumgarten. Winckelmann's writings would soon exert tremendous influence on the humanistic-classical epoch and its representatives Goethe, Humboldt, Herder, and others.

Lessing's *Laokoon* (1766) was another influential aesthetic essay in which its author set out to clarify the relationship between the visual and the literary arts through a detailed analysis of the Laokoon sculpture. Lessing argued for a fundamental differentiation between the visual and poetic arts based on the nature of their aesthetic signs. While painting is spatial, poetry is temporal. From this difference Lessing concludes that literature is the superior art, for it has a wider variety of materials at its disposal, because unlike painting, it never arrests an image in a moment of time, but can always overcome even the most gruesome and disturbing moment by another more benign representation. Painting and sculpture are unable to do so, their representations remain fixed, and are thus limited to more acceptable material. Lessing ultimately argues against the Horacian doctrine of *ut pictura poesis,* the theory that views literature as a form of painting. For him, poetry's versatility and richness proves superior over the visual arts, and with his analyses of both modes of representation Lessing helped launch that branch of aesthetics concerned with the materiality of its signifiers, now generally termed media aesthetics, as well as aesthetic semiotics.

Philosophical aesthetics would soon advance from its marginal position in Enlightenment discourse to the center of philosophical debates. For this to happen, however, Enlightenment's faith in the supremacy of analytic reason first had to wane. This form of reason was to be replaced by an aesthetic *Symphilosophie,* a use of thought aimed at the unification of its separate moments. However, the thinkers of the romantic generation no longer saw the highest unity, that is, the unity of the absolute, in operations of analytic reason, but rather in the experience of art. Within one hundred years, the hierarchy of sensuality and reason, aesthetic perception and abstraction had been reversed. Situated between Leibniz and Schelling, the Enlightenment can from one perspective seem more a farewell to an old world than the dawn of a new age.

Notes

[1] For an excellent overview of the employment of the metaphor of light in the philosophical discourse from antiquity to the present, see Hans Blumenberg's essay "Licht als Metapher der Wahrheit. Im Vorfeld der philosophischen Begriffsbildung," in *Ästhetische und metaphorologische Schriften* (Frankfurt a. M.: Suhrkamp, 2001), 139–71. In his article "Aufklärung," Horst Stuke states that the Enlightenment aims at the liberation from all authority that does not survive the questioning by reason. In *Geschichtliche Grundbegriffe. Historisches Lexikon zur politisch-sozialen Sprache Deutschlands,* ed. Horst Brunner et al. (Stuttgart: Klett, 1972), 1: 243–342. Reference on p. 245. For a contemporary document, see e.g., Diderot's article "Fait" (Fact) in his *Encyclopédie.*

[2] Ernst Cassirer argues that the Enlightenment is part of a wider intellectual development in which modern philosophical thought reaches self-consciousness; *The Philosophy of Enlightenment* [1938], trans. F. C. A. Koelln and J. P. Pettegrove (Boston: Beacon Press, 1961), 8.

[3] See Manfred Frank, "Aufklärung als analytische und synthetische Vernunft," in *Aufklärung und Gegenaufklärung in der europäischen Literatur, Philosophie und Politik von der Antike bis zur Gegenwart,* ed. Jochen Schmidt (Darmstadt: Wissenschaftliche Buchgesellschaft, 1989), 377–403.

[4] See Peter Gay, *The Enlightenment.* Vol. 1: *The Rise of Modern Paganism* (New York & London: Norton, 1977), 293.

[5] See the article "Cartésianisme" by Abbé Pestré in Diderot's *Encyclopédie.*

[6] See Thomas Munck, *The Enlightenment: A Comparative Social History* (London: Arnold, 2000), 4.

[7] Cassirer, *Philosophy,* 107.

[8] Regarding this combination of influences from Spinoza and Leibniz, see Jan Rohls's *Geschichte der Ethik* (Tübingen: Mohr/Siebeck, 1991), 308.

[9] Gottfried Wilhelm Leibniz, "De primae philosophiae emendatione, et de notione substantiae" in *Philosophische Schriften.* Vol. 1: *Kleine Schriften zur Metaphysik,* trans. Hans Heinz Holz (Frankfurt a. M.: Suhrkamp, 1996), 199.

[10] Leibniz, "System nouveau de la nature et de la communication des substances, aussi bien que de l'union qu'il y a entre l'ame et le corps," in *Kleine Schriften zur Metaphysik,* 200–227, here 218.

[11] Leibniz, "Eclaircissement du nouveau system de la communication des substances, pour servir de reponse à ce qui en est dit dans le Journal du 12 septembre 1695," in *Kleine Schriften zur Metaphysik,* 226–37, here 234.

[12] On Leibniz's notion of God, Etienne Gilson comments: "As a matter of fact, the God of the *Monadology* was but the Good of Plato, solving the problem of which world to create, by means of the infinitesimal calculus recently discovered by Leibniz," *God and Philosophy* (New Haven: Yale UP, 1941), 99–100.

[13] See Wilhelm Windelband, *Lehrbuch der Geschichte der Philosophie,* 18th ed. (Tübingen: Mohr/Siebeck, 1993), 389.

[14] See Cassirer, *Philosophie,* 140.

[15] Leibniz, "Von der Glückseligkeit," in *Kleine Schriften zur Metaphysik,* 391–401, here 399.

[16] Uwe Wesel, *Geschichte des Rechts: Von den Frühformen bis zum Vertrag von Maastricht* (Munich: Beck, 1997), 365–72.

[17] See Ernst Bloch, "Christian Thomasius. Ein deutscher Gelehrter ohne Misere," in *Naturrecht und menschliche Würde* (Frankfurt a. M.: Suhrkamp, 1961), 315–53, here 343.

[18] See the introduction by Raffaele Ciafardone in the volume *Die Philosophie der deutschen Aufklärung: Texte und Darstellung* (Stuttgart: Reclam, 1990), 11–38, esp. 31.

[19] Moses Mendelssohn, "Über die Frage: was heißt aufklären?" (Regarding the question: what it means to enlighten?), in *Was ist Aufklärung?,* ed. Ehrhard Bahr (Stuttgart: Reclam, 1974), 3–8. Many other contributions to the Enlightenment debate of the 1780s are readily accessible in this volume.

[20] Both Ciafardone, *Aufklärung,* 13–14 and Stuke, *Aufklärung,* 265, arrive at the convincing conclusion that Kant's essay is not typical for the use of the term "Enlightenment" at this time.

[21] Kant, "Beantwortung der Frage: Was ist Aufklärung?" Kant's works are quoted from the *Theorie-Werkausgabe,* ed. Wilhelm Weischedel, 9th ed. (Frankfurt a. M.: Suhrkamp, 1996). According to philosophical citation standards and in order to facilitate the verification of quotes for users of English language editions, I will not give the page numbers of the German edition, but rather the internationally used pagination of the original A and B editions. The above quote can be located on A 481.

[22] Kant, "Was ist Aufklärung?" A 481.

[23] Johann Georg Hamann, "Brief an Christian Jacob Kraus, Dec. 18, 1784," in *Was ist Aufklärung?* 17–22.

[24] Friedrich Schiller, *Über die ästhetische Erziehung des Menschen in einer Reihe von Briefen,* in *Werke in drei Bänden* (Munich: Hanser, 1984), 2: 445–520, here 462.

[25] One must agree with Windelband's assessment that deism on the one hand is an important expression of tolerance and humaneness, but on the other hand it is the anemic state of religion, "ein Kunstprodukt der gebildeten Gesellschaft" (an artificial product of the educated society, *Lehrbuch der Geschichte der Philosophie,* 414).

[26] Lessing, *Nathan der Weise,* in *Werke in drei Bänden* (Munich: Hanser, 1982), 591–735; esp. Act III, Scene 7.

[27] Johann Carl Wezel, *Belphegor oder die wahrscheinlichste Geschichte unter der Sonne* (Frankfurt a. M.: Insel, 1965), 7 and 112.

[28] Lessing, "Die Erziehung des Menschengeschlechts," in *Werke in drei Bänden,* 3: 637–58, here 656.

[29] Lessing, "Die Erziehung des Menschengeschlechts," 638.

[30] See e.g., *Kritik der reinen Vernunft,* B 670, A 642.

[31] *Kritik der praktischen Vernunft,* A 220, A 226.

[32] *Kritik der praktischen Vernunft,* A 226.

[33] Peter Gay points out this dualist view of history that regards the historical past as a bleak register of crimes and cruelty while simultaneously emphasizing that some few epochs of reason and progress allow for the hope that reason can triumph. *The Enlightenment* (note 3), 1: 32–33.

[34] Kant, "Idee zu einer allgemeinen Geschichte in weltbürgerlicher Absicht," A 396.

[35] Kant, "Idee zu einer allgemeinen Geschichte in weltbürgerlicher Absicht," A 409.

[36] Herder, *Auch eine Philosophie der Geschichte zur Bildung der Menschheit* (Stuttgart: Reclam, 1990), 36.

[37] Regarding the Pietist influences on Hamann, see Isaiah Berlin, "The Counter-Enlightenment," in *The Proper Study of Mankind: An Anthology of Essays,* ed. Henry Hardy and Roger Hausherr (New York: Farrar, Straus and Giroux: 1998), 243–68.

[38] Johann Georg Hamann, *Sokratische Denkwürdigkeiten: Aesthetica in nuce* (Stuttgart: Reclam, 1968), 51.

[39] *Sokratische Denkwürdigkeiten*, 81.

[40] Novalis, "Die Christenheit oder Europa," in *Werke in einem Band* (Munich: Hanser, 1981), 526–44, esp. 535–36.

[41] The following is a thumbnail sketch that draws heavily on the material that I develop in detail in the first three chapters of my study *The German Aesthetic Tradition* (Cambridge: Cambridge UP, 2002).

[42] See Peter Gay, *The Enlightenment,* 2: 215.

Johann Christoph Gottsched and Luise Adelgunde Victorie, anonymous painting, ca. 1740.

Gottsched's Literary Reforms: The Beginning of Modern German Literature

Katherine R. Goodman

THE MODERN PERIOD IN GERMAN LITERATURE began in the first third of the eighteenth century when literary imagination became fundamentally rational. Challenges to rationalism have never abated, but in order to remain valid in the new philosophy of the 1720s and 1730s, religious and classical authorities could no longer be taken on faith, they had to be proven to be correct. German rhetoric was rigorously subjected to the rules of logic. Literary genres, poetic imagery, and figurative speech had to adhere to principles of morality and verisimilitude. A new breed of literary critics would soon analyze literary texts as aesthetic objects. By the late-eighteenth century, literature had become self-reflexive.

The inexorable victory of reason was rendered possible by literacy in the vernacular. German linguistic reformers sought to persuade large segments of academia and the aristocracy to use the vernacular (instead of Latin and French) and forcefully developed rules to unify German spelling, grammar, and syntax across regional dialects. Print media became the tool to popularize the new philosophy of reason, and the audience for literary and journalistic texts expanded from the local to the national, from specialists and the elite to generalists and a wider urban audience. Oral culture — including sermons, tales, extemporaneous dramatic productions — lost currency as more readers turned to books. Similarly, visual culture grew relatively less important as affordable texts — without expensive illustrations — were mass produced. As book culture evolved, text increasingly dominated imaginations.

Obviously, such massive changes evolved only gradually over many decades, but in the first half of the eighteenth century no one worked harder for literary reforms in Germany than Johann Christoph Gottsched (1700–1766). He had predecessors, aides and critics, but he was the single most effective mobilizing force for a modern German literature. This "German Fontenelle" was neither an original thinker nor an especially creative poet.[1] He was rather a synthesizer, promoter, and popularizer, arguably the greatest in German cultural history. In these roles his energy, comprehensive vision, and organizational skills have rarely been matched. Gottsched resembled Fontenelle in the breadth of his interests: philosophy, science, linguistics, poetics, rhetoric, history of literature, journalism, translation, pedagogy, and more. He published several journals — both for professional and more general readers — to advance the cause of modern German culture. In addition to his own tireless activity, Gottsched possessed the ability to motivate others. He organized many students and colleagues to help him in his undertakings and referred to them as his "Gehülfen" (associates or apprentices).[2] Among the most gifted of these was his wife, Luise Adelgunde Victorie Gottsched, née Kulmus (1713–1762). Many of his associates carried Gottsched's interests to other parts of Germany and Europe, most notably to Russia, Poland, and Hungary. He maintained an active correspondence with scholars and pedagogues throughout Europe and Germany.

Leipzig as Cultural Center

When Gottsched arrived in Leipzig in 1724 as a student, the Saxon city of around 24,000 inhabitants was one of several culturally significant cities in Germany. Because it was known for its francophile culture of gallantry, contemporaries often referred to Leipzig as "little Paris." Although the Saxon court did not reside there but in nearby Dresden, aristocrats frequently visited Leipzig because it was a major trade center. European traders brought their wares to Leipzig twice yearly, and local manufacturers prospered from the fairs. Among the important objects produced or traded in the city were books. Leipzig also boasted a major university. This combination of trade fairs, book manufacture, and a major university made Leipzig an important intellectual center in Germany. Even other culturally vital cities — shipping centers like Hamburg or the other major publishing center Frankfurt am Main — did not have this unique combination of commerce and learning.

Still, cultural changes came slowly. In 1701, for instance, the progressive philosophy professor Christian Thomasius (1655–1728) was attacked when he argued forcefully against the persecution of people accused of witchcraft in *De Crimine Magiae* (1701). Decades earlier Leipzig law professor Benedict Carpzov (1595–1666) had been one of Germany's most vociferous lawyers arguing for the persecution of "witches." If the 1720s, when Gottsched arrived in Leipzig, it was still professionally dangerous to support the then very modern rationalism of Christian Wolff, professor of philosophy at the University of Halle. Indeed, Gottsched nearly failed an exam in which he took a stand defending Wolff's rationalism before historian Johann Burkhard Mencke (1674–1732) came to his defense. Orthodox Lutheranism dominated the municipality, scholasticism the university.

As elsewhere in Germany that university culture was dominated linguistically by Latin. Indeed, writing from exile in the Netherlands, French philosopher and critic Pierre Bayle chose to compare Leipzig not with Paris, but with Athens — calling it "l'Athenes d'Allemagne" — because of the international standing of the *Acta Eruditorum* (1682–1782), a journal published in the *lingua franca* of Europe by Professor Otto Mencke (1644–1707).[3] Again, it was Christian Thomasius who drew rebukes from his colleagues in 1687 for announcing the first lecture series in the German vernacular.[4]

By the 1720s Leipzig was host to an active community of amateur poets writing in the vernacular. These were by no means all gallant. Occasional poetry was widely written in Germany. Professional men — lawyers, professors, and doctors — and some women wrote poetry for private celebrations, amusements, and ceremonies. They memorialized marriages, promotions, graduations, birthdays, and funerals in verse. They wrote each other letters in verse. These verses might be copied out in one's best handwriting or privately printed and distributed to a friend or friends. Public occasions were commemorated by those seeking attention and rewards for their efforts. Men and women also engaged in writing religious poetry.[5]

In Leipzig, anonymous "street poetry" also flourished — broadsides and scandal sheets mostly in verse — often penned by students and young aspiring gentlemen. Frequently bawdy or slanderous, "pasquills" — particularly popular in Leipzig until they were banned in 1724 — often alluded to actual events and people.[6] The ban was not completely effective and these sheets, sometimes appearing as weeklies, were carried around town, including to the coffee houses, by news-runners, sometimes women.[7] In short, literary activity in the vernacular was very widespread in Leipzig.

Johann Christian Günther and Christiane Mariane von Ziegler

Two Leipzig poets illustrate the texture of literary culture, the status of the vernacular and the forces operating for literary innovation at the time in Germany: Johann Christian Günther (1695–1723) and Christiane Mariane von Ziegler. In 1717 Günther arrived in Leipzig, and Johann Burckhard Mencke became his mentor. Mencke had long been training himself in a simpler, more modern style by translating the early Greek lyric poet Anacreon and writing his own gallant poetry under the pseudonym Philander von der Linde.[8] Anacreon had been influential in the development of French gallant poetry, and Gottsched later tested his own skills translating his verse. Under the tutelage of Mencke and owing to his own native talent, Günther became the most gifted German poet of the age. He was strongly influenced not only by Anacreon, but also by Ovid (in particular by the Roman poet's sophisticated love cycle, *Amores*) and the neo-Latin erotic poetry of Johannes Secundus (1511–1536).⁹ In graceful verses Günther praised wine, women and song:

> Schweig du doch nur, du Helffte meiner Brust;
>   Denn was du weinst, ist Blut aus meinem Herzen:
> Ich taumle so und hab an nichts mehr Lust,
>   Als an der Angst und den getreuen Schmertzen,
> Womit der Stern, der unsre Liebe trennt,
>   Die Augen brennt.¹⁰

[Be still, you who are half my breast, for what you weep is my heart's blood; I'm reeling so and desire nothing but the fear and faithful pain with which the star, which separates our love, burns my eyes.]

Like other gallant poets, he sometimes wrote erotic verse. Günther also expanded the scope of occasional poetry to include social criticism. One of his themes became the plight of poets who could not earn a livelihood from their craft. Günther did not succeed in becoming poet at the court of Augustus the Strong, Elector of Saxony and was obliged to complete his medical degree and find employment as a doctor. While some readers admired his talent, many contemporary critics focused on what they perceived to be immoral behavior, considering the expression of amorous sentiments to have improper, all too personal origins. Allegations to this effect followed him even after he became a practicing physician. Other critics did not like his desire to elevate poetry to a profession, believing that this let to sycophancy and did not really represent "work." (Some poets earned good money from patrons and the subjects of their occasional poetry, while publishers paid few royalties, asserting that it was they who performed the work in printing a book.)¹¹ Günther's graceful verses became well known and admired among the *cognoscenti* after his early death at age twenty-eight, but were still criticized for their perceived superficiality. In the effort to overcome the cumbersome baroque style, German gallant poets foundered on the conflict between the frivolity of the Anacreontic tradition favored by the aristocracy and the earnest moral standards of the learned, religious, middle-class, non-aristocratic audience.

The wealthy and relatively independent patrician, Christiane Mariane von Ziegler (1695–1760), wrote both religious and gallant poetry. The widowed daughter of a former Leipzig mayor, Ziegler hosted a salon in the 1720s and early 1730s. She gathered local patricians, lawyers, academics (among them Gottsched and Mencke), and artists (including Johann Sebastian Bach who set some of Ziegler's lyrics to music) for intellectual amusements in the style of the seventeenth-century Parisian salons.¹² An admirer of novelist and *précieuse* Madeleine de Scudéry (1607–1701), Ziegler translated the Frenchwoman's *Conversations* (1680–92) and the novel *Les Bains de Thermopylae*, which had originally appeared as part of the *Conversations*. Writing verse was a popular form of entertainment for leisure hours. Poetry provided amusement or promoted sociability, sometimes it became a parlor game. Very popular were games in verse. In Ziegler's salon, for instance, echo rhymes provided an amusing way to pass the time. Rhymes for poetic lines were given and each guest wrote a poem using words that rhymed with those of the model.

Shortly after his arrival in Leipzig in 1724, Gottsched began visiting Ziegler's salon. He soon began tutoring her in prosody and, in time, supported her publicly as a writer and a poet. On his recommendation she was invited to become a member of the *Deutsche Gesellschaft* (1730, admitted 1731) and crowned imperial poet laureate (1733). Gottsched's support for Ziegler and other women poets was not totally unselfish, but a modern gesture in keeping with much admired French culture. In the latter part of the seventeenth century the French *modernes* had illustrated the superiority of French culture over the literature of classical antiquity by pointing to the accomplishments of the *précieuses*, notably their neologisms and novels. Gottsched aimed to rival this gallant French achievement in Germany and recognized the hitherto neglected presence and ability of women poets and readers from the upper middle class and educated aristocracy in Germany. Gottsched would strive to involve women, especially as readers, in his literary activities.

Ziegler also advocated expanding the public roles of literary women. In 1728, invoking the names of French women predecessors, largely aristocrats — salonières, novelists, letter writers and gallant poets — as inspiration, she encouraged other German women to publish the poetry they wrote for private affairs and demonstrate their ability in public. In the preface to *Versuch in gebundener Schreib-Art* (Essay in Poetic Form, 1728), a collection of her own religious and gallant poetry, Ziegler ponders the fact that women cannot write nearly as well as men though women are orally very proficient, sometimes even superior to men in their speech:

> Indeß habe ich vielmal der Sache mit Verwunderung nachgedacht, wie es doch zugehen müsse, daß da das Frauenzimmer, so wol bey Hofe, als auch in woleingerichteten Städten, den Ruhm mit Beyfall aller, auch so gar derer gelehrtesten Männer hat, oft besser als jene zu reden, dennoch im schreiben es mit ihnen gar nicht fort wolle, sondern zehn Weiber-Federn nicht an die Schrifft eines einigen in der Gelehrsamkeit angeführten Mannes, ich will nicht sagen in gelehrten, sondern bloß ordentl. Sachen reichen.[13]

> [In the meantime I have often pondered with amazement, how it must come about, that since women, both at court and in well-appointed

towns, earn a reputation with the approval of everyone, including the most learned men, of frequently speaking better than these, still cannot make a go of it at all in writing, rather ten women's quills cannot match the text of a man trained in learning, and I mean only in ordinary matters, never mind in learned ones.]

Ziegler deplored women's lack of education and of formal training in literary matters; the inelegance of her German prose in this passage illustrates her point. Under the influence of Mencke and Gottsched, Ziegler developed a clearer style. The syntax in the preface to her collection of prose letters, *Moralische und vermischte Send-Schreiben* (Moral and Mixed Letters, 1731), is already much more logical and clear:

Die ohne diß zur Spötterey sehr geneigte Welt wird ohnfehlbar bey abermahliger Erblickung eines andern Entwurffs meiner schlechten Gedancken auf die Meynung gerathen, ob hätte ich mich in das Bücher-Schreiben so verliebt, daß ich in Zukunfft nichts als eitel Schrifften häuffig unter das Volck schneyen lassen, und meine Feder in eine immer währende und beständig lauffende Machine verwandeln würde.[14]

[When they see another example of my poor thoughts, worldly people, already so fond of ridicule, will surely form the opinion that I have fallen so much in love with writing books that I plan in future to let my vain texts fall as abundantly as snowflakes among the populace and to transform my quill into a perpetual and constantly running machine.]

Ziegler's subtle irony may conceal the fact that she experienced censure for her publications and that the poetic laurels bestowed on her publicly represented a provocation in some quarters.[15] Like Günther, she was assumed to have engaged in immoral acts.[16] Broadsheets and satires in verse carried the slander throughout Leipzig. Her social status as a patrician was not sufficient to insulate her from such diatribes. Eventually Gottsched tired of defending her and, especially after his marriage in 1735, distanced himself from her. At the same time, in the late 1730s, Ziegler's continued affinity for more sociable and graceful forms of poetry alienated her from the earnestness of Gottsched's reforms.[17] After 1739 she remarried and ceased publishing.

Language and Style from the Baroque to Neoclassicism

The dominant discourses in the early seventeenth century were mainly religious or social — gallant pleasantries, reportage, and celebrations of local events or of wine, women and song. The infusion of literary discourse with principles of rationalism and neoclassicism — secular morality and verisimilitude — had not yet occurred. The German language itself was an obstacle to those who promoted these ideas, as academicians trained in Latin and aristocrats trained in French were ill-equipped to use German with intellectual subtlety.

When Gottsched embarked on his reforms, there was no standard grammar, nor a standard orthography. Differences in regional dialects appeared in poetry, affecting not only rhyme and scansion, but also grammar and even basic coherence. Vernacular stylistic and rhetorical models were, in terms of the classical triad (grand, middle, low), either too high or too low for general and rational discourses on intellectual matters.[18] The high end of the rhetorical scale was represented by students of elaborate Ciceronian structures: the chancery style (*Kanzleistil*) and the Second Silesian School. The former was the style used at the courts in Vienna or Dresden — lengthy, convoluted sentences, replete with foreign loan words and expressions of servile obeisance. The so-called Second Silesian School, literature of the late baroque, had favored elaborate Italian Marinism, found in the poetry of Silesian Christian Hoffmann von Hoffmannswaldau (1616–1679) and erudite Spanish allusion from the dramas of his compatriot, Daniel Caspar von Lohenstein (1635–83). These two styles — the chancery style and the Second Silesian School — shared certain traits.[19] They were rich, even opulent in extravagant and profuse imagery, epithets, synonyms, repetitions, had a vocabulary of foreign (usually French or Latin) extraction, and convoluted syntax with heavy emphasis on periphrasis and subordinate clauses.

The then fashionable gallant literature that emanated from the salons of the *précieuses*, the *modernes*, extended the influence of this language of indirection, circumlocution, and passionate extremes. This was a literature whose primary purpose was sociability — manners and affections; it cultivated a refined, sometimes artificial and affected style of expression. Consider the following sentence written in the introduction to his dictionary for women (1715) by Leipzig lawyer and sometime poet, Gottlieb Siegmund Corvinus (1677–1746):

> Ja wie die Tugend nicht nur ihre Augen auf ein kluges Buch lencket, sondern auch darbey einen blancken Degen in die Hand nimmt, um ihren entbrannten Arm dadurch nicht müßig gehen zu lassen, so wird sie Bellona, als Göttin des Krieges, von diesem wundernswürdigen Parnass auf eine solche Wahlstadt führen, wo ihre Töchter als Heroinen, trotz den berühmtesten Helden kämpffen, Lantz und Schild behertzt führen, ihren zarten und schlancken Leib in einen beschwerlichen Pantzer und Küraß einschliessen, die wollenweiche Stirne mit einem Casquet beschweren, und so wohl die Blitze in ihren schönen Augen, als auch auff der Klinge zeigen, wo diese Heldenmüthigen Dames mit auffgestreifften Armen das Schlachtschwerdt auf beyden Seiten vieltausend Leichen streuen lassen, und sich durch ihren

männlichen und heroischen Geist solche Sieges-Palmen und Oliven-Zweige erfechten, welche mit ihrer rühmens-würdigen Asche nimmermehr verstäuben können, sondern längst in den Tempel der Ewigkeit mit unter die unverwelcklichen Sieges-Cräntze auffgehenget worden.[20]

[For as virtue not only directs her eyes toward a wise book, but in so doing also takes up a shining sword that her flaming arm not remain idle, so will she transport Bellona, goddess of war, from this wondrous Parnassus to a chosen battleground where her daughters, against the most famous heroes, will fight and bravely carry lance and shield, encase their delicate and slender bodies in heavy plate and armor, weigh down their woolly soft brows with caskets and let show flashes from their beautiful eyes as well as their blades, where with outstretched arms these heroic ladies will let their swords strew many thousand bodies on both sides of the battlefield and by their manly and heroic spirit win such victory palms and olive branches as can never be scattered with their fame-worthy ashes, but rather were hung with the never-fading crown of victory in the temple of eternity.]

Such convoluted style was not appropriate for the new ideal of a cultivated communication of genuine sentiment or reasoned discourse.

A New Standard for German: Gottsched's *Deutsche Sprachkunst* (1748)

The development of a common German vernacular was the effort of many minds and imaginations: in the eighteenth century Gottsched was the most important scholar and author figuring in the codification of its grammar, spelling, and syntax. Long desired and discussed, the task of setting the standard was daunting due to regional rivalries and the absence of linguistic standards. When Gottsched arrived in Leipzig in 1724 Mencke supervised the *Deutsch-übende Gesellschaft* (Society for the Practice of German) in Leipzig, which had started as a group of Silesian students who wanted to improve their rhetorical skills in German.[21] It was not an unusual society in Germany, and like similar "Sprachgesellschaften" (language societies) of the seventeenth century, remained largely regional in its impact. In 1727 Mencke's new protégé Gottsched became its *Senior*. This gave Gottsched a position from which to engage in his linguistic activities. With the *Académie Française* in mind, but without any royal mandate, Gottsched redesigned the Society and tried in vain to find a royal patron for it.[22] In the end this society assumed a very different organizational structure, one which reflected the political and cultural situation in Germany. Unlike the French academy, membership in the *Deutsche Gesellschaft* was neither restricted in number, nor was its structure centralized. It had affiliates in other cities and towns — usually university cities, not royal residences (Göttingen, Jena, Greifswald, Königsberg, Helmstedt, Bremen, Bern, Basel, Altdorf, Erlangen, Mannheim and Vienna). Gottsched had hoped the Society would compile a dictionary and a grammar. In the end the dictionary never appeared, but Gottsched produced a grammar.[23] For years he gathered material and authored preliminary articles for the grammar in his journal *Critische Beyträge* (Critical Essays, 1732–44), one of the first professional publications for German philologists and literary scholars and until 1738 the official organ of the *Deutsche Gesellschaft*.

Although not without critics (especially in Silesia and Switzerland), Gottsched's *Deutsche Sprachkunst* (Art of the German Language, 1748) was an enormous success.[24] Fifteen editions had appeared by 1780. As the work gathered momentum and took on canonical authority, it standardized German spelling, grammar, word formation, and syntax and was adopted in many schools throughout the German states. His guiding principles, he claimed, had been the practices of the best authors and nature itself (objectivity). In reality his standard appeared biased as it was based on the Meissen dialect in Saxony. While this irritated some (again, especially Silesians and Swiss), Gottsched's appearance of objectivity, his energy in promoting the plan and no doubt the desire of many to have any reasonable standard carried the argument. As he wrote in the preface to the first edition the *Deutsche Sprachkunst* was designed for youth, those who had not attended university, soldiers, scribes, and young ladies. The *Deutsche Sprachkunst* went through five authorized editions during Gottsched's lifetime and, like his introduction to philosophy *Erste Gründe der Weltweisheit* (Foundations of Worldly Wisdom, 1730), was adopted by schools throughout Germany. Gottsched's most important contribution to a renovation of German literature was his adamant, even dogmatic concern for the promotion and codification of the German language.

Reasonable Oratory: Gottsched's *Grundriß zu einer Vernunfftmäßigen Redekunst* (1729)

Intellectuals had long criticized the extravagances of the late baroque style that persisted into the eighteenth century. As early as 1682 in his *Unterricht von der Teutschen Sprache und Poesie* (Lessons in German Language and Poetry) Daniel Georg Morhof (1639–1691) had excoriated baroque *Schwulst* (bombastic style), but this book had not brought about a radical departure from the late baroque high style. Here, too, Gottsched did more than anyone to establish a German style for the new fashion in literature. One of his earliest publications was the *Grundriß zu einer vernunfftmäßigen Redekunst* (Introduction to a Rational Rhetoric, 1729). In 1736 he published the expanded *Ausführliche Redekunst* (Complete Rhetoric), which provided guidelines for good German prose style. Gottsched turned to classical and French models of prose style that would, in essence, fulfill Aristotle's insistence on clarity. A self-proclaimed disciple of Cicero and Quintilian, Gottsched adhered to the classical triad of styles, referring to them as "natürlich," "sinnreich," and "bewegend" (natural, judicious, and moving).[25] He labored primarily to establish a standard for the "middle" style lacking in German, a style guided by reason, but not devoid of elegance. The stylistic ideals of Gottsched and other Germans in the early eighteenth century replicated those asserted by the French neoclassicist academicians under Louis XIV: conciseness, restriction of imagery and participles, *connexio realis* (connections based not on language [*connexio verbalis*], but on content). Of overriding importance in the consideration of style was the new criterion of reason. It should govern both content and mode of expression. Sentences should not only follow logically, they should also be constructed logically, unfolding in a natural, reasoned way. Language should be appropriate to its content, not redundant, exaggerated, or overly servile.

Quite apart from his influential textbooks, Gottsched's own disciplined style did much to transmit his rhetorical ideals. Whatever he translated or wrote appeared in clear, elegant sentences. His discursive style reached many through two popular moral weeklies (*Die vernünfftigen Tadlerinnen* [The Reasonable Lady Scolds, 1725–26] and *Der Biedermann* [The Upright Man, 1728–29]), several journals (*Critische Beyträge* [1732–44]; *Neuer Büchersaal* [New Library, 1745–50]; *Das Neueste aus der anmuthigen Gelehrsamkeit* [The Latest from the World of Pleasing Scholarship, 1751–62]);[26] and many books.

After their marriage in 1735, Gottsched's wife, sometimes also known as "die Gottschedin," became a generous and effective contributor to these works.[27] For instance, some contemporaries attributed major portions of the *Neuer Büchersaal* to her.[28] Her style certainly rivaled her husband's in clarity and wit, and she must be counted among the major influences on the development of a new German style. In particular, when it was a matter of satirizing exaggerated or illogical style, her lively and humorous imagination was pressed into service. This is found, for instance, in *Die Horatier* (1739), a satire on the rhetorical skills of Lutheran ministers who opposed Wolff's philosophy; in "Schreiben an die Verfasser der critischen Beyträge . . ." (Note To The Authors of the Critical Essays, 1740), a satire on exaggerated prose; in her satire on musical dramas, *Der kleine Prophet von Böhmischbroda* (The Little Prophet from Böhmischbroda, 1753), and a series of satires on southern German clerical (Catholic) rhetoric which appeared in several journals.[29] Luise Gottsched's contributions in this field have remained largely unappreciated.

The New Philosophy: Christian Wolff and Gottsched

Gottsched's poetics owed much to the philosophy of Christian Wolff, whose deductive rationalism was the most important philosophical influence on the young professor. In 1724 alliance with the philosopher Wolff was no trivial matter. The year before, Wolff had been ordered by Friedrich Wilhelm I (r.1713–1740) to leave Halle and his university post within twenty-four hours. Wolff's opponents, Pietists, had convinced the Prussian king that Wolffian philosophy supported insurrection against him. The opportunity to win such an intellect to the university in Leipzig was foiled by orthodox Lutherans and scholastic academicians. One group reviled Wolff's faith in human reason to discern divine truth and bring about happiness, the other his rejection of classical authorities who did not conform to modern insights of reason. It did not matter to them that Wolff's deductive logic concluded that human reason would ultimately yield an understanding of the divine order of the universe.

Gottsched became one of Wolff's staunchest and most vocal advocates. Among Gottsched's earliest popular successes was an introduction to the philosophy of Wolff: *Erste Gründe der Weltweisheit* (1730). Used by students in classrooms, but also by readers outside the classroom — men and women alike — this text became the standard introduction to modern philosophy for many Germans for at least the next fifty years. Through this work alone Gottsched might have earned a place in German cultural history. Due in part to this text, Wolff's philosophy dominated German cultural discourse until the publication of works by Immanuel Kant (1724–1804) at the end of the century.

A New Standard for Literature: Gottsched's *Critische Dichtkunst* (Critical Poetics, 1730)[30]

While Gottsched's absolute faith in the divinity of reason provided the foundation for his linguistic and literary endeavors, his literary tastes were also decidedly influenced by the neoclassical stance of French academician Nicolas Boileau (1636–1711), the defender of the *anciens,* to whom other German poets like Johann von Besser (1654–1729), Erdmann Neumeister (1671–1756), and Freiherr Rudolph Ludwig von Canitz (1654–1699) were likewise attracted. These are the German poets Gottsched frequently cited as models for his compatriots. While these authors had already paid tribute to Boileau, it was Gottsched who more forcefully articulated and successfully popularized neoclassical ideas, most notably in *Critische Dichtkunst*.[31]

At the same time, with his unshakeable faith in the progress of reason and the philosophy of Wolff, Gottsched was the staunchest of modernists. This position was clear already in his first Leipzig publication. For a collection of the poetry by his professor Johann Valentin Pietsch (1725) Gottsched provided an introductory translation of a treatise by theologian Jean le Clerc (1657–1736), "Gedancken über die Poesie und Poesie an sich selbst" (Thoughts on Poetry and Poetry per se, 1699).[32] Le Clerc was concerned with classical authors and with improving poetry in the French vernacular. Only if modern poets wrote in the vernacular, he asserted, could they acquire the stature of the ancients and free themselves of the slavery of imitation. Classical authors might exhibit superior poetical skills, but for Le Clerc their themes, imagery, and philosophy had been rendered obsolete. Le Clerc revealed inconsistencies, illogicalities, and natural impossibilities in texts by Homer, Virgil, Horace, and others. He argued that those who recommended the classics for their moral lessons were in error, for these were often contradictory and did not hold up to Christian scrutiny. Equally important, the authors of these famed texts aimed foremost at seducing the reader with the beauty of their language. They lulled reason to sleep with their pleasant cadences.

Le Clerc's essay focused attention on principles that imbue all of Gottsched's writings on literature. Indeed, implicit in this modernist critique of the classics were the fundamental tenets of neoclassicism: verisimilitude and morality.[33] In accordance with Aristotle, Gottsched also argued that literature should accurately represent nature and reality. The occasional and gallant literature that dominated German culture in the early eighteenth century sought to entertain, to please, and to be sociable. It could not fulfill the high moral purpose that Gottsched and his associates envisioned for it. Its stylistic norms did not and could not accurately represent emotional or natural reality. Whether a text was classical or not Gottsched applied the modern, that is Wolffian, standard of reason. In *Critische Dichtkunst* he replaced the rules of poetics with standards of verisimilitude and decency. However, because he interpreted Aristotle's expectations of verisimilitude in terms of the deductive rationality of Wolffian philosophy, Gottsched's own logical deductions appear to continue the rules of classical poetics.

The key to Gottsched's theory of poetry lies in his understanding of the imitation of nature. To imitate nature plausibly poets should not restrict themselves either to mere description or to mere imitation (of speech, in drama or role poems). Rather, a poet should find a sequence of events, a *Fabel*, that illustrates the invisible workings of reason.[34] Poets do not lie if they misrepresent historical fact as long as they represent philosophical truth. An event is then *plausible* (*wahrscheinlich*), even if not historically accurate. Like Aesop in his fables, poets render the public a service by dressing dry precepts in attractive garments. However, while no one seriously believes in talking animals, it is another matter where witches, ghosts, devils, and angels are concerned. These figures, popular in literature of the late baroque, should be avoided because they are not real. Gottsched faulted Milton and Shakespeare, in part, for having introduced such characters. Representing them in poetry transgresses the principles of imitation and encourages superstition. That is *ir*rational.

Of the many genres for which Gottsched provided historical development and logical principles in *Critische Dichtkunst,* his treatment of tragedy and comedy have most interested literary critics and historians. Unlike Boileau, Gottsched addressed an audience that was primarily non-aristocratic and did not attend the theater. In the face of moral opposition to drama, by 1728 Gottsched began arguing for the potential moral value of theatrical production, calling it "eine Schule der Geduld und Weisheit"[35] (a school for patience and wisdom). In *Critische Dichtkunst* he elucidated the rational principles on which a new, modern theater could be based. Gottsched's expectations of verisimilitude were supported by Aristotle's three unities. A play that disrupted the unity of time, place, or action could not be said to be a good example of the imitation of reality when the illusion of reality was expected. Baroque opera with its elaborate machinery, fantastic events and characters, and intrusive musical accompaniment could not meet his neoclassical requirements for imitating nature. (Indeed, Shakespeare's plays were found wanting for similar faults.) Reason also required characters of mixed morals, neither totally virtuous nor totally sinful.

Because the same philosophical material could receive treatment in different genres, the nature of these determined the character of a text. Since tragedy arouses "admiration, pity and fear," its characters should naturally be worthy, that is noble.[36] The style should also be elevated if it is to inspire awe. Since comedy evokes laughter, its characters should be of low origin and its style may be low. By this reasoning Gottsched sustained, through deductive logic, Aristotle's class distinctions in tragedy and comedy.

Drama Reform:
Die Deutsche Schaubühne (1741–1745)

By the time of Gottsched's death, drama had all but surpassed poetry as the most highly regarded genre. While other literary figures had also certainly been active on behalf of drama reform, Gottsched's efforts went beyond moral justification and theoretical elucidation; they extended into the practical domain. As early as 1727 he had begun to provide a German-language repertoire for theatrical groups to perform.[37] Later Gottsched published a six-volume collection of plays in German, *Die Deutsche Schaubühne* (The German Stage, 1741–1745). Successive volumes contained increasing numbers of original plays in German (as opposed to translations). Among the tragedies in the early volumes he included translations of Racine's *Iphigenie*, Corneille's *Horace* and *Cid*, and Voltaire's *Zayre* and *Alzire*. In 1732 Gottsched published an "original" tragedy, *Sterbender Cato* (Dying Cato), a blend of Addison's *Cato* (1713) and Deschamp's *Caton d'Utique* (1715).[38] This tragedy was intended to serve as a model and inspiration to others. An enormously popular success at the time because of its stand against tyranny, literary historians — quite reasonably — have nonetheless found little to admire in this patchwork tragedy.

Luise Gottsched's adaptation of Guillaume-Hyacinthe Bougeant's *Le Femme docteur ou la théologie Janseniste tombée en quenouille* (1732) as *Die Pietisterey im Fischbeinrocke* (Pietists in Petticoats, 1736) has been viewed more favorably by modern critics, but its contemporary reception was accompanied by considerable tumult. She adapted the Jesuit's criticism of Jansenism (a mystic trend outlawed in the Catholic Church) almost too successfully as a critique of German Pietists, for in various locations the comedy occasioned riots, confiscation of the text and new censorship laws. An innocent clergyman was even arrested as the presumed author, for Luise Gottsched wisely published this satire anonymously.

For Gottsched's *Deutsche Schaubühne* she provided not only translations, but also original plays that established a Saxon tradition of satiric comedy of character types in Germany.[39] Luise Gottsched also became one of the first in Germany to defend what became known as the *sentimental comedy* in England or the *comédie larmoyante* when she translated and defended Françoise de Graffigny's (1695–1758) *Cenie, oder die Großmuth im Unglücke* (Cenie, or Generosity in Misfortune, 1750). Her husband may not have admired Molière's comedies (only one, *Le Misanthrope*, was included in the *Schaubühne*),[40] but Luise Gottsched's dramatic oeuvre reflects the Frenchman's influence. In her comedies she ridiculed cultural pretensions of aristocrats and non-aristocrats (*The Mésalliance,* [*Die ungleiche Heirath,* 1743]); francophilia (*The French Housekeeper,* [*Die Hausfranzösinn, oder die Mammsell,* 1744]); false modesty and greed (*The Last Will,* [*Das Testament,* 1745]); and intellectual pretensions (*The Witling,* [*Der Witzling,* 1747]). Literary historians have often judged these comedies to be somewhat schematic, but newer interpretations suggest there are subtleties that still need to be explored.[41]

Caroline Friederike Neuber and the Reform of the Theater

Secular drama and the novel were considered genres of dubious moral content by many Protestants (especially Pietists) and some Catholics in Germany. German courts generally showed little interest in German plays but favored French drama or Italian opera. Permanent theatrical structures were built only for courts and aristocrats. Churches offered religious plays, and Latin schools had a strong, flourishing tradition of student productions in German. There were wandering minstrels and traveling acting companies extemporizing in pubs, barns, attic spaces, tents, or temporary stages in the market square. Standing theaters for the bourgeois middle class were to develop gradually only in the second half of the eighteenth century.

Actress and theater director Caroline Neuber (1697–1760) and her husband, theater manager Johann Neuber (1697–1759), had been attempting to reform German theater for about five years when they entered into a practical association with Gottsched in 1727. They had performed French neoclassical plays in German translation at courts in Braunschweig, Weissenfels, and elsewhere.[42] The couple had barely taken over the management of Sophie Elenson-Haack-Hoffmann's theater company (in which she had also been the principle actress) when Gottsched approached them with plans to provide new translations. Soon they were also performing Corneille's *Cinna*, Racine's *Iphigenia* (in Gottsched's translation), the second part of *Cid*, and Racine's *Berenice* in various German cities. Original German-language plays conforming to neoclassical standards were added to the repertoire, including Gottsched's *Sterbender Cato* (performed 1731). Some of these had been written by a member of her company, some by Gottsched, his apprentices, or others.

Caroline Neuber reformed theatrical practice to conform to rationalist principles of verisimilitude. At courts in Dresden, Braunschweig, and Hanover she had seen French companies and studied their diction, gestures, and staging. She began disciplining her troupe. To protect the reputation of actors in general, unmarried actresses lived with the Neubers. Insofar as her budget (and contemporary morality) permitted, costumes were historicized. She discarded the crowns and stars made of tinsel and paper. Romans no longer dressed in hoop skirts. Improvisation yielded to memorization. Actors trained their voices to orate rhymed Alexandrines and their bodies to move in pre-determined gestures. The new emphasis on text and author enhanced the possibility of directing a consistent moral to the audience.

When, for financial reasons, the Neubers were obliged to perform older favorite plays, Caroline revised them by omitting the scenes most offensive to new tastes. She invented fresh, rationalized improvisational situations and frequently wrote short plays to precede the main attraction. In these she usually presented allegorical figures who spoke on behalf of theatrical reform. One full-length comedy, a pastoral play titled "Das Schäferfest oder die Herbstfreude" (The Shepherd's Festival, or Autumn Joy), an adaptation of Calderon's *La vida es sueño*) appeared in the *Wiener deutschen Schaubühne* (1754). Neuber's colorful staging of the banning of the *Hanswurst* character from the theater (1737) demonstrated her support for Gottsched's reforms. The *Hanswurst* was a stock comic, often obscene, character of the slapstick variety that could not well be integrated into the high moral role now proposed for the theater. Together the Neubers, Gottsched, and his associates succeeded in drawing the attention of the educated elite to the cultural possibilities of the theater. By the 1740s neoclassical plays had been performed for non-aristocratic audiences in cities like Hamburg, Frankfurt, and Leipzig.

By then, however, Neuber's company was in disarray. As others began reaping the rewards of her innovations, she encountered difficulties obtaining licenses and a suitable stage in Leipzig. When Empress Anna of Russia invited her troupe to Russia, she saw it as a way to salvage her company. But the empress died and Neuber had ruptured her relationship with Gottsched. In Leipzig in September 1741 she performed in the prologue *Der allerkostbarste Schatz* (The Most Precious Treasure), a satire about a learned pedant presumed by many to have represented Gottsched. This performance precipitated the irrevocable break with Gottsched and provided fuel for his detractors. Johann Christoph Rost (1717–65) wrote a bitter satire *Das Vorspiel* (The Prologue, 1742) about Gottsched's alleged attempt to prohibit Neuber's prologue.

The Gottsched Era: An Assessment

Gottsched made a signal contribution to the development of modern literature in German. He labored successfully for the introduction of rationalist principles in philosophy, language, and literature. His introduction to the fundamentals of philosophy; his grammar, rhetoric, and literary handbooks (*Weltweisheit, Sprachkunst, Redekunst,* and *Critische Dichtkunst*) became staples in German schools virtually until the end of the eighteenth century. His efforts to reform the German stage were pathbreaking. However, even though he had urged women of his acquaintance (notably Ziegler and his fiancée, Luise Kulmus) to translate the novels of Scudéry, he ignored the novel in his theoretical writings. But his influence on the development of book culture, also fostered by his numerous journals, was enormous and has yet to be adequately appreciated even today.

Gottsched's historical importance is indisputable, but appreciation for his achievements remains tepid. Wolff's particular brand of modern philosophy, which Gottsched did so much to popularize, is no longer of interest except historically. In the case of language and style, Gottsched's reforms were quickly absorbed into the culture, but with time his role in these reforms was largely forgotten. His efforts on behalf of the theater are often given passing mention only to be followed by the harshest criticism of his literary reforms, characterized most often as pedantic and unimaginative. Arguably this assessment is correct. However these opinions have often colored his reception by literary historians to the neglect of his other achievements and particularly of his critical role in the development of modernity in Germany.

Beginning in the late 1730s and intensifying dramatically around 1740 both Gottscheds faced harsh criticism from critics in Switzerland, Hamburg, and Dresden in particular. Johann Christoph Gottsched's literary reforms had been predicated on the philosophy of the early Enlightenment. International and national developments in literature quickly overcame his position. Influenced by tendencies from abroad, German authors developed an interest in empiricism — Barthold Heinrich Brockes's *Irdisches Vergnügen in Gott* (Earthly Delight in God, 1721–1748) and Albrecht von Haller's *Versuch schweizerischer Gedichte* (Experiment in Swiss Poetry, 1732) are prime examples[43] — and in sensualism — Johann Ulrich König's translation of Dubos's "Réflexions critiques sur la poësie et la peinture" (1727) and Baumgarten's lectures on aesthetics (1750–58 [1742]) are relevant here.[44] In addition, the wealth of images and linguistic formations available in indigenous Pietist texts and discourse began having a strong impact on authors such as Friedrich Gottlieb Klopstock (1724–1803) in the late-1740s when he began publishing.[45] This new language of subjectivity quickly found resonance in young poets like Christoph Martin Wieland, Johann Wilhelm Ludewig Gleim, and Christian Fürchtegott Gellert who emerged as significant literary figures a generation later. Though Gottsched's literary reforms were in time superseded by new developments, that does not alter the significance of his wide-ranging undertakings. His literary reforms laid the foundations for German modernity.

Notes

[1] His contemporaries Gottlieb Stolle (1673–1744) and Carl Günther Ludovici referred to him with this epithet. See Günter Gawlick, "Johann Christoph Gottsched als Vermittler der französischen Aufklärung," in Wolfgang Martens, ed., *Leipzig: Aufklärung und Bürgerlichkeit*, Wolfenbüttler Studien zur Aufklärung, vol. 17 (Heidelberg: Lambert Schneider, 1990), 199.

[2] For more on Gottsched's use of this term and its context, see Katherine R. Goodman, "Learning and Guildwork. Luise Gottsched as Gehülfin," in *Nonne,*

Königin und Kurtisane, ed. Michaela Holtkamp and Gabriele Jancke (Königstein: Ulrike Helmer, 2004), 83–108.

[3] Quoted in Georg Witkowski, *Geschichte des literarischen Lebens in Leipzig* (1909; rpt. Munich: K. G. Saur, 1994), 87.

[4] Another scandal erupted two years later when students with pietist leanings conducted *collegia* at the university in the vernacular, and men and women from the town attended. See Hans Leube, *Orthodoxie und Pietismus: Gesammelte Studien* (Bielefeld: Luther Verlag, 1975), 185–89. Between 1713 and 1725 philosopher Christian Wolff wrote works in German, but returned thereafter to Latin to reach a larger audience among European intellectuals.

[5] There were a number of aides available to those who wished to acquire the rudiments of prosody. There existed scores of handbooks in the Renaissance tradition of *Poetices libri septem* by Julius Caesar Scaliger (1484–1558) and Martin Opitz's famous, concise *Buch von der deutschen Poeterey* (Book on German Poetics, 1624). One could consult an *aerarium* (*Schatzkammer*, treasury) for poetic words or phrases, but many collected their own. Rhyming dictionaries were much used, and one might also consult popular anthologies for examples of various subgenres of poems in the popular *florilegia* (*Blütenlese*, bouquets), for instance, Männling's *Lohensteinius sententiosus* (1710).

[6] Georg Witkowski, *Geschichte des literarischen Lebens,* 250–51.

[7] Gottlieb Siegmund Corvinus, *Frauenzimmerlexicon* (1715; rpt. Frankfurt a. M.: Insel, 1980).

[8] In part under Mencke's influence, by 1717 (when Günther arrived) Leipzig had evolved into a center for gallant lyric poetry. Among others who admired Anacreon's simple elegance and clarity and cultivated their own "middle" style by translating him are Daniel Wilhelm Triller (1695–1782), Johann Friedrich Christ (1700–1756), Friedrich von Hagedorn (1708–1777), Barthold Heinrich Brockes (1680–1747), Johann Wilhelm Ludwig Gleim (1719–1803), and Gotthold Ephraim Lessing (1729–1781). In 1734 Gottsched translated Anacreon into unrhymed verse (*Critische Beyträge,* 152–68). Among the new literary models in Leipzig were also light French odes; indeed in France, England, and Italy the elegant poetry of Anacreon had been translated at least a century earlier. Anne Dacier translated his poetry into prose in 1681, but a third edition with verse translations added appeared in 1716. Most agreed that the Greek poet was not very profound. See Herbert Zeman, *Die deutsche anakreontische Dichtung: Ein Versuch zur Erfassung ihrer ästhetischen und literarhistorischen Erscheinungsformen im 18. Jahrhundert* (Stuttgart: Metzler, 1972), 57–96.

[9] Zeman, *Die deutsche anakreontische Dichtung,* 67–68.

[10] Johann Christian Günther, "Abschieds-Aria" in *Werke,* ed. Reiner Bölhoff (Frankfurt a. M.: Deutscher Klassiker Verlag, 1998), 862.

[11] See Günther's contemporary detractor, Gottfried Ephraim Scheibel, *Die unerkannten Sünden der Poeten* (Leipzig: Teubner, 1734), 182–91. Publishers usually paid a fixed rate on a per page basis.

[12] Georg Christian Lehms refers to other gallant women poets in Leipzig in his lexicon, so there may well have been other imitations of French salons as well; see Lehms, *Deutschlands Galante Poetinnen* 145.

[13] Christiane Mariane von Ziegler, *Versuch in gebundener Schreib-Art* (Leipzig: Braun, 1728), 8r-v.

[14] Christiane Mariane von Ziegler, *Moralische und vermischte Send-Schreiben* (Leipzig: Braun, 1731), a6r-v.

[15] Women who wrote religious and occasional poetry for private use were already an affront to many contemporaries. How much more offensive was one who permitted her gallant poetry to be published and received public honors for it.

[16] For more on Ziegler, see Katherine R. Goodman, *Amazons and Apprentices: Women and the German Parnassus in the Early Enlightenment* (Rochester, NY: Camden House, 1999), 168–95.

[17] Notable in this regard is her translation of P. Cerceau's defense against critics of his poetry who claim it lacks high moral purpose, "Vertheidigung des P. Cerceau wegen des Zeitvertreibes den er zuweilen darinn findet, nach des Marot Art Verse zu machen" ("Defense of P. Cerceau on account of the leisure he sometimes finds in writing verses in the manner of Marot," 1739). In the late 1730s she translated various other texts from the French that supported her views: Madeleine de Scudéry's *Conversations* (1735) and *Bains de Thermopylae* (probably at Gottsched's request), Fontenelle's *Der Dibutadis an Polemon* and *Thamire* (1739), Henriette de Coligny, Countess de la Suze's *Ergasis und Edone, oder Arbeit und Wohllust* (1739), and Chevalier de Méré's *De la vraie honête* (1739). See also Goodman, *Amazons and Apprentices,* 94–195.

[18] Cicero's designation of three levels of style — plain (for instruction); grand (for moving souls); middle (to delight) — had long been known in Germany via Renaissance poetics, most notably Julius Caesar Scaliger's *Poetice* (1561). The complex periods of Cicero (as opposed to the more concise Seneca) remained influential in Germany longer than in France, where they lost most of their exemplary stature in the seventeenth century. See Eric A. Blackall, *The Emergence of German as a Literary Language 1700–1775* (Cambridge: Cambridge UP, 1959), 149–77.

[19] Blackall traces both to the influence of Cicero and notes the irony of Gottsched identifying himself with the style of Cicero. Blackall divides Seneca's style into two categories: the "curt" and the "loose." It is the latter that he finds closer to that which Gottsched developed (50–53 and 76).

[20] Gottlieb Siegmund Corvinus, *Frauenzimmerlexikon* (1715; Frankfurt a. M.: Insel, 1980), preface.

[21] It had begun as the *Görlitzische Poetische Gesellschaft* in 1697 and became the *Deutschübende poetische Gesellschaft* in 1722.

[22] The *Académie Française* was founded nearly 100 years earlier, in 1635, when Cardinal Richelieu offered his protection to a group of intellectuals meeting regularly in a private home. Richelieu hoped to counteract the influence of the salons and the *précieuses* in the formation of French language, literature, and culture. By 1672 the academy had come directly under the protection of Louis XIV and met in the

Louvre. Membership was restricted to 40 and had to be approved by the king. Its charter stated that it owed respect to its protector. The academy was explicitly charged with the production of a dictionary, grammar, and handbooks for rhetoric and poetics. Gottsched clearly had this model in mind when he reorganized the *Deutsch-übende Gesellschaft*, see Detlef Döring, *Die Geschichte der Deutschen Gesellschaft in Leipzig: Von der Gründung bis in die ersten Jahre des Seniorats Johann Christoph Gottscheds* (Tübingen: Niemeyer, 2002).

[23] In 1730 Gottsched was elected member of the *Societät der Wissenschaften* in Berlin, and the head of the "teutsche Zunft," Paul Ernst Jablonski (1693–1757) wrote asking his advice on their plans to produce a dictionary and a grammar of German. Gottsched responded that he — and the Leipzig *Deutsche Gesellschaft* — would produce them. He had planned to have contributors for the dictionary from all over Germany, but this enterprise never materialized. He was more successful with the grammar.

[24] Five additional editions appeared in the next thirty years: 1749, 1752, 1756, 1762, 1775. After the rights expired in 1776, further editions appeared. In all there were fifteen by 1780. It was translated into Latin, Russian, Polish, and French and formed the basis for Wendeborn's *Elements of German Grammar* (1774). Indeed it was still in print at the beginning of the nineteenth century.

[25] Blackall, *Emergence of German*, 154.

[26] See the essay by Helga Brandes in this volume.

[27] Usually articles in these journals were not signed, so it is difficult to determine who wrote them. Many of Luise Gottsched's translations and original works appeared under her name. The most controversial, however, did not: *Die Pietisterey im Fischbeinrocke* (1736) and *Die Horatier* (1739) appeared anonymously.

[28] Gabriele Ball, *Moralische Küsse: Gottsched als Zeitschriftenherausgeber und literarischer Vermittler* (Göttingen: Wallstein, 2000), 171–200.

[29] *Critische Beyträge* (1743), *Der neue Büchersaal* (1747, 1750), and *Das Neueste aus der anmutigen Gelehrsamkeit* (1751–54, 1756). For a complete listing of articles in this series, see Edith Krull, *Das Wirken der Frau im frühen deutschen Zeitschriftenwesen* (Berlin: Lorentz, 1939), 29–30, 41–42, 47–48.

[30] In accordance with contemporary practice, the word *critisch* in this title meant precisely that literature would be judged by the most exacting standards of reason.

[31] This work proved very popular and there were three new editions in the next twenty years: 1737, 1742, 1751.

[32] "Parrhasiana ou Pensées diverses . . ." Pietsch had been a doctor who wrote poetry in his leisure time. In 1717 he became professor of literature in Königsberg and later introduced Gottsched to Horace when the eager student requested guidelines on how to write poetry. Le Clerc was a protestant theologian (born in Geneva) and editor of three journals published in the Netherlands. Gottsched reissued the translation fifteen years later, in 1740, toward the beginning of his dispute with the Swiss Bodmer and Breitinger. Johann Christoph Gottsched, "Des berühmten Johann le Clerk Gedanken über die Poeten und Poesie an sich selbst." In *Critische Beyträge* 24 (1740): 531–600.

[33] See Gordon Pocock, *Boileau and the Nature of Neo-classicism* (Cambridge: Cambridge UP, 1980), 5.

[34] Johann Christoph Gottsched, *Versuch einer Critischen Dichtkunst* (1751; rpt. Darmstadt: Wissenschaftliche Buchgesellschaft, 1962), 142–51; Part I; Section iv; Paragraphs 1–9.

[35] Gottsched, "Akademische Rede, Die Schauspiele, und besonders die Tragödien sind aus einer wohlbestellten Republik nicht zu verbannen" in vol. 9.2 of *Ausgewählte Werke*, ed. P. M. Mitchell (Berlin: Walter de Gruyter, 1976), 494.

[36] Gottsched, *Versuch einer Critischen Dichtkunst*, 164; Part 1; Section iv; Paragraph 25.

[37] He was probably aided by members of the *Deutsche Gesellschaft* (including Christiane Mariane von Ziegler) who were then meeting as the *Scherzende Gesellschaft* (Jovial Society). This group amused itself producing translations.

[38] Originally Gottsched intended to translate Addison's play in its entirety, but changed his mind when he could no longer support its structural irregularities (in neo-classical terms). In the end he translated the first three and a half acts from Deschamps and the last one and a half from Addison. Roughly 186 lines are original. Gottsched wrote two fully original tragedies: *Die parisische Bluthochzeit König Heinrichs von Navarra* (1745) and *Agis, König zu Sparta* (1745), but *Sterbender Cato* remained the most popular.

[39] Susanne Kord disputes the traditional interpretation of Luise Gottsched's comedies as "Typenkomödien" (comedies of type). See Susanne Kord, *Little Detours: The Letters and Plays of Luise Gottsched (1713–1762)* (Rochester, NY: Camden House, 2000), 71. Kord suggests a radical difference of literary judgment between Johann Christoph and Luise Gottsched. For more on the relationship between the Gottscheds, see Katherine R. Goodman, "Of Gifts, Gallantries and Horace. Luise Kulmus (Gottsched) in her early Letters," *Women in German Yearbook* 17 (2001): 77–102, and Detlef Döring, "Luise Adelgunde Victorie Gottsched (1713–1762)" in *Sächsische Lebensbilder* 5, ed. Gerald Wiemers (Stuttgart: Verlag der Sächsischen Akademie der Wissenschaften zu Leipzig, 2003), 213–46.

[40] Gottsched found them a slightly exaggerated, frivolous, and a little too ready simply to amuse, rather than edify. Luise Gottsched had translated *Misanthrope* as she did *Der Verschwender* and *Der poetische Dorfjunker* by Philippe Néricault Destouches (1680–1754); *Die Widersprecherinn* by Charles Rivière Dufresny (1648–1724); and *Das Gespenst mit der Trummel* by Joseph Addison (1672–1719). Earlier she had also translated Addison's *Cato* (1735).

[41] Luise Gottsched also wrote one tragedy, *Panthea* (1750), about fidelity in marriage. Her comedies appeared anonymously, but her tragedy appeared under her name. For more on Luise Gottsched, see Goodman, *Amazons and Apprentices*, 196–252; Kord, *Little Detours;* and Goodman, "Of Gifts, Gallantries, and Horace."

[42] These were three by Nicolas Pradon: *Regulus, Brutus,* and *Alexander;* and Corneille's *Cid*.

[43] See the essay by Rosmarie Zeller in this volume.

[44] See the essay by Kai Hammermeister in this volume.
[45] See the essay by Kevin Hilliard in this volume.

First issue of the moral weekly Die vernünftigen Tadlerinnen, *1624. The inscription under the frontispiece reads "Weh dem der thöricht ist und dennoch klug will heißen" (Woe to the silly who wants to be wise).*

The Literary Marketplace and the Journal, Medium of the Enlightenment

Helga Brandes

EVERY ERA CREATES ITS OWN MEDIA, and the history of media is as old as that of mankind. After or besides the traditional "human" medium (especially the messenger, the preacher, the teacher, the storyteller), the medium of construction (the castle, park, etc.), and the medium of writing (letter, sheet, wall), the early modern age developed the print medium (book, newspaper, journal, broadsheet, poster, calendar, almanac, and so on).[1] The eighteenth century was the epoch of the journal, and was followed by the mass and electronic media of the nineteenth and twentieth centuries (the daily press, telephone, telegraph, record, film, television, and computer). The journal, the periodical literature of the eighteenth century, provided the key medium for bourgeois society; this chapter focuses on the journal as a new medium in the era of Enlightenment. The major classes of journals presented here are the moral weeklies, women's magazines, the calendar and almanac, and review journals — all of which played an important role in restructuring the public sphere toward a bourgeois public and had a significant share in developing the literary market and a public middle-class culture.[2]

The Literary Marketplace

In the eighteenth century the literary market consisted of, above all, authors, the book trade, journals, literary critics, and the reading public. Major changes occurred in a rapid expansion of the market as reflected in the catalogues of the Leipzig and the Frankfurt book fairs. In 1763, the number of new titles listed in these catalogues had risen since 1721 by 265; during the next forty years from 1763 to 1805 the rate of new titles grew tenfold (2,821 more books appeared in 1805 than in 1763). Around 1740 about 750 new titles entered the market annually; during the 1780s and 1790s there were about 5,000 each year.[3] The market growth of what was then placed under the rubric *Schöne Literatur* (*belles lettres*) was especially substantial: in 1740 *belles lettres* comprised 6 percent of the total list and was in sixth place among the different subject groups; in 1770 it moved into second place with 16.5 percent of the market share, and in 1800 it topped the list with 21.5 percent. Between 1730 and 1740, 176 new journals were founded; 754 between 1741 and 1765, and 2,191 between 1766 and 1790.[4] New journals cover the German landscape "wie Gebirgsschnee" (like mountain snow), the writer Ludwig Wekhrlin (1739–1792) remarked in 1780. Publishing in France similarly progressed at a rapid pace, especially under the influence of the Revolution. In 1788 one could choose among ten or so Paris and provincial journals; in 1789 there were about 200 titles, and that number had doubled by the following year: the revolution had unleashed a paper flood.[5]

What were the reasons for this growth of printed matter, especially in the field of imaginative literature? First, the nature of publications had changed: the dominance of Latin gradually gave way to German publications. At the beginning of the century 60 percent of all books were still written in Latin; by 1735 this picture had changed, as 75 percent of all books were then in German. Along with the process of secularization came a steep decline in theological and religious books. In 1735 they still comprised 40 percent, in 1800 only a mere 6 percent of total reported book production, while the proportion of scientific and philosophical books rose steadily to 40 percent; *belles lettres* from 3 percent in 1700 to 27 percent in 1800.[6] The novel in particular flourished.

The interest in reading increased with new subject matters, and learned books as well as devotional ones were gradually replaced by entertaining, popular texts. The ideas of the Enlightenment lent themselves to a popularization of its goals. This popularization was made possible by the rapid increase in reading ability among large sectors of the bourgeoisie. Women's literacy increased dramatically for the first time in the old regime. If around 1700 a literate woman from the middle classes was something of an exception, by the end of the century there were warnings by educators and journalists against a reading mania (*Lesewut*). Around 1700 only 5 percent of the German population or approximately 80,000 to 85,000 people are estimated to have been literate, but by 1800 we count between 350,000 and 550,000 potential readers (or an increase of about 25 percent).[7] The proliferation of reading societies reflects this development. The number of poets and writers, both male and female, also increased. In the 1760s there were about 2,000 to 3,000 authors, in the 1790s about 7,000, and in 1810 about 12,500; many women authors were obliged to remain anonymous to protect their social standing.[8] According to Reinhard Wittmann,[9] the fifty-year process of the author's emancipation from patronage had come to an end around 1800 when honoraria according to market value were becoming the rule.[10] But it was still a long road to free, independent authorship. The professionalization of the book trade brought with it a change from the antiquated exchange system to a cash trade which facilitated book production and marketing. Last but not least the institutionalization of literary criticism stimulated the literary market by steering readers to books of the new genres and educating the reading public about literary matters.

The eighteenth century was the "century of the journal" and saw the "birth of the journalist."[11] The term *Zeit-Schrift* (journal) as *Verschriftlichung von Zeit* (scripting of the times) was documented for the first time in 1751 when Peter von Hohenthal used the term in the preface to his *Oeconomische Nachrichten;* it became a standard term only several decades later.[12] This term *Zeitschrift* can mean in German a journal, periodical, or (daily) newspaper. The characteristics of a journal (*Zeitschrift*) in the eighteenth century were: periodicity (regular appearance — weekly, monthly, quarterly, yearly), public accessibility, topicality (specializing in certain themes, for example, education, fashion), variety in type, form, and presentation in order to engage and entertain the reader. The average print run of 500 to 700 was small; the eighteenth-century journal was not yet the mass medium it became during the nineteenth century, especially with the *Zeitung* (newspaper) that appears in much shorter intervals, usually daily. The *Zeitung* is the faster medium, striving for actuality, dissemination of political news and facts, and favoring information, news reports, editorials, and commentary. The eighteenth century distinguished between a general audience journal and the special subject one, such as the scientific and scholarly journals for a learned public of professionals that still dominated the market in the seventeenth century. The first 'universal' journal for scholars was *Acta Eruditorum* (Transactions of the Learned), founded in 1682 in Leipzig and modeled after the first scientific journal as we know it today, the French *Journal des Sçavants* (1665–1701); the first German-language journal was *Monatsgespräche* (1688–1690), founded in in Leipzig by Christian Thomasius. The number of German-language journals rose from around 70 titles before 1700 to roughly 300 to 400 in 1750, to over 1,000 during the 1780s; in 1830 more than 7,000 titles were in circulation.[13] The following discussion includes the most important categories of journals.

The Moral Weeklies

Moral weeklies in the tradition of John Addison and Richard Steele's *Tatler* (1708–11), *Spectator* (1711–12), and *Guardian* (1713) flourished especially in the first half of the eighteenth century and the fashion spread throughout Europe. Among the most important German-language moral weeklies were: *Die Discourse der Mahlern* (Discourses of the Painters, Zurich 1721–23),[14] *Der Patriot* (Hamburg 1724–26), *Die Vernünftigen Tadlerinnen* (The Reasonable Women Critics, Halle/Leipzig 1725–26), *Der Biedermann* (The Gentleman, Leipzig 1727–29), *Die Matrone* (The Matron, Hamburg 1728–

30), *Der Freymäurer* (The Freemason, Leipzig 1738), *Der Weltbürger* (The World Citizen, Berlin 1741–42), *Der Freydenker* (The Freethinker, Danzig 1741–43), *Der Fremde* (The Stranger, Kopenhagen/Leipzig 1745–46), *Der Gesellige* (The Socialite, Halle 1748–50), *Der Mensch* (Man, Halle 1751–56), *Der Freund* (The Friend, Ansbach 1754–56), *Der Nordische Aufseher* (The Nordic Overseer, Copenhagen, Leipzig 1758–60), and *Der Hypochondrist* (The Hypochondriac, Schleswig 1762). Wolfgang Martens's groundbreaking research has uncovered 107 German-language moral weeklies and some 57 similar journals, published mostly in such urban centers as Zurich, Hamburg, and Leipzig.[15] Martens provided the first detailed study of these journals, as serious research into and appreciation of the moral weeklies' importance for the social, literary, mental, and media history of the eighteenth century has come rather late.

These journals became the most important medium for the Enlightenment, propagating a new thinking without old prejudice. Their criticism of prejudice was based on the concept of natural law, that all human beings were fundamentally equal, and that reason, morality, and virtue were essential. Because it was considered irrational, superstition was singled out for mockery. The moral weeklies propagated an understanding of the world, of mankind, and of all things through reason. Typically, these journals were interested in women's affairs, demonstrated emancipatory tendencies, urbanity, and cosmopolitanism. They prepared the way for the idea of tolerance in the era of Lessing. An entire generation of writers contributed to this genre as editors, contributors, and critics, as for example Johann Jakob Bodmer, Johann Jakob Breitinger, Johann Christoph Gottsched und his wife Luise Adelgunde Victorie, Johann Wilhelm Ludwig Gleim, Johann Elias Schlegel, Gotthold Ephraim Lessing, Gottlieb Wilhelm Rabener, Nikolaus Dietrich Giseke, Justus Friedrich Wilhelm Zachariae, Samuel Gotthold Lange, Immanuel Jakob Pyra, Johann Peter Uz, Johann Friedrich von Cronegk, Meta Klopstock (née Moller), Heinrich Wilhelm von Gerstenberg, Johann Georg Hamann, and Josef von Sonnenfels.

The moral weeklies were intended to reach a broad segment of the bourgeois reading public, as anybody could purchase them without being a member of a certain club, as was the case with for instance with the Masonic journal. These publications appeared regularly, on a weekly basis, and initially editors and contributors usually remained unnamed, or assumed fictitious names. These publications were rather short-lived, rarely remaining in print for more than two years; they appeared in 500 copies on the average, the exceptions being the *Die Vernünftigen Tadlerinnen* in 2,000 copies and *Der Patriot* with at times as many as 6,000 copies printed. Following the same external format, each article typically consisted of eight pages (one-half sheet) dedicated to a single topic. Themes covered diverse areas of knowledge and human endeavors (reason and passion, world-wisdom, education, society, aesthetics, language, poetry, and so on). They had one goal — to promote virtue — and they thus often seem repetitive. Religious issues gradually gave way to worldly, everyday questions; the process of secularization in the eighteenth century was also manifested in the medium of the journal. Political and ephemeral matters were excluded because the editors and authors wished to convey lasting values in a general framework; the lack of interest in contemporary issues was a symptom of their aspiration for timelessness. Without losing their relevance, the weeklies could then later appear a second time bound together in yearly volumes with an index, some even in several reprints, features they shared with the book.

The moral weeklies eschewed costly illustrations (copperplate engravings) that would have raised the modest price of 6 *Pfennige* per issue; some used decorative signets. This simplicity in appearance fit the rather monotonous and repetitive content. But a colorful array of text forms compensated for the lackluster content: letters, dreams, poems, fables, songs, epigrams, dialogues, exemplary stories, parables. The fictive authorship offered the opportunity to write in a subjective, lively style, hiding behind the mask of anonymity. Instead of a didactic style, the more successful moral weeklies developed an increasingly conversational tone in an effort to distinguish them from the contemporary book (though the booklike character of the early moral weeklies was still clearly evident); this tone was intended to establish a close relationship with the readership. The request for letters to the editor belongs to those journalistic features that have endured until the present day. In sum, the moral weeklies represent the transition from the genre "book" to the medium "journal."

The message of the moral weeklies reflected the optimism, the belief in progress and in the perfectibility of men of Enlightenment philosophy, and the new morality of the bourgeoisie. Thus, while they furthered the development of a public sphere, they never went so far as to advocate social change. Rather, they accepted the existing feudal order and emphasized the social barriers separating the bourgeoisie from the lower classes as well from the aristocracy. Accordingly, the courtly, gallant lifestyle was mocked in its tendency toward superficiality and mere etiquette; typical vices of the feudal lords such as vanity, luxury, indulgence, and idleness were derided. But they also suggested that one keep one's distance to the servant class, to the peasants, and craftsmen: these persons were supposedly uncouth, uneducated, and lacking in refinement. One should only socialize with persons of one's own estate, of the educated middle class. This was the class to which the readership of the weeklies predominantly belonged: ministers, scholars, physicians, refined merchants, professors, judges, and — for the first time in the history of the journal — bourgeois women. The latter were addressed directly as readers.

The moral weeklies presented a virtuous, edified image of the human being. The enlightened individual was characterized by prudence, equanimity, discretion, and self-possession. Referring to the teachings of ancient philosophers (Plato, Seneca, Cicero, Marcus Aurelius), they praised the "golden mean" as the best way to achieve happiness through virtue. The moral person is honest, modest, and temperate, avoids extremes and thus sets himself apart from the wicked, the squanderer, the tight-wad, the idler, the indefatigable—all of whom were caricatured in the moral weeklies in the tradition of Theophrastus and La Bruyère. These values and attitudes (asceticism, self-control, stoicism) reflect the social and economic aspirations of the rising bourgeoisie; "Protestant ethics" (Max Weber) constituted a program even at this early date. The moral weeklies presented the socio-psychological interdependency of emotional control and economic success characteristic of the early eighteenth-century bourgeoisie as a "process of civilization" (Elias).[16] Thus, basic emotional values dominate in love and friendship rather than wild passion or destructive desire; "reasoned love" (*vernünftige Liebe*, Thomasius) resembling friendship appeared as guarantor of lasting marital happiness. Friendship was valued above all other virtues. In a similar vein, the moral weeklies presented nature not as a wild, elemental force, but as a tamed, domesticated expression of a rational order. An enlightened readership saw its ideal of nature realized in the highly structured English landscape garden. That which was "civilized" was at the same time the natural, the rational.

The canon of values of the early Enlightenment included the expression of a high degree of self-confidence and self-assurance. The moral weeklies thus were able to criticize a wide range of social abuses. Besides criticism of the nobility, they attacked social evils such as the ruinous system of providing for the poor, empty conventions such as dueling, antiquated customs, and ceremonial events, and, above all, the educational system (illiteracy, tutors, schools) and women's lack of education. The prominent poets and scholars Bodmer, Breitinger, and Gottsched were vocal defenders of women's education in the early phase of the 1720s. They criticized prejudice, questioned traditional gender roles and relationships and no longer accepted the lack of education of bourgeois women as "ordained by nature." Rather, they argued, women had to be compensated for their lack of schooling through appropriate measures such as reading and acquiring collections of books. They made recommendations for appropriate reading for women in so-called *Frauenzimmer-Bibliotheken* (women's libraries), voluminous lists that were intended to help them along on the road to a better education. As the recommended titles in these lists indicate, such "libraries" were mostly encyclopedic, comprising books from various areas of knowledge.[17]

Thus it does not come as a surprise that a number of moral weeklies presented a fictive female editor or title figure in order to reach women more directly, as, for example, in *Die Vernünftigen Tadlerinnen*, *Die Patriotinn* (1725?), *Die Matrone* (1728), *Die vor sich und ihre Kinder sorgfältigen Mütter* (Mothers Caring for Themselves and Their Children, 1731–32), *Die Braut* (The Bride, 1742), *Die Deutsche Zuschauerin* (The German Female Spectator, 1748), and *Die Frau* (1756–57). Also, the earlier discussion of the *querelle des femmes*, the ongoing European discussion about the role of women, was revived in a humorous way: "Ob es denn eine so gantz ausgemachte Sache sey, daß die Manns-Personen Menschen wären? [...] die Leugnung dieser Streit-Frage wäre das beste Mittel sich an denen zu rächen, die bisher die Menschheit der Weiber in Zweifel gezogen haben"[18] (Is it is such a well-established fact that male persons are indeed human beings? [...] Denying this polemical question would be the best way to take revenge on those who until now have cast doubt on the human status of women). The enlightened woman, not really the learned woman, was the ideal in the early moral weeklies, only later to be superseded by the *fair* woman under the influence of Rousseau.

Literary criticism and questions of language played an important role in the moral weeklies, as it was the order of the day to educate the readership in good taste. Baroque rhetoric and bombastic language (Hoffmannswaldau, Lohenstein) were out, but Martin Opitz, Friedrich Rudolf Ludwig von Canitz, and Johann von Besser were praised for their work — being based "in reason" — the poet Johann Christian Günther for his elegant style. The cultivation of a good style and a pure language was important; Gottsched attacked the German penchant for employing French words and the mixing of languages (in *Die Vernünftigen Tadlerinnen*), while the Swiss Bodmer and Breitinger, equally concerned with matters of language, argued for preserving regional dialects, a colorful language, and the power of imagination (*Discourse der Mahlern*).

The Women's Journal

During the last third of the eighteenth century specialized journals addressed to women began appearing: *Iris* (1774–76 [1778]) edited by Johann Georg Jacobi and Wilhelm Heinse;[19] and *Die Akademie der Grazien: Eine Wochenschrift zur Unterhaltung des schönen Geschlechts* (The Academy of the Graces, a Weekly for the Entertainment of the Fair Sex, 1774–76, 1780) edited by Christian Gottfried Schütz. There were also several such journals now edited by women: *Für Hamburgs Töchter* (For the Daughters of Hamburg, 1779) by Ernestine Hofmann; *Wochenblatt für's Schöne Geschlecht* (A Weekly for the Fair Sex, 1779) by Charlotte Henriette von Hezel; and *Papiere einiger Freunde* (Papers of Several Friends, 1780–83) by Dorothea Lilien.

As women assumed editorship of significant journals, middle-class women took a step toward more autonomy, self-esteem, and social recognition. Hence, while these women had already been entering the literary market as authors in appreciable numbers, their new roles as journal editors or contributors would enhance their influence: they entered into a more intensive communication with their readers than had existed before and increased their audience considerably. They could develop new skills and prove their ability as literary managers, organizers, and businesswomen negotiating with publishers, printers, and booksellers, and, as journal editors, soliciting contributions and subscribers to their journals. It is true that Luise Gottsched — her husband's "skillful helpmate" — had contributed some pieces to the second edition of the *Vernünftigen Tadlerinnen* (1738). But it was quite a way from contributor to editor to (modern) journalist, and participation in the communicative sphere was an important step in their "long road to emancipation."[20]

The first women's journals followed closely the model of the moral weekly. By the 1770s female readership had grown considerably and the literary fashion of sensibility provided more opportunity for women's literary activities. The most successful women's journals were Sophie La Roche's *Pomona für Teutschlands Töchter* (Pomona, for Germany's Daughters, 1783–84) and Marianne Ehrmann's *Amaliens Erholungsstunden* (Amalia's Leisure Hours, 1790–92) which will be discussed in more detail to illustrate the changing characteristics of this genre of journal.[21]

Pomona's editor, Sophie von La Roche (1730–1807), had already become a prominent author in her own right after the success of her novel *Die Geschichte des Fräuleins von Sternheim* (The History of Lady Sternheim, 1771). Her new journal appeared from January 1783 to December 1784. Considering herself already in the "autumn of her life," she named the journal for the Roman goddess of fruit and fruit trees. The reception of her impressive oeuvre and especially that of her journalistic activities was overshadowed for a long time by the condescending attitude of prominent contemporary male authors.[22] Goethe, calling her "Pomona" in a letter to Schiller of 24 July 1799, opined: "Sie hebt das Gemeine heraus und zieht das Vorzügliche herunter und richtet dann das Ganze mit ihrer Sauce zu beliebigem Genuß an"[23] (She elevates the common, pulls down the excellent, and mixes everything with her sauce for everybody's taste). Representative for older scholarship is Hugo Lachmansky, who wrote in his Berlin dissertation about *Pomona:* "Und wie durch welke Herbstreviere schreitet man auch durch die blütenlose Öde dieser Zeitschrift"[24] (We find only a desert without flowers like the withered fall landscape). But recent scholarship, especially Ulrike Weckel's monumental study of German women's journals, now stresses the journals' literary merits, its importance for women's presence in the public sphere and in the process of women's self-fashioning.[25]

Pomona enjoyed a wide and receptive audience, comparable to Jacobi's *Iris*, to which Goethe as well as La Roche contributed.[26] Johann Georg Jacobi (1740–1814) in turn published in *Pomona* along with many other prominent writers of the day; noteworthy among the many female contributors were: Sophie Albrecht (1757–1840), poet, actress and dramatist; the poet Philippine Engelhard (née Gatterer, 1756–1831); Elisa von der Recke (1754–1833), essayist and poet; and the novelist Caroline von Wolzogen (1763–1847).

In her preface "An meine Leserinnen" (To My Women Readers), La Roche explained the conceptual design distinguishing her journal from the women's journals edited by men: "*Das Magazin für Frauenzimmer und das Jahrbuch der Denkwürdigkeiten für das schöne Geschlecht* — zeigen meinen Leserinnen, was teutsche Männer uns nützlich und gefällig achten. *Pomona* — wird Ihnen sagen, was ich als Frau dafür halte"[27] (The *Magazine for Women* and the *Yearbook for Memorabilia for the Fair Sex* show my readers what German men consider useful and entertaining for us. *Pomona* will tell you what I as a woman think about it). La Roche did not need to legitimize her editorship, as Marianne Ehrmann did more than a decade later. With her program of combining the useful with the entertaining, La Roche stated literary and educational goals for her journal, a project that was to be neither a learned nor an ephemeral one. She also set her journal apart from the moral weeklies whose popularity was then waning.

While the moral weeklies presented to their readers each week a different theme from a number of areas in the well-chosen, easy to read format of eight pages, the monthly *Pomona*, with its roughly one-hundred pages per issue, did not always make optimal use of the medium, but presented several lengthy essays and stories (some of thirty pages and more), showing in comparison to the standards of the journal form pronouncedly epic characteristics. La Roche demonstrated her journalistic skills, integrating different text forms in her journal, such as travel accounts, letters, moral tales, and poems. As a sign of her close connection with her women readers, she introduced a section of "Letters and Responses" and published actual letters, while the moral weeklies mostly used fictive letters.

Pomona provided descriptions of other countries, each issue focusing on one nation, to educate its readers to become "world citizens" (1784, 2: 167). The journal regularly acquainted its readers with a literary genre or form, such as the novel, tragedy, comedy, allegory, fable and so on, and made reading recommendations now and then, but no longer published entire lists, as the moral weeklies had done with the *Frauenzimmer-Bibliotheken*. And while the latter had the goal of improving bourgeois man by propagating an ideal, social being, the woman's journal pursued a gender-specific aim: the moral education of women by creating a distinctively feminine gender role. In the "Letters to Lina" column that appeared in every issue, "Pomona" instructs her younger cousin in all questions concerning "woman's destiny," such as choosing the right husband, being a bride, marrying, raising children, and performing household duties. The originally emancipatory impetus of *Pomona* gave way to gender-specific female socialization. While the moral weeklies preferred generalizations of moral characteristics, *Pomona* introduced a more subjective style and even included some of editor Sophie La Roche's biographical details and personal accounts. By specializing in women's topics and by individualizing its content, *Pomona* exhibited considerable eagerness to be effective; with its concretized heroines "Sophie," "Lina," or "Pomona," it offered models for identification to its readers. Yet this detracted from a more encyclopedic oriented presentation of knowledge as was offered in the moral weeklies. The more exclusive concentration on women was thus coupled with a diminishing emancipatory potential.

Pomona reflected the transition from progressive, enlightened thinking to Rousseau's sentimental natural philosophy in the conception of woman that changed from "woman as a human being" to "woman as an essentially feminine being." Earlier the moral weeklies had still protested against restricting women to the house when, for instance, Johann Jakob Bodmer declared in 1721 in his journal: "Es ist in Wahrheit der gröste Affront für das weibliche Geschlecht / daß man es in die Circkel der Kamer / der Kuchen / der Stuben / und der Kunckel einschrancket; Ich sehe keine klärere Consequentz als diejenigen / welche man daraus machen kan / daß die weiblichen Seelen unedler als die männlichen / ich sehe aber auch nichts absurders und falschers als dieses"[28] (It is in truth the greatest affront to the female sex to restrict it to the circle of bedroom, kitchen, sitting room, and spinning wheel; I see no clearer consequence from this than that women's souls are seen as less noble than those of men, but I also see nothing more absurd and wrong than this). About sixty years later, La Roche's declaration proclaiming woman's voluntary return into the house — as a human being second to the male — signaled woman's role change in the era of sensibility. *Pomona*'s loss of emancipatory content served to stabilize traditional hierarchical, patriarchal family structures.

During the last decade of the eighteenth century, Marianne Ehrmann (1753–1795) issued two women's journals, *Amaliens Erholungsstunden* (Amalia's Leisure Hours, 1793–95) and *Die Einsiedlerin aus den Alpen* (The Female Hermit from the Alps, 1793–94);[29] the successful journals had each a press run of about 1,000 copies. Marianne Ehrmann supported herself and for several years also her husband with the publication of these journals. She was thus one of the first professional female journalists in Germany, where the profession of author-journalist was slowly gaining acceptance. Sophie La Roche was clearly considered a creative writer, while Ehrmann became known as a journalist beyond Germany because of her tracts *Müßige Stunden eines Frauenzimmers* (A Woman's Leisure Hours, 1784) and *Philosophie eines Weibes* (A Woman's Philosophy, 1784).[30]

The very subtitle to *Amaliens Erholungsstunden,* "Teutschlands Töchtern geweiht" (Dedicated to Germany's Daughters), indicated Ehrmann's interest in La Roche's journal,[31] but notwithstanding several parallels (enlightened tendencies, criticism of prejudice, variety of topics) Ehrmann gave her journal her own stamp. Compared with *Pomona, Amaliens Erholungsstunden* employed journalistic strategies more effectively: the articles are shorter, more precise, and more rhetorical. A "feurige und muntere Schreibart"[32] (spirited and lively style of writing) is intended to arouse the interest of the readers. The format of the periodical is attractive: a colorful variety of copper engravings, music, poems, letters, dialogues, and moral stories enliven the magazine. The editor was fond of dialogues and dramatizations, perhaps recalling her earlier work on the stage. Here we find definite beginnings of a modern journalistic style in the communicative structure, the dialogues with female readers, and the resonance from the readership. Specifically feminine subject matters increased compared with *Pomona,* leading to an even greater fixation on established gender roles and to a renunciation of emancipatory aspects when stressing woman's human character. The image of woman is more conservative, at times more controversial and ambivalent than in the early moral weeklies.

Marianne Ehrmann used her journals as a means to integrate various discourses. The journal became a forum for women to exchange opinions and experiences. *Amaliens Erholungsstunden* assumed more journalistic quality by presenting more real-life situations and stories. The editor — like La Roche before her — mentioned details of her own biography or personal experience, leaving aside the moral weeklies game of fictitiousness. Such fictionalizing tendencies were replaced by direct references to reality. This new form approached the modern form of the editorial. Symptomatic for the historical transition from the aesthetic-fictional to a journalistic structure of the women's journal was the editor's signature as "Amalia Ehrmann" under several articles. While the moral weeklies still eschewed reference to contemporary events, *Amaliens Erholungsstunden* referred directly or indirectly to timely issues including occasionally political ones. Thus, the strictly conservative journal rejected the French Revolution; religion, the authorities, and the class structure were not questioned, and the journal was not in any way politicized.[33]

Moreover, the instruction of women was no longer an important subject in this journal; literary and aesthetic education was all but forgotten in favor of presenting woman's role as that of wife, mother, and companion. *Amaliens Erholungsstunden* came closer to Rousseau's construction of gender dichotomy than *Pomona* had done. Woman appeared here again as passive, humble, submissive, and emotional, man as active, strong, superior, and rational. The medium for education has turned into a medium for entertainment and ideology. An emphasis on women's moral and domestic responsibilities, her virtue and chastity provided the underpinnings for the exemplary stories and the deterring accounts (popular topics were the debauched damsel or the fallen woman). Accordingly, the "Einfluß des schönen Geschlechts auf Staatsgeschäfte und Staatsgegebenheiten" (influence of the fair sex on public business and matters of state) — thus the heading of one article — remained congruent with woman's "destiny," limited to the family as "the smallest cell of the state" (1791, 2: 275). Women should care for the "welfare of the individual family," for this is "the foundation of the state." They should leave it to the men "für Deutschlands Freiheit und Wohl zu wachen" (to watch out for Germany's freedom and well-being, 1791, 2:276).

Woman and the public sphere have now been separated more than earlier in the century. La Roche still considered her editorship a normal activity, while Marianne Ehrmann made excuses for her public appearance as transgressing the norm; her writing was, she insisted, only a pursuit during her leisure hours. It seems as if at the end of the eighteenth century prejudice against women's publishing had increased again after an intermittent phase of liberalization. *Amaliens Erholungsstunden* no longer displayed the carefree attitude and immediacy that *Pomona* could muster. However, with her special communicative strategies, Marianne Ehrmann succeeded in "gently" criticizing society. When she did take exception to the traditional image of woman, she used subtle subversive strategies (self-protection, accommodation, and circumlocution).[34] For instance, she condemned women's lack of education by having a man complain about it. She hoped to garner men's acclaim for improving women's education with pragmatic arguments (an educated woman serves the welfare of her husband, her children, and the household) rather than through arguments of principle (the equality of everyone requires education for all human beings). Thanks to these strategies, Marianne Ehrmann was able to publish for two years rather unencumbered; only in the third year did problems with the publisher Cotta arise. More and more editorial responsibility was taken away from her, and the share of male contributors increased, among them the famous naturalist and travel writer Georg Forster (1754–1794), the director, actor, and dramatist August Wilhelm Iffland (1759–1814), and the head of a military academy and writer Konrad Gottlieb Pfeffel (1736–1809). Toward the end of 1792 she disassociated herself from the publisher. During the subsequent financial disputes the publisher, Cotta only addressed Ehrmann's husband Theophil, since a woman could not represent herself legally at the time. The publisher profited from the good reputation of Ehrmann's journals and started a sequel in 1793, *Flora, Teutschlands Töchtern geweiht* (Flora, Dedicated to Germany's Daughters), which lasted until 1803.

The journals of the two editors, La Roche and Ehrmann, reflected the slow dissolution of the emancipatory image of woman in the early Enlightenment over the course of the eighteenth century. The enlightened, sensible woman of La Roche was transformed into a rather ambivalent, contradictory one in search of new understanding of gender roles personified by Marianne Ehrmann. Women's journals, as has been seen, illustrate the development of the medium, its journalistic forms. Sophie La Roche and Marianne Ehrmann paved the way for women journalists in the nineteenth century.

From the Calendar to the Almanac of the Muses

Recording time officially, calendars go back to Roman times; later additions to the calendar, such as weather predictions, dates of religious holidays, planting times, phases of the moon, and even narrative pieces were added as *practica* serving the farmer's practical needs and desire for reading material. This type of calendar was introduced in Germany by the reformer Paul Eber in 1551. The historical calendar can be traced back to the Gregorian calendar; with its cyclical structure into which the events could be entered, it served well the homogeneous view of history during the Renaissance.[35] Calendars flourished in the early modern period, and some of the more interesting ones include those produced by Grimmelshausen in the second half of the seventeenth century. Strictly speaking, they did not belong to the new media of the eighteenth century. But they were still popular then and spawned a specialized type, the so-called almanac of the Muses (*Musenalmanach*) or "pocket book" (*Taschenbuch*).

In the eighteenth century the popular calendar (*Volkskalender*) was a household staple that served as a kind of reference guide through the year. The added matter of rare, curious, and sensational stories as well as actual events made it the most popular reading material for the masses. The anonymously published calendar was still typically divided into the actual calendar table and the *practica*, as was the case with the *Curieuser und immerwährender Astronomisch-Meteorologisch-Oeconomischer Frauenzimmer-Reise- und Hand-Calender* (Remarkable and Eternal Astronomical-Meteorological-Economic Travel and Home Calendar for Women, 1737).[36] The calendar's baroque subtitle read:

> Curieuser und immerwährender Astronomisch-Meteorologisch-Oeconomischer Frauenzimmer-Reise- und Hand-Calender. Worinnen abgehandelt sind: Die angenehmsten und nöthigsten Materien, so in einem Calender vorkommen, und von alten Haußwirthen und neuen Naturkundigern in der Haußwirthschafft, Feld- und Garten-Bau aus der Witterung und denen vier Natur-Reichen, auch bey der Gesundheit zu beobachten sind. Wie auch Die Messen, Märckte, ankommende und

abgehende Posten in denen vornehmsten Städten, Rechnungs-Müntz-Gemäß-und andere unentbehrliche Nachrichten, ingleichen die aeromatrische Machinen auf die beste Art zu verfertigen, angetroffen sind. Dem endlich Ein vielfältig-approbirtes Wäsch- und Küchen-inventarium, mit unterschiedenen hierbey sehr nöthigen Künsten vor Frauenzimmer und Hauß-Wirthe, und andere Gemüths-ergötzende Nachrichten beygefüget und mit saubern Figuren erklähret ist. Mit einer Vorrede von Mademoiselle Sidonia Hedwig Zäunemann.

[In which is dealt with: The most pleasant and useful matters that belong into a calendar: to be observed by experienced farmers and new practitioners in the household in domestic tasks, in field work, gardening, the weather and the four seasons, and concerning health and well-being. Also to be found are news about the fairs, markets, post days in the major cities, accounting, moneys, measurements, and other indispensable news, for instance how aerometric machines can best be constructed. And finally a much acclaimed table for laundry and kitchen inventory, with the different, very necessary information for ladies and lords of the house been added, as well as other pleasant instructions, all explained in clear drawings. With a preface by Mademoiselle Sidonia Hedwig Zäunemann.]

With the preface by the Erfurt poet Sidonia Zäunemann (1714–1740), the publisher addressed this calendar to women, the new market of a growing female middle-class readership. But it was mostly a rehash of older material from the European household literature (*Hausväterliteratur*).[37] Such a calendar conveyed practical knowledge and lore for everyday activities according to the seasons, the work, and religious holidays in the old European tradition. In spite of its store of superstition (such as astrology) on the one hand, its real-life experience and current practices on the other made the calendar a medium for disseminating new and actual information throughout the population. Its empirical perspective on daily life and on the working world went along with enlightenment tendencies to focus on the labors of this world, assisting in the process of secularization.

Although calendars (also called almanacs) included various entertaining topics and sub-genres (anecdotes, fashion reports, court scandals, medical advice), they also tended to specialize (calendars for certain professions, for a certain class or group, for a certain subject matter). In the second half of the eighteenth century a new type of belletristic calendar evolved in the form of the successful French publication *Almanach des Muses* (1765–1833).[38] An anthology, a "poetic florilegium," published annually, this *Almanach* favored poems and also included excerpts from dramas, epics, and yet unpublished pieces along with a calendar table and illustrations. Following the French example, the first German *Musenalmanach* (1770–1804) appeared in Göttingen edited by Heinrich Christian Boie (1744–1806) and Friedrich

Wilhelm Gotter (1746–1797). This was followed shortly thereafter in Leipzig by the *Almanach der deutschen Musen* (1770–1781) edited by the Göttingen professor of philosophy and oriental languages Johann David Michaelis (1717–81) and Christian Heinrich Schmid (1746–1800).[39] In 1772 poems appeared for the first time by Gottfried August Bürger (1747–1794), Johann Heinrich Voss (1751–1826), Matthias Claudius (1740–1815), and Johann Gottfried Herder (1744–1803). Another well-received almanac appeared in Göttingen, the *Taschenbuch zum Nutzen und Vergnügen nebst Göttinger Taschen Calender* (Almanach for Benefit and Pleasure, with Göttinger Almanach, 1778–1797) edited by the Göttingen professor Georg Christoph Lichtenberg (1742–1799). These almanacs were published in a duodecimo or even smaller format that easily fit into a pocket (thus the name *Taschenbuch*). It has been estimated that there were more than 2,000 such volumes on the market between 1750 and 1860.[40]

Since bourgeois women had come to dominate literary readership by the end of the eighteenth century,[41] literary almanacs were often addressed to them, as was the *Leipziger Taschenbuch für Frauenzimmer zum Nutzen und Vergnügen* (Leipzig Almanac for Women's Benefit and Pleasure, 1784–1820).[42] It appeared yearly in the favored duodecimo format and became a popular companion for women. In the preface, the editor introduced himself and his fictitious family to the readership — young women, wives, and daughters — and announced reviews by his "son" Carl. These books were not works of art, but rather books "worthy" of being read by women. Not unlike the calendar, the almanac offered an encyclopedic variety of useful, informative, and entertaining topics, from news about aristocratic figures, moral essays, and literary pieces, to household tips on coffee, meat selection, or family celebrations. Reading recommendations were especially detailed emphasizing literature, moral tales, and novels by contemporary writers such as (in 1784) Gottlieb Konrad Pfeffel, the moralists Johann Martin Miller (1750–1814) and Joachim Heinrich Campe (1746–1818), the authors of women's novels and educator Madame de Genlis (1746–1830), and Sophie La Roche. This was less a literary program than an ideological effort to teach "female virtues," and the almanac functioned as a medium for the socialization of the female readership.

While the journals in the Enlightenment had a rather cosmopolitan orientation, this orientation changed toward one of increasing patriotism under the pressure of political events during the last third of the eighteenth century. In this vein, the *Leipziger Taschenbuch für Frauenzimmer* presented "The Nation's Great Men," essays on "The Germans" and the German national character was praised:

> Ihren Charakter krönte eine unverstellte Redlichkeit, die nur in dem einzigen Falle von ihnen wich, wenn dadurch das Heyl ihrer Nation

befördert werden konnte. Noch ist diese Tugend der Vorzug ihrer spätern Nachkommen vor andern Völkern geblieben. Wohl ihnen, wenn sie nie von ihnen weichen! Er ist ein Deutscher — hieß, er ist ein ehrlicher redlicher Mann, und wem er sein Wort und den biedern Handschlag gegeben hatte, der konnte ihm trauen. (1784, 181)

[Their character was crowned by a sincere honesty, which departed from them only when in this manner the saving of their nation could be advanced. This virtue is still their offspring's advantage over other people. Hail to them! May they never lose it! 'He is a German' meant he is an honest man and he to whom the German had given his word and handshake could trust in him.].

By contrast, the almanac painted the picture of a Turk in a nationalistic vein, as the Turkish nation was clearly devalued: "Sie sind ohne Gelehrsamkeit, ohne Bücher, und werden übel erzogen. Sie bekümmern sich nicht um die Ursachen der Dinge, überlassen sich auf der einen Seite ihrer Gewohnheit, und auf der andern auf ein unvermeidliches Schicksal" (1784, 187; The Turks lack erudition, books, and are educated poorly. They do not care about the origin of things, give way to their habits on the one hand, and to an unavoidable fate on the other).

While such national prejudices were common lore in the eighteenth century, the increasing interest in present day matters in the journals generally went hand in hand with a nationalistic emphasis.[43] While the moral weeklies introduced a practical, worldly enlightenment and the women's journals served increasingly as a forum for gender discourse, the almanacs highlighted yet another facet of eighteenth century publishing media: the tendency to employ *belles lettres*.

The Review Journal

The literary journal served yet another area: bourgeois-cultural reasoning and critique, a prominent feature of the eighteenth century that Kant had aptly called "the age of criticism" (in the preface to his *Critique of Pure Reason*). When the enormous increase in book production in the late eighteenth century made an overview of the literary market increasingly difficult, assistance in orientation for the readership became a necessity. This niche was filled by a new periodical type, the review journal. It followed the tradition of the learned journal (for example the *Acta Eruditorum* (1682–1782) and the *Göttingischen Zeitungen von gelehrten Sachen* [1739–present]),[44] an informative periodical for scholars about new research. Literary criticism was also present in other eighteenth-century journals, especially in the moral weeklies. In the modern newspaper it has received a special section that exists to the present day: the *Feuilleton*. In the eighteenth century special journals for literary reviews catered to the interests of the middle-class readership and to the enlighteners' efforts to elevate the reader's taste and judgment. Such journals became an important medium of communication during the late phase of the Enlightenment.[45] It was their task and achievement to survey literary production and to select the most important works; they had to publish quickly in order to remain current. At times, they merely related the contents of a book and neglected to engage in a critical review. Herder, for example, would admonish: "Ein wahrer Kunstrichter in einem solchen Journal muß nicht Bücher, sondern den Geist beurteilen"[46] (A true critic in such a journal should not judge books but their spirit).

Pierre Bayle's *Dictionnaire historique et critique* (1697), translated into German by Johann Christoph Gottsched with substantial help from his wife Louise Adelgunde Victorie Gottsched (Leipzig 1741–44), was influential in the rise of literary criticism, as were English models like the debate about Alexander Pope's *Essay on Criticism* (1711). Since the 1730s journals for literary criticism had gained acclaim in Germany; examples include *Beyträge zur critischen Historie der deutschen Sprache, Poesie und Beredsamkeit* (Contributions to A Critical History of the German Language, Literature, and Style, 1732–44) edited by J. Chr. Gottsched; *Sammlung critischer, poetischer, und anderer geistvollen Schriften, zur Verbesserung des Urtheils und des Wizes in den Wercken der Wolredenheit und der Poesie* (A Collection of Critical, Poetic, and Ingenious Writings for the Improvement of Judgment and Wit in Works of Good Style and Literature, 1741–44) edited by Gottsched's Swiss competitors Bodmer und Breitinger; *Bemühungen zur Beförderung der Critik und des guten Geschmacks* (Essay in Promoting Critique and Good Taste, 1743–47) edited by Christlob Mylius and Johann Andreas Cramer; *Crito: Eine Monat-Schrift* (The Critic, a Monthly, 1751) edited by the literary club "Dienstags-Compagnie" in Zurich, or the *Magazin der deutschen Critik* (Magazine of German Criticism, 1772–76), edited by Gottlob Benedikt von Schirach. The following became the most important ones and will be touched on here: *Briefe, die neueste Literatur betreffend* (Letters Concerning the Most Recent Literature, 1759–65), edited by Gotthold Ephraim Lessing, Moses Mendelssohn, Friedrich Nicolai, and Nicolai's *Allgemeine Deutsche Bibliothek* (The General German Library).

Briefe, die neueste Literatur betreffend (1759–65) presented a critical, selective overview of new, contemporary literature. The idea for this journal was Lessing's (1729–1781), who had returned to Berlin in 1758 and came in close contact with the young and enterprising Berlin publisher Christoph Friedrich Nicolai (1733–1811) and the enlightened Jewish philosopher Moses Mendelssohn (1729–1786);[47] the journal became the common enterprise of literary friends, with Lessing, Mendelssohn, and Nicolai as editors. The program differed from Nicolai's more scholarly *Bibliothek der schönen Wissenschaften und der freyen Künste* (Library of the Beautiful Sciences and the Liberal Arts, 1757–1765),[48] and the *Literaturbriefe* (as they are usually referred to) concentrated on German-language publications in the area of science, philosophy and *belles lettres* (leaving aside the other arts). The epistolary form had been used successfully by the *Mercure galant,* and the *Literaturbriefe* were written as fictive letters addressed to a Prussian officer who had been wounded in the Seven Year's War (he was the young poet and friend Ewald von Kleist who died in 1759) to inform him about ongoing literary events. The journal appeared weekly in altogether 333 segments, of which Lessing authored the first several in his always witty, ironic, and conversational style that the other editors tried to emulate in their articles. As early as September 1760 Lessing gave up his editorship in order to assume a post as army secretary in Breslau. Nicolai and Mendelssohn took over and were later joined by the patriotic Berlin author Thomas Abbt (1738–1766); the professor of philosophy and aesthetics Johann Georg Sulzer (1720–1779) also contributed some letters. The accent shifted from literature to philosophy and aesthetics, and the tone became less polemical. Nicolai's contribution went far beyond that of being the organizer and publisher, his reviews of *belles lettres* and comments on aesthetic theory presented in the unsystematic way of the journal contained fundamental reflections.[49] The *Literaturbriefe* gave rise to literary feuds, as with Gottsched in the famous Seventeenth Letter, with the then already popular and prominent Wieland, or the comic writer Johann Jakob Dusch (1725–1787). The journal praised above all writers of their own taste and conviction, the Schleswig poet and dramatist Heinrich Wilhelm von Gerstenberg (1737–1823), the patriotic poet and literary mentor Ludwig Gleim (1719–1803), and Ewald von Kleist (1715–59). For Lessing the journal also served as a sort of advertising tool when discussing his own writings. The *Literaturbriefe* together with a number of other review journals in the 1760s to the 1780s provided an important forum for the literary, philosophical, and scientific discourse of the Enlightenment.

The most influential review organ of the late Enlightenment was Nicolai's *Allgemeine Deutsche Bibliothek* (1765–1805).[50] The *ADB* sought to create a cultured, literary public in Germany by presenting reviews of literary and scholarly works for the middle-class readership. It was a unique, ambitious undertaking of encyclopedic proportions that reviewed some 80,000 books in some 256 volumes during the forty years of its existence. Nicolai presided over this enterprise except for the years from 1792 to 1800 because of difficulties with the Prussian censors. (Between 1792 and 1800 Carl Ernst Bohn edited the journal in Hamburg.) Planned as a quarterly journal, it appeared often in irregular intervals with up to eighteen issues (of the sizable volume of twenty sheets) annually in an edition of 2,500 copies, slowly decreasing to 2,200 in 1783, and 1,250 in the 1790s.

Nicolai's intent was to have all new publications reviewed, regardless of subject matter, as he introduced his journal to the public in its first edition: "Dieses Werk soll seiner Absicht nach eine allgemeine Nachricht, von der ganzen neuen deutschen Literatur vom Jahre 1764 an, in sich enthalten. Man wird also darin von allen in Deutschland neu herauskommenden Büchern, und andern Vorfällen, die die Literatur angehen, Nachricht zu erteilen suchen"[51] (This work intends to contain a general announcement of the entire new German literature starting with the year 1764. We shall inform about all new books published in Germany and about other literary events as well). Nicolai even included translation (in shorter reviews) and allowed most room for the books deemed of major importance for the entire country. Because of the lack of one cultural center for all German-speaking lands, the journal was to serve as a medium for rallying a cultural unity.

At the beginning in 1765, Nicolai had a steady group of ten reviewers; during the last years there were some 150. Altogether there were some 433 reviewers active in this journal, among them some well-known writers and scholars like Herder, Mendelssohn, Campe, the collector of folk tales Johann Karl August Musäus (1735–1787), and Adolph Freiherr von Knigge (1752–1796), but these reviewers were not identified and the reviews were signed only with a code. Not surprisingly, Nicolai made many enemies with his journal's often severe criticism, among them Kant, Fichte, the philosopher and novelist Friedrich Heinrich Jacobi (1743–1819), the Swiss popularizer of religion and physiognomy Johann Caspar Lavater (1741–1801), and Goethe. In turn, the journal was labeled a "review factory" and Nicolai was said to live not only *for* but mostly *on* the Enlightenment.[52] Nicolai's aim was to convey an enlightened understanding of literature that served a moral and useful purpose. He showed little interest in new trends such as the individualism and sensibility becoming fashionable in the 1770s in literature and art. Other journals thus emerged with a more voguish approach than Nicolai's, which clung to the more learned, sober, and instructive type of review. Also, with the rapidly expanding book market (already in 1769 there were 1,300 new titles) it became impossible to review all new books; the claim to complete coverage could no longer be maintained. A competitive venture, the *Allgemeine Literatur-Zeitung* (1785–1849) founded in Jena by Friedrich Justin Bertuch,[53] Christian Gottfried Schütz, and Christoph Martin Wieland, suffered the same fate. With the increasing differentiation and specialization of the scholarly disciplines and aforementioned mushrooming literary texts, it was no longer possible to present an encyclopedic review of the entire book market. Specialized journals for all scientific, cultural, and literary areas took their place. These *reviews* of the nineteenth century replaced the encyclopedic with selectivity.

The eighteenth-century journals were remarkable in paving the way for literary and cultural developments. They stimulated the process of literary club formation (reading societies). Moreover, they provided a new means of communication and fostered the development of new genres (books for girls, magazines for women, journals for entertainment, moral stories, satires, essays, for instance). Unlike any other medium in the eighteenth century, the journals aided the construction of a social identity by effectively propagating a bourgeois worldview. They became the most popular medium and most effective for the Enlightenment, a "school for the nation," even if their political effect was rather limited to preparing a bourgeois public sphere because of the territorial fragmentation and absolutistic princely rule in eighteenth-century Germany.

— Translated by Barbara Becker-Cantarino

Notes

[1] See Werner Faulstich, *Die bürgerliche Mediengesellschaft, 1700–1830* (Göttingen: Vandenhoeck & Ruprecht, 2002), 253 et passim.

[2] Faulstich, *Die bürgerliche Mediengesellschaft,* 9–10, 11–15, and 225.

[3] Reinhard Wittmann, *Geschichte des deutschen Buchhandel: Ein Überblick* (Munich: Beck, 1991), 111–12.

[4] Wolfgang von Ungern-Sternberg, *Schriftsteller und literarischer Markt,* in *Hansers Sozialgeschichte der Literatur.* Vol. 3: *Deutsche Aufklärung bis zur Französischen Revolution 1680–1789,* ed. Rolf Grimminger (Munich: Hanser, 1979), 1: 135. John McCarthy writes: "Of more than 6,000 journals appearing between 1700 and 1790 [. . .], 323 literary and 1,101 magazines for light reading matter" can be documented; "Literarisch-kulturelle Zeitschriften," in *Von Almanach bis Zeitung: Ein Handbuch der Medien in Deutschland 1700–1800,* ed. Ernst Fischer et al. (Munich: Beck, 1999), 177. On the topic of the book and journal market, see also Helga Brandes, "Buch- und Zeitschriftenmarkt, Frauenzimmer-Journale und Literaturkritik im 18. Jahrhundert," in *Zeitdiskurse: Reflexionen zum 19. und 20. Jahrhundert,* edited by Roland Berbig, Martina Lauster, and Rolf Parr (Heidelberg: Synchron, 2003), 301–317; here 301–304.

[5] Jean Paul Bertaud, *C'était dans le journal pendant la Révolution française* (Paris: Librairie académique Perrin, 1988), 9. See also Albert Ward, "The Evidence of the Leipzig Book-fair Catalogues," in his *Book Production, Fiction, and the German Reading Public 1740–1800* (Oxford: Clarendon, 1974), 29–58.

[6] Hans-Albrecht Koch, "Buchhandel," in *Literatur Lexikon: Begriffe, Realien, Methoden,* ed. Volker Meid (Gütersloh: Bertelsmann Lexikon Verlag, 1992), 13: 138.

[7] Rudolf Schenda, *Volk ohne Buch: Studien zur Sozialgeschichte der populären Lesestoffe 1770–1910* (Munich: dtv 1977), 444–45; Rolf Engelsing, *Analphabetentum und Lektüre: Zur Sozialgeschichte des Lesens in Deutschland zwischen feudaler und industrieller Gesellschaft* (Stuttgart: Metzler, 1973), 62; and Rolf Engelsing, *Der Bürger als Leser: Lesergeschichte in Deutschland 1500–1800* (Stuttgart: Metzler, 1974).

Wittmann, *Geschichte* 179, arrives at different figures. He views the "reading revolution" in the eighteenth century not so much in quantitative terms (a rise in literacy from 2 percent to only 4 percent), but as a qualitative one, as an intensification of reading. Reinhard Wittmann, *Geschichte des deutschen Buchhandels: Ein Überblick* (Munich: Beck, 1991).

[8] Barbara Becker-Cantarino, *Der lange Weg zur Mündigkeit: Frau und Literatur in Deutschland von 1500–1800* (Stuttgart: Metzler, 1987), 278–84.

[9] Wittmann, *Geschichte* 159.

[10] See Hans J. Haferkorn, "Zur Entstehung der bürgerlich-literarischen Intelligenz und des Schriftstellers in Deutschland zwischen 1750 und 1800," in *Deutsches Bürgertum und literarische Intelligenz, 1750–1800*, ed. Bernd Lutz (Stuttgart: Metzler, 1974), 113–275; and John McCarthy, "Rewriting the Role of the Writer: On the 18th Century as the Age of the Author," *Leipziger Jahrbuch zur Buchgeschichte* 5 (1995): 13–37.

[11] Wolfgang Martens, "Die Geburt des Journalisten in der Aufklärung," in *Wolfenbütteler Studien zur Aufklärung*, ed. Günter Schulz (Bremen: Jacobi, 1974), 1: 84–98.

[12] Faulstich, *Die moderne Mediengesellschaft* 226; Jürgen Wilke, *Literarische Zeitschriften des 18. Jahrhunderts (1688–1789)*, Sammlung Metzler, vols. 174 and 175 (Stuttgart: Metzler, 1978), here 1: 26.

[13] Jürgen Wilke, *Grundzüge der Medien- und Kommunikationsgeschichte: Von den Anfängen bis ins 20. Jahrhundert* (Cologne: Böhlau, 2000), 72–75 and 94–98.

[14] See the essay by Rosmarie Zeller in this volume.

[15] Wolfgang Martens, *Die Botschaft der Tugend: Die Aufklärung im Spiegel der deutschen Moralischen Wochenschriften* (Stuttgart: Metzler, 1968), 500–44. See also Helga Brandes, "Moralische Wochenschriften," in *Von Almanach bis Zeitung*, 225–32.

[16] Norbert Elias, *Über den Prozeß der Zivilisation*, 14th ed. (Frankfurt a. M.: Suhrkamp, 1989).

[17] See Peter Nasse, *Die Frauenzimmer-Bibliothek des Hamburger 'Patrioten' von 1724: Zur weiblichen Bildung in der Frühaufklärung* (Stuttgart: Akademischer Verlag Hans-Dieter Heinz, 1976), 90–125.

[18] *Die Vernünftigen Tadlerinnen* (1725) 1: 7.

[19] The last issue of *Iris* dated 1776 appeared only in 1778.

[20] Becker-Cantarino, *Der lange Weg zur Mündigkeit*.

[21] See Helga Brandes, "Das Frauenzimmer-Journal: Zur Herausbildung einer journalistischen Gattung im 18. Jahrhundert," in *Deutsche Literatur von Frauen, vol 1: Vom Mittelalter bis zum Ende des 18. Jahrhunderts*, ed. Gisela Brinker-Gabler (Munich: Beck, 1988), 1: 452–68; the detailed study by Ulrike Weckel, *Zwischen Häuslichkeit und Öffentlichkeit: Die ersten deutschen Frauenzeitschriften im späten 18. Jahrhundert und ihr Publikum*, Studien und Texte zur Sozialgeschichte der Literatur, vol. 61 (Tübingen: Niemeyer, 1998); and Helga Brandes, *Buch- und Zeitschriftenmarkt*, 304–11.

[22] See the bibliography and commentary by Barbara Becker-Cantarino in *Sophie La Roche: Herbsttage. Nachdruck der Ausgabe von 1805* (Karben: Verlag Petra Wald, 1999), afterword, pages *15–*53.

[23] Goethe, Hamburger Ausgabe, 4th ed. (Munich: Beck, 1960), 14: 13.

[24] Hugo Lachmansky, *Die deutschen Frauenzeitschriften des 18. Jahrhunderts,* Diss. (Berlin, 1900).

[25] Ulrike Weckel, *Die ersten deutschen Frauenzeitschriften,* 75–100 and 513–43.

[26] *Iris* had a press run of 800–1,000 copies. See Jürgen Wilke, *Literarische Zeitschriften,* 2: 119.

[27] *Pomona für Teutschlands Töchter. Speier 1783–1784* (Rpt. Munich: K. G. Saur, 1987), 1: 7. Jürgen Vorderstemann's introduction to this reprint of the entire journal (in 4 volumes) is very informative. Subsequent references to this edition in the text. See also Ruth Dawson, "The Monthly *Pomona* and Its Audiences," in her *The Contested Quill: Literature by Women in Germany 1770–1800* (Newark: U of Delaware P, 2002), 122–31.

[28] *Die Discourse der Mahlern, Zürich 1721–23* (Rpt. Hildesheim: Olms, 1969), 1, 8: 7.

[29] Reprint, edited by Annette Zunzer, Schweizer Texte. Neue Folge, vol. 15 (Bern: Haupt, 2002). See also Britt-Angela Kirstein, *Marianne Ehrmann: Publizistin und Herausgeberin im ausgehenden achtzehnten Jahrhundert* (Wiesbaden: Deutscher Universitäts Verlag, 1997); and Helga Stipa Madland, *Marianne Ehrmann: Reason and Emotion in Her Life and Works,* Women in German Literature, vol. 1 (New York: Peter Lang, 1998).

[30] A second edition and a French translation appeared only a year later in 1785. Ehrmann was later forgotten until her rediscovery in the twentieth century by Edith Krull, *Das Wirken der Frau im frühen deutschen Zeitschriftenwesen* (Charlottenburg: R. Lorentz, 1939).

[31] La Roche must have served as a model, since Ehrmann had played in Vienna on several stages under the pseudonym "Sternheim."

[32] *Amaliens Erholungsstunden* (12 vols.) Tübingen 1790–92. Here, 1791, 2: 268.

[33] During the 1790s political journals originated in Germany in response to the French Revolution, such as the Jacobin journals *Das Neue Graue Ungeheuer* (1795–97); *Die Schildwache* (1796/97); *Die Geißel* (1797–99); *Obskuranten-Almanach* (1798–1800); and Joseph Görres, *Das Rothe Blatt* (1798) and *Der Rübezahl* (1798/99). Among the important anti-revolutionary journals were: Leopold Alois Hoffmann, *Wiener Zeitschrift* (1792/93), Ludwig Christian von Grolmann, Ernst August Anton von Göchhausen et al., *Eudämonia, oder deutsches Volksglück: Ein Journal für Freunde von Wahrheit und Recht* (1795–98). See Helga Brandes, "'Ein Volk muß seine Freiheit selbst erobern . . .' Rebmann, die jakobinische Publizistik und die Französische Revolution," in *Francia: Forschungen zur westeuropäischen Geschichte* 18.2 (1991): 219–30.

[34] See Brandes, *Das Frauenzimmer-Journal* 464–68.

[35] See Jan Knopf, "Kalender," in *Von Almanach bis Zeitung,* 45–61.

[36] (Erfurt: Ernst Michael Funke, 1736). This was the sixth edition; the date 1719 on the title page may indicate the calendar's first appearance.

[37] This calendar took its materials especially from the encyclopedic economic guide by Johann Coler, *Calendarium Perpetuum et Sex Libri Oeconomici* (1609, first collected edition); see Helga Brandes, "Frühneuzeitliche Ökonomieliteratur," in *Die Literatur des 17. Jahrhunderts*, ed. Albert Meier (Munich: Hanser, 1999), 470–84.

[38] Wolfgang Bunzel,"Almanache und Taschenbücher," in *Almanach bis Zeitung*, 24–35.

[39] Michaelis was the first translator of two Richardson novels into German: *Geschichte der Clarissa, eines vornehmen Frauenzimmers* (Göttingen 1768–1770) and *Geschichte Herrn Carl Grandison. In Briefen entworfen* (Leipzig 1754–1755), and he was the father of Caroline Schlegel-Schelling.

[40] York-Gothart Mix, *Die deutschen Musenalmanache des 18. Jahrhunderts* (Munich: Beck, 1987), 16.

[41] Erich Schön, *Der Verlust der Sinnlichkeit oder die Verwandlungen des Lesers. Mentalitätswandel um 1800* (Stuttgart: Klett, 1987).

[42] Leipzig: Adam Friedrich Böhme, 1784; subsequent references to this edition in the text. See also the catalogue of women's almanacs by Lydia Schieth, *"Fürs schöne Geschlecht": Frauenalmanache zwischen 1800 und 1850* (Bamberg: Staatsbibliothek Bamberg, 1992).

[43] This was also evident in the title with several new journals then appearing with "German" in the title, mostly after French models like *Der Teutsche Merkur* (1773–1810) edited by Christoph Martin Wieland and the *Deutsche Museum* (1776–91) edited by Heinrich Christian Boie and Christian Konrad Wilhelm von Dohm. It was continued under the title *Neues Deutsches Museum* (1789–91), edited by Boie.

[44] Since 1817 it was published under the title *Göttingische gelehrte Anzeigen*.

[45] See Wilke, *Literarische Zeitschriften*, 1: 79–91; and Helga Brandes, *Buch- und Zeitschriftenmarkt*, 312–17.

[46] Johann Gottfried Herder, "Über die neuere deutsche Literatur. Erste Sammlung von Fragmenten. Eine Beilage zu den Briefen, die neueste Literatur betreffend. 1767," in *Herder. Sämmtliche Werke*, ed. Bernhard Suphan (Rpt. Hildesheim: Olms, 1978), 1: 142–43.

[47] See the landmark study by Alexander Altmann, *Moses Mendelssohn: A Biographical Study* (U of Alabama P, 1973); and Allan Arkush, ed., *Moses Mendelssohn and the Enlightenment* (Albany: State U of New York P, 1994).

[48] In 1766 the journal was renamed *Neue Bibliothek der schönen Wissenschaften und der freyen Künste* and edited by Christian Felix Weisse, later (with vol. 29) by Johann Gottfried Dyck. It lasted until 1805.

[49] See the comments by Wolfgang Albrecht in *Friedrich Nicolai. "Kritik ist überall, zumal in Deutschland nötig": Satiren und Schriften zur Literatur* (Munich: Beck, 1987), 526–27.

[50] *Allgemeine Deutsche Bibliothek*, usually abbreviated as *ADB*, was the title from 1765 to 1792 under the editorship of Nicolai; from 1793 to 1805 it was *Neue Allgemeine*

Deutsche Bibliothek, or *NDAB.* From vol. 107, 1792 until 1800, the editor was the Hamburg publisher Carl Ernst Bohn. Because of Prussian censorship, Nicolai had no choice but to have the journal printed in Hamburg where less stringent censorship prevailed. In 1801 Prussia lifted the ban and Nicolai resumed editorship with vol. 56, until 1805 when the occupation of Berlin by Napoleon's troops forced the closing of his business. See the chapter "The *Allgemeine Deutsche Bibliothek* as the Centerpiece of Nicolai's Program of Enlightenment and His Firm," in the excellent study by Pamela E. Selwyn, *Everyday Life in the German Book Trade: Friedrich Nicolai as Bookseller and Publisher in the Age of Enlightenment, 1750–1810* (University Park, PA: Pennsylvania State UP, 2000), 251–97.

[51] *Allgemeine Deutsche Bibliothek. Des ersten Bandes erstes Stück* (Berlin: Nicolai, 1765), 1.

[52] Klaus L. Berghahn, "Von der klassizistischen zur klassischen Literaturkritik 1730–1806," in *Geschichte der deutschen Literaturkritik (1730–1980),* ed. Peter Uwe Hohendahl (Stuttgart: Metzler, 1985), 52.

[53] See Gerhard R. Kaiser and Siegfried Seifert, eds., *Friedrich Justin Bertuch (1747–1822): Verleger, Schriftsteller und Unternehmer im klassischen Weimar* (Tübingen: Niemeyer, 2000).

Frontispiece of Anna Louise Karsch, Auserlesene Gedichte *(1664), with her portrait (inscribed Anna Louise Dürbach, her maiden name).*

Religious and Secular Poetry and Epic (1700–1780)

Kevin Hilliard

Sacred and Secular

THE STORY OF THE EIGHTEENTH CENTURY cannot be plotted as a simple, smooth development toward a secular understanding of the world and man's place in it, let alone as the "rise of modern paganism" (Peter Gay)[1] — a phrase that applies with even less force to Germany than it does to France or England. If secular beliefs were growing in boldness and authority, and secular attitudes gaining ground in the life of society, it is no less true that Christianity continued to exert a strong hold on people's hearts and habits. It seems an apt expression of the tendencies of the age, therefore, that of the two great epic poems written in Germany in the eighteenth century, one was a religious epic, and the other a secular romance.

Sacred Epic: Klopstock, *Der Messias*

The twenty cantos and almost 20,000 lines of *Der Messias* were written by Friedrich Gottlieb Klopstock (1724–1803) over a twenty-five year period between 1748 and 1773. It was thus itself an epic undertaking that from the beginning captured the imagination of the German reading public. For devout Christians, it was the answer to their prayers: in an age of dangerous freethinking, here was the long-awaited poet who would sing the "Helden-Geschichte von JEsu von Nazareth"[2] (heroic story of Jesus of Nazareth). For more aesthetically minded critics, Klopstock was the poet who at last provided Germany with the great epic every national literature needed to be worthy of standing alongside the ancient Greek and Roman traditions. What is more, he had written it in the long hexameter verse favored in classical literature, and was thus the first modern to have risen to the challenge set by Homer and Virgil. When at last his labors were complete, Klopstock could therefore boast that in *Der Messias* the elevation of language and religion had erected an eternal monument to his name (an obvious echo of Horace, *Odes*, 3.30).[3]

Posterity, however, has not been as kind to Klopstock's epic as he clearly expected. The power of his poetic language is recognized. Many of the poem's local effects are of a considerable sublimity, as in this Homeric simile describing the Pharisee Philo's black mien as he rises to his feet to speak out against Christ in the priestly council:

> So, wenn auf unerstiegnen Gebirgen ein nahes Gewitter
> Furchtbar sich lagert, so reißt sich eine der nächtlichsten Wolken,
> Mit den meisten Donnern bewaffnet, entflammt zum Verderben,
> Einsam hervor. Wenn andre den Wipfel der Zeder nur fassen,
> Wird sie von einem Himmel zum andern waldichte Berge,
> Wird hochtürmende meilenlange Königsstädte
> Tausendmal donnernd entzünden, und sie in Trümmern begraben.[4]

> [So when on mountains unclimb'd encamps tremendous a nigh storm,
> One of the black huge clouds, most arm'd for destroying, advances
> Bulging alone: while others but seize the tops of the cedars,
> This from the east to the west shall enkindle centennial forests,
> Fire the haughtily-towering league-long cities of monarchs,
> Burying homes of men in ashes and ruin, with thund'rings Thousandfold].[5]

But the plan of the whole "wants proportion, cohesion, interest, and unity," as William Taylor of Norwich put it in his *Historic Survey of German Poetry* in 1830.[6] If Christ's Passion, which occupies the first ten cantos, lacks dramatic focus, the Resurrection and Ascension described in the remaining ten are even poorer in incident. Klopstock therefore pads out the action with the reactions of a host of what Taylor, perhaps unkindly, calls "celestial loiterers, the angels, patriarchs, and prophets" (1:279), who indulge in such a "multiplicity of pietistic rhapsodies" that "even Saint Theresa" would "weary" of them (1:283).

It is doubtful whether there are many now who would dissent from these views. Yet to see the work only in this way is to read with secular expectations and a secular understanding of what an epic poem ought to be — a way of reading that Klopstock himself anticipated when he said that the freethinker would see in his work only "ruins" where a true Christian would admire a "majestätische[r] Tempel"[7] (majestic temple). The *fabula*, the "argument" of the poem, is not really constituted by the events described in the Gospel. It is nothing other than what German theology calls *Heilsgeschichte*, the history of salvation, from the beginning to the end of time. Indeed time itself, in this view, is only a human concept, inadequate to the nature of the covenant made between God the Father and Son from the beginning, in a timeless present (Canto 1.83–135). It is for this underlying reason that there can be no real action in the poem. Everything essential cannot be other than it has been, is, and will be for evermore. The only action remaining is that of a dawning awareness in creation of the sublime fact of salvation, rippling outward along the great chain of being, upward from inanimate nature through the consciousness of embodied or disembodied spirits in their varying degrees of insight to the hierarchy of angels. This growing awareness *is* the story. It is told in a hundred variations: in the "dramatic" episodes like the healing of Samma (Canto 2), in the remorse of the penitent devil Abbadona (a long drawn-out subplot that for decades had a tender-hearted readership on tenterhooks, before coming to a theologically bold conclusion in the prospect that he would be saved on Judgment Day), in the conversion of the good pagan Portia (Cantos 7 and 15), in the joyful surmises of the patriarchs, prophets, and angels — but just as much in the more subtle stirrings of emotion in all these witnesses and bystanders. For it is in the soul of the believer, and only there, that the work of salvation is finally completed. It is there that the "Taten der Seele" (deeds of the soul, Canto 6.7) are performed that *are* the workings of salvation. And it is this that accounts for the lyrical and inward quality of the work that has been observed over and over again, most memorably in Schiller's famous account of Klopstock in *Über naive und sentimentalische Dichtung* (On the Naïve and the Sentimental in Poetry, 1796).

Secular Epic: Wieland, *Oberon*

No one could accuse Wieland's *Oberon* (1780) of lack of incident. A rollicking romance in the manner (and the stanzaic form, a loose-limbed *ottava rima*) of Ariosto's epic *Orlando Furioso*, with no shortage of violence, sorcery and erotic interest, it takes its hero, the knight Hüon of Bordeaux, from the court of Charlemagne to that of the Caliph of Baghdad and back again, with shipwreck on a desert island and captivity in Algiers thrown in for good measure.

No one who had observed the early career of Christoph Martin Wieland (1733–1813) could have imagined that he would produce anything like this in his mature years. In the 1750s he belonged to the party of the "Alpinisten,"[8] as their enemies mockingly called the high-minded group around the Swiss critics Bodmer and Breitinger (see the essay by Rosmarie Zeller in this volume). He worshipped the poetry of Bodmer's early *protégé* Klopstock, and in particular his *Messias:* "Über [. . .] Klopstocks ersten fünf Gesängen [. . .] vergaß ich Essen und Trinken, Spiel, Schlaf, mich selbst und die ganze Welt"[9] (reading Klopstock's first five cantos I forgot about eating, drinking, sleeping, cards, myself and the whole world). By the late 1760s, however, his conversion to a benign Epicureanism had gone so far that when Klopstock, in 1771, set up a reading society (*Lesegesellschaft*) in Hamburg, he explicitly forbade the reading of Wieland's *risqué* stories.[10]

William Taylor was as enthusiastic about *Oberon* as he was cool toward *Der Messias:* it was Wieland's "master-piece [. . .] — the child of his genius in moments of its purest converse with the all-beauteous forms of ideal excellence [. . .] — an epic poem, popular beyond example, yet as dear to the philosopher as to the multitude" (2:9). One of its attractive features is its humor. This is not merely an adventitious admixture. Wieland was aware of the gap that modern civilization had opened up between the heroic manners and beliefs of warrior or chivalric cultures and the prose of modern life, and exploited it to humorous effect.[11] In a philosophical age, the whole nature of belief in the ideal fictions of the past had changed — indeed the awareness that they *were* fictions could no longer be suppressed. That is why Wieland cannot keep a straight face in the exordium to his poem. Having started in the traditional manner, with an invocation of his muse and a summary of the poem's argument (which, however, he presents in a deliberately helter-skelter fashion), he pulls up short:

> Doch, Muse, wohin reißt dich die Adlersschwinge
> Der hohen trunknen Schwärmerei?
> Dein Hörer steht bestürzt, er fragt sich was dir sei,
> Und deine Gesichte sind *ihm* geheimnisvolle Dinge.
>
> Komm, laß dich nieder zu uns auf diesen Kanapee,
> Und — statt zu rufen, ich seh, ich seh,
> Was niemand sieht als Du — erzähl uns fein gelassen
> Wie alles sich begab.[12]

[But Muse, whither is the eagle's pinion of high, delirious enthusiasm taking you? Your listener stands nonplussed, he asks what the matter is with you, and your visions are mysteries *to him*. Come, settle down next to us on this sofa, and instead of crying "I see, I see" what no one sees but you — take your time and tell us how everything happened.]

In having his muse plummet from the heights of poetic rapture to the banality of an eighteenth-century drawing-room (that "Kanapee" strikes a deliberately anachronistic note), Wieland is recapitulating, in a comic key, the transformation undergone by philosophy and esoteric learning in the course of the century, as they were taught to forsake their former haunts and instead "dwell in Clubs and Assemblies, at Tea-Tables, and in Coffee-Houses" (as the famous passage from no. 10 of the *Spectator* put it).[13] He takes account, that is to say, of the mental horizons of a public that is at ease in the modern world, and whose social and intellectual interactions are conducted in the currency of good manners and common sense. Confronted by this public, and indeed sharing its values — among them a lively sense of what is and what is not probable in the modern world — Wieland narrates his epic in the ironic awareness that epic is in fact no longer possible, since the ground for belief in its superhuman exploits and supernatural machinery is no longer present. Correspondingly, the elevation of the epic stanza Wieland inherits from Ariosto is constantly undercut by colloquialisms and a prosaic, conversational loosening of meter, line-length and line-divisions — a far cry from the stately formality of Klopstock's hexameters.

Lyric Poetry: Aesthetic and Social Determinants

Epics were written only by the most ambitious of poets, who were not afraid to enter the lists with Homer, Virgil, Ariosto, or Milton. It is therefore not surprising that only few such poems were attempted in the period. Lyric poetry, by contrast, was produced in great profusion. "Niemahls ist unser geliebtes Deutschland so voller Poeten gewesen als itzund"[14] (never has our beloved Germany been so full of poets as now), wrote one critic in 1734. Johann Heinrich Campe estimated in 1788 that there were twenty thousand "Versemacher" (versifiers) in Germany — far too many, in his view.[15] One standard bibliography — itself a digest of a much more voluminous work — lists approximately 250 new titles of poetry between 1700 and 1780.[16] But these are only the ones its compilers considered to be of potential significance for literary history. Many more are not listed. Moreover, counting only single-authored books is seriously to underestimate the total. Thousands of poems were printed either as single fly-sheets or published in anthologies and journals.[17] Hymns, too, continued to be written in large numbers, and the new genres of the church cantata and oratorio (Bach!) generated further demand for religious verse.[18] Opera and the *Singspiel* had to be supplied with arias and songs (see the essay by Sarah Colvin in this volume). Yet more poetry is hidden away in letters and other manuscript sources. Finally, there was an unquantifiable mass of oral poetry, now lost (except where ethnographic pioneers like Herder or Goethe collected surviving examples), glimpses of which we catch in the memories of contemporaries such as Günther, who recalls hearing an old serving woman in his childhood singing a song of the Thirty Years' War while he sat listening spellbound by the hearth.[19]

Gathering this profusion of forms under the heading of "lyric poetry" is to suggest a likeness of purpose and manner that the poetry of the time did not possess. The notion of lyric as the third major poetic genre, after epic poetry and drama, was itself only gradually developing in the period. In most theoretical writings of the time there is merely a greater or lesser number of miscellaneous poetic forms, collectively differentiated from epic and drama, if at all, only by their relative brevity. The ode jostles with the elegy and the song, the *rondeau* is cheek by jowl with the epigram, the sonnet competes for attention with the cantata, with no evident conceptual or formal principle uniting them all.

Part of the problem was that no form that had ever been invented could be discarded (though early in the eighteenth century, theorists did decide that the solemn jocularity of Baroque acrostics and figure poems — poems whose layout forms an image on the page — was in poor taste). This meant that there was no single authoritative model to which poets could turn. Horace might help with the ode, but was of little use where a sonnet was required. Of course the ancients were regarded as exemplary, in a general and honorific sense. But in 1700 or 1730, a poet who aspired to a "classical" style was committed to little more than a certain purity of diction and restraint in the use of poetic figures. Themes and sentiments were recycled from the reservoir of classical and humanist poetry. Contemporary French (Boileau, Jean-Baptiste Rousseau) and English (Pope, Thomson, Gray) poets were admired and imitated, not least in their verse forms, as the long Alexandrine line favored by poets of the seventeenth century gradually gave way to blank verse or four-beat iambic or trochaic lines. Only in the 1740s did a more conscious classicism begin to take hold, when a succession of minor poets were nominated for the title the "German Horace" (some of whom, in the 1750s and 1760s, actually did succeed in sounding something like him, as the deliberate imitation of his strophic forms was added to the widespread influence of his sentiments). The rules (*praecepta*) of rhetoric, with its clear and practical distinctions between the plain, the middle, and the elevated style were as important as any models (*exempla*). Those contemporary German poets whose work the critics most frequently praised — Hagedorn, Haller, Gellert, Klopstock — were cited as much for exemplifying one of these levels of style to perfection as for their own more individual virtues. As classically educated poets with a thorough grounding in rhetoric, these writers understood their craft in the same way.[20]

However, academic poetics and criticism were increasingly falling behind the times in their understanding of the dynamics of literary production. Changes in mentality, but also in the social function of literature and in the literary market, were leading to a new relationship between poets and their readers.

The market for imaginative literature expanded considerably in the course of the eighteenth century.[21] The middle classes were becoming consumers of culture in growing numbers, as they acquired the means and leisure to afford and enjoy things that previously had been the preserve of the learned professions or the nobility. Leisure itself was a luxury whose benefits the urban middle classes increasingly came to desire and acquire for themselves.[22] Social visits, balls, concerts, plays, outings, and passing the time in the new coffeehouses — "Conzerte, Maskeraden, Komödien und Opern" and the "caffeetisch"[23] — were among the pleasures the middle classes now laid claim to. But more private and intimate forms of leisure were sought out, too. The desire for comfort and ease found no more eloquent expression than in the introduction of the sofa ("Sofa" or "Kanapee" in German) to the domestic interiors of the eighteenth century:

> Das Canapee ist mein Vergnügen,
> Drauf ich mir was zu Gute thu;
> Da kann ich recht vergnüget liegen
> In einer ausgestreckten Ruh'.[24]

[The sofa is my pride and joy. I take my fill of pleasure resting on it, stretched out at full length.]

The sofa, with its suggestion of oriental voluptuousness, was the appropriate place for amorous dalliance ("Hier scherzt der kleine Amor [...] / Auf einem weichen sopha" [*sic*] — here the little Amor plays, on a soft sofa).[25] But it was also the site for no less voluptuous pleasure of reading, as we have already seen in Wieland's *Oberon*, where the poet's Muse was gently taken by the hand and led to the sofa to tell her tale. In Goethe's *Die Leiden des jungen Werthers*, too, Werther reads aloud to Lotte as they sit side by side on the "Canapee."

Literacy and leisure were both on the increase, as was the use of one to fill the other. Reading societies (*Lesegesellschaften*) sprang up all over Germany. Reading was becoming a favorite pastime — and not just among the middle classes. It was growing in the lower classes, too, as a contemporary writer observed: "Schon wandelt allmählig die populär gewordene Litteratur aus den Zimmern, unter die Treppe, und mir ist eine Lesegesellschaft bekant, zu welcher ein Paar Kutscher gehören"[26] (Gradually literature has begun appealing to ordinary people and has left the drawing rooms and moved below stairs; I know a reading society which has a couple of coachmen as members). Whereas in 1690 it could be said of literary production that "der Gelehrte producirt und der Gelehrte konsumiert des Buchhändlers Waren"[27] (the bookseller's wares are produced and consumed by scholars), by the middle of the eighteenth century those without higher learning (Latin) were beginning to form the majority (a shift in balance that is reflected in the steady decline in the proportion of Latin titles published). Within this more or less leisured and literate, but not necessarily learned reading public, women constituted a prominent group. The fictional Lotte had many real-life counterparts: "Ein Dichter findet sehr leicht Leser. — Vielleicht findet er noch leichter Leserinnen"[28] (A poet easily finds male readers. Perhaps he finds female readers more easily still). In 1735 the poet Anna Teuber exhorted her "sisters" (Schwestern) to nourish and cultivate the delight they took in books ("Bücher-Lust").[29] Most would have needed no encouragement: as another woman writer said, "Die Seele wird vergnüget / Wenn sich der muntre Fuß zum Bücher-Schranck verfüget"[30] (the soul rejoices when the foot, with lively step, proceeds to the book-cabinet).

Here, then, were the beginnings of the modern reading public, a "Lesewelt" (world of reading), as it came to be called.[31] Within this world, what counted was no longer erudition, but taste, that *je ne sais quoi* of tact, ease, sensitivity, and judgment that could be found in women as easily as in men, and in the unscholarly more than in the learned. It was for this "feminized" public — curious, pleasure seeking, avid for novelty — that authors now increasingly began writing. The demand was there; the supply adapted to satisfy it. As the century wore on, the new reading crowded out the old. If in 1735 Anna Teuber still recommended the Bible as the book women should read above all others, the "literary works of intelligent men" ("was kluge Männer tichten") did not lag far behind.[32] By 1771, the positions were reversed, according to Müller von Itzehoe: "Gellert, [Ewald von] Kleist, Ges[s]ner, Thomson, Klopstock, Yorick [that is, Sterne]" had taken the place of the catechism in "polishing the understanding" and "forming the moral character" of contemporary readers.[33]

The prominence of poets in particular is conspicuous in Müller's list. Until the rise of the popular novel in the latter third of the century, poetry was indeed the staple fare of many readers, especially if one includes narrative poems like the *Fabeln und Erzählungen* (Fables and Stories) by Christian Fürchtegott Gellert (1715–1769), the best-selling German book of the eighteenth century. Short poems were easily produced and easily consumed. Poetry provided suitable entertainment and matter for discussion at social gatherings.[34] There was a ready market for anthologies and almanacs of verse; moral weeklies and other journals published their share of poems as well.[35]

As we have already seen, there was no shortage of poets and versifiers to meet the demand. Universities were a fertile breeding ground.[36] The survival of pragmatic genres like the devotional and especially the occasional poem lowered the threshold for entry to the market. Until the decline of the occasional poem in the 1760s and 1770s, many poets began (and indeed ended) their careers as authors of poems marking weddings, baptisms, funerals, birthdays, graduations and other social occasions (bombarding the rich, one critic complained, with unwanted poems in the hope of financial reward or preferment).[37] Although the satirists frequently mocked occasional poetry, it served a real social need, both for recipients and authors. For writers with no other hope of employment or worldly success, it could be a lifeline. Thus for Anna Louisa Karsch (1722–91), one of the most remarkable poetic talents of the century, the small sums she earned as a young woman with her occasional verse made the difference between eating and going hungry, until her poems finally brought her to the attention of patrons who provided for her more amply.[38]

Even poets whose circumstances were less precarious had to be adept at exploiting whatever opportunities the writing of poetry offered. If it was desirable to impress potential or actual patrons in the higher and highest reaches of society, it was equally important not to neglect the business end of the market. Thus Brockes, taking stock of the past year in his (customary) New Year's poem for 1735, proudly reports having received intelligence that his poems have been read "an Höfen, ja so gar / [von] Gekröhnten Häuptern" (at court, and by monarchs themselves), but also notes with satisfaction that the fourth part of his *Irdisches Vergnügen in GOTT* (Earthly Delight in God, 1736) has already gone into a second edition, within the space of barely more than a year since its first.[39] Later poets such as Gleim and Klopstock were canny operators in the literary market. Neither the change in the composition of the reading public nor the corresponding change in taste escaped them. Erudition was out — or if it was to be acceptable, it had to be "anmuthig" (graceful).[40] Hagedorn, who was a highly learned man, proclaimed "Ich [habe] es [. . .] oft für eine nicht geringe Glückseligkeit gehalten, daß es niemals mein Beruf gewesen ist, noch seyn können, ein *Gelehrter* zu heissen"[41] (I have often thought it a not inconsiderable blessing that it never has been, and never could be my calling, to bear the name *scholar*). Other equally well-educated poets made a similar display of their indifference to learning. Bodmer crossly wrote in a letter that Klopstock despised scholarship, as if it were merest pedantry.[42] Klopstock was always eager to hear what impression his works made on "Ungelehrte" (the unscholarly).[43] Among these, again, he had his eye on women especially — admittedly not only for the purposes of market research. He sent a female correspondent this account of one reading he gave from his poetry: "Es [ist] eine ungemein süße Sache [. . .] wenn man von liebenswürdigen Leserinnen zugleich geliebkoset, u. zugleich verehrt wird. Ich habe von Lazarus u Cidli oft vorlesen müssen mitten in einem Ringe von Mädchens, die entfernter wieder von Mannspersonen eingeschloßen wurden. Man hat mich mit Thränen belohnt"[44] (It is a mightily sweet thing to be treated simultaneously with tenderness and respect by amiable female readers. I repeatedly had to read [the episode] of Lazarus and Cidli [from *Der Messias*], sitting in the middle of a circle of girls, who in turn were surrounded by a circle of men. I was rewarded with tears).

This is an apt image of the composition of the public in the middle of the century. The effect on this occasion was all Klopstock's. But his relationship with his readers was only the most striking example of how sensitive a medium poetry was for creating, receiving, reinforcing, and recycling currents of feeling and emotional dispositions within the new "Lesewelt." Poets exploited the new literary market to create communities of readers for whose thoughts and sentiments their works provided a stimulus and outlet.

Varieties of Lyric

Five main trends can be discerned. The first tendency is to colonize the new-found terrain of leisure from the direction of religious practice and sentiment. What is being offered here is a kind of poetic worship: poetry becomes an aestheticized extension of devotional literature, mingling edification and aesthetic rapture. Brockes's *Irdisches Vergnügen in GOTT* and then Klopstock's religious odes and his great hymns in free verse (1758–61) are variations of this tendency.[45] As God's majesty is its ultimate object, the sublime is its organizing principle.[46]

The second revolves around an ideal of gentlemanly urbanity and learning lightly worn.[47] Poetry's function, in this view, like that of literature in general, is to nourish and discipline sound reason and good taste, and to promote a cheerful sociability between those (of both sexes) so instructed and informed. The themes range from questions of practical philosophy to satirical comments on social foibles and follies; virtue is praised, vice condemned. The temper is equable and optimistic. Friedrich von Hagedorn (1708–54), lauded by his contemporaries for his ability to combine "muntres Scherzen / Mit Wissenschaft"[48] (raillery and learning) incarnated this urbane ideal for an earlier, Wieland for a later generation.[49] "Witz" (less "wit" than sprightly "intelligence") is its formal principle, Horace its presiding genius.

This eudemonistic tendency (Hagedorn proclaimed man's "Recht vergnügt zu seyn"[50] [right to pleasure]) could easily modulate into a third, more frankly hedonistic key. Under Hagedorn's influence, the verse of the so-called Halle circle — Johann Wilhelm Ludwig Gleim (1719–1803), Johann Peter Uz (1720–96), Johann Nikolaus Götz (1721–41)[51] — celebrated and stimulated the human propensity toward pleasure-seeking ("der Durst der Menschen nach Vergnügen").[52] The poetry of "Nebenstunden," that is, moments of leisure,[53] suspends allegiance to the work ethic and celebrates the simple pleasures of life. Prompted by the contemporary revival of Anacreontic verse in France, Gleim and others identify these pleasures as wine, women, and song. To the jibe that in reality they were abstemious, chaste, and tunelessly untalented, one might reply that the criticism misses the point at least on the first two counts: the license of poetry to fantasize and fictionalize was not the least of the freedoms they were asserting. The formal principle of this kind of poetry — sometimes called "rococo" by literary historians — is a kind of unstudied grace and charm.

The fourth tendency, which is associated chiefly with Klopstock's secular poetry (*Oden,* 1771), takes themes from these last two and plays them through again — but this time with feeling. For Klopstock, poetry came from the heart rather than from reason. This is the sentimental turn in German (and not only German) literary history. The beloved is celebrated in verse, but in a wholly chaste and seraphic vein.[54] Love, friendship and the pleasures of life are again praised, but in a more enthusiastic key than before (for example "Elegie" ["Der du zum Tiefsinn . . ."], "Das Rosenband," "An Gleim"). Many new emotional effects are gained by exploiting what Gellert called "the pleasures of discontentment."[55] Thus, for instance, poems about friendship will be transposed into a melancholy minor key, with the poet imagining himself being the only survivor at the grave of his companions, the sorrow at their early death mingling with the pleasure his memory of their happiness together still gives him ("Die frühen Gräber," [The Early Graves], "Die Sommernacht" [The Summer Night]). Sensibility and a dynamic linguistic expressivity are the hallmarks of this kind of poetry.

The fifth main tendency of German poetry in this period takes its cue from the widening of the literary market to include the sector of the population at the furthest remove from classical learning: the common people. Even before Herder and Bürger, the rugged strength and simplicity of the antique ballad had been praised by Hagedorn,[56] and a consciously simple style practiced by the Anacreontic poets. The next step was to "ventriloquize" what poetry *composed* by the unlearned might sound like. Thus, poets variously adopted the persona of a "Bänkelsänger" or popular fairground balladeer (Gleim), an untutored Prussian soldier (Gleim),[57] and a servingman of plain understanding (Matthias Claudius). Claudius wrote as "Asmus," the "Wandsbecker Bothe" (courier of Wandsbeck). It is symptomatic that his famous "Abendlied" (Eventide Hymn), with its prayer for childlike simplicity ("Laß uns einfältig werden"; cf. Matth. 5:3, 18:3), was reprinted in Herder's *Volkslieder* (Folksongs) of 1778. Others experimented in the same vein.[58] Needless to say, the aesthetic quality this kind of poetry seeks and cultivates is naïveté.

Writing by Women

Of the groups in society who generally did not have access to advanced education, women constituted the only one to speak in their own right in significant numbers.[59] Of course they had to face down considerable prejudice.[60] But the eighteenth century was the age of *Aufklärung* and good at facing down prejudice; many men lent their support to the cause of women's education, women's reading, and women's writing.[61] More damaging than outright prejudice was a subtle gendering of genres, which meant that no woman was likely to attempt an epic (too encyclopedic) or sublime ode (too strenuous).[62] An Anacreontic *erotikon*, already dubiously decent for men, would have been unthinkable for women. But within these limits, the conditions for women writers were not unfavorable. Both the expanding market for poems and volumes of poetry and the shift in orientation toward the needs of a leisured and unlearned public created new opportunities for them.

Much of what they wrote is indistinguishable in theme and style from the general run of eighteenth century poetry (for better or worse). But when they write from a woman's point of view or describe their own experience they add an original and refreshing note. Sidonie Hedwig von Zäunemann's "Landtag, welchen die Königin Eva denen sämtlichen Weibern zum Trost zu Frauenstadt [. . .] gehalten" (Parliament of Women, convened by Queen Eve in Womenstown), a satire on husbands' treatment of their wives, is written with considerable verve.[63] Teuber describes the female scene of writing:

> Die Arbeit lag deswegen nicht,
> Mein Spinnrad ließ mich dennoch schreiben.
> Das Lese-Pult stand im Gesicht;
> Die Lincke mußt am Faden bleiben;
> Die Tafel auf dem Kny; und mit der rechten Hand
> Führt ich den Griffel fort, wenn sich ein Versgen fand.[64]

[My other work was not left undone for all that; my spinning-wheel still allowed me to write. The book-rest stood facing me; my left hand had to keep hold of the thread; the writing-tablet on my knee; and with my right hand I guided the pencil whenever a line came into my head.]

Anna Louisa Karsch touchingly describes the hunger of a nursing child at its mother's breast.[65] Philippine Gatterer worries whether her profile corresponds to the Grecian ideal of beauty — and decides in the end that it is quite good enough. The poems she wrote around the time of her engagement (in 1780) are direct and full of tenderness and warmth.[66] In poems such as these one hears a personal note which is all too often lacking from the more conventional poems written by men in the period. There were advantages in not being expected to know the rules (Teuber writes, "Die Regeln von der Poesie, / Sind mir bishero vest verschlossen,"[67] — [the rules of poetry have been a closed book to me so far]). This conferred a certain freedom — a license to turn the stuff of ordinary experience into poetry — which the women writers of the time were able to exploit with an engaging nonchalance and energy.

The Poetry of Pleasure and the Pleasure of Poetry

"Opulence and Commerce commonly precede the improvement of arts, and refinement of every Sort," Adam Smith wrote, continuing: "Prose is naturally the Language of Business; as Poetry is of pleasure and amusement."[68] Poetry was one of the surplus products of an increasingly commercial and leisured society, and itself a stimulus to enjoyment in and of moments of leisure. Hagedorn, who according to contemporary accounts spent part of every day in a coffee house, captured the relation between productivity and pleasure in his poem "Die Alster," in the opposition between the two rivers of his native town of Hamburg:

> Der Elbe Schiff-Fahrt macht uns reicher;
> Die Alster lehrt gesellig seyn!
> Durch jene füllen sich die Speicher;
> Auf dieser schmeckt der fremde Wein.
> In treibenden Nachen
> Schifft Eintracht und Lust,
> Und Freyheit und Lachen
> Erleichert die Brust.
> [. . .]
> Ertönt, ihr scherzenden Gesänge,
> Aus unserm Lust-Schiff um den Strand!
> Den steifen Ernst, das Wort-Gepränge
> Verweist die Alster auf das Land.
> [. . .]
> Nichts lebet gebunden,
> Was Freundschaft hier paart.
> O glückliche Stunden!
> O liebliche Fahrt![69]

[The shipping on the Elbe makes us richer; the Alster teaches us to enjoy each other's company! The Elbe fills our warehouses; on the Alster we savor imported wine. Harmony and Pleasure board our floating craft, and Liberty and Laughter relieve our cares. Resound, merry songs, from our pleasure-boat to the shore! The Alster banishes ceremonial solemnity and high-flown words to the land. There is no constraint where Friendship joins us together. O happy hours! O sweet progress!]

What is accumulated in hours of work is spent in pleasure; and poetry ("Gesang") is as much an essential ingredient of that pleasure as a way of propagating, commemorating, and storing it up for conscious consumption. Thus real capital is transformed into cultural capital, designed to be spent on leisure and to stimulate and structure its use, whether to more contemplative or (as in Hagedorn's own poem) more immediately hedonistic purposes — which do not exclude moral ones, as his celebration of liberality, sociability and friendship demonstrates.

It would be absurd, of course, to reduce the variety of eighteenth-century German poetry to a single pattern. But the invitation to pleasure that this and many other poems of the period extend is certainly one of the main strands of its genetic code. It forms a double helix with a religious strand running in a clear line from Brockes to Klopstock, from the former's contemplation of God in nature, on walks or in his garden, to the latter's hymnic celebrations of God's living power. For in their own way, these poems, too, are dedicated to "Vergnügen," to pleasure, as the very title of Brockes's *magnum opus* proclaims; and his *Irdisches Vergnügen in GOTT* is matched by Klopstock's famous hymn "Die Frühlingsfeyer" (Celebration of Spring, 1759), which was called an "Ode über die ernsthaften Vergnügungen des Landlebens" (Ode on the Serious Pleasures of Country Life) when it was first published. The links between the two strands are many — Gleim, for instance, can cite "Brokks" in his altogether more worldly "Aufmunterung zum Spatziergehn" (Encouragement to a Walk).[70] And from there it is but a step to the openly erotic poems of Johann George Scheffner, with his "Einladung auf das Feld" (Invitation to the Countryside) and "Ermunterung zum Vergnügen" (Enticement to Pleasure).[71]

If one had to choose a single poem from the period that could be placed at its center of gravity, it might well be Klopstock's "Ode von der Fahrt auf der Zürcher See" (Ode on the Boating Trip on the Lake of Zürich), written, appropriately enough, exactly at the mid-point in the century, in 1750. It takes up Hagedorn's motif of an excursion on the water[72] and his praise of song, sociability, and friendship. At the same time, as its opening lines indicate, it absorbs Brockes's idea of contemplating the grandeur of Creation into its own scheme, which throughout carries a religious subtext:

> Schön ist, Mutter Natur, deiner Erfindung Pracht,
> Auf die Fluhren verstreut; schöner ein froh Gesichte
>   Das den großen Gedanken
>   Deiner Schöpfung noch einmahl denkt.
>
> Von der schimmernden See weinvollem Ufer her,
> Oder, flohest du schon wieder zum Himmel auf,
>   Komm im röthenden Strale,
>   Auf den Flügeln der Abendluft;
>
> Komm, und lehre mein Lied jugendlich heiter seyn,
> Süße Freude, wie du! [. . .]

[. . .]

Jetzt empfing uns die Au in die beschattenden
Kühlen Arme des Walds, welcher die Insel krönt:
　Da, da kamst du, o Freude!
　　Ganz in vollem Maaß über uns

Göttinn Freude! du selbst! dich, dich empfanden wir!
Ja du warest es selbst, Schwester der Menschlichkeit,
　Deiner Unschuld Gespielinn,
　　Die sich über uns ganz ergoß!

[. . .]

Treuer Zärtlichkeit voll in den Umschattungen,
In den Lüften des Walds, und mit gesenkten Blick,
　Auf die silbernen Wellen,
　　That mein Herz den frommen Wunsch:

Möchtet ihr auch hier seyn, die ihr mich ferne liebt,
In des Vaterlands Schoos einsam von mir verstreut,
　Die in seligen Stunden
　　Meine suchende Seele fand,

O! so wollten wir hier Hütten der Freundschaft baun,
Ewig wohnten wir hier, ewig! wir nennten dann
　Jenen Schatten-Wald, Tempe,
　　Diese Thäler, Elysium.[73]

[Fair is the majesty of all thy works
On the green earth, O mother nature, fair!
　But fairer the glad face
　　Enraptur'd with their view.

Come from the vine-banks of the glittering lake —
Or — hast thou climb'd the smiling skies anew —
　Come on the roseate tip
　　Of evening's breezy wing,

And teach my song with glee of youth to glow,
Sweet joy, like thee [. . .]
[. . .]

Soon the green meadow took us to the cool
And shadowy forest, with becrowns the isle.

> Then cam'st thou, Joy, thou cam'st
> Down in full tide to us;
>
> Yes, goddess Joy, thyself: we felt, we clasp'd,
> Best sister of humanity, thyself;
>   With thy dear innocence
>   Accompanied, thyself.[74]
>
> [. . .]
>
> Full of affection, in the airy shades
> Of the dim forest, and with down-cast look
>   Fix'd on the silver wave,
>   I breath'd this pious wish:
>
> "O were ye here, who love me though afar,
> Whom singly scatter'd in our country's lap,
>   In lucky hallow'd hour
>   My seeking bosom found;
>
> Here would we built huts of friendship, here
> Together dwell for ever." — The dim wood
>   A shadowy Tempe seem'd;
>   Elysium all the vale.[75]]

The "Hütten" Klopstock wants to build on the site of the epiphany of joy are a reminiscence of the "tabernacles" of Mark 9:5 (translated as "Hütten" in Luther's New Testament), which Peter wanted to erect to mark the place of Christ's transfiguration. The fulfillment of the ending thus incorporates both Christian and classical elements. But the ode also pays tribute to the power of poetry to channel the emotions toward the conscious consummation of pleasure. For on the boating party, poetry was recited and sung:

> Hallers Doris sang uns[,] selber des Liedes [w]erth
> Hirzels Daphne, den Kleist zärtlich, wie Gleimen, liebt;
>   Und wir Jünglinge sangen
>   Und empfanden wie Hagedorn.
>
> [Hirzel's Daphne, worthy of song herself, sang us Haller's "Doris" — Hirzel, whom Kleist loves as tenderly as he loves Gleim; and we youths sang and felt like Hagedorn.]

This may well be the "widerborstigste und verzwackteste Satz, der vielleicht in der ganzen deutschen Lyrik zu finden ist" (the most rebarbative and convoluted sentence to be found anywhere in German lyric poetry), as Albert

Köster claimed; but as Karl Ludwig Schneider rightly observes, it is also "ein künstlerischer Schwerpunkt des Gedichtes" (a key moment in the artistic composition of the poem),[76] for in the interlacing of names, poetry's ability to create communities of feeling is made manifest. Poetry, for Hagedorn, had been a way of "shortening the long hours" ("die langen Stunden [zu] kürtzen") and the supreme social "pastime and pleasure" ("Zeit-Vertreib und Lust").[77] Klopstock's poem gives it no new functions, but raises these existing ones to a higher power. Poetry strengthens ties of friendship and fellow feeling; it regulates the exchange of their thoughts and emotions and unites its devotees in a shared identity and sense of election.

The feeling thus created seeks no outlet in action, and strives instead only to heighten the intensity of its own self-awareness. But this community of feeling, nourished by poetry, based on the shared enjoyment of leisure, and dedicated to the vindication and pursuit of happiness, may have done as much to further the cause of Enlightenment as many an act of solitary intellectual courage in defiance of tradition, custom, and prejudice. Indeed autonomous acts of individual intellectual courage might not have been possible without the underpinning of a wider and deeper cultural identity, one formed in the shared experiences of the "Lesewelt." This new world of reading was a kind of inner America, an extra-territorial domain and habitat of freedom, access to which was open, in principle, to men and women of any social standing. The expansion of leisure and reading helped create this communal identity in eighteenth-century Germany. Other literary genres no doubt played important roles in the process. But lyric poetry was perhaps the most important of all: portable and ubiquitous (a particular advantage in a divided polity like Germany), often set to music, it could be recited and performed, and its sentiments appropriated, where any two or three were gathered together.

Poetry's explicit messages (for it was, of course, to instruct as well as please, in conformity with the time-honored and much invoked Horatian principle of *prodesse* and *delectare*) were frequently dully virtuous and worthy. But its pragmatic function was to help constitute the public sphere, not only as an arena for earnest debate, but as a place of pleasure and shared experience, where the *right* to pleasure and shared, open-ended, non-instrumental experience was vindicated. In that sense leisure was the true medium of Enlightenment culture. And to that extent lyric poetry, too, which arose out of, and at once filled, structured, and celebrated leisure, had its modest part to play in the unfolding of Enlightenment.

Notes

[1] Peter Gay, *The Enlightenment: An Interpretation. The Rise of Modern Paganism* (London: Weidenfeld & Nicolson, 1966).

[2] *Graf Ludwigs von Zinzendorff Teutscher Gedichte Erster Theil* (Herrnhuth: Im Waisenhause, 1735), "Vorrede."

[3] "An Freund und Feind" (1781), in Friedrich Gottlieb Klopstock, *Oden,* ed. Franz Muncker and Jaro Pawel, 2 vols. (Stuttgart: G. J. Göschen'sche Verlagsbuchhandlung, 1889), 1: 28.

[4] Friedrich Gottlieb Klopstock, *Der Messias,* canto IV, ll. 277–283. In Klopstock, *Ausgewählte Werke,* ed. Karl August Schleiden, 4th edition (Munich: Hanser, 1981), 275.

[5] William Taylor, *Historic Survey of German Poetry,* 3 vols. (London: Treuttel & Würtz, Treuttel Jun. & Richter, 1830), 1: 274. He comments on this "admirable simile": "German hexameters rendered word for word seldom slide into English so well as these" (274).

[6] Taylor 1: 282.

[7] "Von der heiligen Poesie" (1755), in Klopstock, *Ausgewählte Werke,* 997–1009, here 1009.

[8] *Ragout à la Mode oder des Neologischen Wörter-Buchs erste Zugabe* (n. p., 1755), 5–6.

[9] "Briefe an einen jungen Dichter" (Letters to a Young Poet), in Christoph Martin Wieland, *Aufsätze zu Literatur und Politik,* ed. Dieter Lohmeier (Reinbek: Rowohlt, 1970), 75–117 ("Erster Brief" [1782], 77). Wieland puts the words in the mouth of his young poet, but continues: "Alles dies war, von Wort zu Wort, vor 35 Jahren, auch *mein* Fall" (all of this, word for word, was also true in *my* case thirty-five years ago). The first five cantos of *Der Messias* were published in 1751.

[10] Friedrich Gottlieb Klopstock, *Werke und Briefe. Historisch-kritische Ausgabe. Abteilung Briefe,* vol. 5: *Briefe 1767–1772,* ed. Klaus Hurlebusch, 2 vols. (Berlin: de Gruyter, 1989), 1: 263 (Klopstock to Heinrich Wilhelm von Gerstenberg, 22 February 1771).

[11] The genre of mock-epic was based entirely on this principle. It enjoyed a considerable vogue in Germany in the 1740s and 1750s. Friedrich Just Zachariae's *Der Renommiste* (The Boaster, 1744) and *Das Schnupftuch* (The Pocket Handkerchief, 1757, modeled on Pope's *The Rape of the Lock*), are the most notable examples.

[12] Christoph Martin Wieland, *Oberon,* ed. Wolfgang Jahn (Munich: Goldmann, 1964), 10.

[13] *The Spectator,* ed. Donald F. Bond, 5 vols. (Oxford: Clarendon Press, 1965), 1: 44.

[14] Gottfried Ephraim Scheibel, *Die unerkannte Sünden der Poeten* (Leipzig: Teubner, 1734), 4.

[15] Campe, "Statistische Nachrichten von den Progressen der Deutschen im Versemachen," quoted in Wolfgang Promies, "Lyrik in der zweiten Hälfte des 18. Jahrhunderts," in *Deutsche Aufklärung bis zur Französischen Revolution 1680–1789,* ed. Rolf Grimminger, vol. 3 of *Hansers Sozialgeschichte der deutschen Literatur vom 16. Jahrhundert bis zur Gegenwart,* 2nd ed. (Munich: dtv, 1984), 569–604, here 571.

[16] *Der Taschengoedeke: Bibliographie deutscher Erstausgaben,* ed. Leopold Hirschberg and Elisabeth Friedrichs (Munich: dtv, 1970).

[17] See Christian Heinrich Schmid, in the preface to his *Anthologie der Deutschen* (Frankfurt a. M. & Leipzig, 1770), on "fliegende Bogen" and other ephemera (v–vii).

[18] Among the well-known poets who wrote hymns in the period are Gellert, Klopstock, and Claudius. Others whose work was devoted almost entirely to hymn-writing include Nikolaus Ludwig von Zinzendorf (1700–60) and Gerhard Tersteegen (1697–1769); see Robert M. Browning, *German Poetry in the Age of Enlightenment from Brockes to Klopstock,* Penn State Series in German Literature (University Park, PA: Pennsylvania State UP, 1978), 153–81; Hans-Georg Kemper, *Deutsche Lyrik der frühen Neuzeit,* vol. 6, 1: *Empfindsamkeit* (Tübingen: Niemeyer, 1997), 19–95.

[19] Johann Christian Günther (1695–1723), "Die schmerzliche Erinnerung der Jugendjahre" (1722), in *Gedichte 1700–1770: Nach den Erstdrucken in zeitlicher Folge,* ed. Jürgen Stenzel, vol. 5 of *Epochen der deutschen Lyrik* (Munich: dtv, 1969), 93.

[20] Hagedorn, in 1729, could still describe poetry as "eine kräftige Gehülfin der Beredsamkeit" (a noble helpmeet to oratory), *Versuch einiger Gedichte, oder erlesene Proben Poetischer Neben-Stunden* (Hamburg: König & Richter, 1729), preface. Gellert was professor of rhetoric at the University of Leipzig. Hans-Henrik Krummacher illustrates how important rhetoric was for Klopstock's theory and practice: "Friedrich Gottlieb Klopstock," in *Deutsche Dichter des 18. Jahrhunderts,* ed. Benno von Wiese (Berlin: Erich Schmidt, 1977), 190–209. Eric A. Blackall gives a masterly description of how the general rules on the levels of style were put into practice by individual poets in *The Emergence of German as a Literary Language 1770–1775,* 2nd ed. (Ithaca: Cornell UP), 211–75, 314–50.

[21] See the essay by Helga Brandes in this volume.

[22] See Markus Fauser, *Das Gespräch im 18. Jahrhundert: Rhetorik und Geselligkeit in Deutschland* (Stuttgart: M & P Verlag der Wissenschaft und Forschung, 1991), 323, 329. The moralists noted and deplored the way in which the middle classes imitated an "indolent" aristocracy's use of time: "[Die Fürsten] pflegen oft am Mittag aufzustehen. / Jezt aft ein Bürgermann der Fürsten Mode nach" (The princes often get up at noon. Now private citizens ape the fashion of the princes), Sidonia Hedwig Zäunemann, *Die von denen Faunen gepeitschte Laster* (Frankfurt a. M. & Leipzig: Brönner, 1739), 47.

[23] Ludwig August Unzer, "Der Winter" (1772), in *Dichtung des Rokoko,* ed. Alfred Anger, Deutsche Texte, vol. 7 (Tübingen: Niemeyer, 1958), 32.

[24] Anon., in *Gedichte 1700–1770,* ed. Stenzel, 153–54. The poem dates from around 1740.

[25] Unzer, "Der Winter," in *Dichtung des Rokoko,* ed. Anger, 32; similarly in the poem "Das Canapee ist mein Vergnügen," *Gedichte 1700–1770,* ed. Stenzel, 154.

[26] Helfrich Peter Sturz, *Schriften,* 2 vols. (Leipzig: Weidmanns Erben und Reich, 1779–1782), 1: 119.

[27] Adrian Beier, "Kurtzer Bericht von der Nützlichen und Fürtrefflichen Buch-Handlung," quoted in Wolfgang von Ungern-Sternberg, "Schriftsteller und literarischer Markt," in *Deutsche Aufklärung bis zur Französischen Revolution 1680–1789,* ed. Grimminger, 137.

[28] Johann Gottwerth Müller ("von Itzehoe"), *Gedichte der Freundschaft, der Liebe, und dem Scherze gesungen: Zweyter Theil* (Helmstedt & Magdeburg: Hechtel, 1771), 5.

[29] Anna Barbara Teuber, *Vermischte Gedichte* (Brandenburg: Christian Hallen, 1735), "Zueignungs-Schrift, an das Tugendhafte Märckische Frauenzimmer" (dedication to the virtuous women of the March of Brandenburg), n. p.

[30] Sidonia Zäunemann, *Poetische Rosen in Knospen* (Erfurt: Johann Heinrich Nonne, 1738), 592. The untitled poem is dated 1737. On women's reading see Wolfgang Martens, *Die Botschaft der Tugend: Die Aufklärung im Spiegel der deutschen moralischen Wochenschriften* (Stuttgart: Metzler, 1968), 520–42.

[31] *Friedrichs von Hagedorn Poetische Werke,* ed. J. J. Eschenburg, 5 vols. (Hamburg: Carl Ernst Bohn, 1800), 1: vi.

[32] Teuber, "Zueignungs-Schrift, an das Tugendhafte Märckische Frauenzimmer," in *Vermischte Gedichte,* n. p.

[33] "Politur [des] Verstandes" and "Bildung [des] Herzens" (literally the "education of the heart"): Müller, *Gedichte der Freundschaft* 19–20.

[34] "Das Gespräch über die Poesie eignet sich vorzüglich für die gemischte Gesellschaft" (conversing about poetry is particularly suitable in mixed company): *Der Gesellige: Eine moralische Wochenschrift herausgegeben von Samuel Gotthold Lange und Georg Friedrich Meier,* ed. Wolfgang Martens, 3 vols. (1748–50; rpt. Hildesheim: Olms, 1987), 1: 91.

[35] Notable anthologies: *Poesie der Niedersachsen,* ed. Christian Friedrich Weichmann, 6 vols. (Hamburg: Schiller und Kissner [vols 5–6: Herold], 1721–38); *Auserlesene Früchte der Deutschen Poesie,* ed. Heinrich Richard Märtens (Leipzig & Wolfenbüttel: Meißnerische Buchhandlung, 1731); *Anthologie der Deutschen,* ed. Schmid; *Lieder der Deutschen,* ed. Karl Wilhelm Ramler (Berlin: G. L. Winter, 1766); *Auserlesene Stücke der besten Deutschen Dichter,* ed. Friedrich Wilhelm Zachariä, 3 vols. (Braunschweig: Waisenhaus Buchhandlung, 1766–78). On the literary almanacs, see the chapter by Helga Brandes in this volume and York-Gothart Mix, *Die deutschen Musenalmanache des 18. Jahrhunderts* (Munich: C. H. Beck, 1987). Poems in moral weeklies: for example, Klopstock's free verse hymns in *Der nordische Aufseher* (1758–61).

[36] Märtens says that the harvest for his anthology was especially large from "Academien, [. . .] weil solche an poetischen Früchten reich zu seyn pflegen" (from universities, because these tend to be rich in poetic fruit) (*Auserlesene Früchte der*

Deutschen Poesie, "Vorrede," n. p.). Zinzendorf reports that it was common for students to publish their poems (*Teutscher Gedichte Erster Theil*, preface, n. p.). See Promies, "Lyrik in der zweiten Hälfte des 18. Jahrhunderts," in *Deutsche Aufklärung bis zur Französischen Revolution 1680–1789*, ed. Grimminger, 897 n. 333.

[37] Scheibel 193 (in a chapter called "Von der Poeten Betteley" [On the Begging of Poets]). He adds that in one town, printers were forbidden to accept epithalamia for publication when a society wedding was in the offing (193).

[38] Anna Louisa Karschin, *Gedichte und Lebenszeugnisse*, ed. Alfred Anger (Stuttgart: Reclam, 1987), "Nachwort," 188, 195, 199.

[39] Barthold Hinrich Brockes, "Zur Neu-Jahrs-Betrachtung des 1735sten Jahres," in Brockes, *Irdisches Vergnügen in Gott, bestehend in Physicalisch- und Moralischen Gedichten*, vol. 5 (1736; rpt. Bern: Herbert Lang, 1970), 486–510, here 507.

[40] Hence the title of Gottsched's journal *Das Neueste aus der anmuthigen Gelehrsamkeit* (The Latest from the World of Graceful Learning, 1751–1762).

[41] "Schreiben an einen Freund" (1752), in *Des Herrn Friedrichs von Hagedorn sämmtliche Poetische Werke*, 3 vols. (Hamburg: Johann Carl Bohn, 1757), 1: xxi.

[42] See Gerhard Kaiser, *Klopstock: Religion und Dichtung*, Studien zu Religion, Dichtung und Geisteswissenschaft, vol. 1 (Gütersloh: Gerd Mohn, 1963), 24.

[43] Friedrich Gottlieb Klopstock, "Warum Klopstock sein Leben nicht geschrieben habe," in Klopstock, *Sämmtliche Werke* (Leipzig: G. J. Göschen'sche Verlagsbuchhandlung, 1855), 10: 278–80, here 279.

[44] Friedrich Gottlieb Klopstock, *Werke und Briefe. Abteilung Briefe*, vol. 1: *Briefe 1738–1750*, ed. Horst Gronemeyer (1979), 104 (to Maria Sophia Schmidt, 10–11 July 1750).

[45] "Dem Allgegenwärtigen" (To the Omnipresent God), "Das Anschaun Gottes" (Seeing God), "Die Frühlingsfeyer" (The Celebration of Spring), "Der Erbarmer" (The Merciful God), "Die Glückseligkeit Aller" (The Happiness of All).

[46] On the sublime in Brockes, see Browning, 10–11. Drollinger calls him "erhaben" (sublime): "An den Herrn Rahtsherr Brockes, über dessen Irdisches Vergnügen in GOTT," in Karl Friedrich Drollinger, *Gedichte, samt andern dazu gehörigen Stücken*, ed. J. J. Sprengen (Frankfurt a. M.: Frantz Barrentrapp, 1745), 92. Klopstock was a byword for sublimity. On the sublime as a hybrid concept, mingling religious and aesthetic elements, see Hans-Georg Kemper, *Deutsche Lyrik der frühen Neuzeit*, vol. 6.1, 148, 252–62.

[47] "Urbanität [ist] ein gewisser Geschmack der Hauptstadt, eine feine, kaum merkliche Tinktur von Gelehrsamkeit, die man aus dem Umgange mit aufgeklärten und kultivierten Personen angenommen hat," [Johann Jakob Bodmer], "Katastrophen in der Literatur" (Catastrophes in Literature) in *Literarische Pamphlete aus der Schweiz. Nebst Briefen an Bodmern* (Zurich: David Bürgkli, 1781), 12, quoting *Teutscher Merkur*, ed. Christoph Martin Wieland, November 1780. This is in fact a translation of Quintilian, *Institutio oratoria*, 6.3.17: "*Urbanitas* [. . .] denotes language with a smack of the city in its words, accent and idiom, and further suggests a certain tincture of learning derived from associating with well-educated men" (*The*

Institutio Oratoria of Quintilian, trans. H. E. Butler, The Loeb Classical Library, 124–27 [Cambridge, MA: Harvard UP, 1977], 2: 447).

[48] Abraham Gotthelf Kästner, "Anakreontische Ode," in *Dichtung des Rokoko*, ed. Anger, 9.

[49] Hagedorn, *Oden und Lieder* (1747); *Moralische Gedichte* (1750). Wieland, *Comische Erzählungen* (1765); *Musarion oder die Philosophie der Grazien* (1768).

[50] Hagedorn, "Horaz," in *Des Herrn Friedrichs von Hagedorn sämmtliche Poetische Werke*, 1: 68–82, here 68.

[51] Gleim, *Versuch in scherzhaften Liedern* (1744–1745); *Sieben kleine Gedichte nach Anacreons Manier* (1764). Uz, *Lyrische Gedichte* (1749); *Die Oden Anakreons in reimlosen Versen. Nebst einigen andern Gedichten*, ed. Götz (1746) (with original poems by Götz and Uz).

[52] Georg Friedrich Meier, *Gedanken von dem unschuldigen Gebrauche der Welt* (Halle: Hemmerde, 1765), 5. Meier was a professor in Halle, and acquainted with the Halle poets.

[53] For "Nebenstunden" (literally "hours [set] aside"), see the titles of a number of collections of the period: Friedrich Ludwig Rudolf von Canitz, *Neben-Stunden unterschiedener Gedichte* (1700); Johann Georg Eckhart, *Poetische Neben-Stunden* (1721); Friedrich von Hagedorn, *Versuch einiger Gedichte, oder erlesene Proben poetischer Neben-Stunden* (1729); Johann Friedrich Löwen, *Poetische Nebenstunden in Hamburg* (1752). For Hagedorn, poetry was the "Gespielinn meiner Nebenstunden" (playmate of my leisure hours): Friedrich Hagedorn, *Oden und Lieder in fünf Büchern* (Hamburg: Bohn, 1747), 3–4, here: 3.

[54] Of one of Klopstock's love odes Bodmer noted, somewhat doubtfully, "[dass sie] der Messias selbst ohne Unanständigkeit hätte schreiben können, wenn er verliebt gewesen wäre" (that the Messiah himself might have written it without offending against decency, if he had been in love). See Bodmer to Hagedorn, 10 September 1748, in *Friedrichs von Hagedorn Poetische Werke* 5: 208.

[55] "Von den Annehmlichkeiten des Mißvergnügens," quoted by Horst Steinmetz in the "Nachwort" to Christian Fürchtegott Gellert, *Lustspiele. Faksimiledruck nach der Ausgabe von 1747*, Deutsche Neudrucke: Reihe Texte des 18. Jahrhunderts (Stuttgart: Metzler, 1966), 9.

[56] Hagedorn, *Oden und Lieder in fünf Büchern*, "Vorbericht," xvi–xvii. Hagedorn is echoing Joseph Addison, *The Spectator*, no. 70 (*The Spectator*, 1: 298).

[57] Johann Wilhelm Ludwig Gleim, *Romanzen* (Berlin and Leipzig, 1756) and *Preußische Kriegslieder in den Feldzügen 1756 und 1757 von einem Grenadier* (Berlin: Voss, n. d. [1758]).

[58] Klopstock's "Kriegslied, zur Nachahmung des alten Liedes von der *Chevy-Chase-Jagd*" (War Song, Imitating the Old Ballad of Chevy-Chase, 1749), later called "Heinrich der Vogler," with its use of the so-called Chevy-Chase stanza, is the link between Hagedorn's (and Addison's) praise of the "Ballad of Chevy Chase" and Gleim's *Preußische Kriegslieder* (Prussian War Songs) which also employ this form. See also Ewald von Kleist's "Lied eines Lappländers" (Song of a Lapplander, 1758) (*Gedichte 1700–1770*, 282), and Klopstock's "Vaterlandslied" (Patriotic Song, 1770),

which was imitated by Claudius; *Gedichte 1770–1800 nach den Erstdrucken in zeitlicher Folge,* ed. Gerhart Pickerodt, vol. 6 of *Epochen der deutschen Lyrik* (Munich: dtv, 1970), 15, 19–20.

[59] Barbara Becker-Cantarino, *Der lange Weg zur Mündigkeit: Frau und Literatur (1500–1800)* (Stuttgart: J. B. Metzler, 1987), 260–61.

[60] See Friederike Marie Charlotte von Schenk, *Versuche in Gedichten* (Braunschweig: Waysenhaus-Buchhandlung, 1772), "Vorbericht," v–xi.

[61] See e. g., *Auserlesene Früchte der Deutschen Poesie,* "Vorrede": poems by women are included because the editor believes "daß auch unter diesem Geschlechte solche poetische Heldinnen vorhanden [sind], die da im Stande seyn, den Dichtern vom ersten Rang den Lorber streitig zu manchen" (that in that sex, too, poetic heroines are to be found who are capable of disputing the honor of the laurel crown with poets of the first rank). See Becker-Cantarino 260–63.

[62] "An hohe Sachen, habe mich / Aus grosser Furcht, nicht wollen wagen. / Ich dachte: Du versteigest dich, / Die Männer werden dich verklagen / Dieweil du pfuschern willst. Und nehmen endlich dir / Buch, Tafel, Griffel, Dint, Sand, Feder und Papier!" (I did not dare tackle high matters. I thought: you strive beyond your sphere, men will accuse you of meddling in things you don't know about, and will finally take away your book, writing tablet, pencil, ink, sand, quill, and paper!). Teuber, "Zueignungs-Schrift an das Tugendhafte Märckische Frauenzimmer," in *Vermischte Gedichte,* n. p.

[63] *Poetische Rosen in Knospen,* 500–09. On Zäunemann, see Becker-Cantarino, 270–72.

[64] Teuber, "Zueignungs-Schrift an das Tugendhafte Märckische Frauenzimmer," in *Vermischte Gedichte,* n. p.

[65] "Ueber die Begierde des Säuglings" (On the Nursing Infant's Craving, 1764), in *O, mir entwischt nicht, was die Menschen fühlen: Anna Louisa Karsch, Gedichte und Briefe,* ed. Gerhard Wolf, Märkischer Dichtergarten (Frankfurt a. M.: Fischer Taschenbuch Verlag, 1982), 54–55. On Karsch, see Becker-Cantarino, 272–78.

[66] "Grosse und kleine Gedanken über meine Nase" (Large and Small Thoughts about my Nose), in Philippine Gatterer, *Gedichte* (Göttingen: Johann Christian Dieterich, 1778), 227–30. "Das Bekenntniß" (The Confession), "Das Jawort" (Accepting the Proposal), "Der künftige Gemahl" (The Future Husband), "Im Garten" (In the Garden), "Die Treuringe" (The Engagement Rings), "Nach der Trauung" (After the Wedding), in Philippine Engelhard gebohrne Gatterer, *Gedichte. Zwote Sammlung* (Göttingen: Johann Christian Dieterich, 1782), 200–01, 205–11, 219–20.

[67] Teuber, "Zueignungs-Schrift an das Tugendhafte Märckische Frauenzimmer," in *Vermischte Gedichte,* n. p.

[68] Adam Smith, *Lectures on Rhetoric and Belles-Lettres,* ed. J. C. Bryce (Oxford: Clarendon Press, 1983), 137.

[69] *Oden und Lieder in fünf Büchern* 174–75.

[70] *Versuch in scherzhaften Liedern. Zweeter Theil* (Berlin, 1745), 41–44.

[71] *Gedichte im Geschmack des Grecourt* (Frankfurt a. M. & Leipzig: Dodsley und Compagnie, 1771), 147–50 and 151–53. Scheffner invokes Gleim as one of his models ("Der Triumpf," 14).

[72] See Bernhard Blume, "Die Kahnfahrt: Ein Beitrag zur Motivgeschichte des 18. Jahrhunderts," *Euphorion* 51 (1957): 355–84 (Hagedorn, 363–64; Klopstock, 377–79).

[73] *Gedichte 1700–1770,* ed. Stenzel, 243–45.

[74] A more accurate translation would read: "Sister of humanity, playfellow of your innocence."

[75] A more accurate translation would make the closing two lines part of the poet's silent prayer: "The shadowed grove would then a Tempe seem, the vales Elysium." — The translation is by Taylor 1: 246–48.

[76] Karl Ludwig Schneider, "Nachwort," in Klopstock, *Oden: Eine Auswahl,* ed. Karl Ludwig Schneider, 171. Köster is quoted by Schneider, ibid. Johann Kaspar Hirzel and his wife were on the boating party. "Doris" is a poem by Albrecht von Haller. Ewald von Kleist (1715–1759) was the author of the celebrated didactic poem "Der Frühling" (Spring, 1749).

[77] "Die Poesie," in *Versuch einiger Gedichte,* 30–37, here 37.

*Alpine landscape, copperplate after painting
by Caspar Wolf (1735–1798).*

Literary Developments in Switzerland from Bodmer, Breitinger, and Haller to Gessner, Rousseau, and Pestalozzi

Rosmarie Zeller

The Construction of Idyll

THIS ESSAY ON EIGHTEENTH-CENTURY SWITZERLAND analyzes a period in which Switzerland played a more prominent role in the history of European literature and culture than it had in earlier or later centuries. Within the context of the Enlightenment, which ascribed great importance to happiness attained through virtue and self-determination, the myth of Switzerland as a virtuous land of freedom arose, epitomized most famously in Friedrich Schiller's *Wilhelm Tell*. Moreover, Zurich as a Protestant city figured prominently in the formation of the literature of Enlightenment. From 1725 to 1750, Zurich became one of the leading centers of German-language literature, alongside Halle and Leipzig.[1] Zurich was then said to harbor twenty to thirty men of genius within its borders, while Berlin was host to merely three or four.

It is no mere coincidence that Switzerland entered the literary history of the Enlightenment — and not only German but world literature, if we consider such authors as Salomon Gessner (1730–1788), Jean-Jacques Rousseau (1712–1778), and Johann Heinrich Pestalozzi (1746–1827) — because the Enlightenment was a bourgeois movement. In contrast to the baroque period, the Enlightenment no longer relied on the existence of a court as a cultural center, a fact that enabled the bourgeoisie to develop its own literature. Switzerland in the seventeenth century was considered an uncivilized country inhabited by peasants and unrefined people since there existed practically no feudal culture in Switzerland, and certainly no courtly literary culture. But the reevaluation of non-courtly lifestyles allowed for a positive view of peasants and shepherds and thus a stylization of Switzerland into a kind of Arcadia. This essay will discuss Zurich's contribution to the literary theory of Enlightenment and the formation of the Swiss myth and its aesthetic representations.

Zurich Enters Literary History

It is surprising that Zurich should become a center for literary theory and that modern literary developments would arise there, since the Protestant clergy strictly regulated all cultural activities in that city. There was, for example, not a single permanent theater in Zurich. And it is no accident that one of the last pamphlets against the modern genre of the novel, *Mythoscopia romantica: oder Discours von den so benannten Romanen* (Investigation of Romance, Or a Discourse on the So-Called Novels, 1699), was written by a Zurich clergyman who considered reading novels a harmful pastime, this just at the time when Leibniz regarded the novel as representation of God's providence.[2] In a satirical portrayal, Johann Heinrich Füssli (1745–1832) describes the literary culture of his day using Salomon Gessner as his mouthpiece:

> Wenige einzelne große Männer haben vor ungefähr so viel Zeit durch ihre Schriften und noch unendlich mehr durch ihren Umgang im Reich des Geschmacks und des Denkens unter uns Epoche gemacht. Vorher deckte Dunkel das ganze Land der Geister [. . .] Die Dichterzunft war ein elender Bettelorden, und der höchste Punkt ihrer Begeisterung etwa der Beischlaf eines hochadelichen Brautpaares, die Geburt eines Staatsmanns, die Ankonft eines Elefanten oder Kometen. Man reimte eine Lebensregel über jeden Schweinstall.[3]

> [A few great men have recently made history through their writings and much more so through their association with the realm of good taste and of the mind [. . .]. Previously, darkness hovered over the entire realm of the mind. Poets were mere beggars and the high point of their enthusiasm was the marriage of a noble couple, the birth of a statesman, the arrival of an elephant or a comet. They wrote moral verses about every pigsty.]

The men who did away with this outmoded fashion and tried to refine their readers' taste were Johann Jakob Bodmer (1698–1783) and Johann Jakob Breitinger (1701–1776).[4] From 1721 to 1723 they published the first moral weekly in Switzerland, *Die Discourse der Mahlern* (The Discourse of the Painters), revised and reedited in 1746 under the title *Die Mahler der Sitten* (The Painters of Morals).[5] It was one of the early moral weeklies in the German language modeled after Addison's and Steele's *Spectator* (1711–1713), whose French edition Bodmer had seen in France. The two erudite men from Zurich who were to exert great influence on German literature in the years to come intended "die Tugend und den guten Geschmack in unseren Bergen einzuführen"[6] (to introduce virtue and good taste into our mountains) with their weekly. With their moral weekly they sought to introduce the Enlightenment to Switzerland — a country they regarded as one big city, not unlike London — while at the same time stressing the national element. They planned to establish a large network of correspondents who were to report about "seltzame Curiositeten in den Caracteren der Moden [. . .] welche das Schweitzerland vor andern Ländern auszeichnet"[7] (noteworthy and curious new fashions [. . .] that distinguish Switzerland from other countries).

Among these "new fashions" peculiar to Switzerland were "die unterschiedenen Moden der Aufferziehung, die Moden die Jungfern zu caressiren, Hochzeit zu machen, die Ehfrauen zu halten; die Conversationen der Männeren mit den Frauenzimmer; [. . .] der Geschmack für die Eloquenz, Poesie, Gelehrtheit"[8] (the different ways of education, of courtship, wedding ceremonies, treatment of wives, men's conduct with women [. . .] and good taste for eloquence, poesy, and erudition). The journalistic enterprise was not very successful; even in Switzerland it was received with little acclaim; yet a few positive reviews appeared in Germany. Articles s by readers that Bodmer and Breitinger had counted on were not forthcoming. Even if a short run was characteristic for all moral weeklies, the *Discourse*'s limited success probably owed much to the harsh cultural climate in which Bodmer and Breitinger had to operate. Censorship was strict and prohibited entertaining pieces, so that the *Discourse* was rightly considered too learned and didactic and generally lacking in entertainment value.

Already in the *Discourse* many articles dealt with poetry and poetics; according to the journal's program, the public's aesthetic sensibilities were to be honed. The Zurich critics' contributions to poetics and to literary theory were even more important than their efforts to elevate Swiss literature to European standards. These efforts had begun with a prose translation of Milton's *Paradise Lost* (1667) that appeared for the first time as *Verlust des Paradieses* in 1732 and saw five more editions (1742, 1754, 1759, 1768, 1780) with constant revisions by Bodmer. The work on Milton led Bodmer and his Zurich colleague Breitinger, with whom he discussed all poetological questions intensively, to a new understanding of the concept of imitation of nature, the fundamental principle for artistic creation in the early eighteenth century. Since nature is not an objective given but a culturally mitigated concept, the question of whether nature is imitated or not in a specific case is dependent upon the particular views of each critic. Each believed that there are certain literary patterns better suited to following this principle of imitation than others. Here precisely was the beginning of the famous literary feud between the Swiss and Gottsched in Leipzig. Gottsched oriented himself towards French literature and tried to introduce its poetological style to Germany; the Zurich poets looked to the English poet Milton and their followers later also to Shakespeare.[9] Gottsched understood imitation of nature to mean the imitation of empirical reality that can be grasped unmitigated by the senses; the Zurich poets insisted that the concept of imitation could also include probable nature. Gottsched wrote: "Der Poet muß ja nachahmen, nicht aber ganz neue Dinge schaffen"[10] (The poet must indeed imitate, but not create entirely new things), while the Swiss maintained: "denn was ist Dichten anders, als sich in der Phantasie neue Begriffe und Vorstellungen formieren, deren Originale nicht in der gegenwärtigen Welt der würcklichen Dinge, sondern in irgend einem andern möglichen Welt-Gebäude zu suchen sind"[11] (What is poetry other than the formation in our fantasy of new ideas and imaginations whose originals are not to be sought in the present world of real things but in some other possible world). With reference to Milton, this meant that the poet can represent God, the angels, the devil — in short the imaginary and marvelous. The Zurich poets defended vehemently the marvelous, as did Bodmer in his treatise *Critische Abhandlung von dem Wunderbaren in der Poesie* (A Critical Treatment of the Marvelous in Poetry, 1740), mainly a defense of Milton. While Bodmer and Breitinger were rejecting Lohenstein's bombastic style, they saw their concept of poetry embodied in Milton's baroque world. While enlightened readers had objected to the appearance of angels or the transformation of devils into pygmies in *Paradise Lost,* the Zurich poets nevertheless defended these fantasies and thus actually supported a poetic concept of the baroque. It is one of the paradoxes in literary history that this defense of an outmoded way of representation created a new fashion. The introduction of a concept of possible worlds was, above all, progressive; it stands for what is called in modern terms "fictionality."[12] In a rationalistic theory of poetics like Gottsched's *Versuch einer critischen Dichtkunst* (Essay on Critical Poetics, 1732 with subsequent editions in 1737, 1742, 1751) that served an entire generation of poets, the imaginary had no place. Bodmer and Breitinger on the other hand borrowed the concept of possible worlds from Leibniz, probably from its popularizer Christian Wolff.[13] Wolff had explained the concept of possible worlds in a comparison with a novel that creates a possible world by arranging the plot in such a way that nothing improbable takes place. Already in his treatise *Anklagung des verderbten Geschmackes* (Reproach of Bad Taste, 1728), Bodmer had employed this concept for the first time in describing the unique quality of poetry: "Aber ein Scribent bauet sich selbst in seiner erhizten Phantasey neue Welten, die er mit neuen Einwohnern bevölkert, welche von einer andern Natur sind und eigenen Gesetzen folgen. Er dichtet sich neue Personen und neue Beggnissen"[14] (A writer builds for himself in his inflamed fantasy new worlds and populates them with new inhabitants who are of a different nature and follow their own laws. He creates new people and new events). Here the poet becomes a God-like creator of new worlds, as is indicated by the term "erhizte Phantasey" (heated fantasy). Bodmer's friend Breitinger elaborated on the concept of possible worlds in his *Critische Dichtkunst* (Critical Poetics, 1740) by widening the concept of mimesis in his chapter "Von der Nachahmung der Natur" (On the Imitation of Nature). Here he could lay the foundation for a non-mimetic poetry by stating that besides the present world there are numerous other worlds just as true as the present world:

> Alle diese möglichen Welten, ob sie gleich nicht würcklich und nicht sichtbar sind, haben dennoch eine eigentliche Wahrheit, die in ihrer Möglichkeit, so von allem Widerspruch frey ist, und in der allesvermögenden Kraft des Schöpfers der Natur gegründet ist. [. . .]Ein jedes wohlerfundenes Gedicht ist darum nicht anderst anzusehen, als eine Historie aus einer andern möglichen Welt. (Bodmer, Breitinger, *Schriften,* 1:56 and 60)

> [All these possible worlds, though they are not real and not visible, have their own inherent truth grounded in its own possibility (free of all incompatibility) and in the almighty power of the Creator of nature. [. . .] Every well-conceived poem is nothing but a story from another possible world.]

The poet's ability to create possible worlds distinguishes him from the historian and justifies his name as a *poieton,* a creator. With his imagination — "Einbildungskraft" was the contemporary term — the poet can transform possible worlds into fictional ones and thus become the creator of new worlds. These must not be impossible, rather appear probable. Innovation is the poet's instrument for creating possible worlds, for only the new can impress the mind and provide edification. Only the new, the unaccustomed, curious, and extraordinary has the power "die Sinnen und das Gemüthe auf eine angenehm-ergetzende Weise zu rühren.[. . .] Die Neuheit ist eine Mutter des Wunderbaren, und hiemit eine Quelle des Ergetzens"[15] (Bodmer, Breitinger, *Schriften* 1:110; to move the senses and the mind in a pleasantly edifying way.[. . .] Innovation is the mother of the marvelous and thus a source of edification).

Here we find an emphasis on innovation as a precondition for aesthetic effect, while at the same time the moral impact of art is being displaced by the aesthetic, although in actual practice morality was retained. With his emphasis on the principle of innovation, Breitinger recognized novelty as the motor of literary effectiveness and development. He then pleaded for a poetics of innovation that freed poetics from the imitation of patterns.[16] Gottsched, for whom good poetry could only be composed according to rules, could, of course, not approve and was suspicious of a concept of poetry and poetics that was for the most part not normative, but attempted to describe the genuine qualities of art and especially of poetry. The newly praised emphasis on the new and the marvelous, the attention to the "Lustbarkeiten der Einbildungskraft"[17] (pleasurableness of the imagination), and the opinion that it was the poet's task to move the heart rather than to be witty: these ideas made Bodmer and Breitinger the fathers of a young generation of poets who rebelled against the poetics of rules represented by Gottsched. It was also an attack on the gallant, witty rococo poetry. Young Klopstock (1724–1803) wrote in a letter to Bodmer of 10 August 1748:

> Ich war ein junger Mensch, der seinen Homer und Vergil las, und sich schon über die kritischen Schriften der Sachsen im Stillen ärgerte, als mir ihre und Breitingers in die Hände fielen. Ich las oder vielmehr ich verschlang sie; und wenn mir zur Rechten Homer und Vergil lag, so hatt' ich jene zur Linken, um sie immer nachschlagen zu können.[18]

> [I was a young man who read his Homer and Virgil and was already quietly annoyed by the criticalwritings from Saxony when I came across your and Breitinger's writings. I read or rather devoured them; and while I had Homer and Virgil to my right, I had yours and Breitinger's to my left so as to be able to consult them constantly.]

The Zurich poets welcomed Klopstock as an author who transformed their theories into practice. They played an important role in the reception of Klopstock's *Messias;* Bodmer especially generated much publicity in connection with the appearance of the first three cantos. He commissioned sample translations into French and Italian and recommended the new work in his letters to correspondents in Switzerland and Germany. His advocacy was so substantial that Johann Adolf Schlegel called it "schweizerische Abgötterey gegen Klopstocken"[19] (Swiss idolatry toward Klopstock).

The criticism of Gottsched's regular poetics evolved increasingly into a fight against Saxony. Bodmer, who all his life revised the wording of his Milton translation to conform to the literary German of Saxony, pleaded for an elevation of Swiss German to a literary language, because one nation should not become "in der Sprache des andern Knecht"[20] (in its language the servant of another). He even fantasized that Saxons would once have to learn Swiss German in order to read their works. And he concluded: "Dieses würde einer Nation, die sich in Ansehung der bürgerlichen Verfassung aus dem Wirbel des deutschen Reiches loosgemachet hat, vor allen andern wol anstehen"[21] (This would be most fitting for a nation that in view of its national constitution has freed itself from the German empire). This constitutes nothing less than a defense of Switzerland's freedom from the German empire. The opposition to the poetic rules of Saxony was also understood as a struggle for political freedom and independence. This resulted in the conflation of poetics and political myths.

Haller's *Die Alpen* and the Myth of a Free Switzerland

Albrecht von Haller (1708–1777) is one of the most frequently cited authors in the works of Bodmer and Breitinger, especially his didactic poem *Die Alpen* (1729). According to then-contemporary literary critics, German poetry reached new heights with Haller's publication of a slender collection of lyrics entitled *Versuch schweizerischer Gedichte* (Experiment in Swiss Poetry, 1732).[22] The adjective "Swiss" in the title attests to Haller's intentions to demonstrate that the Swiss were educated and on a par with their Saxon contemporaries, a fact that had often been doubted. Bodmer had written to Haller that he was repulsed by the fact "daß man in Sachsen noch nicht wisse, durch welches Werk die Barbaren gescholtenen Schweizer die Deutschen besiegt hätten" (Hirzel, *Hallers Leben,* cxix; that the Saxons were still ignorant of the work with which the so-called barbarous Swiss had surpassed the Germans). On the other hand, Haller was well aware of the linguistic idiosyncrasies of the German spoken in Switzerland to which he wanted to point with his title. In his preface to the third edition (1743) he stressed the problem of the lack of a literary language in Switzerland, stating that he had introduced many linguistic changes: "Die Vorsehung hat mich nunmehro nach Teutschland geführet; ich habe seit sechs Jahren mehr Gelegenheit gehabt, mir das Teutsche bekannt zu machen, das zwar einigermaßen meine Muttersprache ist, aber in meinem Vaterlande viel unreiner und fast seltener gesprochen wird als das ganz fremde Französisch" (*Gedichte,* 246; Providence has now lead me to Germany; during the last six years I have had more opportunity to acquaint myself with the German language that is more or less my mother tongue, but is spoken in my country with less purity and almost with less frequency than the utterly foreign French). Indeed, French was then the everyday language, spoken and written by the upper class bourgeoisie for communication, above all in the canton Bern. Haller, too, had written the notes on his Alpine journey in French. In the preface of the fourth edition of his *Versuch schweizerischer Gedichte* he went even further and wrote: "Aber ich bin ein Schweizer, die deutsche Sprache ist mir fremd, und die Wahl der Wörter war mir fast unbekannt. Der Ueberfluß der Ausdrücke fehlte mir völlig, und die schweren Begriffe, die ich einzukleiden hatte, machten die Sprache für mich noch enger"[23] (But I am Swiss, the German language is foreign to me, and I barely knew the right choice of words. I completely lacked the wealth of expressions and the sophisticated concepts that I wanted to use for embellishment; this made the language even more of a limitation for me). Surprisingly, Haller's "mistakes" vis-á-vis Saxon German did not bother the critic Gottsched, who wrote in his review: "Die Verse sind vor einen Schweizer überaus flüssig und rein"

(Hirzel, *Hallers Leben,* cxxii; The verses are remarkably fluid and pure considering the author is Swiss).

Haller was aware that with his didactic poems he had introduced a new kind of poetry to Germany. In the preface to the fourth edition he wrote that, in his youth, he had been an admirer of Lohenstein, but then he had become acquainted with the English poets (presumably Pope and Shaftsbury) from whom he had taken to heart their "Liebe zum Denken und den Vorzug der schweren Dichtkunst" (*Gedichte,* 148–49; the love for thinking and the preference for a difficult poetry). This meant, he pointed out, that he had to compress many thoughts into few lines, and that he could not leave verses devoid of meaning. Haller strove all his life to achieve in his poetry a high degree of complexity of thought combined with ever more concise wordings and images.

Although Haller maintained that his new poetry had little influence, his collection went through eleven editions during his lifetime, not only in Bern but also in Göttingen (after the first two editions), and without counting numerous pirated editions. The last edition appeared in 1777, at a time when Goethe and a new generation of poets had emerged as a new, rebellious literary force.

Poems with titles like *Gedanken über Vernunft* (Thoughts on Reason), *Aberglauben und Unglauben* (Superstition and Lack of Faith), *Die Falschheit menschlicher Tugenden* (The Duplicity of Human Virtues), and *Über den Ursprung des Übels* (On the Origin of Evil) deal with issues of interest to Enlightenment philosophy, such as the essence of human nature, the signs of genuine virtue and piety, and the relationship between faith and morality. Haller's contemporaries admired and discussed perhaps most the poem *Über den Ursprung des Übels,* while *Die Alpen* remained the most influential poem, one often quoted in travel books. In 1728, Haller, together with his friend Johann Gessner, had taken a trip through the Alps, an unusual, daring journey at the time. Haller used this trip in his poem *Die Alpen* describing the Alps for the first time as a positive experience, a place of beauty, and not, as was customary, as a place of horror, a deserted land or wilderness. As early as 1710, in his *Dream of the Region of Liberty,* Joseph Addison had situated the land of freedom in a mountain valley, a beautiful spot in the midst of rugged mountains, flowery meadows, green trees, and a crystal clear stream.

In 490 Alexandrine verses divided into ten-line stanzas, Haller's poem describes the simple world of the inhabitants of the Alps as a contrast to the spoiled city dwellers, a topic that Haller's compatriot Béat Louis de Muralt had dealt with in his *Lettres sur les Anglois et les François et sur les voiages* (1725). Muralt had mocked and lamented the luxury and lack of morals in the Swiss city of Bern early in the century. In his poem Haller employed already the topoi of bucolic praise through poetry that contrasted moral life in the country to immoral city life, but it was altogether new that the location of his poem was not a fictional Arcadia but Alpine Switzerland.

The concept of "Glückseligkeit" (happiness) was the poem's theme. The Alpine dwellers were presented to the reader in possession of happiness, which was the highest goal of Enlightenment. Haller's achievement in revaluing the Alpine dwellers can be appreciated when compared with Gottsched's words about shepherds: "Unsere Landleute sind mehrentheils armselige, gedrückte und geplagte Leute. Sie sind selten Besitzer ihrer Heerden; [. . .] Zudem herrschen unter ihnen schon so viel Laster, daß man sie nicht mehr als Muster der Tugend aufführen kann" (*Versuch einer Critischen Dichtkunst* 284; Our peasants are mostly impoverished, oppressed and exploited people. They are rarely owners of their flock;[. . .] and so many vices are among them that one can no longer consider them proponents of virtue). Repeatedly, Haller pointed out that his description was "gemalt" (painted) according to real life (in Haller's notes referring to verses 110 and 261). He emphasized this at the beginning of the poem, when after citing the classical models he rejected them and addressed the Alpine dwellers thus:

> Ihr Schüler der Natur, ihr kennt noch güldne Zeiten!
> Nicht zwar ein Dichterreich voll fabelhafter Pracht;
> [. . .] Das Schicksal hat euch hier kein Tempe zugesprochen,
> Die Wolken, die ihr trinkt, sind schwer von Reif und Strahl;
> Der lange Winter kürzt des Frühlings späte Wochen,
> Und ein verewigt Eis umringt das kühle Tal;
> ("Die Alpen," v. 31–38, in *Gedichte*, 22)

[You students of nature still know this golden time!/ Not merely the poet's realm full of fabulous splendor / [. . .] But fate has denied you here that the valley of Tempe[24] known of old, / The clouds you drink are heavy with frost and hail, / A long winter shortens spring's late weeks, / Eternal ice surrounds the cool valley.]

This is no land of milk and honey, no paradise in which the lion sleeps beside the lamb, but a harsh, rocky land. Yet these very rocks guarantee the independence of their country. In this poem, for the first time, the Alps are not seen as an obstacle but as a fence protecting its inhabitants from foreign invaders:

> Sie warf die Alpen auf, dich von der Welt zu zäunen,
> Weil sich die Menschen selbst die grössten Plagen sind;
> (v. 53–54)

[Nature created the Alps to fence you off from the world, / Because men are their own worst enemies.]

It is an image that Schiller's *Wilhelm Tell* will take up again when Tell responds to his son Walter's question about why they do not live in the plain by saying that there people do not own the land and are not free. Disdained by city dwellers, simple folk live in this region in a steady rhythm of work, leisure, and sleep. They are strangers to vice and desire, and are content with what they have. They already live in that state of moral perfection the Enlightenment wished to bring to all people. Repeatedly Haller described the Alpine dwellers' rational, moral and happy way of life:

> Hier herrschet die Vernunft, von der Natur geleitet,
> [. . .] Und hier hat die Natur die Lehre, recht zu leben,
> Dem Menschen in das Herz und nicht ins Hirn gegeben [. . .]
> Entfernt vom eitlen Tand der mühsamen Geschäfte
> Wohnt hier der Seelen Ruh und flieht der Städte Rauch
> (vv. 67, 89–90, 161–62)

> [Here reason rules, guided by Nature.[. . .] And here Nature has instilled the right way to live / Into man's heart, not into his mind. [. . .] Far away from vain pursuits and troublesome business / The soul lives here peacefully and flees the city's smoke.]

The new generation of sentimental poets liked especially the emphasis on the Alpine dwellers' natural und moral life and their innocence. Even love among the sexes is a free and true love unhindered by conventions and special interests. There is no misalliance and no unhappy love, important topics in eighteenth-century literature, and no adultery. The seasons organize the simple Alpine dwellers' life. Spring, summer, and fall are for working, winter is for teaching and learning. The old pass on their knowledge, the young sing unadorned songs that attest to their free spirits. They are not educated like the city dwellers are, but their heart speaks here too. An old man:

> Lehrt, wie die feige Welt, ins Joch den Nacken strecket,
> Wie eitler Fürsten Pracht das Mark der Länder frisst,
> Wie Tell mit kühnem Mut das harte Joch zertreten,
> Das Joch, das heute noch Europens Hälfte trägt. (v. 302–05)

> [Points out how faint nations put their back under the yoke, / And let vain princes pomp consume their lands, / How Tell with bold courage has shaken off the yoke / That half of Europe still bears today.]

Such lines demonstrate Haller's implied criticism of contemporary social conditions for which he was chastised in some quarters.

The Alpine dwellers must live on what the Alps and their treasures provide: the many herbs and flowers provide beauty and are useful. In the interior there are crystals and life-spending water (v. 431). Even if the Alpine world is not a paradise, it provides everything necessary for living and more. The rivers carry gold, but the shepherd disdains it. Instead, he is highly skilled at producing cheese, a process that is described in detail for the first time in a poetic way.[25]

Haller's picture of the peaceful, content, modest and happy Alpine dwellers, whom he frequently called shepherds, was subsequently influential and was often applied to Switzerland as a whole. Likewise his "imitation of nature" — as the eighteenth century called it — was praised. Not only had he presented a people of shepherds, he had also depicted the reality of the Alps, including among other things the famous waterfall of the Staubbach in the Bernese Oberland, later to be visited by thousands of Swiss and European visitors including Goethe. These descriptions aroused much contemporary interest, both critically and with acclaim depending on the critic's poetological position.

Breitinger considered *Die Alpen* proof of his theory that poetry was far superior to painting. In doing so, he was addressing a central issue in the lively discussion about the Horatian principle *ut pictura poesis* in the first half of the eighteenth century. He explicitly pointed to Jean-Baptiste Dubos's theory, which assigned to painting a greater effect on the mind than poetry because painting directly affects the senses while poetry can have an influence on the mind only through imagination or fantasy.[26] Breitinger, on the other hand, was of the opinion that poetry can dominate a person's mind in a totally different way, especially because with his descriptions, choice of metaphors, and tropes the poet can influence the readers' imagination and does not leave him the liberty "mit flüchtigem und ungewissem Gemüths-Auge müssig herumzuschweifen" (*Schriften* 1: 23; to roam randomly with a fleeting and unsteady eye of the mind). Poetic expression including — according to Breitinger — also rhythm, rhetorical figures, style, and the marvelous has a ravishing and enchanting influence upon the senses and the imagination, so that we mean to see the things before us as we read about them. Breitinger cited the description of Alpine plants and flowers in Haller's poem as an example:

> Dort ragt das hohe Haupt am edlen Enziane
> Weit übern niedern Chor der Pöbel-Kräuter hin;
> Ein ganzes Blumen-Volk dient unter seiner Fahne,
> Sein blauer Bruder selbst bückt sich und ehret ihn. (v. 381–84)

> [There a gentian's high head overlooks / The chorus of ordinary plants far and wide; / An entire nation of flowers serves under his banner, / Even his blue brother bows to him with respect.]

Lessing referred to these lines in his *Laokoon* and remarked that it was painted poetry but "ohne alle Täuschung" (without any illusion) and that

Breitinger's praise resulted from the wrong perspective, because a unified vision had not been achieved and thus a vivid impression had not been left as claimed by Breitinger. Finally setting aside the *ut-pictura-poesis* principle in his *Laokoon,* Lessing defined poetry as an art that represents the temporal and transient. He could no longer praise Haller's descriptions that contemporaries had admired so much.[27]

Gessner's *Idyllen* Recalls Arcadia

Published in 1756 and expanded by a second volume in 1772, Salomon Gessner's *Idyllen* were even more popular than Haller's poetry. They went through more than a dozen editions, were translated into several European languages, and were especially successful in France. It was the first literary work in German in the eighteenth century to be famous beyond the borders of the German-speaking world. With his *Idyllen,* Gessner (1730–1788)[28] tried to introduce bucolic forms of classical antiquity into modern literature. The appeal of this genre for an urban and a courtly readership lay in the depiction of a world of unspoiled nature and pure morals in an unaffected language. For Gessner the idyll had its home in a golden age when men were "frey von allen den Sclavischen Verhältnissen, und von allen den Bedürfnissen, die nur die unglükliche Entfernung von der Natur nothwendig machet" (free of all slavish situations, of all those needs which only arose from the unhappy estrangement from nature). Idyll and eclogue represented the life of "glüklicher Leute [. . .] wie sie bey der natürlichsten Einfalt der Sitten, der Lebens-Art und ihrer Neigungen, bey allen Begegnissen, in Glük und Unglük betragen"[29] (happy people [. . .] how they act with the utmost simplicity of customs, way-of-life, and inclinations in all occurrences of happiness and misfortune). There are a Daphne and a Damon who observe a splendid nature after a thunderstorm, there is old Palemon who recounts his happy life once more before being transformed into a cypress tree at the grave of his beloved; there is the shepherd's vow not to love another woman until he sees a girl pass by and he loses his melancholy thinking of nothing else but wanting to find and to kiss her. There is the amorous game between Damon and Phyllis, between Daphnis and Chloe; there is unhappy Chloe, who loves a Lycas unaware of her love, and so on. If the poetic world in Bodmer's and Breitinger's sense is a possible world, it must be the one of these shepherds, a lively counter-world to reality. Gessner inserted many references to the real world seen as difficult and troublesome.

"Der Wunsch" (The Wish, 1756) shows the value system of the idylls most clearly. It is the wish to live "im kleinen Landhaus, beym ländlichen Garten, unbeneidet und unbemerkt" (I, 66; in a small country estate with a rustic garden unnoticed and unenvied). The location is a *locus amoenus:* nut trees provide shade, a cool spring murmurs with playful ducks swimming on it, pigeons, chicken, and singing birds belong into this picture, while gardens produce tasty vegetables. This happy place is contrasted with two other localities, the city, where "Sitten und Verhältnisse tausend Thorheiten adeln" (I, 66: customs and circumstances ingratiate a thousand follies), and the estates of some neighbors, who bring their city ways to the country where they only want to be able to throw big parties without being seen or disturbed. Such men act like the miser Harpax who exploits the peasants. They are far removed from the moral life that the poet strives for. The ideal neighbor in the country is the one who plants his crops, sings happy songs, and tells entertaining stories. It is the type of peasant celebrated by Haller, the peasant who happily and contentedly pursues his work.

This idealized country life also has a sociable side. The poet finds it partly in the right books that show the path to true beauty: "Du schöpfrischer Klopstok, und du Bodmer, der du mit Breitingern die Fakel der Critik aufgesteket hast, [. . .] Und du Wieland, [. . .] oft sollen eure Lieder in heiliges Entzüken mit hinreissen" (I, 70; You creative Klopstock, and you, Bodmer, who together with Breitinger has lit the torch of criticism [. . .] and you Wieland, [. . .] your songs will often bring holy ecstasy). Gleim and Ewald von Kleist are also mentioned, and this indicates the literary frame within which Gessner was moving. The other form of sociability consists of the friends' visits with whom the poet wants to travel through the beautiful countryside and to enjoy the fruits of the garden and a modest glass of wine. But the poet is aware that his dream of the country estate and a life away from the urban, spoiled civilization will not come true.

The shepherd has an eye for the real treasures in nature and observes, albeit with moral overtones: "Aber du blaue Viole, du Bild des Weisen, du stehst bescheiden niedrig im Gras, und streust Gerüche umher, indeß daß geruchlose Blumen hoch über das Gras empor stehn, und pralerisch winken" (I, 63; You blue violet, image of the wise, you stand modestly and low in the grass sending out a scent while odorless plants rise high above the grass and beckon proudly). The shepherd's perception is an aesthetic one when he speaks of the pleasant illusion brought about by a butterfly he at first had taken for a flower: "Welch eine bunte Blume wieget sich dort an der Quelle? So schön und glänzend von Farbe — Doch nein! Angenehmer Betrug! Ein Schmetterling flieget empor, und läßt das wankende Gräschen zurück" (I, 63; What a colorful flower is moving gently back and forth at the spring? So beautiful and shining with color . . . but no! a pleasant delusion! A butterfly rises up and leaves the waving grass behind). This passage also illustrates Gessner's rhythmic language, a language that succeeds in producing the effects required of poetry by Bodmer and Breitinger: it is heightened, different from everyday speech, and elicits the kind of astonishment the theoreticians demanded of literature. Gessner practiced this openly by letting his literary figures express repeatedly their surprise at what they see. He succeeded in representing nature as a source of delight in an emotional language full of exclamations, as when for instance Damon speaks to Daphne:

> Welche unerschöpfliche Quelle von Entzüken! Von der belebenden Sonne bis zur kleinesten Pflanze sind alles Wunder! O wie reißt das Entzücken mich hin! wenn ich vom hohen Hügel die weitausgebreitete Gegend übersehe, oder, wenn ich ins Gras hingestrekt die manigfaltigen Blumen und Kräuter betrachte und ihre kleinen Bewohner; [...] wenn ich die Wunder betrachte, dann schwellt mir die Brust, Gedanken drengen sich dann auf; ich kan sie nicht entwickeln, dann wein' ich und sinke hin und stammle mein Erstaunen dem der die Erde schuf! O Daphne, nichts gleicht dem Entzüken, es sey denn das Entzüken vorn dir geliebt zu seyn. (I, 33)

> [What an inexhaustible source of delight! From the life-giving sun to the smallest plant, all are miracles! When I look from a high hill into the wide landscape below, or when I lie stretched out in the grass looking at the many flowers and plants and their tiny inhabitants [...] when I observe these miracles my chest swells, and thoughts flow freely; but I cannot unfold them, then I cry and sink down and stammer my amazement to Him who created this earth! O Daphne, nothing compares to this rapture except for the rapture to be loved by you!]

But such verses in which the two lovers express their mutual love seem to have raised eyebrows in Protestant Zurich. In connection with the publication of the bucolic novel *Daphnis,* the censorship office intervened as they apparently did not understand that the *Idyllen,* though a literary game, was at the same time deeply moral and represented those virtues that the philosophers of the Enlightenment had preached. Thus, it was no accident that the *Idyllen* were published together with Diderot's *Contes morales,* both in a French and a German version.

Gessner's popularity was not only due to the literary qualities of his work and its convergence with Enlightenment tenets — one of which was the "education of the heart" — but also to the fact that they were read as portrayals of Switzerland. Gessner himself promoted this. He wrote to Gleim: "In einem Lande, wo ein hochgräflicher Graf, oder ein gnädiger Baron den Landmann zum armen Sclaven macht, da mag letzterer kleiner und verächtlicher seyn als bey uns, wo die Freiheit ihn zum besser denkenden braven Mann macht; und ich getraute mir, auf unsern Alpen Hirten zu finden, wie Theokrit zu seiner Zeit, denen man wenig nehmen und wenig leihen dürfte, um sie zur Ekloge zu bilden" (I, 17; In a country where a mighty count or a benevolent baron enslaves the peasant, the latter may appear poorer and more contemptible than in our country where freedom makes him a more thoughtful, honest individual; and I did find such shepherds in the Alps, as did Theocritus in his day, who could be used for an eclogue without changing them much). It is not surprising that many readers traveled to Switzerland to find Arcadia and to admire patriarchal customs and conditions.[30]

In this connection Jean-Jacques Rousseau must be mentioned: Rousseau saw himself as a citizen of a free country and with his descriptions in *Julie ou la Nouvelle Heloïse* (1761) helped fashion a picture of Switzerland as a country of freedom while depicting landscapes very similar to those of Haller's. When St. Preux has to leave his beloved Julie for the first time and goes to Valais, he is not only an observer of how happy the Alpine inhabitants are, but he himself experiences a state of quiet happiness that he was unable to achieve in the lowlands and in the company of men. He praises mountain air as a remedy for body and mind.

Rousseau added the scenery of Lake Geneva to these idealized Alpine landscapes. When St. Preux returns from his travels abroad, the view of Lake Geneva causes a moment of ecstasy, a wave of delight that is recorded in a letter describing the rich and fertile soil, a unique landscape as the most beautiful the human eye has ever seen. Repeatedly connections are drawn between the sublime, the beauty of the landscape and the freedom of the inhabitants. Rousseau's description of the landscape is always accompanied by a depiction of the protagonist's feelings, usually St. Preux's, who describes the Alps and Lake Geneva. The image of idyllic conditions in Switzerland is accentuated by the fact that St. Preux finds patriarchal conditions in Julie's house. Even Lake Geneva and the Genevans are included in this picture of bliss, even though they reveal blemishes such as a great fondness for money. Yet Rousseau sets them favorably apart from the Parisians, because Genevans are by nature moral, and vice only comes from abroad, since they travel frequently and have much contact with foreigners whose way of life threatens their "ancient modesty."

Rousseau localized the novel of love, in which morality overcomes great passion, in a concrete landscape, and connected the plot and the protagonists' conditions with this landscape, as Goethe would do in 1774 in his *Werther*. Nevertheless, a marriage between Julie and her tutor is impossible even in this country of freedom because of class barriers. There is only a short episode of a genuine love relationship in the form of an idyll at the beginning of the novel, a place of rustic simplicity with brooks, bushes, and hedges, a bucolic refuge for the lovers. Like the shepherds in Gessner's *Idyllen*, Julie and St. Preux experience a happy time here, but their happiness cannot last. In Rousseau's world, class barriers continue to be insurmountable.

The Peasants Want a Voice

A treatise with a wide readership further promoted the impressions that Switzerland was a new Arcadia, and that happy people as described by Haller and Gessner were actually to be found there: it was *Die Wirtschaft eines philosophischen Bauern* (Economy of a Philosophical Farmer, 1761). The Zurich physician Hans Caspar Hirzel (1725–1803) was the author of the work, which describes the business and views of a certain Jakob Gujer (1716–1785) (under the name of Kleinjogg), who had a farm close to Uster in the Zurich Oberland. In large parts of his treatise Hirzel lets Kleinjogg speak directly. Kleinjogg trusts God's providence and praises industry and hard work, which should also serve as a model for urban dwellers. His highest goal is, very much in agreement with the Enlightenment, true happiness, the prerequisite for which is contentment, not wealth, power, and honor. Like Rousseau, Kleinjogg believes that man is essentially good but corrupted by society. Therefore, Kleinjogg teaches his children himself to protect them from bad influences. Hirzel writes: "In dem Bewustseyn der Ausübung seiner Pflichten, und der daher entstehenden Gemütsruhe, setzet er seinen Begriff von der Glückseligkeit. In den natürlichen Folgen unserer Handlungen entdeckt er die Belohnungen und Strafen des gerechten Gottes, die Fruchtbarkeit ist die Belohnung eines fleißigen Feldbauer, so wie die Gemüthsruhe einer guten sittlichen Handlung"[31] (Conscious of fulfilling his duties and acquiring peace of mind, he sets an example of happiness. He discovers the rewards and punishments of a just God in the natural consequences of his actions. Rich bounty is the reward of an industrious farmer just as peace of mind is that of a virtuous deed). Soon travelers to Switzerland visited this Kleinjogg, alias farmer Gujer: it was the same curiosity about a rustic, unspoiled state that also generated the interest in Haller and Gessner. Kleinjogg resembled a patriarch living in an earlier, untouched, natural state, seen as an embodiment of Rousseau's unspoiled mankind. He became a model for the mostly urban readership of the treatise.

While an educated writer lent his voice to the peasant Kleinjogg, the farmer Ulrich Bräker spoke for himself. Bräker's autobiography, *Lebensgeschichte und natürliche Ebentheuer des Armen Mannes im Tockenburg* (The Life Story and Natural Adventures of the Poor Man in Tockenburg, 1789), was published by Johann Heinrich Füssli (1741–1832) in Zurich.[32] Füssli had received the manuscript from the clergyman Martin Imhof who took this autobiography as proof that the Enlightenment had then reached the farthest valleys of Switzerland. He commented: "In einem der abgesöndertsten Winkeln des so wenig bekannten [. . .] Tockenburgs wohnt ein braver Sohn der Natur, der, wiewohl von allen Mitteln der Aufklärung abgeschnitten, sich einzig durch sich selbst zu einem ziemlichen Grade derselben hinaufgearbeitet hat"[33] (In one of the remotest corners [. . .] of little known Toggenburg there lives an upright son of nature, who, though completely cut off from all means of enlightenment, has raised himself up to a considerable degree of enlightenment, all on his own). According to clergyman Imhof, Bräker wrote "in der kunstlosen Sprache des Herzens" (in the artless language of the heart) and was an example for the fact that "echte Weisheit und Tugend an kein Land und an keinen Stand unter den Menschen gebunden ist" (true wisdom and virtue are not tied to a social class), that they can often be found in the lonely peasant's hut, and that the source of Bräker's happiness is in his own heart.[34] Bräker was molded into an example of a happy, enlightened, wise man.

But in reality Bräker's life was by no means as happy as it appeared in his autobiography.[35] The son of a small farmer, he grew up in a Pietist family attending school only a few weeks each year. He learned how to write only in his thirtieth year. When only twenty years old, he joined the Prussian army, took part in the Seven Years' War and deserted after the battle at Lobowitz in 1756. He returned home, farmed his small plot in Toggenburg (eastern Switzerland), and established a small wool trade on the side — with little success. His quarrelsome, uneducated wife showed little understanding for her creative husband who would rather read and write than attend to his business. As was customary in his class, he grew up with only a few religious books, but with the help of friends he was accepted into the Moralische Gesellschaft zu Lichtensteig, a reading society in the canton St. Gall, and thus had access to books.[36] He read intensively geographical and historical writings, and he read and wrote commentaries on Shakespeare's plays.

Bräker kept a diary until the end of his life and the diary formed the basis for his autobiography. Initially, his Pietist interest in soul searching may have motivated him to write his autobiography, but the more Bräker turned away from Pietism, the more his joy in writing seems to have taken on a life of its own. Toward the end of his autobiography he remarked tongue-in-cheek: "was soll ich mich selbst tadeln? Wäre das nicht Narrheit auf Narrheit gehäuft?" (Why should I criticize myself? Would that not heap folly upon folly?). When he saw that his life story did not turn out as he had envisioned it, he wondered if he should recast it after Jung-Stilling's famous autobiographical novel.[37] He also mentioned Rousseau's *Confessions* by way of comparison, but opined that his own story did not entail that type of confession; nevertheless he added a chapter entitled "Meine Geständnisse" (My Confessions) in which he told of his fight against desire and passion. He had received a pious education and had gone through hellish fears as a young man because of his fantasies.

It is no coincidence that Bräker — as a person from the lower classes and lacking any formal education — would choose the autobiographical form, the least confining literary genre. Bräker could make use of his readings and follow his models according to the topic at hand. He patterned his writings after the novel, skillfully added direct discourse to his reports, and expressed his emotions, all features typical of the novel of the late eighteenth century. He would describe nature:

> Welche Lust, bey angenehmen Sommertagen über die Hügel fahren — durch Schattenwälder streichen — durchs Gebüsch Einhörnchen jagen und Vogelnester ausnehmen! [. . .] Und welch Vergnügen machte mir nicht jeden Tag, jeder neue Morgen, wenn jetzt die Sonne die Hügel vergoldete, denen ich mit meiner Herde entgegenstieg, dann jenen haldigen Buchenwald und endlich die Wiesen und Waidplätze beschien. [. . .] Wann dann alle anliegenden Gebüsche von jubilirenden Vögeln ertönten und dieselben um mich her hüpften. — O! Was fühlt' ich da! — Ha, ich weiß es nicht! — halt süsse, süsse Lust! Da sang' und trillerte ich dann mit, bis ich heiser ward. Ein andermal spürte ich diesen muntern Waldbürgern durch alle Stauden nach, ergötzte mich an ihrem hübschen Gefieder und wünschte, daß sie nur halb so zahm wären wie meine Geissen, beguckte ihre Jungen und ihre Eyer, und erstaunte über den wundervollen Bau ihrer Nester. (B 380)

[What a joy to drive across the hills on summer days — to roam through shady forests — to chase squirrels in the underbrush and to empty birds' nests! [. . .] and what pleasures every new day brings, every new morning when the sun colors the hills golden, then shines on the forests and finally on the meadows and grazing areas as I am ascending the mountain with my herd — when the bushes echo with the singing of the birds and they fly around me — O, what did I feel then! — I don't know — pleasant feelings! Then I sang and whistled along until I was hoarse. Another time I followed these cheerful forest dwellers into the bushes, delighted in their colorful plumage wishing they would be only half as tame as my young goats, I watched their young and their eggs and marveled at the intricate construction of their nests.]

The description resembles more that of Gessner's idylls than an attempt at realism; after all, a goatherd was at the very bottom of the social ladder in the country, an occupation reserved for the poor and young children. Bräker idealized nature and youth; he represented and glorified his childhood through the filter of bucolic literature. In his narrative he preferred entertaining to sad events, spending over half his autobiography on the time from his youth up to his military service while cutting short his courtship, marriage, business venture, and later life. He wrote about what gave him and his readers pleasure, as, for instance, his amorous adventures. Writing and living in the imaginary seemed to constitute for him a kind of compensation for his dreary life. Compared to the autobiographies of Jung-Stilling and Karl Philipp Moritz, who likewise came from poor and uneducated families, Bräker showed more wit and irony, less inclination to critical self-examination, and no self-pity. His text radiates with humor and appears very spontaneous to the point of being naïve at times, a quality appreciated by contemporary readers in an era of increasing interest in the natural and unaffected. The success of Bräker's autobiography was, in short, largely due to the fact that readers saw in it the realization of the ideal of the simple life propagated by Rousseau, combined with the literary appeal of a naive style of presentation.

A Book for the People

In 1781 Johann Heinrich Pestalozzi's *Lienhard and Gertrud* began to appear, a book that described for the first time the actual life of the peasants, according to contemporaries. Pestalozzi (1746–1827)[38] was strongly influenced by Rousseau in his activities and in his own life.[39] He worked a farm for some time, founded an institution for poor children, and took great interest in the poverty and lack of education of the people in the country. His four-volume novel *Lienhard and Gertrud*,[40] a work greatly indebted to Rousseau's *Emile* and *Contrat Sociale*, incorporated Pestalozzi's progressive ideas for educating the common people. Literature was seen by these writers as an ideal medium to influence people because it reaches the heart and not just the intellect. In his novel, he described the family of Lienhard and Gertrud and the social problems in the village of Bonnal ruled by a selfish and unfair mayor who entices the men to drink in his tavern and to spend their money needed for their household. This leads to neglect and degeneration in the village. Gertrud succeeds in informing the aristocratic landlord Arner about the goings-on in the village. The nobleman takes up the role as patriarch and improves conditions, dismisses the mayor, provides work for the laborers, and improves the economic situation of the village by bringing in a cotton mill. He also introduces a village school, improves the laws and regulations for government and business.

In its first part, the novel is centered on the family and Gertrud conveys the principles of a good education. Christian values are the basis for all behavior. An elementary school is organized according to the principles of industry, openness, loyalty, and common sense. The last step in the educational enterprise concerns the improvement of the community. The peasants learn gradually to take responsibility for their community.[41] Although Pestalozzi emphasized in his preface that he is describing "nature," what he actually designed was a utopia of a better society and, in the sense of Bodmer and Breitinger, a possible world.

While the novel sold well, it did not have the impact envisioned by Pestalozzi, in part because the book was received as an entertaining story rather than as an educational handbook. The book probably did not reach those people for whom it was meant. In Nicolai's *Allgemeiner Deutscher Bibliothek* the book was praised without reservations. The reviewer (probably Karl August Musäus) wrote that Pestalozzi had transformed his ideas of teaching the people very successfully into literature. Even in distant Berlin, where the book was also published, it was praised as popular, close to the actual people in its tone, and entertaining. This way of telling a story had also fascinated the contemporary readers of Bräker's autobiography.

The works and authors discussed here should not be regarded as representing a linear, progressive development within Swiss literature. It is true that the authors discussed were, for the most part, acquainted with one another, read each other's works, corresponded, and were interested in the socio-political project of the Helvetian Society. They shared the political and cultural values that grew out of an urban culture and a national awareness that regarded the Alpine landscape and the simple life of its rural population no longer as a barbaric, uncultured country but as a model of idyllic, patriarchal life. Switzerland had become a mythical modern Arcadia.

— Translated by Barbara Becker-Cantarino

Notes

[1] Still informative is the anthology edited by Max Wehrli, *Das geistige Zürich im 18. Jahrhundert: Texte und Dokumente von Gotthard Heidegger bis Heinrich Pestalozzi* (Zurich: Atlantis, 1943).

[2] Leibniz wrote a review of Heidegger's tract in which he defended the novel.

[3] Johann Heinrich Füssli, *Zürich im Spätrokoko. Briefe des Conte di Sant' Alessandro*, ed. Emil Ermatinger (Frauenfeld: Huber 1940), 132.

[4] Bodmer was the son of a minister and chose the career of a merchant, which led him to France and Italy. He studied Swiss history and taught this subject at the Carolinum, a Zurich Latin School mostly for theologians, from 1731 to 1775. He introduced the works of Dante and Shakespeare and above all medieval literature to a wider reading public. See Albert M. Debrunner, *Das güldene schwäbische Alter: Johann Jakob Bodmer und das Mittelalter als Vorbildzeit im 18. Jahrhundert*, Epistemata, vol. 170 (Würzburg: Königshausen & Neumann, 1996). Breitinger studied theology at the Carolinum where he later taught Greek, Hebrew, logic, and rhetoric. He was a philologist and edited the works of the German Baroque poet, Martin Opitz.

[5] See Helga Brandes, *Die "Gesellschaft der Maler" und ihr literarischer Beitrag zur Aufklärung: Eine Untersuchung zur Publizistik des 18. Jahrhunderts*, Studien zur Publizistik, vol. 21 (Bremen: Schünemann, 1974).

[6] Johann Jakob Bodmer und Johann Jakob Breitinger, *Die Discourse der Mahlern. Vier Theile in einem Band* (1721–1723; reprint, Hildesheim: Olms 1969), unpaginated preface.

[7] *Discourse*, Part 3, no. 12.

[8] *Discourse*, Part 3, no. 12.

[9] I do not wish to reiterate in detail the famous quarrel, but merely point to the contribution by the Swiss poets to a new understanding of literature.

[10] Cited after Wolfgang Bender, *Johann Milton: Episches Gedicht von dem verlohrnen Paradiese. Faksimiledruck der Bodmerschen Übersetzung von 1742* (Stuttgart: Metzler, 1965), 16*.

[11] Johann Jakob Breitinger, *Critische Dichtkunst* (1740; reprint, Stuttgart: Metzler 1966), 1: 59–60.

[12] See Lubomir Doležel, *Occidental Poetics: Tradition and Progress* (Lincoln, NE: U of Nebraska P, 1990), 40–52.

[13] Bodmer's *Anklagung des verderbten Geschmackes* began with praise of Christian Wolff as a profound thinker and great teacher of the German nation who wrote in a scholarly yet understandable language.

[14] Johann Jakob Bodmer and Johann Jakob Breitinger, *Schriften zur Literatur*, ed. Volker Meid (Stuttgart: Reclam, 1980), 39; subsequent references provided parenthetically.

[16] Doležel, *Occidental Poetics*, 49.

[17] Bodmer, *Critische Dichtkunst*, unpaginated preface.

[18] Quoted from the postscript to Breitinger, *Critische Dichtkunst* 23*.

[19] The documents have been reprinted in Friedrich Gottlieb Klopstock, *Der Messias. Gesang I–III*, ed. Elisabeth Höpker-Herberg (Stuttgart: Reclam, 1986). In an announcement of the first three cantos in the *Freymüthigen Nachrichten* (25 October 1748), Bodmer wrote a fictive letter: "Wissen Sie auch schon, was vor einen hohen Ruhm der Himmel der deutschen Muse zugedacht hat? Sie soll ein episches Gedicht in dem Geschmacke des verlohrnen Paradieses hervorbringen, und einen Poeten formieren, der einen gleichen Schwung mit dem Milton nehmen wird; dieser soll keine geringere Handlung zu besingen erwählen als das Werk der Erlösung" (Do you already know what great glory the heavens have bestowed upon the German muse? She is to produce a poem in the manner of *Paradise Lost* and to prepare a poet who can rival Milton; he has chosen no less a topic than the salvation). Quoted from Wehrli, ed., *Das geistige Zürich*, 80.

[20] Johann Jakob Bodmer, "Lob der Mundart," in *Mahler der Sitten* (1746), quoted from Wehrli, ed., *Das geistige Zürich*, 79.

[21] Wehrli ed., *Das geistige Zürich*, 80.

[22] Haller was born in Bern, studied medicine at the universities of Tübingen, Leiden, Paris, and Basel, worked as a physician in Bern from 1728 to 1735, went as a professor of anatomy, surgery, and botany to the University of Göttingen in 1736, where he became a renowned scholar with his scientific publications. He also wrote hundreds of reviews and had a worldwide correspondence. In 1753 he returned to Bern where he held several political offices. He published three political novels in the 1770s, *Usong* (1771), *Alfred* (1773), and *Fabius und Cato* (1774), which were not

very successful. For his biography, see Ludwig Hirzel, *Hallers Leben und Dichtungen* (Frauenfeld: Huber, 1917); for his works, see Christoph Siegrist, *Das Lehrgedicht der Aufklärung*, Germanistische Abhandlungen 43 (Stuttgart: Metzler, 1974), and Karl S. Guthke, *Literarisches Leben im achtzehnten Jahrhundert in Deutschland und in der Schweiz* (Bern & Munich: Francke, 1975).

[23] Albrecht von Haller, *Gedichte*, ed. Ludwig Hirzel (Frauenfeld: Huber, 1917), 249.

[24] Tempe: a valley in Thessaly famous for its lush vegetation and mild climate.

[25] Haller took the description of making cheese from Johann Jakob Scheuchzer, *Beschreibung der Natur-Geschichten des Schweizerlandes* (1706–1708), 2:196. Scheuchzer's was the first description of Swiss cheese production; he credited the healthy life of the Swiss to the different forms of dairy foods.

[26] Jean Baptiste Dubos, *Réflexions critiques sur la poésie et la peinture* (Utrecht, 1732–1736).

[27] Lessing, *Sämtliche Schriften*, ed. Karl Lachmann and Franz Muncker (Stuttgart and Leipzig: Göschen, 1886–1924), 9: 102–4.

[28] The son of a printer, Gessner began to paint and write after breaking off his apprenticeship as a book dealer. In 1761 he became a partner in the Orell publishing company, which took the name Orell, Gessner & Füssli in 1771 and became one of the most important publishing houses in Switzerland. From 1780 on they published the *Neue Zürcher Zeitung*. See *Maler und Dichter der Idylle: Salomon Gessner 1730–1780*. Ausstellungskataloge der Herzog August Bibliothek, vol. 30 (Wolfenbüttel: Herzog August Bibliothek, 1980).

[29] Salomon Gessner, *Idyllen. Kritische Ausgabe*, ed. E. Theodor Voss (Stuttgart: Reclam, 1988), 15. Subsequent references cited parenthetically.

[30] See Uwe Hentschel, "Salomon Geßners Idyllen und ihre deutsche Rezeption im 18. und beginnenden 19. Jahrhundert," *Orbis litterarum* 54 (1999): 332–49; Ulrich Im Hof, *Das Europa der Aufklärung* (Munich: Beck, 1993), 93–98 on the admiration of Switzerland.

[31] Wehrli, ed., *Das geistige Zürich*, 180.

[32] Füssli was a partner in the publishing house Orell, Gessner & Füssli, Bodmer's successor as professor for Swiss History at the Carolinum in Zurich, and later editor of the *Neue Zürcher Zeitung*. Füssli edited Bräker's autobiography, and since neither Bräker's manuscript nor Füssli's edited version has survived, it is impossible to tell how much he changed the original beyond orthographical and grammatical corrections.

[33] Ulrich Bräker, *Sämtliche Schriften. Vierter Band: Lebensgeschichte und vermischte Schriften*, ed. Claudia Holliger-Wiesmann et al. (Munich: Beck, 2000): 357. Subsequent references cited parenthetically.

[34] *Leben und Schriften Ulrich Bräkers, des armen Mannes im Tockenburg*, ed. Samuel Voellmy (Basel: Birkhäuser, 1945), 1: 70.

[35] For his biography see Holger Böning, *Ulrich Bräker: Der arme Mann aus dem Toggenburg. Eine Biographie* (Zurich: Orell Füssli, 1998).

[36] Bräker can serve as an example for the benefit of these reading societies for ordinary people in remote areas; on the other hand it was very unusual that a lower middle class person like Bräker was admitted into a reading society, as he was below the social standing of its members; see Ulrich Im Hof, *Die Entstehung einer politischen Öffentlichkeit in der Schweiz: Struktur und Tätigkeit der Helvetischen Gesellschaft* (Frauenfeld & Stuttgart: Huber, 1983), 132–40, and Gerhard Sauder, "Die Bücher des Armen Mannes und der Moralischen Gesellschaft im Toggenburg," in *Buch und Sammler: Private und öffentliche Bibliotheken im 18. Jahrhundert. Colloquium der Arbeitsstelle 18. Jahrhundert* (Heidelberg: Winter, 1979), 167–86.

[37] Johann Heinrich Jung (1740–1817), the gifted son of a poor country teacher and tailor who became a renowned ophthalmologist and professor at the University of Heidelberg and later at Marburg, wrote his autobiography in the early 1770s under the pseudonym "Stilling" (the quietist). The first part, *Heinrich Stillings Jugend: Eine wahrhafte Geschichte* (Heinrich Stilling's Youth: A True Story, 1777) was published by Goethe and became a great success, starting a wave of autobiographical writings.

[38] See Peter Stadler, *Pestalozzi. Geschichtliche Biographie.* 2 vols. (Zurich: Verlag Neue Zürcher Zeitung, 1988–1993).

[39] See Werner Bänziger, *"Es ist freilich schwer, sein eigenes Bild mit Treue zu malen . . .": Die Autobiographien von Pestalozzi, Zschokke und Wessenberg* (Aarau & Frankfurt a. M.: Sauerländer, 1996), and Peter Hager, *Pestalozzi und Rousseau* (Bern: Francke 1975).

[40] Pestalozzi reworked his novel twice; in 1790–1792 a totally new version appeared in three parts, and in 1819 and later, a revision of the previous one. We discuss and cite from the first edition.

[41] About efforts to introduce such ideals in Switzerland through a "Helvetische Gesellschaft," see Im Hof, *Die Entstehung einer politischen Öffentlichkeit.*

Lessing, Minna von Barnhelm, *Act II, 6: Minna appeals in vain to Tellheim's love. Act III, 7: Tellheim refuses Werner's offer of money. Illustrations of 1770 by Daniel Chodowiecki, the most famous engraver of his day and one of Lessing's Berlin circle of friends.*

Lessing, Bourgeois Drama, and the National Theater

Francis Lamport

FROM THE 1740S ON, Johann Christoph Gottsched's (1700–1766) personal star began to wane.[1] He came under increasing critical attack, both for the narrow rationalism of his views and for his allegedly dictatorial pretensions as sole arbiter of German literary taste; and his partnership with the actress and theater troupe leader Friederike Neuber came to an end when her troupe departed for St. Petersburg in 1740. But Gottsched's achievement and his significance in the history of German drama should not be underrated. Even Lessing, in his blistering attack on Gottsched in the famous seventeenth *Literaturbrief* (Literary Letter) of 1759,[2] sums up the state of the German theater before Gottsched's reform in terms that closely echo Gottsched's own words in the preface to *Der sterbende Cato* (The Death of Cato, 1732). Gottsched had in considerable measure succeeded in generating acceptance for serious, "regular" drama among a public of increasingly "bourgeois" tastes and values; his association with Frau Neuber can be seen as the first step towards the creation of a German National Theater, that distant goal for which, as Goethe's Wilhelm Meister was to observe, so many at that time could be heard to sigh.[3] Gottsched's *Deutsche Schaubühne* (German Stage) of 1740–45 was intended to provide the nucleus of a repertory for such a theater. However, for all the assiduity and, within their limits, the talent of Gottsched and especially of his wife, Luise Victorie Gottsched, as adaptors and translators, and the promise of a number of younger dramatists who built on the foundations Gottsched had laid, something more truly original was needed before their hopes for a national German dramatic revival could be realized. This only appeared with Gotthold Ephraim Lessing (1729–81) and the revolution initiated by his *Miß Sara Sampson* (1755), the first German tragedy with a contemporary bourgeois setting.[4]

Schlegel and Gellert:
Heroic Tragedy and Sentimental Comedy

Johann Elias Schlegel (1719–49) was and is still rightly regarded as the most promising of the generation of dramatists growing up under Gottsched's shadow. In his short life Johann Elias completed five tragedies and drafted sketches for two more; he also produced several comedies and a small but significant body of essays which have earned him the title of "a German pioneer in aesthetics."[5] While still a pupil at the famous Saxon "prince's school" at Schulpforta (1736–37), he began writing tragedies along the lines of classical Latin and Greek models — *Die Trojanerinnen* (The Trojan Women) based on Seneca, and *Orest und Pylades,* based on Euripides' *Iphigenia in Tauris,* but with significant modifications of his own. Both were repeatedly revised, and were published only after his death by his brother Johann Heinrich. In both plays the issue is the execution of a divine command that appears to conflict with nature and humanity: the sacrifice of a human victim, or in *Die Trojanerinnen,* of two — Hecuba's daughter Polyxena and Andromache's son (and Hecuba's grandson) Astyanax. Here cruelty and barbarism triumph, but in *Orest und Pylades* the two friends gain their liberty, together with Orest's sister Iphigenia. The barbarian king Thoas, who has held Iphigenia captive and forced her to sacrifice other Greek captives to the goddess Diana, is himself killed, and as he dies still crying out for revenge, the priest Hierarchus announces the liberation of the Greeks and the abolition of the barbarous practice of human sacrifice:

> THOAS: So stützt der Himmel selbst noch meiner Mörder Sache?
>   Er will — ich soll — verzeihn — ich aber — ich — will Rache. —
> HIERARCHUS: Sein Odem eilt davon, indem er Rache schreyt.
>   Wißt, daß ich Herrscher bin, und ihr befreyet seyd.
>   Hätt euch kein Götterspruch dem nahen Tod entrissen,
>   So hätt euch eure Treu und Tugend retten müssen.
>   Die machen Griechenland von unsrer Feindschaft frey.
>   Wir ehren euren Bund, und dieser Schwester Treu.
>   Hier soll kein Grieche mehr durch uns geopfert werden;
>   Ihr selbst seyd Opfer werth, und Götter auf der Erden.[6]

[Thoas: So even heaven itself supports my murderers' cause? / Heaven wants — me to — forgive — but I — I — will have vengeance — / Hierarchus: His breath takes flight, even as he cries for vengeance. / Know that I rule here now, and that you are released. / Even if a divine pronouncement had not delivered you from imminent death, / Your devotion and virtue must have saved you. / They deliver Greece from our enmity. / We honor your bond, and this sisterly devotion. / No more

Greeks shall be sacrificed by us, / You yourselves are worthy to receive sacrifice, and are Gods upon the earth.]

Goethe was to "humanize" the story still further in his *Iphigenie auf Tauris* (1779/86), but in this early version we already hear the true voice of Enlightenment, the victory of humanity over barbarism.[7]

Schlegel turned to Roman history, or historical legend, in *Dido* and in the unfinished *Lucretia,* then to German, or rather Germanic history in *Hermann* (1740–43). The defeat of the Roman legions under Varus by the Germanic tribes led by Hermann (Arminius) the Cheruskan in the Teutoburg Forest in A.D. 9 was to prove a potent rallying symbol for the emergent "national" consciousness of a Germany which, in the eighteenth century, was still divided into dozens, if not hundreds, of nominally independent political units. The subject was also treated by Klopstock in a series of "bardic" dramas: *Hermanns Schlacht* (Hermann's Battle, 1769); *Hermann und die Fürsten* (Hermann and the Princes, 1784); *Hermanns Tod* (Hermann's Death, 1787), and by Heinrich von Kleist (1777–1810) in his bloodthirsty *Die Hermannsschlacht* (1810), written to rouse the Germans against the subjugation of their country by Napoleon. Schlegel portrays the rebellion of the virtuous, noble if "primitive" Germans against the supposedly superior, but decadent "civilization" of the treacherous Romans: contemporaries saw in this a call for Germany to throw off the cultural domination of France, and the patriotic note undoubtedly helps to account for the degree of popularity *Hermann* enjoyed on the stage. The play is constructed with some skill, but ultimately does not spring to dramatic life, particularly since, in accordance with neoclassical precept, all action takes place off-stage and is merely reported to the audience. Moreover, Varus and his legions make only a brief appearance; the actual conflict in the play lies between those Germans who are loyal to the old tribal ways — Hermann himself, his father Siegmar, and his bride Thusnelda — and those who have given their allegiance to Rome, notably Thusnelda's cynical, self-serving father Segest and Hermann's own Romanized brother Flavius. Hermann himself stands somewhat apart from the action, victorious in his unsullied virtue, and the play arouses little if any real tragic feeling.

To a lesser extent, this is also true of Schlegel's last and most successful tragedy, *Canut,* completed in 1747 in Denmark, where Schlegel had lived and worked since 1743. It was written to celebrate the accession of the Danish King Frederik V, to whom it is dedicated, and its hero, the great eleventh-century king of Denmark and England, is depicted in the guise of an eighteenth-century "enlightened despot." Like Hermann, he is essentially untragic in his triumphant virtuousness, a fault perceived and criticized by contemporary commentators such as Lessing and Nicolai. Dramatic interest centers upon his antagonist Ulfo, an untamable Viking warrior obsessed with military glory and pursuing his envious hatred of Canut by all available means, from treachery and intrigue to violent rebellion. Pardoned by the generous Canut, he rebels again and is finally condemned, but is allowed to die the warrior's death he desires when he falls fighting against Canut's loyal vassal Gottschalk, whom he has attempted to suborn. There had been villains in German tragedy before, even in Schlegel's own dramatic works. But Ulfo has seemed to many critics to embody a new kind of dynamic egoism, foreshadowing the rebellious heroes of the *Sturm und Drang,* Klinger's Guelfo in *Die Zwillinge* (The Twins, 1776), the Moor brothers of Schiller's *Die Räuber* (The Robbers, 1781), or perhaps even Goethe's *Götz von Berlichingen* (1773), like Ulfo the defender of a traditional martial code and of an individual liberty verging on anarchism, against the increasing centralized power of the modern state. Ulfo might even be seen as a proto-Marcusean rebel against the "bad faith" and "repressive tolerance" of the modern state, who finally provokes the king to act against him and thus to reveal the iron fist concealed within the velvet glove: "enlightened despotism" is exposed as "a noble illusion."[8] This is, of course, not what Schlegel intended, but it is certainly true that, not for the first or last time, evil proves dramatically more interesting than good, and Johann Heinrich Schlegel found it necessary to insist, in his preface to his late brother's play, that Canut was intended as the hero and not Ulfo, as many contemporaries had evidently thought (*Ausgewählte Werke,* 606).

Schlegel's originality should not be exaggerated. Like others, he experimented with a variety of settings for tragedy, but all in the distant or legendary past. He remained committed to the "Würde und Majestät" (dignity and majesty) of tragedy,[9] which Lessing was to declare secondary and superfluous to the true tragic effect, and he retained the stately Alexandrine, though his handling of it is superior to that of Gottsched and his other contemporaries. Although in his essays he is ready to point out the inconvenience and implausibility occasioned by a strict observance of the unities of place and time, in practice he adheres to the rules, to the detriment of *Hermann,* for example, as we have observed; and though again in theory he puts forward a more imaginative and less literal-minded conception of "imitation" and dramatic probability than Gottsched, in practice he can be equally pedantic, as in *Orest und Pylades,* where any hint of the miraculous or of actual divine intervention is scrupulously avoided. But his work is more rewarding than most eighteenth-century tragedy in the heroic or elevated mode. Schlegel's comedies also enjoyed considerable popularity. They even include a one-acter in verse, *Die stumme Schönheit* (The Silent Beauty, 1747). In 1740 Schlegel had published an essay defending the use of verse in comedy, against the preference of Gottsched and his followers for prose (*Ausgewählte Werke,* 408–24), but prose remained the norm for this genre. *Der geschäftige Müßiggänger* (The Busy Idler), published in Gottsched's

Schaubühne in 1743, is in the satirical mode favored by Gottsched; its central character embodies the folly indicated by the title, which is held up to ridicule. But in *Der Triumph der guten Frauen* (The Triumph of the Good Ladies, 1749) satire is largely abandoned for sentiment in the new style of comedy which had already made its appearance in England, in such plays as Steele's *The Conscious Lovers* (1722), and in France, with the *comédie larmoyante* (sentimental, or literally "tearful" comedy) of Nivelle de la Chaussée (1692–1754). Plays such as these were beginning to combine an enlightened optimism, a vision of social and familial harmony reflecting a wider, underlying belief in a world ordered by a benevolent providence, with a kind of sensibility that has been generally seen as characteristically "bourgeois" or "bürgerlich," and a style and setting involving some degree of what would later come to be called realism.

Comedy had traditionally drawn its characters from the middle ranks of society and shown them in contemporary, domestic situations, though a certain distance is often maintained by the use of standard neoclassical names (Alceste, Damis, Philinte and the like) alongside German ones. Now these "bourgeois" characters (the term is convenient, if notoriously imprecise) are presented no longer as ridiculous embodiments of folly, vice or antisocial behavior (hypochondria, avarice, or misogyny, for example), but as sympathetic or even admirable figures of social virtue. Thus, in Schlegel's play the "good ladies," Hilaria (disguised as a man, under the name Philinte) and Juliane cure their husbands, the faithless and flirtatious Nicander and the jealous and tyrannical Agenor, of their respective aberrations, and everything ends in happy reconciliation (even though the maid Cathrine skeptically observes: "Die geschwindesten Bekehrungen sind sonst nicht allemal die aufrichtigsten" [*Ausgewählte Werke*, 372; The quickest conversions are not always the most honest]). There is a lively intrigue whose conventional improbabilities — disguises, overhearings, and so on — the sympathetic spectator will willingly overlook, and there is some sharp and convincing dialogue, but there is little that is actually funny or comic in the traditional sense.

The same development can be seen in the comedies of Christian Fürchtegott Gellert (1715–69), the popular professor of poetry, rhetoric, and ethics at the University of Leipzig, whose moral fables and sentimental novel *Das Leben der schwedischen Gräfin von G**** (The Life of the Swedish Countess G***, 1747–48) also enjoyed great success in their day. If in *Die Betschwester* (The Pious Fraud, 1745), as the title indicates, satire predominates, in *Das Los in der Lotterie* (The Lottery Ticket, 1746) and *Die zärtlichen Schwestern* (The Affectionate Sisters, 1747) the emphasis has shifted to sentiment, even tears. In *Das Los* virtue is rewarded: Frau Damon's winning lottery ticket, purloined by her avaricious husband, finds its way back to its rightful owner, who can joyfully exclaim to her niece Carolinchen and the latter's exemplary fiancé Anton: "Sie werden sehen, wie wunderbar das

Schicksal die guten Absichten zu belohnen weis [....] Wenn diese Ehe nicht zärtlich wird: so wird es keine in der Welt" (you will see how miraculously fate contrives to reward good intentions [...] If this marriage does not prove truly affectionate, then no marriage in the world will).[10] But in *Die zärtlichen Schwestern,* where traditional comic satire has almost disappeared, virtue must, at least for one of the sisters, be its own reward. Julchen must learn to recognize that she truly loves her suitor Damis, and give up her mistaken notions of freedom and agree to marriage; but Lottchen must learn that her suitor Siegmund does not truly love her, for he switches his attentions to Julchen after he is mistakenly led to believe that she rather than Lottchen has inherited a valuable estate. One might perhaps expect a final scene of sentimental forgiveness, but no: Siegmund is banished, and Lottchen is forced to renounce her love: "Wie redlich habe ich ihn geliebt, und wie unglücklich bin ich durch die Liebe geworden! Doch nicht die Liebe, die Thorheit des Liebhabers hat mich unglücklich gemacht. Bedauern Sie mich" (*Lustspiele* 110; How honestly I loved him, and how unhappy I have become through love! But it is not love, it is my lover's folly that has made me unhappy. Give me your sympathy). The play thus ends on an almost tragic note;[11] comedy and tragedy, as traditionally understood, are drawing closer together. And if, in the sentimental comedy or "rührendes Lustspiel," contemporary "bourgeois" characters are presented no longer as ridiculous or contemptible, but as models of social virtue, in the middle-class "domestic tragedy" or "bürgerliches Trauerspiel" they are shown as worthy of the *aesthetic* dignity of a tragic fate.

Bourgeois Tragedy and Lessing's *Miß Sara Sampson*

The bourgeois tragedy has often been seen as an inherently unsatisfactory compromise, falling between the two stools of convincing realism and tragic stylization, and it is also often suggested that comedy was the more suitable vehicle for the optimistic worldview of the Enlightenment, for the events of tragedy are hard to reconcile with the Leibnizian-Wolffian-Gottschedian belief in a providentially ordered "best of all possible worlds." The abolition of the "Ständeklausel" (the "class clause," or the requirement that the characters of tragedy be persons of noble rank and consequence) and the adoption of prose dialogue in place of the hitherto universal Alexandrine were nevertheless epoch-making innovations in the history of the drama.

Although purists were inclined to attack the sentimental comedy — Gottsched actually suggested that these so-called comedies would be better designated "bürgerliche Trauerspiele"[12] — Gellert defended them in his inaugural lecture, *Pro comoedia commovente,* delivered in Latin at the University of Leipzig in 1751. In 1754 Lessing presented a German translation to the public in his periodical the *Theatralische Bibliothek*. In his introduction, Lessing comments briefly on the innovations affecting both comedy and tragedy in recent years. Comedy, he says, has risen a few degrees on the social (and emotional) scale, tragedy has fallen a few: the French have introduced the sentimental comedy, the English the bourgeois tragedy (cf. *Lessing* 4:12–13). Here, Lessing is thinking of such English examples as *The History of George Barnwell,* or *The London Merchant* (1731), by George Lillo (1693–1739), or *The Gamester* (1753) by Edward Moore (1712–57), both of which had been translated and successfully performed in Germany.[13]

In the following year Lessing himself established the genre in Germany with *Miß Sara Sampson*, first performed on 10 July 1755 in Frankfurt-on-Oder. His friend the poet Karl Wilhelm Ramler (1723–98) was present with him at the premiere and reported that the audience had "3 ½ Stunde zugehört, stille gesessen wie Statuen und geweint" (quoted in *Lessing* 2: 693; listened for three and a half hours, sat as still as statues, and wept). In this they were following the example of the stage figures, who, with the conspicuous exception of the villainess Marwood, are largely characterized by passivity and copious weeping. Despite this lachrymosity and the sentimental rhetoric with which the characters express themselves, however, occasional modern revivals have shown that the play has not entirely lost its power to move an audience, if no longer as demonstratively. Lessing subsequently maintained that "nur diese Tränen des Mitleids, und der sich fühlenden Menschlichkeit, sind die Absicht des Trauerspiels, oder es kann gar keine haben" (4: 144; only these tears of pity, and of feeling humanity, are the object of tragedy, or it can have none), and that *The London Merchant* was by this criterion far superior as a tragedy to Gottsched's *Sterbender Cato*. Lessing's *Miß Sara Sampson* is often said to be "modeled" on Lillo's play, but their plots are quite different, and Lessing's is much less of a simple cautionary tale. In this respect, although *Sara* undoubtedly set the fashion for bourgeois tragedy in Germany, it is somewhat untypical of the genre. With their greater emphasis on evil and retribution, the next German examples, *Lucie Woodvil* (1756) by Johann Gottlieb Benjamin Pfeil (1732–1800) and *Der Freigeist* (The Freethinker, or in the full eighteenth-century sense of the word, The Libertine, 1757) by the tragically short-lived Johann Wilhelm von Brawe (1738–1758) are both closer to Lillo's play in effect, and more characteristic of the general temper of eighteenth-century German tragedy.[14] Both plays follow Lessing (and Lillo) in the use of English names and settings, and of prose. Wieland's *Clementina von Porretta* (1760), which is more in the tearful vein, is set in Italy, but is a dramatization of an episode from an English novel, Samuel Richardson's *Sir Charles Grandison* (1754), which like all Richardson's novels enjoyed tremendous popularity in continental Europe.

In *Miß Sara Sampson,* much as in Richardson's novel *Clarissa Harlowe* (1747–48), an essentially virtuous heroine makes a single error — eloping with an untrustworthy lover — which proves to have fatal consequences. Her father, Sir William Sampson, sets out in pursuit of the lovers, determined not upon retribution but upon forgiveness and reconciliation, but arrives too late to save her from the murderous revenge of her lover Mellefont's discarded mistress Marwood. Interestingly enough, all the names, down to the appropriately named honest servant Waitwell, are borrowed from the *comedies* of the English dramatist William Congreve (1670–1729), and the setting, in an "elendem Wirtshause" (Lessing 2:11: a wretched inn), is one which hitherto would have been thought suitable only for comedy, if that: tragedy has indeed come several stages down in the world. Nevertheless, though the characters are no longer kings and princes but private individuals, they are still of fairly elevated rank: Sir William Sampson is a baronet — presumably a country squire — and Mellefont moves in fashionable (if dissipated) society, and introduces Marwood to Sara under the name of Lady Solmes. Marwood is the most active and therefore, in a sense, like Schlegel's Ulfo, the most interesting character in the play. The modern reader is also inclined to feel some sympathy for her in her situation — a single mother, abandoned by her lover in favor of a younger and more attractive woman — but there is little doubt that Lessing intends us to see her as the embodiment of selfishness and evil. Where the virtuous characters express their feelings by weeping, Marwood grimaces and gnashes her teeth (2: 83); persuading Mellefont, against his better judgment, to allow her to meet Sara, she first humiliates her rival, then poisons her. However, the dying Sara nobly forgives her murderess, and forbids her lover to seek revenge: "Marwood wird ihrem Schicksale nicht entgehen; aber weder Sie, noch mein Vater sollen ihre Ankläger werden. Ich sterbe, und vergeb' es der Hand, durch die mich Gott heimsucht" (2: 98; Marwood will not escape her fate; but neither you, nor my father shall be her accusers. I die, and forgive the hand through which God afflicts me); and when Mellefont stabs himself in remorse and despair, Sir William declares that "Er war mehr unglücklich, als lasterhaft" (2: 100; he was more unfortunate than vicious).

The note of forgiveness and reconciliation, sounded so strongly throughout *Miß Sara Sampson,* is absent from Pfeil's *Lucie Woodvil.* The orphan Lucie is pregnant by her lover Karl Southwell, but Karl's father Sir Willhelm [*sic*] is implacably opposed to their marriage. In desperation, and prompted by her unscrupulous maidservant Betty, Lucie poisons Sir Willhelm, only to discover, too late, the reason for his opposition — the fact that she is his own illegitimate daughter. She rushes offstage to stab first Betty, then herself, in both cases fatally, and Karl goes mad. All this has sprung from Sir Willhelm's guilty secret (which has been heavily hinted at throughout the play), and so a kind of poetic justice can be seen to operate; even so, the world depicted seems less the work of a benevolent providence than, as Karl describes it, an "elendes Gewebe von Unsinn und Bosheit"[15] (a wretched web of senselessness and wickedness). And in Brawe's *Freigeist,* evil seems triumphant. The feeble "hero" Clerdon (the weak, indecisive male protagonist is a standard feature of the genre) vacillates between the promptings of his true friend Granville, urging him to return to the paths of religion and virtue, and those of his secret enemy, the diabolical tempter Henley, a kind of bourgeois Iago hell-bent on Clerdon's destruction. Henley is victorious: Clerdon kills Granville, who forgives him with his dying breath, and then — on stage this time — kills Henley and himself; but Henley has, literally, the last word: "Ich sterbe! — Doch mein Feind stirbt mir zur Seiten — ich bin gerächt — o Triumph! o Rache!" (*Anfänge* 332: I die! — But my enemy dies beside me — I am avenged — o triumph! o revenge!). It could almost be a deliberate reversal of the humane optimism of Schlegel's *Orest und Pylades.*

Despite the success of *Miß Sara Sampson* and *Lucie Woodvil* (*Der Freigeist* had to wait some years for performance), heroic neoclassical tragedy was not yet dead. In 1755 Friedrich Nicolai, Berlin bookseller and publicist, friend of Lessing and tireless promoter of Enlightenment values of a rather narrowly rationalistic stamp, offered in his periodical *Bibliothek der schönen Wissenschaften und der freyen Künste* (Library of the Polite Sciences and Liberal Arts), a prize for the best new German tragedy. Brawe submitted *Der Freigeist,* but unsurprisingly, given Nicolai's conservative taste, the prize went to a heroic tragedy, *Codrus,* by another young dramatist who, like Brawe, died at a tragically early age a mere two years later, Johann Friedrich von Cronegk (1731–1757). *Codrus* tells the story of the legendary last king of Athens, who sacrifices himself in fulfillment of a prophecy that his death will save his city from the invading Dorians. *Codrus* is by modern standards a tedious piece, but it enjoyed some success on stage, as did Cronegk's second tragedy, *Olint und Sophronia,* a Christian martyr tragedy set at the time of the Crusades. Cronegk died before finishing this work, and it was completed by the Viennese writer Cassian Anton von Roschmann-Hörburg (1739–1806) in 1764; it was in Roschmann's version that *Olint und Sophronia* was chosen for the opening of the Hamburg Nationaltheater three years later. Brawe did manage to complete his second tragedy, *Brutus,* this time in the heroic mode, yet remarkable for being written neither in Alexandrines nor in prose, but in the unrhymed iambic pentameter or "blank verse" of the English drama. Wieland also adopted blank verse for his historical tragedy *Lady Johanna Gray,* adapted from *Lady Jane Gray* (1715) by the English dramatist and poet laureate Nicholas Rowe (1674–1718); this work achieved the distinction of being the first play in blank verse to be performed in a German-speaking theater when it was staged in Zurich in 1758. Brawe's *Brutus* had to wait until 1770 for its first and apparently its only performance, in Vienna; the public (and probably the actors) were not yet ready for what only a few years later was to establish itself as the standard verse-form of classical drama in German.

Christian Felix Weisse

The most prolific and successful tragedian of the generation, however, was undoubtedly Christian Felix Weisse (1726–1804). His best-remembered work is probably *Richard III* (1759), if only due to Lessing's adverse criticism in the *Hamburgische Dramaturgie* — despite which the play remained a favorite until the last years of the century. After *Rosemunde* (1761, set in sixth-century Italy), Weisse abandoned Alexandrines for blank verse in *Die Befreiung von Theben* (The Liberation of Thebes, 1764) — though this play appears never to have been performed — and in his last verse tragedy, *Atreus und Thyest* (1766), staged in Leipzig in 1769; he then turned to prose in *Romeo und Julie* (1767), freely adapted from Shakespeare, and *Jean Calas* (1774), on that recent, notorious miscarriage of justice which had aroused such widespread sympathy and indignation throughout Europe, and provoked Voltaire to his campaign against the "infamy" of the Catholic Church. Weisse was also a successful writer of comedies and *Singspiele* (plays with spoken dialogue and musical numbers, the forerunners of Mozart's German operas and Beethoven's *Fidelio*),[16] but, thanks probably to Lessing's strictures, these have been almost totally neglected by subsequent critics.[17]

The polarization of good and evil characters we have observed in Schlegel's tragedies and in the bourgeois tragedy is even more pronounced in the work of these dramatists. Cronegk's Codrus and Olint, Brawe's Brutus, and Wieland's Lady Johanna Gray are full of noble sentiments, devoted and ultimately willing, even eager, to sacrifice themselves for some heroic idea, be it patriotism, religion, duty, or in the most abstract and general sense "virtue" (the word "Tugend" itself is uttered with monotonous frequency). Weisse, on the other hand (personally the mildest of men, enjoying an exemplary family life and a respectable professional career as a taxcollector), was fascinated by the dramatic potential of evil, and, particularly in his *Richard III*, Queen Rosemunde, and Atreus, created flamboyantly villainous protagonists who revel in vengeance and murder. All these tragedies continue to observe the neoclassical unities, more or less strictly, as indeed do the bourgeois tragedies of Lessing and his followers. The result (as in Schlegel) is a general sacrifice of plausibility: characters come and go often for no good reason, simply to observe the unity of place or the *liaison des scènes*, and themselves call attention to the unlikely scene of action or to the fact that the action is beginning at an improbably early hour of the morning, so as not to overstep the unity of time. *Richard III*, for example, is set entirely within the Tower of London, beginning "when scarce the youthful day is breaking through the dark" (*Lessings Jugendfreunde*, 6), but with Richmond's army only a day's march away. Action is banished off stage, though we hear the screams of the murdered princes and Richard subsequently enters brandishing a bloody dagger, and the final act is a prolonged sequence of lamentation over the horrors of the murder, on the part of the female characters and Lord Stanley, scarcely mitigated by the news of Richard's defeat and death at the hands of Richmond. In the original version of the play Richmond himself does not appear, a defect Weisse remedied in a subsequent revision.[18]

As Lessing observed, Weisse has completely sacrificed the broad historical panorama of Shakespeare's *Richard III* in favor of a private, personal tragedy in the French manner. Weisse claimed in fact not to have studied Shakespeare's play before writing his own, though the dream of his murdered victims which Richard recounts in the opening scene resembles that of Shakespeare's Richard on the eve of the battle of Bosworth (Weisse does not let us see the ghosts for ourselves), and the scene in act 3 in which Richard pays court to Princess Elizabeth (a character who does not appear on stage in Shakespeare's play, but who has an important part in Weisse's) strongly recalls the wooing of Lady Anne by Shakespeare's Richard.

Lessing: Theory and Experiment, 1756–60

Lessing, his own practice in *Miß Sara Sampson* notwithstanding, strongly criticized the portrayal of extremes of virtue and vice in heroic tragedy. In correspondence with Nicolai and his other Berlin friend, the great Jewish philosopher Moses Mendelssohn, he describes the stoic protagonists of heroic tragedy as "schöne Ungeheuer" (4: 173; beautiful monsters); in his *Literaturbriefe* of 1759 the characters of Wieland's *Lady Johanna Gray* are sarcastically, and rather unfairly, dismissed as "ein liebes frommes Mädchen . . . ein lieber frommer Vater . . . ein lieber frommer Gemahl . . . eine liebe fromme — ich weiß selbst nicht was" (5: 206; a dear, pious girl . . . a dear, pious father . . . a dear, pious husband . . . a dear, pious — I really don't know what). In the opening pages of the *Hamburgische Dramaturgie* (1767), Lessing is similarly unmoved by the Christian martyrs of *Olint und Sophronia* who "[halten] gemartert werden und sterben, für ein Glas Wasser trinken" (4: 237; think no more of being tortured and dying than of drinking a glass of water). Characters such as these cannot truly engage our sympathy. But he is even more critical of Weisse's Richard, who is "unstreitig das größte, abscheulichste Ungeheuer, das jemals die Bühne getragen. Ich sage, die Bühne: daß es die Erde wirklich getragen habe, daran zweifle ich" (4:

574; indisputably the greatest, most abominable monster that the stage has ever borne. I say, the stage: that the earth ever bore it, I doubt) — and of the undeserved suffering of his innocent victims. The portrayal of such rampant evil can only cast doubt on the goodness of divine providence, which it is the dramatist's duty to make manifest:

> Das Ganze dieses sterblichen Schöpfers sollte ein Schattenriß von dem Ganzen des ewigen Schöpfers sein; sollte uns an den Gedanken gewöhnen, wie sich in ihm alles zum Besten auflöse, werde es auch in jenem geschehen. (4: 598)
>
> [The whole created by this mortal creator should be an image of the whole created by the eternal Creator; should accustom us to the thought that just as in the one everything is resolved for the best, so it is in the other.]

Lessing begins to set out his theory of tragedy (which never attained the form of a complete and coherent treatise) in correspondence with his Berlin friends Mendelssohn and Nicolai in 1756–57.[19] Lessing's arguments can be seen to a large extent as a vindication of the bourgeois tragedy as represented by *Miß Sara Sampson,* but the correspondence ranges widely, touching upon the correct interpretation of key terms in Aristotle's doctrine of tragedy — the "pity and fear" and "purgation" or "purification" (*eleos, phobos, katharsis*) of the *Poetics* — and drawing on examples from both ancient (Greek) and modern tragedy. From the beginning, Lessing is implacably opposed to the heroic mode of tragedy favored by his friends, and to the sentiment of "admiration" it sought to arouse in its audience. The plays themselves spell out the message: thus, the last line of *Codrus* tells us that his death demands no tears, but begs for admiration (Cronegk, *Schriften* 1: 226: "Sein Tod will nicht beweint, er will bewundert seyn"). Lessing, however, insists that true tragedy seeks to arouse only tears of pity, and that it thereby fulfills the moral purpose that he, like most writers of the period, unquestioningly accepts that it must have.[20] Nicolai, apparently less conservative in this respect, held that tragedy should only seek to arouse strong passions; any moral effect could only be secondary, and the Gottschedian insistence on a specific moral lesson, or the supposedly Aristotelian doctrine that tragedy sought "die Leidenschaften zu reinigen oder die Sitten zu bilden" (4: 156; to purify the passions or to improve morality) was responsible for the poor quality of most German tragedy. Lessing agrees that a tragedy need not seek to inculcate a particular lesson, but holds that the arousal of pity in the audience is itself morally improving:

> *Der mitleidigste Mensch ist der beste Mensch,* zu allen gesellschaftlichen Tugenden, zu allen Arten der Großmut der aufgelegteste. Wer uns also mitleidig macht, macht uns besser und tugendhafter, und das Trauer-

spiel, das jenes tut, tut auch dieses, oder — es tut jenes, um dieses tun zu können. (4:163; letter to Nicolai, November 1756)

[*The most compassionate man is the best man,* the most disposed to all social virtues, to all kinds of magnanimity. Therefore, whoever makes us compassionate, makes us better and more virtuous, and tragedy, which does the one, also does the other, or — it does the one, in order to do the other (Lessing's emphasis).]

To this end, the tragic protagonist must of course be a virtuous person, but not unfeeling or stoically impassive, like Gottsched's Cato or Schlegel's Canut; and he or she must have committed some error or fault, some *hamartia* as Aristotle had called it, so that "sein Character und sein Unglück [ein] *Ganzes* ausmachen" (4:192; his character and his misfortune add up to a whole). Sara's elopement would fall under this description.

About this time, Lessing also encountered the dramatic works of the French *encyclopédiste* Denis Diderot (1713–84), who by example and precept was challenging the established neoclassical style, calling for new dramatic forms to bridge the gap between comedy and tragedy, and employing a much more realistic manner of presentation. Lessing promptly set to work translating Diderot's work into German, and *Das Theater des Herrn Diderot* appeared in 1760. This first edition appeared anonymously, but in a second edition, published in 1780, Lessing acknowledged his authorship and the influence Diderot had on his own work.[21] The nature and extent of this influence has been much disputed, but it would seem that Lessing found in Diderot confirmation of the move that he had made in *Miß Sara Sampson,* replacing heroic neoclassical tragedy with a new, more realistic form of serious, contemporary bourgeois drama.

In the late 1750s, however, Lessing was also experimenting with other possibilities for tragedy, employing a variety of settings, classical and exotic, and of styles, including blank verse. He even attempted a tragedy on the old German story of Doctor Faust, and published a fragment of it in the famous seventeenth *Literaturbrief* of 1759.[22] It is in this essay that he denounces Gottsched's reforms and declares that, left to itself, the Germans' taste in drama would much more closely resemble that of the English than of the French. But the only one of these experiments to reach completion, the brief one-act tragedy *Philotas* (1759), although it retains the prose of *Miß Sara Sampson,* reverts to ancient Greek characters and setting, though the story is apparently Lessing's own invention. It appeared in the middle of the Seven Years' War (1756–1763), in which Prussia under its king Friedrich II (Frederick "the Great") faced a formidable coalition led by Austria under the Archduchess Maria Theresia. The war gave rise to a great outburst of patriotic feeling in Prussia and in the Protestant states of Germany in general, and *Philotas* was generally taken to be a celebration of patriotic self-sacrifice in the spirit of Cronegk's *Codrus:* the young prince Philotas, captured by the enemy king Aridäus, restores (as he believes) his lost honor and the military fortunes of his country by killing himself. But it is now generally agreed that Philotas's suicide is seen by Lessing not as a noble deed like that of Codrus, but, as Aridäus declares, as an act of tragic folly, of "wütende Schwermut" (2:124; raging melancholy), the senseless squandering of a young life full of promise. A number of productions of the play (hitherto rarely performed) in recent years have also interpreted it in this light. Lessing could hardly remain untouched by the war, and served in a non-combatant capacity as secretary to General Tauentzien, commander of the Prussian forces in Silesia. But he wrote on 14 February 1759 to the poet Gleim, Prussian patriot and author of popular verses in ballad style celebrating Friedrich's campaigns, that he regarded patriotism as "a heroic weakness that I am very happy not to share."[23] It was allegedly Lessing who read out the proclamation of peace in Breslau (now Wrocław, in Poland) in 1763; the story is unsubstantiated, but has the ring of truth.

Minna von Barnhelm

Lessing's next completed play was one which Goethe would describe as "the truest product" of the Seven Years' War and as a work based on real life and on specific historic events, and as such one that had an immense impact.[24] The play was not a tragedy of war, but a comedy of peacemaking — his most successful and still most frequently revived play, the comedy *Minna von Barnhelm*.

Lessing had begun his playwriting career as a student in Leipzig with half-a-dozen comedies, one of which, *Der junge Gelehrte* (The Young Scholar), had been staged by Frau Neuber in January 1748. These apprentice comedies, as one may call them, run the gamut of available comic styles, from satire to sentiment, as they had been established by the Gottscheds and extended by Schlegel and Gellert. They are similarly set in a recognizable but unspecific contemporary, bourgeois German milieu, but their characters bear the familiar distancing mixture of neoclassical and German names, the latter generally reserved for women and servants. In *Minna von Barnhelm,* however, everything is specific. The action takes place in the (unnamed, but unmistakable) Prussian capital, Berlin, in the immediate aftermath of the Seven Years' War. Hero and heroine are respectively a Prussian officer, Major von Tellheim, and a Saxon heiress, Minna von Barnhelm (both, we notice, of aristocratic rather than bourgeois rank) — Prussia and Saxony having been on opposite sides in the war, and Saxony subject to a harsh Prussian occupation. The principal male characters all wear the blue uniform of the Prussian army, and manifest that Prussian rigidity which can be admirable in its concern for dignity and honor, but can too easily be taken to excess: as the maid Franziska tells Tellheim, in his uniform and boots he looks "gar zu brav, gar zu preußisch" (1:661; far too upright, far too Prussian). Tellheim's noble and generous treatment of the conquered Saxons has earned him Minna's love, but also the suspicion of the Prussian authorities, who have accused him of corruption. Disgraced and impoverished, too proud to accept the help of his willing friends, Tellheim believes that he can no longer marry Minna, but she refuses to give him up. What ensues is in fact a comedy of intrigue, with mutual deceptions and misunderstandings leading almost to the brink of disaster, before all is resolved by the convenient arrival of a letter from the Prussian king announcing Tellheim's rehabilitation, and of Minna's uncle, Count von Bruchsall, to set the seal on their engagement. These developments are paralleled by the less complicated whirlwind romance of their subordinates, Minna's pert maid Franziska Willig and Tellheim's doughty sergeant-major Paul Werner (it is again significant that even the subordinate characters have *surnames*). Providence is truly benevolent: as in Gellert's *Das Los in der Lotterie,* we are invited to observe "wie wunderbar das Schicksal die guten Absichten zu belohnen weiß" (cf. above, pp. 151–52). The action is in fact highly conventional, even artificial, but the grounding of characters and situation in a precise contemporary reality offers an unprecedented illusion of solidity and gives the play, paradoxically, a more lasting, even universal appeal than those of Lessing's predecessors, which now seem irretrievably of their own time. The double betrothal of Prussian and Saxon further adds a note of patriotic appeal — not of martial heroism but of pacific reconciliation. The scenes between Minna and Tellheim are emotionally highly charged, as Minna's love beats against the rock of Tellheim's pride, but there is also broad comedy in the opening scene between Tellheim's curmudgeonly servant Just and the obsequious landlord of the inn where the action is set, and in act 3, where there is a show-stopping scene featuring a vain and foolish Frenchman who mangles the German language: the whole play is both more genuinely serious and more genuinely comic than any of its predecessors. The dialogue throughout is supple and lively, worlds away from the rhetoric of *Sara* and *Philotas,* and Lessing seems totally at ease with his material and his technique.

The Hamburg Nationaltheater and Lessing's Hamburgische Dramaturgie

Lessing began *Minna von Barnhelm* in 1763, in the immediate aftermath of the war, and the title page proclaims the play to have been completed in that year, but in fact it was shelved in favor of other projects and not completed until four years later, when it was to prove the most successful production of the Hamburg Nationaltheater. This short-lived enterprise (it was commonly referred to as the "Hamburger Entreprise") was the result of an initiative by a group of private citizens, led by a minor writer, Johann Heinrich Löwen (1727–71). Löwen and others had long advocated the establishment of publicly subsidized theaters in Germany, which would raise standards by freeing the drama from the vagaries of uninformed public taste, would educate the public in turn and, above all, present plays in German (not in French or Italian as was done at court theaters) and thus encourage the growth of native playwriting talent. But to achieve all this would mean appealing for support to the German princes, most of whom, notably Frederick the Great of Prussia, while happy to patronize German painters, architects and musicians, were indifferent or hostile to German literature and drama. One notable exception was Duke Christian Ludwig II of Mecklenburg-Schwerin, who in 1751 appointed J. F. Schönemann and his troupe as official court players (*Hofschauspieler*); and in Schwerin Konrad Ekhof (1720–78), the greatest German actor of his day, established an academy for actors designed to improve both professional standards and the social standing of the players, who were still all too often regarded as social pariahs. Löwen was encouraged by the example of Schwerin, not least because he was married to Schönemann's daughter, and also by the posthumous publication in 1764 of Schlegel's essays, *Schreiben von Errichtung eines Theaters in Kopenhagen* (Letter on the Establishment of a Theater in Copenhagen, *Ausgewählte Werke* 553–58) and *Gedanken zur Aufnahme des dänischen Theaters* (Thoughts Toward the Improvement of the Danish Theater, *Ausgewählte Werke* 559–85). King Frederik V (1746–66) had brought new encouragement to the arts, especially the theater, which had been suppressed under his pietistic predecessor Christian VI. Löwen reiterated Schlegel's proposals in his *Geschichte des deutschen Theaters* (History of the German Theater, 1766), calling again for recognition of the theater as a civic institution, subsidized and strictly controlled by the state; it is in this work that he first uses the term "Nationaltheater." He still seems to have hoped, against all evidence, to touch the conscience of the King of Prussia, but when the opportunity arose to create something along the lines he wanted in Hamburg, he decided to take his chance.

The actor-manager Konrad Ackermann had built a theater just off the Gänsemarkt (the "Goosemarket," where Lessing's statue now stands), but was in financial difficulties. Hamburg was, after Vienna and Berlin, the third largest city in the German-speaking world, with over 90,000 inhabitants at the time. It was also a Free Imperial City with a republican, if by no means democratic, constitution, subject to no territorial prince, but governed by a Senate selected from among its own citizens. The Hamburg Nationaltheater would therefore be a bourgeois institution in the truest sense of the word. It would not, however, be publicly subsidized but dependent on private capital, for the Senate remained as indifferent to the arts as the princes. Löwen found a group of private citizens willing to support his venture, and a consortium was set up to take over the theater from Ackermann. However, none of the members possessed any actual theatrical expertise, and Ackermann remained in practical control. This would soon prove a source of trouble, as Ackermann was already the object of jealous intrigues on the part of several members of his company.

The Nationaltheater opened officially on 22 April 1767 with *Olint and Sophronia:* a curious choice, one might think, but one that reflects the continuing status of heroic tragedy as the most prestigious of dramatic genres. Within months, however, the enterprise began to founder. Several reasons have been adduced for this. Löwen himself has been saddled with much of the blame, perhaps unfairly, as a well-meaning literary intellectual with no real understanding either of the theater or of business.[25] The venture rested on shaky foundations. Official public support — a key feature of Löwen's scheme as originally conceived — was lacking. Nor were the members of the consortium among the leading business names of the city; one or two of them indeed had shady financial pasts, and they could not command the necessary credit. Faction and intrigue continued, and the hoped-for new playwriting talent failed to appear — Löwen had originally proposed that a prize be offered annually for the best new play, but this was never implemented, and the repertory remained dominated by French plays and plays in the French style. The success of *Minna von Barnhelm*, outstanding though it was, achieving more performances than any other single play, came too late to save the venture, and within two years the "Enterprise" had failed and Ackermann resumed full formal control. But although the Hamburg venture was, on the face of things, a failure, it was a not unworthy attempt to achieve a worthy goal, and we owe to it not only the completion and first production of *Minna von Barnhelm*, but also the production of Lessing's most sustained and substantial work of dramatic criticism, the *Hamburgische Dramaturgie*.

One might well add that we owe to it the very form of the *Dramaturgie*, for the *Dramaturgie* is not a systematic treatise, but takes its shape from that of the theatrical repertory, even if commentary on individual plays soon gives way to general reflections of an increasingly theoretical nature. Lessing was engaged by the Nationaltheater to produce a twice-weekly "critical register" of the productions, but soon Lessing's criticisms began to lag weeks, then months behind the actual performances; the actors and not least the redoubtable leading lady Sophie Hensel complained; a pirated edition appeared in Leipzig, causing Lessing first to suspend, then to abandon serial publication. The last parts appeared at Easter 1769, after the Nationaltheater had formally ceased to exist; but the fiction of twice-weekly serial publication in individual dated numbers ("Stücke") is maintained to the end, providing a convenient means of reference to what, as Lessing himself points out, is "nichts weniger, als ein dramatisches System"[26] (anything but a dramatic system). Lessing soon realized that the enterprise lacked sound foundations. His letters of the time to friends such as Nicolai reveal his increasing disillusionment, and in the final numbers he openly expresses his bitter disappointment, particularly at the failure of what for him must have been the most important of Löwen's hopes, the fostering of new German playwriting talent:

> Über den gutherzigen Einfall, den Deutschen ein Nationaltheater zu verschaffen, da wir Deutsche noch keine Nation sind! Ich rede nicht von der politischen Verfassung, sondern bloß von dem sittlichen Charakter. Fast sollte man sagen, dieser sei: keinen eigenen haben zu wollen. Wir sind noch immer die geschwornen Nachahmer alles Ausländischen, besonders noch immer die untertänigen Bewunderer der nie genug bewunderten Franzosen. (4:698)

> [What a generous notion, to create a National Theater for the Germans, when we Germans are not yet a nation! I am not speaking of the political constitution, but merely of our moral character. One might almost say that this consists in not wanting to have one of our own. We are still the sworn imitators of everything foreign, still especially the humble admirers of the never sufficiently admired French.]

Lessing is harsh in his criticism of the French and what he had in the seventeenth *Literaturbrief* called the "Frenchified" ("französierend," 5:71) German theater. His strictures on the plays of Cronegk and Weisse have already been mentioned. Voltaire, the dramatist most frequently performed at the Nationaltheater, is repeatedly attacked, and his understanding of human character is compared unfavorably with that of Shakespeare (Nos. 11, 15). But Lessing's previous enthusiasm for the English style of drama, with its complexity and variety, has now abated: "die englische Manier in diesem Punkte, zerstreuet und ermüdet uns" (No. 13, 4:288; the English style we find in this respect distracting and wearisome), and Lessing also rejects the Shakespearian mixture of genres, the "komische Tragödie, gotischer Erfindung" (No. 70, 4:557; the comic tragedy, of Gothic invention). The great villain of the *Dramaturgie*, however, is Corneille, who is castigated for the unnatural plot and characters of his *Rodogune* (Nos. 29–32) and above all, as critic and commentator, for his presumption in departing from the true doctrine of tragedy, as laid down for all time, as Lessing now proclaims, by Aristotle. Developing and refining the theory of tragic pity first set out in his correspondence with Mendelssohn and Nicolai, Lessing now maintains with grand rhetorical flourish that "die Tragödie, mit einem Worte, ein Gedicht ist, welches Mitleid erreget" (No. 77, 4:588; tragedy is, in a word, a poem that excites compassion). And whereas in the correspondence Lessing and his friends had agreed in rejecting the notion of *katharsis* ("Reinigung"),[27] he now insists that by this Aristotle had meant nothing other than the "Verwandlung der Leidenschaften in tugendhafte Fertigkeiten" (No. 78, 4:595; the transformation of passions into virtuous behavior), which, his faith in the necessary moral function of tragedy unshaken, he envisages as the true goal of the tragedian's art. It is for this detailed exegesis of Aristotle's doctrine of tragedy that the *Dramaturgie* is perhaps most renowned, though critics remain divided on whether Lessing is correct in his interpretation, or is merely claiming Aristotelian authority for his own independently formulated theory, one which moreover bears the stamp of eighteenth-century sensibility and which Aristotle himself would have found quite alien.[28] Whatever the truth of this, it is noteworthy that whereas Corneille — and indeed Lessing himself on an earlier occasion — could frankly admit departure from Aristotelian authority, Lessing now finds it necessary to insist on the infallible and timeless validity of the Aristotelian tradition.

He also seeks to reconcile the theories of Aristotle and his old ally Diderot; for despite his hostility to the drama of Corneille and Voltaire, which has been stressed by generations of patriotic German critics, Lessing praises Diderot's sentimental comedy *Le Père de famille*, and while criticizing Diderot's theories in certain respects, he clearly regards Diderot's bourgeois realism as the most, if not the only, promising development of dramatic art in his own time. Lessing also commends the bourgeois tragedy in connection with a performance of his own *Miß Sara Sampson,* in which Madame Hensel as Sara (it was one of her favorite roles) "starb ungemein anständig" (No. 13. 4:293; died with exceptional propriety). And in his condemnation of Weisse's Richard, Lessing maintains that Aristotle himself held that the tragic hero must be portrayed as "mit uns von gleichem Schrot und Korne" (No. 75, 4:580–81; of the very same stuff as ourselves), though this refers to a sense of common humanity rather than to social equality as such.

Deeply disillusioned with the failure of the "Enterprise" and, so he claimed, with the theater altogether, Lessing left Hamburg in April 1770 to take up appointment as librarian to the Duke of Braunschweig-Wolfenbüttel. He remained in this post for the rest of his life, despite further disappointments and frustrations, and despite offers of engagement in Mannheim and Vienna, where attempts were again being made to establish national theaters. These met with slightly better success — the Palatine Nationaltheater in Mannheim bears that name to the present day, and the Burgtheater in Vienna was to become the foremost German-speaking theater in the early years of the nineteenth century — but Lessing felt, as he wrote to his brother in May 1777, that "Mit einem deutschen Nationaltheater ist es lauter Wind" (talk of a German National Theater is so much hot air).[29] But he was still to produce two more dramatic masterpieces, the tragedy *Emilia Galotti,* the greatest if most problematic of his bourgeois dramas, in 1772, and the "dramatisches Gedicht," the blank verse parable play *Nathan der Weise*, in 1779, two years before his death at the age of fifty-two.

Emilia Galotti

Both these works go back to plans made some years earlier, in the case of *Emilia Galotti* in that earlier period of experiments in tragedy, the late 1750s. On 21 January 1758 he wrote to Nicolai that he was planning "eine bürgerliche Virginia" (a bourgeois Virginia), a modernized and, so he claimed, "de-politicized" version of the old Roman story of the plebeian Virginius, who had killed his daughter with a butcher's knife (the only weapon at hand) rather than see her carried off as a slave by the tyrant Appius Claudius. Nothing came of this at the time; Lessing took it up again in Hamburg, but failed to complete it; he finally returned to it in 1771 in Wolfenbüttel. The finished play was performed in Braunschweig on 13 March 1772 in the presence of the Duke and Duchess, and published and reprinted three times in the same year. Lessing stayed away from the premiere, pleading toothache, and never saw the play performed. But contemporaries felt that here, at last, was a German tragedy that could stand comparison with the best work of other nations. Lessing's friend Johann Arnold Ebert (1723–1795, Professor at the Caroline Academy in Braunschweig) hailed him as a German Shakespeare (*Lessing* 2:709). Goethe was more reserved in his judgment, but his own tragic hero Werther has *Emilia Galotti* lying open on his desk when he commits suicide.[30]

Like *Miß Sara Sampson*, *Emilia Galotti* deals with the fate of a young woman, on the threshold of life and sexual awakening, who leaves — in this case, is forcibly removed from — her paternal home and the security of traditional familial and moral values it represents, and is thus exposed to a dangerous wider world of instability, passion, selfish desires, and revenge. The play is set in Italy, but Lessing's petty Italian absolutist state could stand for any number of contemporary German ones, even Braunschweig-Wolfenbüttel itself. Emilia, daughter of Colonel Odoardo Galotti and fiancée of Count Appiani, arouses the desire of the ruling Prince. The Prince's unscrupulous henchman Marinelli has Appiani assassinated and Emilia abducted to the Prince's country retreat. Odoardo arrives, but is seemingly powerless to remove her from the Prince's power. She declares that she would rather die than remain at the mercy of her would-be seducer. With a dagger thrust into his hands by Countess Orsina, the Prince's discarded mistress — who hopes that Odoardo will act as the instrument of her revenge by killing the Prince — he stabs his daughter in the heart. The Prince, like Aridäus in *Philotas*, is horrified:

DER PRINZ. Grausamer Vater, was haben Sie getan?
ODOARDO. Eine Rose gebrochen, ehe der Sturm sie entblättert.
— War es nicht so, meine Tochter?
EMILIA. Nicht Sie, mein Vater — Ich selbst — ich selbst —
(2: 204)
[THE PRINCE. Cruel father, what have you done?
ODOARDO. Plucked a rose before the storm stripped its petals. —
Was it not so, my daughter?
EMILIA. Not you, my father — I myself — I myself —]

The disposition of the principal characters — father, daughter, lover, ex-mistress — closely resembles that of *Miß Sara Sampson,* though new figures are added, notably the heroine's mother and fiancé. The main divergence from the earlier play, however, is that the moral conflict between virtue and vice is in *Emilia Galotti* at the same time a social, even a political conflict. The would-be seducer is the highest authority in the land, with the power of life and death over his subjects, as we are forcibly reminded by the exchange between the Prince and his minister, Camillo Rota, at the end of act 1:

DER PRINZ. Was ist sonst? Etwas zu unterschreiben?
CAMILLO ROTA. Ein Todesurteil wäre zu unterschreiben.
DER PRINZ. Recht gern. — Nur her! geschwind.
CAMILLO ROTA *(stutzig und den Prinzen starr ansehend).*
Ein Todesurteil, sagt' ich.
DER PRINZ. Ich höre ja wohl. — Es könnte schon geschehen sein.
Ich bin eilig. (2: 142)
[THE PRINCE. What else is there? Anything to sign?
CAMILLO ROTA. There is a death sentence to sign.
THE PRINCE. Yes, gladly. — Just let me have it, quickly.
CAMILLO ROTA. *(taken aback, and staring fixedly at the Prince):*
A death sentence, I said.
THE PRINCE. Yes, I heard you. — I could have done it by now.
I am in a hurry.]

Like the principals of Lessing's earlier bourgeois dramas, the Galottis are not exactly "middle class" (the completed play is, incidentally, not designated "bürgerliches Trauerspiel" by Lessing), but they are not technically of the nobility and cannot ultimately resist the Prince, and Count Appiani is disposed of so that he cannot come to his fiancée's assistance. It is unsurprising that, from the time of the play's first appearance, many have been unwilling to accept Lessing's repeated assurance that his treatment of the Roman source was "von allem Staatsinteresse befreit" (free of all political interest).[31] In the original story, as recounted in Livy's history of Rome and treated by a number of modern European dramatists, Virginius's killing of his daughter had been the signal for a popular uprising leading to the overthrow of the tyrant. Nothing of the kind happens here: the Prince banishes his evil counselor Marinelli, but he himself remains in power, and Odoardo gives himself up to the Prince's justice. The only hint of possible rebellion occurs in act 3, when Claudia Galotti, Emilia's mother, arrives in search of her daughter with a crowd of people in support, but a word from Marinelli suffices to disperse them: "Zurück da! ihr!" (2: 171; Back there, you!). Their threatened appearance may constitute a suggestion of what might happen if the Prince does not mend his ways; but even this is a reading perhaps colored by post-French Revolution hindsight.

Other considerations prevent a too simple reading of the play in terms of class conflict. Emilia, dimly aware of her own sexual awakening, is undoubtedly in some degree (as Goethe was the first to suggest) attracted to the Prince, even over the dead body of her worthy but sexually unexciting fiancé. What finally provokes Odoardo into striking the fatal blow is her confession to her father that "Ich habe Blut, mein Vater; so jugendliches, so warmes Blut, als eine. Auch meine Sinne, sind Sinne. Ich stehe für nichts" (2:202; I have blood, father, blood as youthful and warm as any woman's. My senses too are senses. I can answer for nothing) and her own appeal to the example of Virginius. Critical disagreement over this conclusion is unabating: is Emilia's virtual suicide to be welcomed as a liberation, *admired* even as an act of self-assertion or even of sublime self-transcendence, or is it to be regarded like the suicide of Philotas as an act of "wütende Schwermut" (raging melancholy)?

Controversy also surrounds the portrayal, in this play and bourgeois tragedy in general, of the bourgeois family and of the value system it supposedly embodies. Seen traditionally as the exemplification of the values of Enlightenment and sensibility, and as a model of ideal social relations in miniature,[32] the patriarchal bourgeois family has more recently come under attack, particularly from feminist critics, as an oppressive institution devoted to the repression and marginalization of women.[33] Lessing does not idealize the Galotti family — the blustering, puritanical father, the wife whom he dismisses (perhaps not entirely fairly) as an "eitle, törichte Mutter" (2: 149; vain, foolish mother) — nor the in many ways admirable, but morose and melancholic Appiani whom they consider an ideal match for their daughter, no doubt in part for the social advancement they hope it will bring them. Lessing had portrayed an ideal father-figure in the loving, forgiving Sir William Sampson, who "würde lieber von einer lasterhaften Tochter, als von keiner, geliebt sein wollen" (2:12; would rather be loved by a depraved daughter than by none at all); Odoardo Galotti seems originally to have been conceived as a deliberate antitype — the father who kills his daughter because, as Lessing had written to Nicolai, "ihre Tugend [ihm] werter ist, als ihr Leben" (2: 202: her virtue is worth more to him than her life). But at the end of the play he at last gains a kind of pathetic dignity, almost as much a tragic victim as Emilia herself. In the course of its long genesis *Emilia Galotti* has (not unlike *Canut* in this respect) outgrown its author's intentions, and gained thereby a tantalizing ambiguity — which does not make it a less successful tragedy, but a more truly modern one.

Nathan der Weise

Nathan der Weise is also a family drama, but it is at least in externals far removed from bourgeois realism. It is a sublime comedy of mistaken identities, with all the improbable revelations and coincidences that implies, set in Jerusalem at the time of the Crusades (the scene also of *Olint und Sophronia,* which Lessing had criticized so severely for its Christian bias). A Jewish girl, the foster-daughter of the wise merchant Nathan, and a Christian Knight Templar discover that they are in fact brother and sister, and the children of the Muslim Sultan Saladin's long-lost brother. The play grew out of the theological controversies in which Lessing became increasingly embroiled in the 1770s; indeed it owes its completion to the censorship which put a stop to the increasingly ferocious war of words Lessing was waging against various representatives of Lutheran orthodoxy, in particular Pastor Goeze of Hamburg. Forbidden to engage in further direct theological polemic, Lessing turned, as he said, to "meiner alten Kanzel, . . . dem Theater" (2:719; my old pulpit, the stage). But he assured his brother Karl that "Es wird nichts weniger, als ein satirisches Stück, um den Kampfplatz mit Hohngelächter zu verlassen. Es wird ein so rührendes Stück, als ich nur immer gemacht habe" (2: 719; It will be in no way a satirical piece, designed to leave the field of battle with scornful laughter. It will be as touching a piece as I have ever composed), and the conclusion is indeed not so far in spirit from the comedies of Schlegel, Gellert, and Diderot. There is good-humored satire in the play, directed chiefly at its Christian characters: the brusque, hot-headed Templar (referred to at one point as a "deutscher Bär": [2: 234; a German bear]), Recha's well-meaning but bigoted Christian nurse Daja, even the "fromm[e] Einfalt" (2:316; *sancta simplicitas*) of the Lay Brother Bonafides, but there is no "Hohngelächter," unless it be for the evil Patriarch, head of the Christian church and a recognizable caricature of Pastor Goeze, whose appearance as "ein dicker, roter, freundlicher Prälat" (2: 295; a fat, red-faced, amiable prelate) belies his inhuman dogmatism and intolerance. The play centers on the famous ring parable that Lessing took from an episode in Boccaccio's *Decameron*. Nathan is summoned before Sultan Saladin and challenged (much as Lessing was challenged by Goeze, or Moses Mendelssohn by the evangelizing Swiss zealot Lavater) to state unambiguously which of the three great religions is the true one: Christianity, Judaism or Islam. Nathan responds by telling the story of three litigious brothers, each claiming to have inherited from their father the ring with its magic opal which

> [. . .] hatte die geheime Kraft, vor Gott
> Und Menschen angenehm zu machen, wer
> In dieser Zuversicht ihn trug. (2: 276)
>
> [. . . had the secret power
> To make that man agreeable to God and man
> Who wore it in that faith.]

But the wise judge before whom they press their claims concludes that on the evidence of their present behavior all their rings must be forgeries, and sends them away to make the power of the true ring manifest by their conduct:

> Es strebe von euch jeder um die Wette,
> Die Kraft des Steins in seinem Ring' an Tag
> Zu legen! komme dieser Kraft mit Sanftmut,
> Mit herzlicher Verträglichkeit, mit Wohltun,
> Mit innigster Ergebenheit in Gott,
> Zu Hülf'! (2: 280)
>
> [Let each one of you vie in competition
> To make the power that's within the stone
> In his ring manifest! And let him help that power
> With gentleness, with heartfelt sociability,
> Benevolence, and humble self-surrender
> To God!]

No one religion is *the* true one, but all great religions can guide men towards the truth — which, as Lessing says elsewhere (8: 33), is ultimately the province of God alone — and right conduct matters more than dogmatic faith. The parable scene is the turning point of the play, for Nathan wins Saladin's friendship and support, which ensures the eventual happy ending. The plot itself enacts the meaning of the parable by bringing all the characters together in a familial embrace with which the play ends. But the play is not only a plea for religious toleration or an assertion of universal brotherhood. Rather, as Mendelssohn said, it is a "Lobgedicht auf die Vorsehung" (poem in praise of providence),[34] or indeed a "Schattenriß von dem Ganzen des ewigen Schöpfers" (an image of the whole created by the eternal Creator) much like the one Lessing, in his *Dramaturgie,* declared it was the dramatist's duty to produce (4: 598). As in *Minna von Barnhelm,* as indeed in

Schlegel's and Goethe's Iphigenia dramas, divine providence rewards those who act in good faith to bring about a happy solution. The conclusion is utopian, but expresses the noblest ideals of the Enlightenment; and as Lessing wrote in the preliminary advertisement of his play (2:749), it was not the fault of providence alone if the world did not always measure up to those ideals.

The relationship between Lessing's mature dramas and his dramatic theories has engaged a good deal of critical attention. Lessing himself acknowledged the productive role of criticism in his work (4: 694), and some commentators have argued that the plays are designed to "put the theories into practice," but this is not really plausible; at most they can be seen as essays in practical criticism, experiments in dramatic form. No systematic theory of the bourgeois tragedy precedes the appearance of *Miß Sara Sampson*, and Lessing's "theory of comedy" amounts to little more than a few scattered observations, though *Minna von Barnhelm* can indeed be seen to be in accord with them. Here, "wahre Komödie" (true comedy) both makes us laugh and stirs our emotions (4: 56), and allows us to laugh at the failings of a man while still respecting his human qualities (4: 362). In *Minna von Barnhelm* and *Emilia Galotti* Lessing lends his characters depth and solidity by portraying them in their social contexts — their *conditions*, as Diderot called them — despite the fact that Lessing is critical of precisely this aspect of Diderot's dramatic theory in the *Dramaturgie* (4: 628–32). Lessing often appears in the *Dramaturgie* to be firmly, even dogmatically attached to the traditional distinction between the dramatic genres as laid down by Aristotle, but *Nathan der Weise* transcends these distinctions, and Lessing acknowledges this in the new generic designation, "Ein dramatisches Gedicht" (a dramatic poem).

The new term points to another innovative feature of Lessing's last play: his adoption of verse rather than prose. In the late 1750s, Lessing had, like others, experimented with blank verse, but he had hitherto written his completed plays in prose, and indeed, with *Minna von Barnhelm* and *Emilia Galotti*, had perfected his technique of prose dialogue. Now he moves beyond it, setting another example, which was to be taken up by Goethe and Schiller in the 1780s and by their successors in the new, reconstituted drama of German classicism. But even his verse is relatively easy and colloquial, eschewing the grand manner, yet still able to encompass a range of effects including sentiment, humor and wit. Goethe and Schiller were undoubtedly inspired by Lessing's example, but they were to make of the medium something much grander and more formal: Goethe's blank verse in *Iphigenie auf Tauris* is the true successor of Schlegel's Alexandrines. But in their early, *Sturm und Drang* tragedies, Goethe's *Götz von Berlichingen* and *Clavigo*, Schiller's *Die Räuber* and *Kabale und Liebe* (Intrigue and Love), they follow and develop further the techniques of prose realism which Lessing had introduced. Lessing's plays are of pioneering significance, landmarks in the history of German drama. But they are also works of enduring theatrical vitality, the first German plays that remain part of the living repertory of the German stage today. For a man who claimed "Ich bin weder Schauspieler, noch Dichter" (4: 694; I am neither an actor nor a poet), they reveal a remarkable grasp of theatrical technique. Lessing gradually relaxes his observance of the unities: *Minna von Barnhelm* moves between different rooms in the same inn, *Emilia Galotti* between the Prince's palaces and the Galottis' house — the contrast of decor underscoring the social differentiation between the two worlds — and *Nathan der Weise* between a number of different locations in its fanciful Jerusalem. Time and place are no longer treated mechanically, but as essential dimensions of the dramatic action.[35] In his dialogue he proves himself a master of both prose and verse and offers rewarding parts to actors and actresses. Even today, critics and theatrical directors alike are constantly discovering new and fruitful interpretations of his work. Whatever the merits of the dramatists who preceded him, it is with Lessing that the German drama comes of age.

Notes

[1] See the essay "Gottsched's Literary Reforms: The Beginning of Modern German Literature" by Katherine Goodman in this volume.

[2] Lessing, *Werke*, ed. Herbert Göpfert et al., 8 vols. (Munich: Hanser, 1970–78), 5:70–73. All Lessing quotations are from this edition, and references are given parenthetically either as *Lessing* followed by volume and page number or, in discussions of major works, simply by volume and page number.

[3] Goethe, *Wilhelm Meisters theatralische Sendung* (Wilhelm Meister's Theatrical Mission, ca. 1777), in *Sämtliche Werke,* Münchner Ausgabe, 2.2: 46. The fullest account of the idea of a German National Theater is: Roland Krebs, *L'Idée de "Théâtre national" dans l'Allemagne des lumières,* Wolfenbütteler Forschungen, vol. 28 (Wiesbaden: Harrassowitz, 1985). See also W. H. Bruford, *Theatre, Drama and Audience in Goethe's Germany* (London: Routledge and Kegan Paul, 1950).

[4] Of general critical books on eighteenth-century German drama, Horst Steinmetz, *Das deutsche Drama von Gottsched bis Lessing: Ein historischer Überblick* (Stuttgart: Metzler, 1987), is a useful overview. On tragedy, Robert R. Heitner, *German Tragedy in the Age of Enlightenment* (Berkeley and Los Angeles: California UP, 1963), is exhaustive; Peter-André Alt, *Tragödie der Aufklärung,* Uni-Taschenbücher, vol. 1781 (Tübingen and Basel: Francke, 1994), discusses selected examples. On comedy, see Eckehart Catholy, *Das deutsche Lustspiel von der Aufklärung bis zur Romantik* (Stuttgart: Kohlhammer, 1982). On Lessing see my *Lessing and the Drama* (Oxford: Oxford UP, 1981), and for up-to-date bibliographical information Wolfgang Albrecht, *Gotthold Ephraim Lessing,* Sammlung Metzler, vol. 297 (Stuttgart: Metzler, 1997).

[5] E. M. Wilkinson, *Johann Elias Schlegel, a German Pioneer in Aesthetics* (Oxford: Blackwell, 1945; rpt., Darmstadt: Wissenschaftliche Buchgesellschaft, 1973).

[6] Johann Elias Schlegel, *Werke*, ed. Johann Heinrich Schlegel, 5 vols. (Copenhagen and Leipzig, 1764–73; reprint, Frankfurt a. M.: Athenäum, 1971), 1: 68. A convenient modern edition is J. E. Schlegel, *Ausgewählte Werke*, ed. Werner Schubert (Weimar: Arion Verlag, 1963), cited hereafter as *Ausgewählte Werke*, here 123.

[7] Gerhard M. Schulz, *Die Überwindung der Barbarei: Johann Elias Schlegels Trauerspiele* (Tübingen: Niemeyer, 1980).

[8] "Eine hochherzige Illusion," Schulz 97. Cf. also the more radically deconstructive reading by Thomas Wirtz, *Gerichtsverfahren: Ein dramaturgisches Modell in Trauerspielen der Frühaufklärung* (Würzburg: Königshausen & Neumann, 1994), 340–417.

[9] See Schlegel's essay, "Von der Würde und Majestät des Ausdrucks im Trauerspiel" (On the Dignity and Majesty of Expression in Tragedy), *Werke*, ed. Johann Heinrich Schlegel, 3: 213–40.

[10] C. F. Gellert, *Lustspiele* (Leipzig, 1747; reprint, ed. Horst Steinmetz, Stuttgart: Metzler, 1966), 368.

[11] Fritz Brüggemann, ed., *Die bürgerliche Gemeinschaftskultur der vierziger Jahre*, II: Drama, Deutsche Literatur in Entwicklungsreihen: Reihe: Aufklärung, vol. 6 (Leipzig: 1933), introduction, p. 31.

[12] Gottsched, *Versuch einer critischen Dichtkunst*, 4th ed. (1751; rpt., Darmstadt: Wissenschaftliche Buchgesellschaft, 1966), 644.

[13] For a brief account of these in their English context, see Janet Todd, *Sensibility: An Introduction* (London: Methuen, 1986), 38–40.

[14] Cf. Cornelia Mönch, *Abschrecken oder Mitleiden: Das deutsche bürgerliche Trauerspiel im 18. Jahrhundert. Versuch einer Typologie* (Tübingen: Niemeyer, 1993).

[15] Pfeil, *Lucie Woodvil*, act 5, scene 9, in Fritz Brüggemann, ed., *Die Anfänge des bürgerlichen Trauerspiels in den fünfziger Jahren*, Deutsche Literatur in Entwicklungsreihen: Reihe Aufklärung, vol. 8 (Leipzig 1934), 268; the same volume also contains *Miß Sara Sampson, Der Freigeist*, and the German version of *The London Merchant*.

[16] See Sarah Colvin's essay in this volume, "Musical Culture and Thought."

[17] *Codrus* appeared in Cronegk's posthumously published *Schriften* (Leipzig 1760), but has never to my knowledge been reprinted. *Olint und Sophronia* (with Roschmann's continuation), *Brutus, Richard III* and Weisse's Singspiel *Der Teufel ist los* are contained in Jacob Minor, ed., *Lessings Jugendfreunde*, Kürschners Deutsche Nationalliteratur, vol. 72 (Berlin: Spemann, n.d.). For a further selection of Weisse's tragedies, see Fritz Brüggemann, ed., *Das Drama des Gegeneinander in den sechziger Jahren*, Deutsche Literatur in Entwicklungsreihen, Reihe Aufklärung, vol. 12 (Leipzig 1938), with a lengthy introduction which also discusses Cronegk's tragedies. *Romeo und Julia* is in Fritz Brüggemann, *Die Aufnahme Shakespeares auf der Bühne der Aufklärung*, Deutsche Literatur in Entwicklungsreihen, Reihe Aufklärung, vol. 11 (Leipzig 1937).

[18] Weisse, *Richard III,* revised version ed. D. Jacoby and A. Sauer, Deutsche Literaturdenkmale des 18. und 19. Jahrhunderts, vol.130 (Berlin: Behr, 1904).

[19] See *Lessing,* 4:153–227.

[20] Cf. Kurt Wölfel, "Moralische Anstalt. Zur Dramaturgie von Gottsched bis Lessing," in Reinhold Grimm, ed., *Deutsche Dramentheorien: Beiträge zu einer historischen Poetik des Dramas in Deutschland* (Frankfurt a. M.: Athenäum, 1971), 45–122.

[21] D. Diderot, G. E. Lessing, *Das Theater des Herrn Diderot,* ed. Klaus-Detlef Müller, Reclams Universalbibliothek, vol. 8283 (Stuttgart: Reclam, 1986). The prefaces only are contained in *Lessing* 4:148–51.

[22] *Lessing,* 5:70–73, and cf. 2: 487–89.

[23] "eine heroische Schwachheit, die ich recht gern entbehre." Lessing, *Werke und Briefe,* ed. Wilfried Barner et al. (Frankfurt a. M.: Klassiker-Verlag, 1985), 11. 1:311–12.

[24] Goethe, *Dichtung und Wahrheit* II, 7, in *Werke,* Münchner Ausgabe, 16: 304–05.

[25] Cf. Krebs (note 3), 322–29.

[26] No. 95, *Lessing* 4: 670. The fullest account in English is still J. G. Robertson, *Lessing's Dramatic Theory* (1939; reprint, New York: Benjamin Blom, 1965). Robertson is, however, excessively critical of what he sees as Lessing's lack of originality (echoed in this by Krebs 433).

[27] See Mendelssohn's summary of their discussions in *Lessing* 4: 219–21.

[28] Cf. Stephen Halliwell, *Aristotle's Poetics* (London: Duckworth, 1986), 312–14.

[29] Lessing, *Werke und Briefe,* ed Wilfried Barner et al., 12:79.

[30] Goethe, *Die Leiden des jungen Werthers* (1774), *Werke,* Münchner Ausgabe 1.2: 299.

[31] *Lessing,* 2:707 (Letter to Karl Lessing, 1 March 1772). Cf. the original letter to Nicolai, *Lessing* 2: 702.

[32] See, for example, Bengt Algot Sørensen, *Herrschaft und Zärtlichkeit: Der Patriarchalismus und das Drama im 18. Jahrhundert* (Munich: Fink, 1984); Günter Sasse, *Die aufgeklärte Familie: Untersuchung zur Genese, Funktionalität und Realitätsbezogenheit des familialen Wertsystems im Drama der Aufklärung* (Tübingen: Niemeyer, 1988).

[33] See, for example, Gail K. Hart, *Tragedy in Paradise: Family and Gender Politics in German Bourgeois Tragedy, 1750–1850* (Columbia, SC: Camden House, 1996).

[34] Quoted in Richard Daunicht, *Lessing im Gespräch* (Munich: Fink, 1971), 581.

[35] On this aspect of Lessing's dramatic craftsmanship, see especially Peter Pütz, *Die Leistung der Form: Lessings Dramen* (Frankfurt a. M.: Suhrkamp, 1986).

Flute concert at Sanssouci. Historical painting by Adolph Menzel (1852) shows C. P. E. Bach at keyboard, Friedrich II on flute, Quantz and Graun.

Musical Culture and Thought

Sarah Colvin

"Haben die Deutschen einen Nationalcharakter in ihrer Music, und worinn besteht er?" (Do the Germans have a national character in their music, and if they do, what is it?). This is the question posed in 1783 by Carl Friedrich Cramer in his *Magazin der Musik*;[1] it was almost certainly alive in the minds of many of his contemporaries. In the early years of the eighteenth century musical culture in the German-speaking areas had already begun defining itself in contradistinction to still powerful influences from abroad, particularly from Italy (although these influences, as we shall see, remained important throughout the century). German and Austrian music lovers were already justly proud of their sacred music, produced by such distinguished composers as Dietrich Buxtehude (1637–1707) in northern Germany and Johann Josef Fux (1660–1741) in Vienna. They would soon become aware of the name of Johann Sebastian Bach (1685–1750), who from 1708 was establishing his reputation as chamber musician and organist to the Duke of Saxe-Weimar, before moving in 1723 to his famous post as director of music for Leipzig. But the development of a secular musical culture, too, already well under way in the seventeenth century, and continued through the eighteenth. Particularly in the northern German states, German-language opera was emerging; by 1705, George Frederic Handel (1685–1759) had written his first opera score for Hamburg. Other great names in music history would emerge, including Josef Haydn (1732–1809), Wolfgang Amadeus Mozart (1756–91), and Ludwig van Beethoven (1770–1827).

A notable feature of the eighteenth century (and one that again has its roots in the seventeenth) is the democratization of musical culture. The consumption of music as a secular pastime shifted from being a privilege enjoyed almost exclusively by those at court to a commodity available to the urban bourgeoisie, in concert halls and civic operas. Thanks to the development of fully written-out notation for new instruments, such as the fortepiano, music moved into the homes of amateurs, and was no longer reserved for professionals who could master the old-style improvised continuo. The German-speaking middle classes had a strong sense of national identity, and their appropriation of musical culture in the course of the century helped further the sense of a developing "Germanness" in their national music. This sense was fueled by the achievements of the great composers and the growing international reputation of Austro-German music. By the century's end, the notion of a specifically German contribution to European musical culture had emerged, a contribution manifest not only in the instrumental forms (sonata and symphony) commonly associated with the period, but just as importantly, in church music (the masses and oratorios of Mozart and Haydn) and in opera.

Musical Centers

More than most artistic forms, music and opera in the eighteenth century depended on space and money. To host singers, an orchestra, and sometimes dancers, opera needed an opera house or theater, or at the very least a large hall. Even chamber music demanded not only a fair-sized chamber but musicians (who usually wanted pay) and space for their instruments. Space and money tend to be in the hands of the ruling classes, so the story of eighteenth-century musical culture in Germany is to some extent the story of the German courts. Wealthier merchant cities like Leipzig and Hamburg certainly played their part in the development of German music: Germany's first commercial opera house opened in Hamburg in 1678, and Leipzig was for many years home and employer to Johann Sebastian Bach.

The fashion for opera and other lavish musical events at eighteenth century courts, however, stemmed not only from individual rulers' love of music, but also from the scope such events offered for spectacle, splendor, and political self-presentation. In the civic context, even free cities within the Empire, such as Hamburg, had an interest in maintaining relations with the princely elite;[2] but opera in particular is an ideal vehicle for *Repräsentation*, the public display that is still perceived by those in power as one part of heading a country or state, and was therefore of special interest to the ruling classes. One of the first things Friedrich the Great did after acceding to the Prussian throne in 1740 was to have an opera house built, complete with a canal system for cascades and waterfalls.[3] Dresden had already erected its new opera near the Zwinger in 1719; the theater was one of the largest in Europe, seating 2,000 and costing nearly 150,000 Thaler. Church music, too, may have a representative function: when, for example, an emperor attended a grand mass at one of Vienna's magnificent churches, he was simultaneously underlining the significance of the faith associated with Habsburg rule.

Some of the smaller courts also managed to maintain a lively musical culture, notably Braunschweig-Wolfenbüttel, Mannheim, Ansbach, Weissenfels, Bayreuth, and Hanover. But many of the smaller principalities were pressed for funds, and the most prestigious musical centers established themselves at the larger and more powerful courts: in the south, at the Habsburg court in Vienna and the Bavarian court in Munich; in the north, at the electoral Saxon court in Dresden and the Brandenburg-Prussian court of the Hohenzollerns in Berlin. Even here, however, the cultural process was regularly disrupted by political events. Wars in particular were expensive, and consumed funds that otherwise would have been available for music and the arts: in the eighteenth century notably the War of the Spanish Succession (1701–1714), which sent the Elector of Bavaria into exile; the War of the Austrian Succession (1740–1748), which stymied musical development in Vienna in the mid years of the century; and the Seven Years' War (1756–1763), a reaction against the Prussian occupation of Silesia which caused financial and hence musical troubles for Berlin and Dresden.

Dresden

Musical culture, both at the courts and in cities, flourished wherever it found a powerful patron. In Dresden, Augustus the Strong (1670–1733; from 1697 simultaneously August II of Poland) was a keen patron of the arts with a particular fondness for opera-ballet. In 1731, Augustus invited Johann Adolf Hasse (1699–1783), one of the best-known opera composers of his age, to become his musical director (*Kapellmeister*). Faustina Bordoni (1700–88), the celebrated Venetian mezzo-soprano, was also employed by the electoral court, and she and Hasse married in the first year of Hasse's tenure.

The Dresden court staged magnificent festivals with dance, fireworks and music. For the wedding of his son Friedrich August to the Emperor's daughter, Maria Josepha, celebrated in Dresden in 1719, Augustus created the most extravagant kind of entertainment available: a firework drama, composed on the theme of Jason and the Golden Fleece. Friedrich August II (August III of Poland) continued the tradition established by his father when he acceded to the throne in 1733. There was, therefore, ample employment for Hasse and Bordoni, as well as for many additional musicians and artists at court; but the state coffers were under considerable pressure. Dresden's financial situation was aggravated by the Seven Years' War, so that when the younger August died in 1763 (and with him the personal union of Saxony and Poland), Faustina Bordoni and Kapellmeister Hasse found themselves in a court up to its ears in debt, and were promptly declared redundant. They jointly received a 12,000 Thaler payoff, with no pension.[4] Theirs was a high-profile case, but not unique: musicians' posts at court were sometimes better paid, but frequently less stable than appointments in towns and cities.

Berlin

Berlin, too, was a cultural as well as political center, and under Friedrich the Great (Friedrich II, 1712–86) the Prussian court rivaled Dresden in musical activity. When Friedrich succeeded his father, the "Soldier King" Friedrich Wilhelm I, in 1740, he commissioned a new opera house, and sent his musical director Carl Heinrich Graun (1703/4–1759) to Italy to find singers. Before he was recruited by Friedrich, Graun had sung tenor roles at the opera in Braunschweig, and had written six operas for that theater, one of which, *Lo specchio della fedeltà* (The Mirror of Loyalty), had been performed on the occasion of Friedrich's marriage to Elisabeth Christine of Braunschweig-Wolfenbüttel in 1733. Friedrich's own Berlin opera, the famous *Linden-Opera* which still stands in replica (the opera house was rebuilt after a catastrophic fire in 1843, and again after it was completely destroyed by bombing during the Second World War) on the avenue Unter den Linden in modern Berlin, opened in 1742 with a performance of Graun's *Cesare e Cleopatra,* composed for the occasion with a libretto after Pierre Corneille (1606–1684), *Le mort de Pompée* (1644). Friedrich was not only a patron of music, however; he was himself a composer and librettist. He composed around 120 sonatas for flute, four concertos, and numerous arias and cantatas. He also wrote at least two, and perhaps as many as eight libretti.[5] Of these, *Montezuma* (1755) is the best known, and unusual for its time because it deals not with a classical subject, but with a piece of fairly recent history. Only partially derived from the play *Alzire* (1736) by Friedrich's contemporary, Voltaire (1694–1778), *Montezuma* tells the story Mexico's colonization from a standpoint that is highly critical of the Christian invader, Cortez. Written in French, the libretto was translated into Italian by the court poet Giampietro Tagliazucchi (*fl.* 1749–63), and set by Graun.[6] It is considered one of Graun's best works for the opera stage.

Remarkable at the court of Friedrich the Great was the Prussian ruler's preference for German composers and musicians (though not, initially, singers) over their Italian counterparts. Largely because of the fashion for opera, Italian musicians were in vogue, and were perceived at many courts as necessary jewels in the ruler's crown. Italian *Kapellmeister* at German courts could expect to earn up to four times as much as their German colleagues.[7] Even though the central European borders were, culturally speaking, fluid, and many German composers worked in Italy for periods in their lives (Hasse, for example, as well as Handel and Mozart), the preferential treatment of Italian musicians at the Imperial courts gave rise to resentment. The attendant sense of injustice finds literary expression at the beginning of the century in a satirical novel by Johann Kuhnau (1660–1722). Kuhnau, a composer, was cantor at Leipzig's Thomasschule, and hence the city's senior musical director. In one of his three novels, *Der musicalische Quack-Salber* (The Musical

Quack, 1700), he tells the story of a Swabian musician who poses as an Italian in order to find employment at a German court, even going to such lengths as sending letters to himself under an Italian name, Caraffa. It is soon revealed that Caraffa is no more than an Italianized form of his ridiculous German name: Theuer-Affe. As the title suggests, he is also a musical fraud or "quack," and only survives as a musician because automatic respect is accorded his Italian persona. Kuhnau is criticizing a society prejudiced toward things foreign: "pflegen sich die Leute," the narrator tells us, "ohnedem in ihrem Urtheile also zu übereilen, daß, wenn sie etwas von einem frembden sehen und hören, sie immer solches vor besser und schöner halten, als was ein Bekandter und Einheimischer zu thun gewhonet [sic] ist"[8] (people tend, anyway, to make such hasty judgments that they believe anything foreign they see or hear is better and more beautiful than what a familiar, local person is accustomed to doing). *Der musicalische Quack-Salber* is an emperor's new clothes-style story that mocks both the perpetrator of the fraud and those who fail to recognize it. The novel is linguistically innovative and written with verve and humor.

Given the fashion for things Italian, Friedrich the Great was making a national-political as well as an artistic statement when, alongside Graun, he chose to employ at his court the Bohemian Benda brothers, Franz and Georg (1709–1786 and 1722–1795 respectively), both violinists as well as composers, and the German composer Johann Joachim Quantz (1697–1773). Quantz, author of *Versuch einer Anweisung die Flöte traversière zu spielen* (1752; On Playing the Flute),[9] served Friedrich for forty-five years, among other things as his flute teacher. Carl Philipp Emanuel Bach (1714–1788) is another name associated with Berlin, a composer then regarded more highly in some circles than his now more famous father, Johann Sebastian. The younger Bach served Friedrich for nearly thirty years, not always willingly, as a number of (unsuccessful) applications he made for posts outside Berlin suggest. His primary task at the Prussian court was to provide keyboard accompaniment for Friedrich's flute performances. Although he was based in Dresden, Hasse, too, saw his operas and other compositions performed in Berlin and Potsdam, and he and Faustina Bordoni both spent time by royal invitation at Friedrich's court. In 1771, Friedrich summoned the singer Gertrud Elisabeth Schmähling (1749–1833), whose later married name was Mara. Schmähling, along with Corona Schröter (1751–1802; an actress and singer much admired by Goethe), had trained in Leipzig at a school established by Johann Adam Hiller (1728–1804), the notable *Singspiel* composer, for the purpose of developing German song by training talented singers at no cost. Schmähling was finally able to persuade Friedrich that Germans could, after all, sing. The soprano (widely known as "die Mara") was prima donna in Berlin, and went on to become one of the most famous European singers of the age.

Mannheim

German musicians also predominated at Mannheim's Catholic court. Elector Karl Philipp (1661–1742) moved the Palatinate court to Mannheim in 1720 and set about establishing a royal center that was architecturally and musically outstanding. Alessandro Galli-Bibiena (1687–1769) designed the opera house, which opened in 1742 as part of the celebrations for the marriage of Karl Philipp's heir, Karl Theodor (1724–1799) to his granddaughter, Elisabeth Auguste. Karl Theodor was as active a musical patron as his predecessor, and by 1778 Mannheim had an astounding ninety singers and instrumentalists on its payroll.[10] Karl Theodor engaged the composer and violinist Johann Stamitz (1717–1757) to lead the Mannheim orchestra. It was a remarkably large orchestra by the standards of the day: in 1756 Stamitz had twenty violins, four each of violas, cellos, and double basses; two each of flutes, oboes and bassoons; four horns, a trumpet, and two kettledrums.[11] It was also renowned for its innovative virtuosity and dynamic range — the famous "Mannheim crescendo." Comprised of musicians who were themselves also composers and wrote symphonies and other works for their orchestra, the so-called Mannheim School was assembled under Stamitz's energetic leadership. The symphonic form in particular was a strength of the Mannheim School; the symphonies of Mozart and Beethoven clearly reveal its influence. But musical culture in Mannheim declined after Karl Theodor moved the court to Munich in 1778, taking most of his musicians with him.

Munich

Munich, seat of the Dukes of Bavaria, had entered the eighteenth century in a troubled state, politically and artistically. Following the Battle of Höchstadt in 1704, its court musicians were either dismissed or went into French exile with their Elector, Maximilian II Emanuel (1662–1726), whose political alliance with France had provoked Imperial displeasure. Maximilian returned in 1715 after the Peace of Baden, and was soon re-addressing the business of court music. He had brought back with him a number of French musicians, including the oboist Jacques Loeillet (1685–1748), and in 1720 he engaged one of Italy's most famous castrati, Antonio Bernacchi (1685–1756), for his opera. Max Emanuel's successor, Elector Karl Albrecht (1697–1745, later Emperor Charles VII), was forced to focus at least some of his energies on the War of the Austrian Succession, but his son, Maximilian III (1727–1777), another royal musician and composer, was able to devote himself to opera at his court. Munich's new opera house, the Residenztheater, replaced the old theater on the Salvatorplatz for performances of *opera seria* and ballet in 1753; among others, operas composed by Maximilian's sister, the Saxon Electress Maria Antonia Walpurgis (1724–1780) were performed there. Maria Antonia was a singer trained by the famous Neapolitan teacher Nicola Antonio Porpora (1686–1768; Porpora had also taught Metastasio and Farinelli), as well as a keyboard player and the composer of two operas (for which she wrote her own libretti), occasional cantatas, and free-standing arias. Her *Talestri, regina delle Amazzoni* (Thalestris, Queen of the Amazons) premiered in Munich in 1760, one in a long line of Amazon operas on German and Italian stages.

Vienna

The most splendid center of opera and music drama, however, was Vienna, the administrative center of the Empire. A series of emperors, including Leopold I (1640–1705), Joseph I (1678–1711), and Karl I (1685–1740) were themselves composers of opera, oratorio, church and chamber music, and all three participated in court ballets.[12] Leopold's second wife, Claudia Felicitas of Tyrol, played keyboard and sang, and Faustina Bordoni was a favorite of Charles's daughter, Archduchess Maria Theresa (1717–80), with whom she performed duets during a stay at the Viennese court in 1725–26. The most famous Italian castrato, Farinelli (Carlo Broschi, 1705–82), also visited and sang in Vienna.

In 1698, Leopold had appointed one of the most distinguished composers of the time, Johann Joseph Fux, to the post of court composer. From 1715 to 1740, Fux held the post of *Hofkapellmeister* (director of court music) at Vienna, which brought him responsibilities in church music (he composed numerous masses and oratorios) as well as in opera and other secular forms. He had studied in Rome with Bernardo Pasquini (1637–1710), the Tuscan composer who was central to the development of Roman opera and oratorio, and when he returned to Vienna was keen to contribute Italian-style operas and oratorios to the musical culture of the court. Fux's best-known opera is *Costanza e Fortezza* (Constancy and Fortitude; the imperial motto), which he composed with a libretto by Pietro Pariati for the crowning of Karl VI as King of Bohemia in 1723. Using Livy as his source, Pariati tells a story around the Etruscan siege of Rome, and weaves contemporary political allusions into his text. The coronation ceremony was in Prague, where a special open-air theater was built by the Viennese court architect (and brother of Mannheim's Alessandro), Guiseppe Galli-Bibiena (1695–1757) for a performance that would employ around one hundred singers and two hundred players;[13] sadly, the sixty-three-year-old Fux's gout seems to have prevented him from attending, and he had to delegate to his assistant the task of conducting this magnificent event.[14]

Fux's most enduring work, however, was his treatise on counterpoint, the *Gradus ad Parnassum sive manuductio ad compositionem musicae regula-*

rem (Steps to Parnassus or a Guide to Regular Musical Composition, 1725). The work was translated into German with the title *Gradus ad Parnassum: Anführung zur regelmässigen musikalischen Composition* in 1742 by Lorenz Christoph Mizler von Kolof (1711–1778). The *Gradus* is in itself a conservative piece of writing, celebrating and solidifying what had already been in European music, rather than looking forward to its future: in it, Fux examines the *stile antico* associated with the Italian Renaissance composer Giovanni Perluigi Palestrina (1525–1594). In its effects, however, the *Gradus* had quite a different dynamic and influenced a generation of composers who were to shape music's development like few before them. Haydn used it to teach himself counterpoint, and both Mozart and Beethoven relied on the principles Fux outlined.[15]

Civic Activity: Hamburg

Opera, in Italian generally designated *dramma per musica,* had spread from Italy across Germany during the seventeenth century, and was well established as a popular form of entertainment in court and civic settings by the beginning of the eighteenth. Whereas court operas were usually performed in Italian, Hamburg was the major center of German-language opera, home to the opera house called the Theater am Gänsemarkt. The new opera had opened its doors in 1678. Hamburg's trading links to Venice, where the first public opera house ever, the Teatro S. Cassiano, opened in 1637, were among the many factors (the city's affluence was another) which helped the Hanse town to become host to Germany's first commercial opera house. Hanover followed suit in 1689, Braunschweig in 1690, and Leipzig in 1693. The Theater am Gänsemarkt collapsed financially in 1738, and was demolished two years before the new Ackermannsches Komödienhaus was constructed (1765; renamed the Deutsches Theater in 1797), where the new-style German *Singspiele* of Mozart, Karl Ditters von Dittersdorf (1739–1799) and Antonio Salieri (1750–1825) played for Hamburg in the late years of the century.

The name inextricably connected with the Hamburg opera is that of Reinhard Keiser (1674–1739), a composer now primarily known for his influence on Georg Friedrich Händel (1685–1759). Händel arrived in Hamburg in 1703, aged eighteen, and composed his first opera *Almira, Königin von Castilien* (1705). In 1706 he left Hamburg for Italy, and on his return was appointed *Kapellmeister* to the electoral court in Hanover. When his Hanoverian master was crowned George I of England in 1714, Händel (who had already enjoyed some extended trips to the English capital, not always at George's pleasure) settled in London as Handel.

Hamburg was also home to the one of the most prolific and influential music theorists of the eighteenth century, a tenor and composer whose body of work and energetic literary style indicates that he was as much a writer as he was a musician: Johann Mattheson (1681–1764). The author of a number of important theoretical works, Mattheson also established the first music periodical to be published in Germany, the *Critica Musica,* which appeared in Hamburg in twenty-four issues between 1722 and 1725. Like Handel, Mattheson was drawn by the opera house: he sang there from 1696, moving from boy soprano to tenor roles (he took the lead male role in Handel's *Almira*). His own first opera, *Die Plejades, oder Das Sieben-Gestirne* (*The Pleiad, or the Seven Stars*) was performed there in 1699, when he was eighteen.

The *Collegium musicum*

A relatively new institution in the eighteenth century was the *Collegium musicum* (music society). *Collegia* were organizations of civic musicians, focused on performance rather than theory, which in some cities were already extant in the sixteenth and seventeenth centuries. Hamburg's was founded in 1660 by the organist of the *Jakobikirche,* Matthias Weckmann (?1619–1674). Leipzig, with the advantage of an established university, acquired a particularly prominent *Collegium musicum* in 1702 through the efforts of one of its students, Georg Philipp Telemann (1681–1767). The Leipzig *Collegium,* later directed by J. S. Bach, provided weekly public concerts for the city, twice weekly at fair times, as well as performing operas.[16] Telemann was also, briefly, musical director of the Leipzig opera, before he left to become *Kapellmeister* to the court at Sorau (now Polish Zary).

In the civic context, the director of music was sometimes designated *Kapellmeister,* sometimes *Stadtkantor.* The responsibilities of an individual holding such a post included producing and directing both church music and music for civic occasions, and often teaching responsibilities at a local school. Opera was not usually among the duties of a civic director of music (this was a major difference between the post of *Hofkapellmeister* and that of *Stadtkantor,* since much of the former's time would be taken up with operatic activity at the court). One notable exception to this rule is Telemann, who in 1722 threatened the city of Hamburg with resignation unless he was also allowed to work with the opera house, and thereby became both *Stadtkantor* and the musical director of the Theater am Gänsemarkt. After his death he was succeeded as cantor by his godson, C. P. E. Bach, who thereby finally escaped Friedrich's Prussian court and his unsatisfying role as chief accompanist to a flautist king.

Women and Music

While the involvement of noblewomen in courtly musical culture, as performers and spectators, was taken for granted, the position of women as musicians and music lovers in the civic context was markedly different. In bourgeois circles, institutions such as the *Collegia musica* were making music ever more accessible to the general public; but middle-class women did not have the same rights of access to public music-making as men. The *Collegia* were usually organized by students, and at that time students were, by definition, men. Advertising his concert series for 1779–80, Göttingen's academic concert master, Johann Nikolaus Forkel (1749–1818), announced that there would be a charge of half a Thaler per concert for "Liebhaber der Musik" (music lovers); but "Damen sind frey" (ladies go free).[17] The assumption is clearly that ladies will accompany (male) music lovers. In a society where women attend public concerts as escorts, we need not expect to find them as public performers. As always where there is a rule, there are notable exceptions: Maria Anna ("Nannerl") Mozart (1751–1829) was one, a gifted keyboard player who toured with her father Leopold (1719–87) and her brother Wolfgang Amadeus (1756–1791) in the 1760s; Maria Theresia von Paradis (1759–1824) another. After 1769, Nannerl Mozart, who was also a composer, was obliged by her parents to abandon her concert tours and stay at home with her mother; she married in 1784. Von Paradis, blind from childhood, was a pianist, organist, singer, and composer, and has the distinction of being the only woman listed among the most proficient instrumental artists living in Germany in Forkel's Leipzig-based *Musikalischer Almanach für Deutschland* (1782–84).[18]

Certain types of instruments were considered more suitable than others for women players. The clavichord and piano, the harp and the glass harmonica were generally viewed as acceptable, as was singing. The glass harmonica, an instrument played using the vibrations produced on glass by the player's fingers, enjoyed a sudden, but fleeting popularity in the late eighteenth century, not least as the result of a concert tour by another blind virtuosa, Marianne Kirchgässner (1769–1808). In 1791, Mozart composed his quintet (K617) for glass harmonica, flute, oboe, viola, and cello in response to Kirchgässner's performance. The least acceptable instruments for female musicians were the cello and the organ (unseemly use of the legs), and trumpet and timpani (too military);[19] but even the violin, viola, and woodwind instruments were frowned upon in the hands of women. Blowing an instrument was considered unseemly, and excessive use of the arms or legs in performance was to be avoided; a respectable woman did not draw attention to her body in public. Hence the popularity of keyboard instruments and others that could be played in a sitting position, keeping the body fairly static.

In the earlier eighteenth century, women as performers were especially unwelcome in churches. Paul's veto on women's speech in church (1 Corinthians 14:34) was considered equally applicable to their singing, hence the use of boy sopranos and castrati in ecclesiastical music. Working at the cathedral in Hamburg, Johann Mattheson pioneered the use of women's voices in church, at first only possible if the singers' bodies were kept out of view; but, as Mattheson notes with typical acerbic wit, "zuletzt [. . .] konte man sie nicht genug hören und sehen"[20] (in the end people could not get enough of hearing and seeing them). Johann Hiller was another staunch supporter of women as active participants in church music, and made a point of providing training for singers such as Gertrud Schmähling and Corona Schröter at his school in Leipzig. But developments for women in music were slow, not least because music was not considered essential to a woman's education before the nineteenth century. Indeed, an amateurish grasp of singing and playing was preferable to serious ambition as a musician or theorist, since the latter could only interfere with a woman's housewifely duties.

Music Theory

The eighteenth century saw a proliferation of writing about music, and the musical treatise can be seen as an art form in itself, related to but also separate from musical practice. Germany led Europe in the production of musical literature; the major publishing centers were Leipzig, Frankfurt am Main, Hamburg, Berlin, and (later in the century) Vienna. Berlin-based publications included the first journal devoted to reviews of musical compositions, *Der critische Musikus an der Spree,* edited by Friedrich Wilhelm Marpurg (1718–95). In Leipzig, Mizler von Koloff was editor of the journal the *Neu eröffnete musikalische Bibliothek* (Newly-opened Musical Library), published between 1738 and 1754, and it was Leipzig, too, that in 1732 saw the publication of the first lexicon of music ever to be printed in German: Johann Gottfried Walther's *Musicalisches Lexicon oder Musicalische Bibliothec.* This 650–page tome records a vast array of musical knowledge from A for alto voice to Z for Zurita (Laurentia de), a seventeenth-century Spanish woman musicologist.[21] Other notable works include Forkel's *Allgemeine Geschichte der Musik* (A General History of Music), published in Leipzig in two volumes (1788 and 1801), the first work of its kind in German, giving wide coverage of musical history to the sixteenth century.

Music's power to affect the human spirit is of particular interest to theorists. Kuhnau's *Musicalische Quack-Salber* opens with a serious reminder of music's potential: in a direct address to his reader, the composer-novelist places music first among the liberal arts, arguing that it has a marvelous power over the human spirit, and can both melt hearts and soothe the savage breast (5; "daß ihre Krafft in den menschlichen Gemüthern wunderbar ist, und [. . .] die Felsen-steinerne [*sic*] Hertzen und die viehischen und unbändigen Begierden öffters erweichen, zäumen und besänfftigen kan"). Kuhnau is referring indirectly to the Aristotelian notion of music's potential to touch human emotions (in German, the *Affekte*). The musician stirs emotion by feeling it, and music touches the affections by imitating them, Johann Adolph Scheibe (1708–76) tells us in his *Compendium Musices Theoretico-practicum* (before 1736; A Theoretical and Practical Compendium of Music).[22] In a discursive prologue to his libretto *Simson* (Hamburg 1709), Barthold Feind (1678–1721), one of Hamburg's most prolific librettists and opera theorists, explains that the body is influenced by the movement of the blood and the Cartesian "Lebens-Geister" (vital spirits), which stimulate certain emotional responses according to the temperament of the listener.[23] The affections provide human beings with a bridge to virtue: they are, in fact, "die wahre Materie der Tugend" (15; the true material of virtue), asserts Johann Mattheson, Feind's contemporary in Hamburg, in *Der Vollkommene Capellmeister* (1739; The Accomplished Director of Music). The didactic tone betrays that both Feind and Mattheson have their roots in the seventeenth century; while the next generation were still aware of and interested in the affective power of music, their notion of its function has shifted. C. P. E. Bach still reminds performing musicians that they must be prepared to immerse themselves in all the *Affekte* they wish to arouse in their audience, but his concerns are clearly less with the achievement of virtue than with capturing the hearts of listeners and winning applause (*Versuch über die wahre Art das Clavier zu spielen*, Drittes Hauptstück, 122–23).

Another favorite subject is musical rhetoric. Mattheson, describing the principles of composition in *Das neu-eröffnete Orchestre* (1713; A New Look at the Orchestra), maps out a rhetoric of music: "es gehören [. . .] zu einer Composition dreyerley: Invention, (die Erfindung) Elaboratio, (Die Ausarbeitung) Execution, (die Ausführung oder Aufführung)" (there are three basic elements of composition: invention [the idea], elaboration [the development of the idea], execution [the presentation or performance]),[24] and Leopold Mozart, preparing his *Versuch einer gründlichen Violinschule* (1756; A Violin Primer), urges players and composers to be aware of breaks or *Einschnitte* (*incisiones*) in the melody.[25] As well as Mattheson's work, Leopold had consulted the influential works on rhetoric of the Enlightenment theorist Johann Christoph Gottsched (1700–66).[26] One of the most extensively discussed features of eighteenth-century musical rhetoric is the use of figures, or musical analogies, which can add depth and meaning to an accompanying text (and are therefore of particular interest in opera, oratorio, and songs). Mattheson, whose acerbic style makes him an entertaining theorist, discusses the issue at some length, but also pours scorn on the modish use of figures to illustrate a text like "zitterndes Glänzen der sprudlenden Wellen" (shivering shine on the foaming waves) because of the technical problems which sound-painting on certain vowels causes for the singer: "wegen des hi, hi, hi, und hu, hu, hu, im Zittern und Sprudlen, sehr wiederlich klinget" (*Capellmeister*, 201–202; because of the hi, hi, hi, and ho, ho, ho, in shivering and foaming; it sounds terrible). The *Capellmeister* was one of the most widely-used theoretical works of the eighteenth century, and was still being used by Beethoven at the beginning of the nineteenth.[27]

Music or Text? The Score Versus the Libretto

Early libretti were intended to be read as programs during a performance, as printing and sales records, and tallow spots on the texts suggest (the latter from tapers held to aid reading in a dark auditorium). One of the most hotly debated topics in the development of opera is the relationship between text and music, music and text. Which should lead, and which follow? Plato's claim that speech has priority over harmony and rhythm led early Italian theorists of opera, such as Gioseffo Zarlino in his influential *Le istitutioni harmoniche* (1558), to contend that music must take its meaning from the text, and that only music involving the voice can have affective power.

Writing in the early eighteenth century, Barthold Feind makes his position clear: "eine Opera ist ein [. . .] Gedicht/ so in die Music gesetzet/ als welche der Verse wegen allhier gebrauchet wird/ nicht aber ümgekehret"[28] (an opera is a [. . .] poem, set to music, and the music is used because of the verse, not the other way around). Mattheson, as a composer, sees things from a different perspective. In his *Critica Musica*, he writes a lively commentary on a text by Heinrich Bokemeyer (1679–1751), a cantor in Wolfenbüttel who expresses views similar to Feind's. To Bokemeyer's claim that the words are the noblest and best part of a piece of music ("das edelste und vornehmste Stück einer guten Music") Mattheson responds spiritedly: he is not prepared to stand for relegating music to the status of a textual prop. He even suggests that music will do perfectly well without text, and in this he anticipates imminent developments in music theory; for by the mid-eighteenth century there is a tangible shift in the perception of the relation of music to text, and the corresponding relationship between composer and poet. In his history of European opera and song, Christian Gottfried Krause (1719–1770) argues for an egalitarian approach, but nevertheless notes a trend toward honoring the composer over the librettist: "Es ist wahr," he admits, "von einem Singstück hat der Poet nicht allemal den größten Ruhm"[29] (it is true that the poet is not greatly recognized for his contribution to an opera). Later in the century, Mozart is in no doubt. While composing *Die Entführung aus dem Serail* (The Abduction from the Seraglio, 1782), he writes to his father, Leopold, in October 1781 that the composer has the upper hand, because in opera poetry must be like an obedient daughter to the music ("bey einer opera muß schlechterdings die Poesie der Musick gehorsame Tochter seyn").[30]

The logical next step is to dispense with poetry altogether. The gradual liberation of music from text, after a century and a half during which music drama predominated, is an important development in the latter part of the eighteenth century. At its end we find Johann Gottfried Herder (1744–1803) in *Kalligone* (1800) pleading for music's right to emancipate itself completely from language. The recognition of music without words as an art form as communicative and meaningful as poetic language is one of the major developments in the history of musical ideas.

German and Italian Opera in the Early Eighteenth Century

Developments in German and Italian opera in the earlier eighteenth century are interwoven, not separate. Composers traveling and working in Italy brought back the latest styles and storylines from Italian *opera seria* and *opera buffa*. German composers regularly set Italian libretti, and in Hamburg Keiser introduced a hybrid form, using Italian arias in German language texts. In this situation, the dividing line between German and Italian opera is blurred. Two examples must suffice here to illustrate some of the manifold interworkings of German and Italian opera in the early part of the century: Keiser's *Fredegunda* (1715; German text by Johann Ulrich König, 1688–1744), and Telemann's *Die ungleiche Heyrath,* also called *Pimpinone* (1725; German text by Johann Philipp Praetorius, ?1696–?1766).

Fredegunda was a "dream team" collaboration between the high-profile Reinhard Keiser and an equally prominent poet-librettist: "den berühmten Johann Ulrich König" (the famous Johann Ulrich König), Christoph Martin Wieland (1733–1813) calls him.[31] König was co-founder of Hamburg's *Teutschübende Gesellschaft* (Society for the Use of German), established in 1715 in a reaction against the ornate style of the late seventeenth century, with the aim of purifying the German language. In the same year, *Fredegunda* premiered in Hamburg. It was to become one of the most successful operas ever played on the Hamburg stage, with regular performances up until the opera's closure in 1738.

Fredegunda is based on a Venetian opera, *La Fredegonda,* composed by Francesco Gasparini (1661–1727) with a libretto by Francesco Silvani (1660–?1742), first performed at Venice's Teatro S. Cassiano in 1705. The material is historical, drawn from the story of Frédegunde, mistress and then wife of Chilpéric I of Neustria (the area around the Seine and Loire ruled by the Franks in the sixth to the eighth century). König clearly follows Silvani in choosing one virtuous woman (Galsuinde) from the rather complex history to set against the scheming Fredegunda; and, like Silvani, he reverses the historical record when he has Fredegunda perish at the opera's close, while Galsuinde survives. (The historical Frédegunde had her rival Galswinthe strangled in her bed.)[32]

Particularly interesting about this opera is how it interacts not only with its Venetian source, but with other Italian predecessors. In the opera's penultimate act, Fredegunda appears on stage in the metaphorical guise of Medea. The references to Euripides are clear when she asserts her destructive power with reference to Colchis, Mycenae, and Argos. Medea is, alongside the Amazons, one of the most popular figures in early opera: *Medea in Atene*, by Antonio Gianettini (1648–1721) and Aurelio Aureli (1652–1708) was written for Venice in 1678, and had been performed with a German parallel translation at the Wolfenbüttel opera in 1688 and 1692. Christian Heinrich Postel (1658–1705) adapted the opera in German for the Hamburg stage in 1695. This gives us a double line of influence, for where Gasparini and Silvani will certainly have known Gianettini's and Aureli's opera, Keiser and König will have been equally familiar with Postel's version. In the second act of Postel's text, Medea makes her appearance on a chariot drawn through the air by two serpents, and at the end of the fourth act of *Fredegunda*, König has his anti-heroine depart in a remarkably similar chariot, drawn through the air by snakes.

The opera also has its distinctively German elements, however. For all his stylistic criticism of the seventeenth-century school dramatists in the *Teutschübende Gesellschaft*, König betrays his own roots in the pedagogical tradition of theater in his introduction to his libretto. He explains that the historical material has been manipulated so as not to diverge from the proper didactic purpose of a play, which is to show vice punished and virtue rewarded ("um nicht von dem rechten Zweck eines Schau-Spiels abzukommen/ welcher allezeit dahin gehen soll/ daß das Laster bestrafft/ die Tugend aber belohnt werde").[33] Vice is punished in the figure of Fredegunda who is sent to hell, and virtue rewarded in Galsuinde who regains her errant royal husband.

Hybrid German and Italian form is at least as characteristic of German comic opera in the eighteenth century as it is of serious opera. Italian comedy informed developments in the German-speaking territories in a kind of pincer movement, coming up through the "low" folk performances of the sixteenth and seventeenth centuries, when the *commedia dell'arte* players toured Germany, but also down through the "high" *opera seria* (with their comic *intermezzi* or entr'actes) that were performed at the German courts, into German-language opera and *Singspiel*.

Telemann's *Die ungleiche Heyrath; oder, Das Herrsch-süchtige Camer Mädgen* (The Unequal Marriage, or the Bossy Chambermaid, 1725) is a German *intermezzo* that clearly demonstrates the influence of the *commedia dell'arte*. The *commedia's* mode of joking was subversive in the carnivalesque manner, and it was customary for the lower classes to get the better of their masters, and for women characters to triumph over men. Character types from the *commedia* are immediately perceptible in *Die ungleiche Heyrath*, where a wealthy old merchant (here Pimpinone; in the *commedia* often called Pantalone) is duped by his spirited female servant, Vespetta.

The Italian influence on German opera does not, of course, end in the early eighteenth century. In 1768 Haydn wrote his best known opera, *Lo Speziale* (The Apothecary), for the inauguration of the new opera house at Eszterháza, with a libretto adapted from the original (1752) by Carlo Goldoni (1707–93). Mozart, too, set a libretto by Goldoni (*La Finta semplice*, The Pretend Simpleton; written by Goldoni for Venice in 1764, set by Mozart in 1768) and others by Metastasio, as well as adopting Lorenzo Da Ponte as his chief collaborator for the later operas. With the development of *Singspiel*, however, the importance of Italy recedes, and French, English, and ancient Classical sources become at least as important in the development of German-language music theater.

Reform

Christoph Willibald Gluck (1714–87) is generally cited as the reformer of opera, but the story of opera reform in the eighteenth century begins earlier than the 1760s, when Gluck wrote his first so-called reform operas. Early attempts to reform opera in fact begin where opera itself began, in Italy, with a group of librettists led by the Venetian scholar Apostolo Zeno (1668–1750). Zeno's reaction was to streamline and simplify: basing his libretti on the French classical dramas of Pierre Corneille and Jean Racine (1639–99), he constructed plots that adhered to the Aristotelian unities of time, place, and action. His aim was to create libretti that could equally well be performed as dramas without music. In 1714, Karl VI invited Apostolo Zeno to the Habsburg court to fill the post of imperial poet and historian. There the Venetian's notions influenced another Italian poet, who was later the most celebrated librettist of *opera seria* writing in eighteenth-century Europe: Pietro Metastasio (1698–1782). In the course of the century his libretti were set to music by practically every opera composer of note, including Mozart. *La clemenza di Tito*, for example, a drama of imperial magnanimity, was written by Metastasio for Vienna in 1734, and was first set by the vice-*Kapellmeister*, Antonio Caldara (1670–1736), for the name day of Karl VI. It was subsequently set around forty times by different composers, including

Hasse in 1735, Gluck in 1752, and (in a revised version) Mozart in 1791, for the coronation of Leopold II in Prague.

Metastasio arrived at Vienna in response to an imperial invitation of 1730, and remained there until his death. He had the advantage of being a more musical librettist than Zeno, and this gave him an ability to write effective arias where Zeno preferred to concentrate on operatic dialog, the recitative. In the spirit of reform, Metastasio's arias are simple and carefully placed in order to avoid becoming the kind of distracting events, primarily designed to showcase a particular singer's talents, that were regarded by reformers as the bane of conventional opera. Metastasian libretti alternate recitative and aria in a way that enables a progression of the action, and this is in keeping with reform notions of a more natural, realistic event.

German-language opera, too, was attracting criticism by the early eighteenth century. Its conventional features included stock comic figures, in Germany the *Hanswurst* in particular; at least one strand of action depicting the battle of the sexes; at least one set of lower-class characters; and the use of local dialect, particularly by the fool or clown. All of these features were also characteristic of *intermezzi*, but now they were no longer kept separate from the opera proper, but were included as one strand in an often highly complex plot. By the end of the seventeenth century, the clown or fool was well on his way to being the undisputed ruler of vernacular opera. It is a mixture of the problems of plot and the predominance of the fool that leads the famous literary theoretician, professor, and literary reformer Johann C. Gottsched, in his *Versuch einer Critischen Dichtkunst vor die Deutschen* (A German Poetics, 1730), to dismiss opera as the most nonsensical work the human mind ever invented ("das ungereimteste Werck, so der menschliche Verstand jemahls erfunden").[34] Gottsched was not himself a musician, and his objections to opera are not primarily musical. His concern is with the text, which offends his rationality: his famous complaint is that one may take only one's ears, and not one's powers of understanding, to the opera.[35] In opera, music has taken over, and the result, in Gottsched's view (which does not seem entirely unreasonable when one looks at many of the texts), is the degeneration of the libretto.

It is therefore very much in the spirit of the time that C. W. Gluck began his program of opera reform with the intention of re-privileging poetry. In Vienna, Gluck had come into contact with Metastasio. His first opera, *Artaserse,* performed in Milan in 1741, was a setting of a Metastasian libretto, and in May 1748 Gluck's and Metastasio's *Semiramide riconosciuta* was performed to inaugurate the new Burgtheater. But Handel's English oratorios and the French *tragédies lyriques* of Jean-Baptiste Lully (1632–87) and Jean-Philippe Rameau (1683–1764) inspired Gluck to develop elements in his own operas that diverge from the prescriptive Metastasian scheme to permit more profound characterization.

In the reform libretto, simplicity and naturalness, and an emphasis on the human element were the key. In Gluck's first "reform" operas, *Orfeo ed Euridice* (1762), *Alceste* (1767), and *Paride ed Helene* (1770), composed to libretti by Calzabigi, he outlines their program or manifesto for the reform of opera. Like other reformers before him, he makes the central point that the influence of *prime donne* and *primi uomini* in opera must be countered, particularly their demands for prominent and lengthy arias in which they can demonstrate their art. Music should function to support the text and the development of the action, and crucial recitatives should not be interrupted by decorative aria or orchestral inserts; instead, simple melodies ("una bella semplicità") should characterize the score.

Gluck's best-known and most admired operas are his two Iphigenias: *Iphigénie en Aulide* (1774) and *Iphigénie en Tauride* (1779), both written for Paris. During the most successful phase of his career Gluck was, in fact, reforming French rather than German opera. Since becoming court composer in 1764, he was based at Vienna, but French opera had long been his interest, and his own *opéra comique*, called *La rencontre imprévue* (The Unexpected Meeting) had premiered in Vienna in January 1764. During a visit to Paris in March of the same year he met Charles-Simon Favart (1710–1792), the prominent librettist of Parisian comic opera. By the early 1770s, Gluck had conceived of a project to reform the *tragédie lyrique*, and he created for Paris French versions of his own *Orfeo* (*Orphée et Eurydice*, 1774) and *Alceste* (1776), as well as the French-language *Armide* (1777) and his two *Iphigénies*. Like Zeno before him, Gluck worked with classical models: *Iphigénie en Aulide* was adapted for him from Racine's drama by Marie François Bailli du Roullet (1716–86), while *Iphigénie en Tauride* was based on Euripides, brilliantly adapted by the first-time librettist Nicolas François Guillard (1752–1814).

Towards the end of his life, Gluck did have plans for a German opera: a setting of the patriotic play *Hermanns Schlacht* (Hermann's Battle, 1769) by Friedrich Gottlob Klopstock (1724–1803). He had begun composing the text in 1669, but then abandoned the project, and the music is now unfortunately lost.[36] Even though the project for a German opera was never realized, Gluck was influential in Germany, because his work shook a previously unshaken belief in the primacy of Italian opera, and fed a growing sense of the possibility of German creative genius in the field. This possibility was also felt by many involved in the development of a new form of German-language opera: the *Singspiel*.

Singspiel

It is commonly noted that German *Singspiel* in the eighteenth century is a hybrid form, deriving from Italian comic opera of the seventeenth century, (which in turn depends on conventions established in the *commedia dell'arte*), French *opéra comique*, and English ballad opera. But *Singspiel* also has German origins in the German-language comic operas of the late seventeenth and early eighteenth centuries. These have their roots not only in Italian opera but in early modern German dramatic comedy such as the Shrovetide plays (*Fastnachtspiele*), which began to be written down in the fifteenth century.[37]

John Gay's *Beggar's Opera* of 1728 is generally cited as the first English ballad opera. Gay's piece was so popular that it soon found imitators, notably Charles Coffey, in *The Devil to Pay, or the Wives Metamorphos'd* (1731), which was performed in Berlin in 1743, translated by the Prussian diplomat Caspar Wilhelm von Borck (1704–1747). Another version by Christian Felix Weisse (1726–1804), titled *Die verschmähten Weiber oder Der Teufel ist los,* was performed in Leipzig by Gottfried Heinrich Koch's theater company in 1752, with music by Johann Georg Standfuß (d? after 1759). Gottsched's attempts to have the piece removed from the Leipzig stage only enhanced its popular appeal,[38] and it played there again in 1766, this time with the title *Die verwandelten Weiber oder Der Teufel ist los* and with new music by Johann Hiller, the composer who came to be Weisse's primary collaborator. The libretto for this performance is no longer extant.

The popularity of the work established the *Singspiel* as an up-and-coming form. Weisse and Hiller were soon its most prominent creators, following up *Die verwandelten Weiber* with further successes, including *Lottchen am Hofe* (*Lottchen at Court*, 1767; after a French libretto by Favart, *La caprice amoureux, ou Ninette à la Cour*, 1755) and *Die Jagd* (*The Hunt*, 1770), which was first performed by the Koch company at Weimar. The latter was dedicated to Duchess Anna Amalia of Sachsen-Weimar (1739–1807), herself a composer and a keen patron of *Singspiel*. *Lottchen*, with its sentimental plot and its juxtaposition of female rural innocence (in the heroine) with male ruling-class depravity (displayed by Astolph, Duke of Lombardy), sets a tone that characterizes Singspiel and light opera in the late eighteenth century. It gives the kind of semi-comic portrayal of gender relations in the feudal system that is also a feature of *Die Jagd*, and, a little later, of Mozart's *Le Nozze di Figaro* (The Marriage of Figaro, 1786) and *Don Giovanni* (1787).[39]

Wieland and the *Singspiel*

After Weisse and Hiller, the best-known partnership in German *Singspiel* is that of Wieland and Anton Schweitzer (1735–87). From 1769, Schweitzer was musical director of the Seyler theater company, and his collaboration with Wieland began while the troupe was based at Weimar on the invitation of Anna Amalia. Wieland was in residence at the court, and quickly involved Schweitzer in his plans for German language opera; for Anna Amalia's birthday in 1772, Schweitzer set Wieland's pastoral libretto, *Aurora*. In 1773, *Alceste* followed, a serious opera in five acts with a libretto that was closely based on Euripides. *Alceste* was a demonstration of Wieland's vision for German *Singspiel*, and attracted much attention as a through-composed, serious opera written in the vernacular. On the strength of it, Wieland and Schweitzer were commissioned to write an opera for Mannheim, and in 1777 they produced *Rosamunde*, a bloodthirsty tale of love and jealousy that premiered in 1780.

Wieland's project was to develop a national form of opera. In this he was not always taken seriously: Goethe created a merciless persiflage of *Alceste's* classical pretensions in his farcical play *Götter, Helden und Wieland* (Gods, Heroes, and Wieland, 1774). Wieland was undeterred, however, and in his own journal, the *Teutsche Merkur* (1773–1810), published his "Versuch über das deutsche Singspiel und einige dahin einschlagende Gegenstände"[40] (An Essay on the German Singspiel and Some Related Topics, 1775), in which he claims that the *Singspiel* more closely resembles ancient tragedy, especially that of Euripides, than any other form of theater, including opera. He goes on to complain about those who are still old-fashioned enough to think that the German language is not suited to singing, and addresses the problem of nomenclature in sung theater. Wieland advocates leaving "opera" as a designation to the Italians and French, and claiming and developing *Singspiel* as Germany's national form. *Singspiel*, he asserts, would suit modern Enlightenment Germany not least because (unlike the more extravagant types of opera) it is affordable in the bourgeois civic context. It is, in short, "ein öffentliches Vergnügen von der edelsten Art und gewiß nicht ohne nützlichen Einfluß auf Geschmack und Sitten"[41] (a public form of entertainment of the noblest kind, and certainly not without a beneficial influence on public taste and habits).

More lastingly influential on German *Singspiel* than Wieland's essay, however, was a non-musical project: his edited collection of fairy tales, called *Djinnistan oder Auserlesene Feen- und Geister-Mährchen* (Djinnistan or Selected Tales of Fairies and Ghosts), which appeared in three volumes between 1786 and 1789. The stories collected in *Djinnistan* were extremely popular, and fed the imaginations of *Singspiel* librettists, not least Schikaneder's when he was writing *Die Zauberflöte*.[42] In Austria, the librettist, composer, and theater director Emanuel Schikaneder (1751–1812) was active in developing what was later called the *Wiener Singspiel*. Characteristic of *Wiener Singspiel* is a predominance of music and singing over spoken text, largely because the performers (unlike those employed by the touring companies of northern Germany) were formally trained singers.[43] The sense of *Singspiel* as a potential "national" form is present in Vienna as it is in the north: in 1778, Joseph II opened a "Teutsches Nationalsingspiel" at the Burgtheater. The project was not a success, possibly because of the wide variety of opera available to audiences in Vienna. One of the more successful pieces to play at the Nationalsingspiel was Mozart's "komisches Singspiel," *Die Entführung aus dem Serail*, which premiered there in 1782; a year later, however, the theater closed, only to re-open in 1785. Great successes were scored by the composer Karl Ditters von Dittersdorf, whose operetta *Doktor und Apotheker* (1786) played seventy-two times in Vienna before the end of the century and was performed across Germany and at London's Drury Lane.[44] This Romeo and Juliet-style story ends not in tragedy, but with the outwitting of both sets of parents, so that marriage contracts are signed for the young couple. In the 1780s, Dittersdorf was more popular with the Viennese public than Mozart; musically, he is remembered for his ability to write long, dramatically effective finales.

When the company collapsed again in 1788, Viennese *Singspiel* moved to the suburban stages. It was on one of these, the Theater an der Wieden, that *Die Zauberflöte* opened in September 1791.[45] The title was inspired by one of the stories from Wieland's *Djinnistan* collection, called *Lulu, oder Die Zauberflöte*. It was given by Schikaneder's company, and Schikaneder himself played the comic role of the bird-man Papageno. This is not the place to attempt an analysis of an opera which has been more frequently and variously interpreted than any other in the Western repertoire. *Die Zauberflöte* shows us, in the parallel stories of Tamino and Pamina, and Papageno and Papagena, that we have choices in life and love: to confine ourselves to the material, corporeal, and comforting, or explore the limits in a sometimes painful spiritual quest. Mozart's music makes clear that both paths are acceptably and sympathetically human — Papageno's engaging songs are among the opera's best known. The opera is perhaps most remarkable for its idealistic evocation of Masonic thought in a society where Freemasonry was neither established nor accepted, and for its ahistorical suggestion that a woman, Pamina, might become an initiate. It was an immediate success: Schikaneder's company gave 200 performances by 1800, and the libretto was soon translated into other European languages, including Dutch, Russian, French, Italian, and English.

Goethe's *Singspiele*

One of the great admirers of *Die Zauberflöte* was Goethe, who supervised its performance in Weimar in 1794. The similarity of Sarastro's order with this *Turmgesellschaft* (Society of the Tower) in the *Wilhelm Meister* novels has received considerable critical attention over the years.[46] Goethe took a particular interest in *Singspiel,* and had himself been experimenting with the new style of music theater, producing a number of his own libretti.

Goethe attended performances by the Koch troupe while a student in Leipzig and became acquainted with Weisse and Hiller. In March 1775, his first libretto, *Erwin und Elmire,* inspired by Oliver Goldsmith's *The Vicar of Wakefield* and designated *Ein Schauspiel mit Gesang* (A Play with Song) was published in the journal *Iris*. It tells the story of a young man who becomes a hermit after being spurned by his beloved; eventually Erwin's father, Bernardo, intervenes, and the lovers are reunited. In a final trio, Elmire expresses her contrition and gratitude for Erwin's forgiveness, promising to devote the remainder of her life to him, while Erwin generalizes happily, "O Mädchen, Mädchen, was macht ihr uns nicht vergessen!"[47] (Oh you girls, the things you make us forgive and forget!). A number of different composers set the piece, including Johann André (1741–99), Duchess Anna Amalia, and, in a revised version, Goethe's friend Johann Friedrich Reichardt (1752–1814), who also provided settings for the later *Singspiele, Jery und Bätely* (1779) and *Claudine von Villa Bella* (1776, revised 1788). *Jery und Bätely* was originally intended by Goethe for another composer friend, Philipp Christoph Kayser (1755–1823); but Kayser never managed to produce a score.

Erwin und Elmire, although certainly not one of Goethe's better-known works, was very successful in its day. In the late 1770s and early 1780s it played in Weimar, Munich, Vienna, Berlin, and Frankfurt am Main. In the Weimar production of 1777 (for which Anna Amalia wrote the music), Corona Schröter took the role of Elmire; Schröter also played the Swiss mountain maiden Bätely in a 1780 production of *Jery und Bätely,* and she herself composed the score for Goethe's next *Singspiel, Die Fischerin* (1782), which opens with the famous ballad *Erlkönig* (King of the Elves).

The *Singspiel* that preceded *Jery und Bätely, Lila* (1776), designated *Ein Feenspiel* (a fairy play), is particularly interesting for the connections that can be drawn from it to two of Goethe's major projects, one finished, the other unfinished: the two-part drama *Faust,* and the libretto he started as a sequel to Mozart's and Schikaneder's *Zauberflöte*. *Lila* tells the story of a woman who, believing her husband dead, has lost hope and faith, and with them her health and a portion of her sanity. Even when the "dead" man stands before her, she refuses to believe her eyes; instead, she retreats to a corner of the family's large estate to nurture her delusions. A friendly doctor called Verazio (the truth teller) disguises himself as a wise wandering hermit, a popular figure in early German-language opera, and eventually effects a cure by persuading her that she can save the husband she presumes dead through her own courage and determination. Verazio impels the entire family to participate in a kind of fairy-tale ballet, so that Lila can be induced to "rescue" them from the clutches of a fictive ogre. She thereby passes the test of love that (in her own imagination; that is the central oddity of the piece) permits a reunion with her husband.

It is often suggested that Goethe has not been properly recognized as a writer of *Singspiel* because he never found a composer to match his own genius.[48] He is not alone, however, in failing to find recognition as a librettist. Weisse, Wieland, and a host of other writers have also been largely ignored in this capacity by literary scholars. Wieland's perceptive remark in his "Versuch über das deutsche Singspiel," "daß die Musik gleichsam die *Sprache* des Singspiels ist"[49] (that music is, so to speak, the *language* of Singspiel [emphasis in original]), goes a long way toward explaining the phenomenon. A successful libretto will of necessity curtail some elements in the text to make space for the music. An element of the aesthetic quality of the whole is given over to the music, and will therefore be perceived as absent if the text is considered in isolation. To get the full effect, we need to experience the opera, not just the libretto, because in fact the music does much of what literary scholars would normally expect a text to do. This is why it has been said that libretti lie at the edge of literature.[50]

Musical Orientalism and Mozart's *Entführung aus dem Serail*

The reports and souvenirs brought home by European travelers in the seventeenth and eighteenth centuries fascinated those who stayed at home, and by the early eighteenth century orientalism — in interior decoration, clothing, literature, and music — was all the rage. Those who could afford it had portraits painted of themselves and their families in oriental garb: Maria Theresia, for example, had an etching of herself and her daughter in Turkish costume made in 1745 by Jean Etienne Liotard (1702–1789).

Turkish-style music was fashionable throughout the century, although its actual stylistic authenticity is more than doubtful. In his *Ideen zu einer Ästhetik der Tonkunst* (Ideas on Aesthetics of Music), Christian Friedrich Daniel Schubart (1739–91) tells an anecdote of a concert of Turkish music performed in honor of the Turkish ambassador's visit to Berlin — the diplomat allegedly shook his head at the sound, and said simply that it was not Turkish.[51] Often called "Janissary" music after the elite Ottoman troops, the *yeni çeri,* European versions of Turkish music imitated some of the sounds produced by military bands in a way that suited Western taste. Typical *alla turca* style includes triangles, cymbals, bass drums and bells, and is characterized by frequent shifts between major and minor keys, unison sections, and repeated short melodies.[52]

A Janissary chorus is one feature of Mozart's orientalist *Singspiel, Die Entführung aus dem Serail*. For many years Vienna was a frontier city between the Holy Roman and Ottoman Empires, and twice under siege (in 1529 and in 1683). In the late eighteenth century the Holy Roman Empire's Islamic counterpart again entered the public eye because Russia and Austria sought to divide the Ottoman territories between them. A general partition was contemplated in 1781, a year before Mozart's opera was first performed for the visit of the Russian ambassador in Vienna. Preparations were also under way for a centenary celebration of the Austrian victory of 1783.[53] Therefore, the level of public interest was probably higher in Vienna, where Mozart was writing, than in the northern German territories. By the late eighteenth century, however, interest in the Islamic world was no longer linked to a real sense of religious or territorial threat; what remained was a kind of delicious fascination, an exoticizing interest that one sees in the spectacle, and, to some extent, the music of Mozart's opera.

Mozart and Stephanie are not the only composer and librettist partnership that produced "Turkish" operas in the eighteenth century. Earlier works include Gluck's comic opera *La rencontre imprévue* and its thematic twin *L'incontro improvviso* composed by Haydn for Eszterháza (1775; text by Karl Frieberth, 1736–1816). Mozart quotes the overture to *La rencontre* in his *Rondo alla turca* from the A major Piano Sonata (1778; K331), and the opera's plot, with its star-crossed lovers, a servant called Osmin, and a magnanimous Sultan closely resembles that of *Die Entführung*. Mozart had himself attempted an opera on a Turkish theme once before, although *Zaïde* (1779–80; K334) remained unfinished. But *Die Entführung* also has a German-language predecessor: the two-part opera *Cara Mustapha* (1686) composed nearly a century before for the Hamburg opera house by Johann Wolfgang Franck (1644–?1710) with a libretto by Lucas von Bostel (1649–1716). In *Cara Mustapha*, a real sense of a Turkish threat is still apparent, and Mozart's opera becomes more readily understandable when we examine its historical predecessor.

Cara Mustapha is more overtly political than *Die Entführung*. It focuses on events leading up to the Battle of Kahlenberg (which concluded the Siege of Vienna on 12 September 1683) — but, predictably for the opera stage, its action centers on passion, not politics. Two kinds of stereotypically "Turkish" passion are displayed by its characters: passionate love (the erotic drive) and a will to commit violence. Where in Franck's and Bostel's opera both of these passions are located in one central character (Mustapha), Mozart and Stephanie divide them between the Pasha, who is in the grip of erotic passion for Konstanze, and his servant Osmin, who is driven by violent fantasies. Osmin is the semi-comical incorporation of notions of the barbaric, violent orient, and in this he is related to Monostatos, Sarastro's black servant in *Die Zauberflöte* (who is also prone to bouts of erotic passion, as his attempted rape of Pamina shows). Sarastro sings a virtuous, paternal bass; but in *Die Entführung* and *Cara Mustapha,* Turks are morally and vocally the lowest of the characters, and the deep bass of Osmin in the former opera and Mustapha in the latter can be read emblematically.

Die Entführung also finally shows us an admirable Muslim in the figure of the pasha (who is, in fact, an exiled European). Stephanie alters his source material to the effect that Belmonte is revealed to be not the pasha's son, but the son of his enemy, thus rendering Pasha Selim's clemency all the more admirable.[54] Franck and Bostel similarly portrayed a virtuous Turkish counterpart to Mustapha in the figure of Ibrahim.[55] Certainly the popular eighteenth-century idea of the virtuous barbarian is pre-dated by seventeenth-century portrayals of noble Turks: Soliman in the play of that name by the Saxon dramatist August Adolph von Haugwitz (1654–1706) is another example.[56] It has been argued that Mozart's achievement, at the conclusion of *Die Entführung aus dem Serail,* is to recode "Turkish" music, which had previously been used only to convey barbarism or to mock the Muslim Other, as celebratory. The music of the final chorus is in C major, and celebrates the triumph of Enlightenment values alongside or within the person of Pasha Selim. This was so influential that "Turkish" musical devices (cymbals, drums, and melodic conventions associated with Janissary music) came to be recognized as celebratory, for example as they are used in Beethoven's Ninth Symphony.[57]

Lieder (Songs)

Alongside and interacting with the German *Singspiel* in the eighteenth century, the German Lied was developing. The term "Lied" designates a solo song with a written keyboard accompaniment, and this in itself marks the form as a phenomenon of the mid-eighteenth century and beyond. Earlier keyboard players (of the kind addressed by the younger Bach in his *Versuch über die wahre Art, das Clavier zu spielen*) would, as a matter of course, have found themselves faced with a figured bass line rather than written-out musical notes. The great advantage of a written-out accompaniment, and one which certainly contributed to the explosive popularity of the Lied, is that, unlike continuo, it is accessible to the musical amateur. This made the new-style Lieder ideally suited for small-scale family or personal entertainment in the homes of the eighteenth century's prospering middle classes. The rise of the Lied went hand-in-hand with another important development in the later eighteenth century, of the fortepiano, or pianoforte. Invented by Bartolomeo Cristofori (1655–1731), this instrument was sometimes called *Hammerklavier*, because it produced notes using a hammer mechanism. From the 1760s, the fortepiano took over as the standard domestic keyboard.

It has been argued that Lieder played their part in the social and moral education of the middle classes not only by mirroring their values, but also by bolstering their confidence as an emerging class.[58] This is certainly suggested by titles of songbooks in the late eighteenth century, such as Reichardt's *Wiegenlieder für gute deutsche Mütter* (Lullabies for Good German Mothers, 1798). Their popularity is testified to in Friedrich Wilhelm Marpurg's *Anleitung zur Musik überhaupt, und zur Singkunst besonders* (Introduction to Music and the Art of Singing, 1763): in an introduction, Marpurg declares that he has faith in the usefulness of his book because it is being published at a time when all the world is learning to sing.[59]

The song collection usually cited as marking the beginning of Lieder development in the eighteenth century is *Sperontes Singende Muse an der Pleisse* (Sperontes' Singing Muse on the [River] Pleisse), published in Leipzig in 1736 and edited by Johann Sigismund Scholze (pseud. Sperontes, 1705–1750). Scholze's collection of texts and tunes was enormously popular (it appeared in several editions) and at the same time heavily criticized, primarily on the grounds that the type and rhythm of the music he selected did not fit the style or the natural rhythm of the texts. As a response and corrective, other collections appeared, including the *Oden mit Melodien* (1753–55) of Christian Gottfried Krause, edited in collaboration with the poet Karl Ramler (1725–1798). Ramler selected simple texts on topics such as rural bliss, love, and friendship; Krause set some of the Anacreontic poems himself, but also enlisted Graun, Franz Benda, C. P. E. Bach, Quantz, and Johann Friedrich Agricola (1720–1774) as composers. The collection was published in Berlin, which soon became the center of the northern German Lied: over the next seventy years, three "Berlin schools" developed with three generations of composers. Marpurg, whose *Berlinische Oden und Lieder* appeared in three parts between 1756 and 1763, belonged to the first generation, as did Krause. *Von der musikalischen Poesie*, Krause's history of music theater with its detailed analyses of poetry and forms of song, was the founding theoretical text for the first Berlin Lied school.

The simplicity of folk-style poetry was thought to render it particularly suited to song. Herder was influential on this point; while teaching in Riga, he made the acquaintance of the Latvian folksong,[60] and in his essay "Auszug aus einem Briefwechsel über Ossian und die Lieder alter Völker" (Excerpt from Correspondence on Ossian and the Songs of Ancient Peoples, first published in *Von deutscher Art und Kunst*, 1773), he champions folk poetry, conjuring an idealized image of untrammeled peoples creating wild, sensuous song ("je wilder, d.i. je lebendiger, je freiwirkender ein Volk ist [. . .], desto lebendiger, freier, sinnlicher, lyrisch handelnde müssen auch, wenn es Lieder hat, seine Lieder sein!" [the wilder, that is, the more alive and free a people is . . . the more alive, free, sensual and lyrical must its songs (if it has songs) be]).[61] The ideal is simple, even childlike, and in German exemplified for Herder by Luther. In fact, the chorale had already influenced the development of German song. Hymn-like songs for church and home use, such as Quantz's *Neue Kirchenmelodien,* published in 1760 with texts by the novelist Christian Fürchtegott Gellert (1715–1769), were as popular as their secular counterparts.[62] Herder's own anthology of folksongs (*Volkslieder*) appeared in two volumes in 1778 and 1779, and included songs from across Europe as well as from Madagascar and Peru, all in German translation.

The move towards Herder and Ossian, however, also signals a move away from the Anacreontic style and toward the poetic styles of *Empfindsamkeit* (Sensibility) and *Sturm und Drang* (Storm and Stress). This was the focus of the second Berlin generation, which included Goethe's friend and collaborator Johann Reichardt, as well as the master mason and composer Carl Friedrich Zelter (1758–1832; conductor of Berlin's famous choir, the *Singakademie*) and Johann Abraham Peter Schulz (1747–1800). Schulz's influential collection *Lieder im Volkston* appeared in three parts between 1782 and 1790, further establishing the fashion for folk style. His preface to the work was particularly influential: in it, he maintains that his intention is to write songs primarily of the people rather than primarily artistic ("mehr volksmäßig als kunstmäßig"), and coins the phrase "Schein des Bekannten" (appearance of familiarity) to describe what is essential in folk style.[63] The notion of the "Schein des Bekannten" came to epitomize the classical Lied aesthetic.

In the more musically conservative context of Switzerland and Austria, the Lied developed more slowly, and figured bass accompaniments persisted until the end of the century.[64] In Austria, Maria Theresia Paradis, Haydn, and Mozart published German songs in the 1880s, although the otherwise prolific Mozart composed only thirty-four in total. His setting of "Das Veilchen" (K476; The Violet) from Goethe's *Singspiel, Erwin und Elmire,* composed in 1785 and published in 1789, is his most famous, and to the regret of many the only Goethe poem he ever set.

Church Music

The histories of secular and church music in the eighteenth century cannot be separated from one another. A court *Kapellmeister* or a civic *Kantor* might well find himself charged with responsibilities in both areas, and there are overlaps in form and style.

Inevitably, church music (which is often vocal) was influenced by opera. In Hamburg, the pastor of the Jakobikirche, Erdmann Neumeister (1671–1756), caused a stir with the publication of his *Madrigalische Cantaten* (Madrigal Cantatas, 1700), which contained no texts from Scripture and no chorales, but poetic texts in the operatic style. In 1704, Reinhard Keiser followed this with his passion oratorio *Der blutige und sterbende Jesus* (Jesus, Bleeding and Dying); again, church music without Scripture, but instead with a libretto written by Christian Friedrich Hunold (pseud. Menantes, 1681–1721). Keiser was also the first composer to set what was to become the most popular of all passion oratorio texts: *Der für die Sünden der Welt gemartete und sterbende Jesu* (Jesus, Martyred and Dying for the Sins of the World, 1715), written by the city senator, Barthold Heinrich Brockes (1680–1747). Brockes's passion was set again by Mattheson and Telemann in 1718, and by Handel in 1719, among many others; its dramatic form, with sung parts and some symbolic characters, anticipates the famous Bach passions later in the century.

Church music reflects the religious divide between the southern areas of the Empire controlled by the Catholic Habsburgs, and the northern areas which had become Protestant during the Reformation. The Protestants were also internally divided. Martin Luther believed profoundly in the importance of music as part of divine worship, and Lutheranism was a driving musical force in churches; but Calvinists and Pietists objected to the excessive use of church music. They also considered opera a corrupting influence, by contrast with the more liberal Lutheran churches, who were prepared to set religious texts to music from popular arias.

The name most frequently associated with northern German church music at this time is Johann Sebastian Bach. Bach was an organist and a devout Lutheran, whose organ works show the influence of his great northern German predecessor, Dietrich Buxtehude. Bach never wrote an opera, although his passions are operatic, and alongside church cantatas he wrote secular cantatas which he titled *dramma per musica,* such as *Phoebus and Pan* (1731; BWV 201, text by Christian Friedrich Henrici [1700–1764]; pseud. Picander, after Ovid) and the so-called Coffee Cantata (c. 1734–35; "Schweigt still, plaudert nicht," BWV 211 [Be still, do not chatter]).

Eighteenth-century cantatas tended to combine arias and recitative sections; characteristic of the German cantata was a mix of biblical and poetic texts, although some of Bach's still use a plain chorale text in the old Lutheran style. Today they are listened to as individual works of art, but Bach's church cantatas were composed to be one functional component in the larger event of the religious service. This included a sermon lasting at least an hour, which was introduced and concluded with either a two-part cantata or two separate compositions.[65] In 1725, Bach set to music nine cantata texts written by the Leipzig poet Christiane Mariane von Ziegler (1695–1760).

Ziegler expresses enthusiasm for the working partnership in a poem she sent Bach, called "Antwort-Schreiben" (A Letter of Response):

> Du weist, daß mich nichts mehr als die Music kan laben,
> Denn dieses Element ernehret Seel und Geist.
> Es kan mir in der That kein größrer Dienst geschehen;
> Als wenn ich, wie du selbst davon kanst Zeuge seyn;
> Vom lieben Noten-Volck mich soll umringet sehen;
> Ich räumte, gieng es an, ihm alle Zimmer ein.[66]

> [You know that nothing quickens me more than music; / Because it is an element that nourishes soul and spirit./ Indeed, I know of no greater service/ Than when (as you yourself can witness)/ I Find myself surrounded by the sweet company of musicians./ If I could, I would give them every room in my house.]

Soon, however, to Ziegler's disappointment, Bach began working with Henrici (Picander), Gottsched's literary competitor and arch-enemy in Leipzig. Bach and Henrici collaborated on an annual series of cantatas, and von Ziegler concludes the second volume of her poetry collection with a piece called "Abschied an die Poesie" (Farewell to Poetry) that can be read as either witty or embittered. In it, she announces her retreat from the field of poetry on the grounds that men are more blessed by the muses, and the efforts of a woman must, therefore, be in vain.[67]

It was Henrici, too, who wrote the recitatives and arias for Bach's St. Matthew Passion (*Matthäus-Passion,* BWV 244), which takes its text from Chapters twenty-six and twenty-seven of the Gospel of St Matthew, and was first performed for Good Friday, 1727. The earlier Passion, the St. John (*Johannis-Passion,* BWV 245) was first performed in Leipzig in 1724; Bach's version of the gospel story incorporated words from Brockes's famous passion. Bach also composed a St. Mark Passion in 1731, for which the music is now largely lost. St. Matthew's gospel was particularly popular among composers of passions, which, like cantatas, were traditionally performed in two parts, before and after a sermon. St. Matthew's account lends itself to such a division and, in its focus on the meditative aspects of the story, to lyrical musical composition.[68] Other notable German composers to produce St. Matthew passions were Bach's great Protestant predecessor Heinrich Schütz (1585–1672) in 1666 and Telemann in 1730.

At the Catholic courts, the most prominent church composers of the century include Fux, Caldara, and Mozart in Vienna; Hasse at Dresden; and Haydn at Eszterháza, and later in Vienna. Fux was Vienna's most prolific and influential composer of masses in the earlier part of the century, although he also wrote oratorios with the librettist Pietro Pariati. Because opera was not permitted during Lent, oratorios — musical settings of sacred texts that follow the conventions of opera, performed in church — were substituted. The form of the oratorio varied in different areas: the Hamburg form of the passion oratorio has already been discussed. For Handel in London, oratorio was a three-act musical drama on a biblical subject, with a chorus, that could be performed as a concert outside the church context: the *Messiah* (1742) is his most famous. Antonio Caldara, the assistant *Kapellmeister* at Vienna, set sacred oratorio texts by the court poets, Metastasio and Zeno, including *Il Battista* (1727) and *Gerusalemme convertita* (1733); and in Dresden Hasse composed Italian-language sacred oratorios for the Catholic ceremonials at the Saxon court, works that were so successful they were also performed in Protestant churches in the second half of the eighteenth century.[69] Hasse's *La conversione di Sant'Agostino* (1750) is the setting of a libretto by Electress Maria Antonia, showing Augustine's conversion in five stages.

As a church composer, Haydn is best known for his late masses and oratorios. The Mariazell Mass in C (the *missa cellensis* of 1782) was written for Eszterháza, but his six great masses were written after he had retired and returned to Vienna, and include the Nelson Mass (*missa in angustiis*, 1798) performed in front of the British admiral in 1800. His last two oratorios were *Die Schöpfung* (The Creation, 1798) and *Die Jahreszeiten* (The Seasons, 1801), written for Vienna in collaboration with Gottfried van Swieten (1733–1803), a wealthy patron and librettist who both sponsored the oratorios' performances and provided the texts. Van Swieten also sponsored a performance of Handel's *Messiah* for Vienna, in an arrangement by Mozart.

Mozart himself wrote his famous Mass in C minor (K427) not for Vienna but for Salzburg, where it was performed in 1783 with his new wife, Constanze, singing one of the solo parts. The mass is remarkable for its mixed style — Mozart uses both the modern cantata style and old-fashioned counterpoint — but also for its beauty, most apparent perhaps in the lyrical *Et Incarnatus* section. His *Requiem* was, notoriously, never completed; he was still working on it at the time of his death in December 1791, and the music was finished by his pupil Franz Xaver Süssmayr (1766–1803). A great deal of paper and ink has been expended on the puzzle of how much, precisely, Süssmayr contributed to the work.

Music Across the Borders: A European Culture

In this essay I have concentrated largely on the German-speaking areas. Even so, no tidily "German" narrative emerges: we find Gluck writing music for Paris; Hasse for Venice, Naples, and Dresden; Haydn at Eszterháza, and Handel in London; the Italian singer Faustina Bordoni in Dresden, Metastasio and Zeno at Vienna; Jommelli in Stuttgart, and French actors, singers, and dancers performing opera-ballet at the Dresden court. Given the geographical spread of the Holy Roman Empire, these kinds of European interworkings were practically inevitable, and "German" musical culture in the eighteenth century developed alongside and out of the cross-border influences from Italy, France, Bohemia, England, and Poland, ruled for much of the century by the Electors of Saxony.

The numerous courts of the Empire were important musical centers, but by the end of the eighteenth century, "high" musical culture was clearly no longer the provenance of the courts and churches. In music theater, Italy's dominating influence was countered by the popularity of the vernacular *Singspiel*. At the eighteenth century's end Italian opera remained popular especially in the South, but it now had serious competition. In some places, the move from Italian to German was forced rather than natural; as a clear signal of the ruler's dedication to the cause of German-language music theater, Karl Theodor opened a Hof- und Nationalbühne in Mannheim in 1775 and inaugurated it with a performance of Wieland's and Schweitzer's German *Singspiel, Alceste*. Similarly, in Munich, the Elector actively sought to shift the artistic focus from Italian to German by founding a Deutsches Schauspiel and Deutsche Oper. Ten years after his move to the Munich court, in 1787, Karl Theodor took the radical step of banning Italian opera there.

The growing financial security and confidence of the middle classes in the eighteenth century paved the way for musical culture to flourish in the civic and domestic context. *Collegia musica* made high-quality music available in performance to anyone who could pay a modest sum to hear it, and civic choirs encouraged personal participation (initially of men, later also of women) in the music-making process. The emergence of musical periodicals alongside the more expensive and less accessible monographs widened access to ideas about music: in 1798, Johann Friedrich Rochlitz (1769–1842) became the first editor of the *Allgemeine Musikalische Zeitung*, published in Leipzig by Breitkopf & Härtel. This weekly publication, which survived until 1848 and is still an important resource for modern musicologists, published reviews, articles, and new scores by contemporary composers.

It is noteworthy that the most specifically "German" musical developments in the eighteenth century are text-based: the new Lied (which is remarkable for the lack of foreign influence on its development), and the *Singspiel*, which provides the foundations for German opera in the nineteenth century. One of the great Lieder composers of the nineteenth century, Franz Schubert (1797–1828), was influenced by his now little-known eighteenth-century predecessor, Johann Rudolf Zumsteeg (1760–1802). Zumsteeg notably set Schiller's poems and ballads, and his use of recitative made a strong impression on the young Schubert.[70]

The social status of the composer was changing fundamentally in this period. During the earlier part of the eighteenth century, the composer was seen primarily as a craftsman: on a mid-century opera libretto the name of composer, if he was identified at all, was likely to be in small print alongside the librettist. By its end, the composer as artist was far more prominent.[71] This is at least in part because the rise of *Singspiel* and the Lied helped produce a sense of the German national capacity for artistic creation in the field of music; but also because the eighteenth century saw some of Germany's and Austria's greatest international musical successes linked with the names of J. S. Bach, Mozart, and Haydn. At the very end of the period, the traditions established by these composers were carried over into the nineteenth century by Ludwig van Beethoven, and some of their achievements were immortalized, with a certain nostalgia, by nineteenth-century writers such as E. T. A. Hoffmann (1776–1822), in his "Ritter Gluck," or "Don Juan."[72]

Notes

[1] Carl Friedrich Cramer, ed., *Magazin der Musik*, vol. 1, (Hamburg 1783), 348; cited in Peter Schleuning, *Der Bürger erhebt sich: Geschichte der deutschen Musik im 18. Jahrhundert*. 2nd revised ed. (Stuttgart: Metzler, 2000), 273.

[2] Dorothea Schröder, *Zeitgeschichte auf der Opernbühne: Barockes Musiktheater in Hamburg im Dienst von Politik und Diplomatie (1690–1745)* (Göttingen: Vandenhoeck & Ruprecht, 1998).

[3] Thomas Baumann, "The Eighteenth Century: Serious Opera," in *The Oxford Illustrated History of Opera*, ed. Roger Parker (Oxford: Oxford UP., 1994), 47–83, here 48.

[4] Schleuning, 19.

[5] For a fuller list and a discussion of the problems of attributing authorship to some works, see Ernst Eugene Helm, *Music at the Court of Frederick the Great* (Norman: U of Oklahoma P, 1960), 41–66.

[6] Published as Carl Heinrich Graun, *Montezuma: Oper in 3 Akten*, ed. A. Mayer-Reinach. Denkmäler deutscher Tonkunst, vol. 15 (Leipzig: Breitkopf & Härtel, 1904).

[7] Geoffrey Webber, "German Courts and Cities," in *Companion to Baroque Music*, ed. Julie Anne Sadie (London: Dent 1990), 149–58, here 151.

[8] Johann Kuhnau, *Der musicalische Quack-Salber* (1700; rpt., Berlin: Behr, 1900), 13. A scholarly facsimile edition with extensive introduction has also been published: *Der musikalische Quacksalber*, edited by James N. Hardin, vol. 3 of Johann Kuhnau, *Ausgewählte Werke* (Bern: Peter Lang, 1992).

[9] Johann Joachim Quantz, *Versuch einer Anweisung die Flöte traversière zu spielen*. Trans. Edward R. Reilly, *On Playing the Flute*, 2nd ed. (New York: Schirmer, 1985).

[10] Roland Würtz, "Mannheim," in *New Grove Dictionary of Music and Musicians* (London: Macmillan, 1980), 11: 622–69, here 625.

[11] Donald Jay Grout and Claude V. Palisca, *A History of Western Music*. 4th ed. (London: Dent, 1988), 564.

[12] Sara Smart, "Ballet in the Empire," in *Spectaculum Europaeum: Theater and Spectacle in Europe (1580–1750)*, ed. Pierre Béhar and Helen Watanabe-O"Kelly (Wiesbaden: Harrassowitz, 1999), 547–70, here 552.

[13] Herbert Seifert, "Costanza e Fortezza," in *The New Grove Dictionary of Opera*, 4 vols. (London: Macmillan 1992), 1: 970.

[14] Julie Ann Sadie, ed., *Companion to Baroque Music* (London: Dent, 1990), 252.

[15] Leonard G. Ratner, *Classic Music: Expression, Form and Style* (London: Schirmer, 1980), 109.

[16] Emil Platen, "Collegium Musicum," in *Die Musik in Geschichte und Gegenwart: Allgemeine Enzyklopädie der Musik, Sachteil*, 2nd ed. (Kassel: Bärenreiter, 1995) 2: 946–51.

[17] Johann Nikolaus Forkel, *Ankündigung seines akademischen Winter-Concerts* (Göttingen: Johann Christian Dieterich, 1779), 11.

[18] Johann Nikolaus Forkel, *Musikalischer Almanach für Deutschland auf das Jahr 1784* (rpt. Hildesheim: Olms, 1974), 151.

[19] Schleuning, *Der Bürger* 182–84.

[20] Johann Mattheson, *Der Vollkommene Capellmeister* (1739; rpt. Kassel: Bärenreiter, 1954), 3, chapter 26, paragraph 19.

[21] Reprinted as Johann Gottfried Walther, *Musicalisches Lexikon oder Musicalische Bibliothec. Neusatz des Textes und der Noten*, edited by Friederike Ramm (Kassel: Bärenreiter, 2001).

[22] Johann Adolph Scheibe, *Compendium MUSICES Theoretico-practicum*. Reprinted as an appendix to Peter Benary, *Die deutsche Kompositionslehre des 18. Jahrhunderts* (Leipzig: Breitkopf & Härtel, 1961). Benary dates the work as pre-1736. In the quotation, italics designate words in Roman type as opposed to *Fraktur*.

[23] Barthold Feind, "Von Erregung der Gemüths-Bewegungen in Schau-Spielen," prologue to *Der Fall des grossen Richters in Israel/ SIMSON*, music by Christoph Graupner. Reprinted in *Die Hamburger Oper*, edited by Reinhard Meyer (Munich: Kraus, 1980–84), I, 255–333.

[24] Johann Mattheson, *Das neu-eröffnete Orchestre* (Hamburg: Benjamin Schillers Witwe, 1713). Microfilm facsimile Ann Arbor: UMI books on demand, 1993.

[25] Leopold Mozart, *Versuch einer gründlichen Violinschule* (Augsburg: Lotter, 1756), 107–8. Reprinted Leipzig: Breitkopf & Härtel, 1956, and translated by Edith Knocker as *A Treatise on the Fundamental Principles of Violin Playing* (Oxford: Oxford UP, 1985).

[26] Mark Evan Bonds, *Wordless Rhetoric: Musical Form and the Metaphor of the Oration* (Cambridge, MA: Harvard UP, 1991), 60–61.

[27] See Richard Kramer, "Notes to Beethoven's Education," in *Journal of the American Musicological Society* 28 (1975), 95.

[28] Barthold Feind, *Deutsche Gedichte* (1708; rpt. Bern: Lang, 1989), 80.

[29] Christian Gottfried Krause, *Von der Musikalischen Poesie* (Berlin: J. F. Voss, 1752), 49.

[30] Wilhelm A. Bauer and Otto Erich Deutsch, eds., *Mozarts Briefe und Aufzeichnungen* (Kassel: Bärenreiter, 1963), 3:167.

[31] Christoph Martin Wieland, "Ueber einige ältere deutsche Singspiele, die den Namen 'Alceste' führen," in Wieland, *Werke* (Berlin: Hempel, n.d.), 29:75–100, here 96.

[32] Article "Frédegunde," in *Dictionnaire d'histoire de France Perrin*, eds. Alain Decaux and André Castelot (Paris: Librairie académique Perrin, 1981).

[33] Johann Ulrich König, *Fredegunda*, reprinted in *Die Hamburger Oper*, ed. Reinhard Meyer (Munich: Kraus, 1980–84), 2: 519–74.

[34] Johann Christoph Gottsched, *Versuch einer Critischen Dichtkunst vor die Deutschen* (Leipzig: Breitkopf, 1730), 604. See Gloria Flaherty, *Opera in the Development of German Critical Thought* (Princeton: Princeton UP, 1978), 95.

[35] Johann Christoph Gottsched, *Gesammelte Schriften* (Berlin: Gottsched-Verlag, 1903), 3: 224–25.

[36] Gerhard Croll and Winton Dean, "Christoph Willibald Gluck," in *New Grove Dictionary of Music and Musicians* (London: Macmillan, 1980), 7: 455–75, here 464–66.

[37] Sarah Colvin, *The Rhetorical Feminine: Gender and Orient on the German Stage, 1647–1742* (Oxford: Clarendon, 1999), 238–43.

[38] Gloria Flaherty, "Bach's Leipzig as a Training Ground for Actors, Musicians, and Singers," in *Music and German Literature: Their Relationship since the Middle Ages*, ed. James M. McGlathery (Columbia, SC: Camden House, 1992), 100–19, here 110.

[39] Both texts by Da Ponte, the latter after Pierre Augustin Caron de Beaumarchais, *La Folle Journée, ou Le Mariage de Figaro* (The Day of Madness, or the Marriage of Figaro, 1778).

[40] Christoph Martin Wieland, "Versuch über das deutsche Singspiel und einige dahin einschlagende Gegenstände." The essay first appeared in *Teutsche Merkur* 3 (1775), 63–87 and 4:156–73. Reprinted in Wieland, *Werke* 38, 126–53, here 132–33.

[41] Wieland, "Versuch" 130.

[42] Peter Branscombe, "Christoph Martin Wieland," in *New Grove Dictionary of Opera* (London: Macmillan, 1992), 4:1154.

[43] Hans-Albrecht Koch, *Das deutsche Singspiel* (Stuttgart: Metzler, 1974), 71–72.

[44] Thomas Baumann, "Karl Ditters von Dittersdorf," in *New Grove Dictionary of Opera* (London: Macmillan, 1992), 1: 1182–84, here 1182.

[45] See also the essay "Enlightenment in Austria: Cultural Identity and National Literature" by Franz M. Eybl in this volume.

[46] Koch, *Das deutsche Singspiel* 90.

[47] Johann Wolfgang von Goethe, *Erwin und Elmire, ein Schauspiel mit Gesang*. Reprinted in Goethe, *Singspiele*, ed. Hans-Albrecht Koch (Stuttgart: Reclam, 1974), 5–32, here 31.

[48] See for example Koch, "Nachwort" 285–324, here 290.

[49] Wieland, "Versuch" 133.

[50] Sandra Corse, *Opera and the Uses of Language: Mozart, Verdi, and Britten* (London: Associated UP, 1987), 14.

[51] Christian Friedrich Daniel Schubart, *Ideen zu einer Ästhetik der Tonkunst* (Rpt. Leipzig: Reclam, 1977), 253.

[52] See Gunther Joppig, "Alla Turca: Orientalismen in der Europäischen Kunstmusik vom 17. bis zum 19. Jahrhundert," in *Europa und der Orient 800–1900*, ed. Gereon Sievernich and Hendrik Budde (Gütersloh: Bertelsmann, 1989), 295–304.

[53] Volkmar Braunbehrens, *Mozart in Vienna, 1781–1791* (New York: Grove, 1990), 74.

[54] See Thomas Betzweiser, "Die Europäer in der Fremde: Die Figurenkonstellation der *Entführung aus dem Serail* und ihre Tradition," in *Mozarts Opernfiguren: Grosse Herren, rasende Weiber, gefährliche Liebschaften*, ed. Dieter Borchmeyer (Bern: Haupt, 1991), 35–48.

[55] On the consequences see Colvin, *The Rhetorical Feminine*, 66.

[56] August Adolph von Haugwitz, *Soliman*, in Haugwitz, *Prodromus Poeticus, Oder: Poetischer Vortrab* (1684; rpt. Tübingen: Niemeyer, 1984).

[57] Timothy D. Taylor, "Peopling the Stage: Opera, Otherness, and New Musical Representations in the Eighteenth Century," in *Cultural Critique* 36 (1997): 55–88, here 74.

[58] Walter Wiora, *Das deutsche Lied* (Wolfenbüttel: Möseler, 1971), 113–16.

[59] Friedrich Wilhelm Marpurg, *Anleitung zur Musik überhaupt, und zur Singkunst besonders* (1763; rpt. Leipzig: Zentralantiquariat der DDR, 1975).

[60] Peter Branscombe, "Herder, Johann Gottfried," in *New Grove Dictionary of Music and Musicians* (London: Macmillan, 1980), 8: 504.

[61] Johann Gottfried Herder, "*Auszug aus einem Briefwechsel über Ossian und die Lieder alter Völker*," in Herder, *Werke* (Berlin: Dümmler, n.d.), 5: 345–72, here 349 and 370.

[62] J. W. Smeed, *German Song and its Poetry, 1740–1900* (London: Croom Helm, 1987), 34.

[63] Johann Abraham Peter Schulz, "Vorrede" to the *Lieder im Volkston*. Reprinted in *Das deutsche Lied im 18. Jahrhundert: Quellen und Studien*, ed. by Max Friedländer (Stuttgart: Cotta, 1902), 1: 256.

[64] Smeed, *German Song and its Poetry*, 40.

[65] Hans Joachim Kreutzer, "Bach and the Literary Scene in Eighteenth-Century Leipzig," in McGlathery, ed., *Music and German Literature*, 80–99, here 85.

[66] Christiane Mariane von Ziegler, *Versuch in gebundener Schreib-Art,* 2 vols. (Leipzig: Joh. Friedrich Brauns sel. Erben, 1728–1729), 148.

[67] Kreutzer, "Bach," 88.

[68] Paul Steinitz, "German Church Music," in *Opera and Church Music 1630–1750,* ed. Anthony Lewis and Nigel Fortune. New Oxford History of Music, vol. 5 (London: Oxford UP, 1975), 557–776, here 621.

[69] Hellmuth Christian Wolff, "Italian Oratorio and Passion," in Lewis and Fortune, *Opera and Church Music* 324–50, here 347.

[70] G. Maier, "Zumsteeg, Johann Rudolf," in *New Grove Dictionary of Music and Musicians* (London: Macmillan, 1980), 20: 716–17, here 717.

[71] Mark Evan Bonds, *Wordless Rhetoric: Musical Form and the Metaphor of the Oration* (Cambridge, MA: Harvard UP, 1991), 56.

[72] I am indebted for this reference to Professor Andrew Barker.

Sophie La Roche, ca. 1772. Drawing by an anonymous artist.

The Era of Sensibility
and the Novel of Self-Fashioning[1]

Anna Richards

"EMPFINDSAMKEIT" (sensibility), a cultural trend underpinned by Shaftesbury's theory of an innate moral sense and influenced by the confessional literature of Pietism, encouraged the frequent expression and analysis of emotion as a means of exercising and demonstrating virtue.[2] In the novel of sensibility, authors focused more on the private and inner lives of characters than on external adventures or wider social developments, and emphasized those values, such as friendship, domestic harmony, and sympathy, that were particularly prized by the emerging middle classes. In the challenge it posed to the "immoral" ways of the courtly aristocracy, the sentimental novel at first had progressive implications. As critics have argued, however, its progressiveness was limited: the sentimental novel was ultimately a symptom of the retreat of the middle classes from any sphere of public influence into the safe haven of the family.

Sentimental novels bear witness to the polarization of gender roles that accompanied this retreat into the private sphere. Early Enlightenment thinkers argued that both sexes should be guided by their reason, and advocated improved education for girls, but by the end of the eighteenth century, under the influence of Rousseau, medical writers, educationalists, and philosophers had come to associate traits such as sensitivity, sympathy, and closeness to nature with the female sex in particular. They argued that women were "undivided," plant-like creatures, whose role was to offer emotional succor to their families, and who had little need of formal learning.[3]

"Empfindsamkeit" was most prevalent in German literary culture between the 1740s, when Klopstock and Gellert's first works appeared, and the 1770s, the decade that marks the highpoint of the trend. Sentimental elements can be found in novels both before and long after these dates, however. This essay traces the history of the sentimental novel by examining six exemplary works from the time of Johann Gottfried Schnabel (1692–ca. 1750), author of *Wunderliche Fata einiger Seefahrer* (Strange Fates of Some Seafarers, 1731–43) to that of Friederike Helene Unger, who wrote *Bekenntnisse einer schönen Seele* (Confessions of a Beautiful Soul, 1806). In doing so, the essay does not provide a revised evaluation of the political impact of the sentimental novel. Rather, it illustrates how "Empfindsamkeit"—often dismissed by today's readers as moralizing and overly self-conscious—allowed authors to depict characters and their fashioning with increasing psychological sophistication. The article also reexamines the gender politics of sentimental fiction, and asks whether the relationship between women and "Empfindsamkeit" is as restrictive as it might first appear, or whether sensibility could have had an emancipatory impact on the portrayal of female characters or on women novelists.

Novels of Adventure and Johann Gottfried Schnabel

During the seventeenth century the novel emerged as a distinct literary genre in Germany, ranging from voluminous courtly novels to the picaresque, but it was in the eighteenth century that German authors began to create novels of European stature. More than any other kind of literary work, it contributed to and profited from an enormous growth of the reading public, a shift in reading habits from intensive to extensive reading, and a secularization of people's preferred reading matter. The popularity which the "Robinsonade" enjoyed from the 1720s on is evidence that these changes were already under way by then. In 1720, Daniel Defoe's shipwreck tale *The Life and Surprizing Adventures of Robinson Crusoe* (1719) was translated into German and became the first in a series of English novels formatively to influence eighteenth-century German literature. Instead of "gallant" novels, the often frivolous stories of flirtation and sexual dalliance most popular at the beginning of the century, many German authors followed Defoe in composing adventure stories. Like the picaresque novels of the seventeenth century, these works recounted a series of dramatic happenings at a speedy narrative pace, but they reflected a more middle-class, "enlightened" view of the world. Rather than simply being the victims of an external fate, for example, heroes influence events through their own moral behavior. The beginnings of the sentimental novel can be traced to the "Robinsonade."

The most famous "Robinsonade" was Schnabel's *Wunderliche Fata einiger See-Fahrer,* more commonly known as *Insel Felsenburg* (Felsenburg Island), published in four volumes between 1731 and 1743 under the pseudonym "Gisander." The first volume is complete in itself and generally considered the most successful. The story is narrated first by Eberhard Julius, a sensitive young man who, after suffering various misfortunes in Europe, is summoned by his great-great-uncle Albertus to the distant Island Felsenburg. There he discovers a utopian community of hard-working, Christian souls living a simple but fulfilled life over whom Albertus rules with enlightened benevolence. The first-person life stories of Albertus and several other islanders make up most of the rest of the volume. They tell of apparitions, premonitions, shipwrecks, kidnappings, murders, incest, bestiality, and cannibalism--happenings narrated successively with little pause for reflection, in a style characterized by lengthy, complex sentences, words of French origin, an emphasis on detail and enumeration, and at times, extraordinary brutality.

It is little wonder that in the early eighteenth century, as in the preceding century, the genre of the novel had (by and large) a low reputation. It was believed that such salacious and violent elements as are found in the *Insel Felsenburg* could corrupt morals. Furthermore, detractors (many of them clergy) argued that novels immersed readers in fantasy worlds that were a dangerous diversion from "real life." To defend themselves against this accusation, authors frequently insisted in prefaces that their works were genuine autobiographies or authentic documents, and titled them "Geschichten" (histories) rather than "Romane" (novels) to reinforce the point. Schnabel's preface, in which the "editor" explains that he was given the manuscript by an author and that readers must decide for themselves how much of it to believe, is unusual. If Schnabel chooses not to justify his narrative through an unqualified assurance of its authenticity, however, its potentially corrupting influence is more than counterbalanced by the moralizing tone with which he overlays even the most gruesome tales. Evil characters are punished; the good are rewarded; the sentimental values of friendship, domestic intimacy, sexual continence, a puritanical faith in God, and a sympathy testified to by tears prevail. Any political message in the novel arises from its moral thesis, and consists in a criticism of the sinful ways of Europe, in particular of the French nation and the aristocracy.

Like most of the novels discussed here, the *Insel Felsenburg* was popular with readers when first published but is seldom read today.[4] "Sentimental" on the one hand, the novel is also accused by modern critics of excessive rationality. They refer to the "utilitarian thinking" of new arrivals on Felsenburg, who happily sacrifice their partners to others and take new ones to help populate the island. Rolf Allerdissen argues that for Schnabel, the head always rules the heart,[5] while Rolf Grimminger writes that Schnabel's characters are endowed with little psychological complexity.[6] However, Schnabel does not always portray his characters' decisions and actions as automatic and unproblematic. Rather, a combination of rational and sentimental elements allows him on occasion to shed light on the psychological processes that precede them.

The events surrounding the arrival of the first group of settlers on the island illustrate this point. The Frenchman Lemelie murders Concordia's husband Van Leuven, and himself dies shortly afterward. The intense grief Concordia suffers after her husband's death makes her a perfect representative of "Empfindsamkeit." But her feelings stand in the way of her union with Albertus, now the island's only other human inhabitant. Soon after Van

Leuven's murder, one of the monkeys Albertus has domesticated is killed. The grief of the monkey's "widower" and children is indescribable, according to Albertus: for forty-eight hours they lie still and neither eat nor drink. But then their mood improves and the simian "widower" sets out to find a new bride. This incident is clearly intended to illustrate the healthy mourning process. The monkey's "rational" decision to remarry does not testify to a lack of feeling, nor, on the other hand, is his intense grief a self-indulgent immersion in emotion that inhibits action: on the contrary, it is a prerequisite for it. It is in this light that the reader is to interpret Concordia's decision, arrived at soon after the return of the monkey with his new partner, to accept Albert as a second husband.

Men and women have distinct roles in the *Insel Felsenburg*. Female characters are important primarily in their capacity as wives and mothers to the island's population. But there is little evidence of the distinct polarization of gender characteristics that would be common later in the century. Concordia's sensibility, for example, is shared in equal measure by Albert, who pulls his hair out in grief when Van Leuven dies. It was with the works of Samuel Richardson (1689–1761), the second decisive English influence on eighteenth-century sentimental fiction in Germany, that the figure of the sentimental heroine became particularly popular. For Richardson, the novel was a vehicle for psychological investigation and a means to educate readers in moral matters. In epistolary novels such as *Pamela, or Virtue Rewarded* (1740–41, *Pamela, oder die belohnte Tugend*, 1742) and *Clarissa: The History of a Young Lady* (1747–48, *Die Geschichte der Clarissa, eines vornehmen Frauenzimmers*, 1749–53), he concentrated on the private lives of middle-class figures, rather than on the external adventures or courtly intrigues that had been the concern of many novels. He portrayed idealized female protagonists possessed of extreme sensibility and a determination to uphold their beliefs in the face of opposition.

Gellert, *Leben der schwedischen Gräfin von G****

Christian Fürchtegott Gellert (1715–1769) was familiar with *Pamela*, and his *Leben der schwedischen Gräfin von G**** (Life of the Swedish Countess of G***), published anonymously in 1747–48, is the first German novel in the tradition of Richardson. The first part of the novel is a first-person account by the eponymous Countess in which she tells of her marriage to the Count von G., their domestic bliss, his supposed death, and her remarriage to his bourgeois friend "R." These events find a shocking echo in the incestuous marriage of the Count's illegitimate daughter Marianne to her brother Carlson, Carlson's death, Marianne's subsequent marriage to his friend Dormund, who turns out to be Carlson's murderer, and her suicide. When the Count, who is not dead after all, reappears, "R" relinquishes the Countess to him. Part Two consists of letters from the Count describing the hardships of his long imprisonment in Russia and the compensation he found in his close friendship with the Englishman Steeley, and of the Countess's description of daily life in the happy community of like-minded, sentimental friends with whom she and her husband now spend their days. The story ends with the death of the Count, and then of "R."

The novel's breathless succession of dramatic events is evidence of its debt to the adventure novels that still prevailed during this period, but, as in the case of Richardson, Gellert's real interest lay in the inner lives of his characters; his narrative tone is intimate and conversational. Although many of his figures belong to the minor aristocracy, Gellert, like Richardson, demonstrates that virtue rather than social standing determines true nobility. The novel further resembles the works of Richardson in its didactic intent. In keeping with the philosophy of early Enlightenment thinkers, it shows that faith in God can ensure happiness even in the face of multiple misfortunes, while passionate, rebellious emotions like those harbored by Marianne and Carlson are destructive. The Countess's optimistic, Leibnizian worldview allows her to diagnose even the deaths of her aunt and Carlson as "lucky" or as "welcome news."[7]

The *Schwedische Gräfin*, though immensely popular in its day, has not, on the whole, met with a favorable reception from modern critics. In addition to its "sermonizing" moralizing tone, they have criticized its "overburdened" plot, lack of narrative cohesion, and "heavy overlay of sentimentality."[8] The characters, it is argued, are "cardboard ideals"[9] who do not develop.[10] Feminist critics have pointed out that the Countess's life is defined by men. Excepting a brief description of her education, the novel begins with her first marriage and ends with the death of her husbands; in fact in the second part, her story is almost subsumed by that of the Count.[11]

The way the characters encourage, experience and describe their emotions may appear excessively self-conscious to the modern reader. In the midst of charitable actions they think of the pleasure reflecting on them will provide afterward, and during their happy hours they purposefully conjure up memories from the past in order to experience the "Wollust" (delight) of being "empfindlich gerührt" (tenderly moved).[12] Intense feelings, often referred to as "indescribable," testify to the depth of their sensibility. The following lines, in which the Countess describes her reaction to the Count's death, are typical: "Ich will meinen Schmerz über seinen Tod nicht beschreiben. Er war ein Beweis der zärtlichsten Liebe und bis zur Ausschweifung groß. Ich fand eine Wollust in meinen Tränen"[13] (I don't want to attempt to describe my pain at his death. This pain was proof of the most tender love, heightened even to excess. I delighted in my tears). Moreover, the supposedly self-deprecating statements the Countess makes may appear self-serving or insincere. Her apology, for example, for the simplicity and meagerness of her wedding, which will doubtless disappoint other brides, is clearly meant to enhance rather than detract from the virtuous image she seeks to portray. But it must be borne in mind that it was uncommon at this period for a novel to have a first-person narrator of the "weaker" sex, whose proper sphere of influence was not thought to extend to the public act of autobiography. In having the Countess analyze her motives, assert her virtues, and reject supposedly female faults such as vanity, Gellert is demonstrating her worthiness for the role.

Like Schnabel, however, Gellert refrains from emphasizing differences between men and women at length. His male characters may go into politics or battle while the women stay at home, and the Countess may insist that she admires her husband for instilling in her the desire to subordinate her will completely to his, but she has been trained by her uncle in the art of independent thinking, and she and the other women spend their days studying and conversing as equal partners with the men. Their maternal role receives little attention; the Countess's relationship with daughter, for example, is barely mentioned. As in the *Insel Felsenburg,* male characters display as much emotion as do women.

Not only does the novel convey a less restrictive image of women than critics have suggested, the moral values it upholds are less abstract than has been supposed. On occasion at least, they are adapted to and even relativized by the characters' experiences, as the Marianne-Carlson episode illustrates. When the Countess and R. discover that Marianne and Carlson are brother and sister, they sympathize with rather than blame them. They both wish the news had never been revealed, even though this would have meant that Carlson and Marianne continued to live in incest. The Countess is critical of Caroline, Marianne's mother, when she insists that the couple part because, justified as the advice may be, Caroline speaks "too early" for them to accept such a course of action.[14] R.'s way of dealing with the situation is preferable, based as it is on an understanding of Carlson and Marianne's psychological needs: he suggests that the advice of scholars be sought before any decision is taken, not because he genuinely needs to be informed of the "right" response, but because he believes the process itself will act as a kind of medicine for the young couple. In the end, Carlson decides to go to battle and in doing so to rely on God to answer their dilemma by sparing or ending his life, a solution to which Marianne agrees. Although the Countess is aware that the pair are deceiving themselves in believing themselves resigned to God's will, she is grateful for the peace of mind their behavior offers them: "Welche glückselige Dienste leistet nicht der Irrtum in gewissen Umständen!" she exclaims (What happy service does not error afford us in certain circumstances!).[15] Gellert advocates a moral code that makes allowances for the circumstances and psychological states of individuals.

Gellert's *Leben der schwedischen Gräfin von G**** did much to divest the genre of the novel of its disreputable associations and contributed to the widening of the genre's readership.[16] In fact, its popularity was such that several new editions were published, and the novel was translated into many different languages.[17] A veritable "Gellertomanie" was born. It was not until some years after the appearance of Gellert's novel, however, that the trend for sentimental novels in the style of Richardson really caught on in Germany.

Wieland, *Geschichte des Agathon*

Christoph Martin Wieland's (1733–1813) novel *Geschichte des Agathon* (History of Agathon) is not part of this trend. In this third-person narrative, first published in 1766–67 and revised in 1773 and 1794, Wieland reacts against moral-sentimental novels such as Richardson's.[18] The present discussion is devoted to the original edition,[19] which is generally thought to be the first German Bildungsroman, that is, a novel depicting the various experiences shaping the character of the young protagonist. It is also a philosophical and political novel and contains elements borrowed from the adventure and courtly traditions.[20] *Agathon* is set in ancient Greece, but the moral and philosophical stances of the characters are rooted firmly in the late eighteenth century. Thus, the eponymous hero, an extraordinarily handsome young man who is brought up to be a priest in a temple at Delphi, is a Platonic idealist whose "Schwärmerei" (enthusiasm) can be seen as an extreme form of sensibility. After falling in love with Psyche and rejecting the advances of a priestess, Agathon flees the temple, rediscovers his father, and lives as a man of means in Athens, where he works for the good of the republic until political rivals succeed in banishing him from the state. He is captured by pirates and sold as a slave in Smyrna to the sophist Hippias, whose philosophy resembles that of eighteenth-century materialist thinkers. Hippias resolves to convince Agathon of the superiority of his way of life and succeeds in engineering a union between Agathon and the hetaera Danae, but Danae and Agathon fall deeply in love and Danae is more converted to Agathon's view of the world than he to hers. Determined to disillusion Agathon, Hippias tells him about Danae's sexual history. The devastated Agathon leaves for Syracuse, where his attempts to reform the tyrannical ruler Dionysius meet with some initial success, but where rivals, once again, finally get the better of him. He retires to Tarent, an idealized republic presided over by an old friend of his father's, and there rediscovers Psyche, who turns out to be his sister, and a reformed Danae, who offers him her friendship.

Contrary to what the happy ending might suggest, Wieland rejects the "novelistic" in this novel. On several occasions, ironic reference is made to the conventions of popular novels and the *Geschichte des Agathon* is distinguished from them. To insist that a work was an authentic document in order to avoid the negative associations of the novel was a typical narrative device of eighteenth-century authors. What is different about Wieland's novel is that, at the same time as he calls it a "Geschichte" rather than a "Roman" and claims its origin is an ancient Greek manuscript, Wieland draws attention to its fictional nature. Influenced by the works of the English novelist Henry Fielding (1707–1754), Wieland creates a self-conscious, playful narrator, who reflects at intervals on the process of narration, renounces responsibility for the story's unrealistic conclusion and, taking the gesture made by Schnabel a step further, asserts in his preface that he doubts anyone will accept the story as authentic and that he leaves it up to the reader to make of it what he/she will. The tone may be playful, but Wieland's point is a serious one. The novelistic, the narrator explains, is to be replaced, not with the "real," but with the "realistic." An author must depict a course of events that *could* happen, but need not *have* happened, in the world as we know it, and characters must be neither improbably good nor improbably bad, because readers must be able to identify with them if they are to learn from them.

This most self-conscious of novels is not without contradictions of its own. After establishing probability rather than historical reality as the principle for selecting narrative events, Wieland's narrator explains that the reader must also accept happenings that appear extremely improbable, since life can be stranger than fiction; and although he insists that characters should be "average" in moral terms, he shies away from presenting an average hero, insisting on the contrary that the reader would find it hard to think of anyone who, under the same circumstances, would have acted more virtuously than Agathon.[21] But Wieland's emphasis on fiction's ability to illuminate "die verborgenern Triebfedern" (*A* 356; the more hidden motivating forces) of human nature would prove central to the development of the novel in the eighteenth century. While *Agathon* was received with disapprobation by many of Wieland's contemporaries, others, such as Christian Friedrich von Blanckenburg (1744–1796), recognized the importance of his analysis of human nature.[22] In 1774, Blanckenburg discussed *Agathon* in his *Versuch über den Roman* (Essay on the Novel), a highly significant theoretical work which did much to raise the status of the genre. Overlooking those aspects of Wieland's novel that were superfluous to his theory, such as its engagement with political and philosophical debates, Blanckenburg used it to illustrate the argument that novelists should direct their attention away from external events and concern themselves instead with the inner state of realistic characters.[23] For Blanckenburg, the novel was a psychological genre.

Like many thinkers of the period, Wieland asserts the influence of bodily processes on personality. Although German psychological and medical writers of the late eighteenth century seldom embraced materialist philosophy in the extreme form propagated by French philosophers such as Julian Offray de la Mettrie (1709–1751), many of them were convinced of the interdependence of psychology and physiology, or of what a contributor to the empirical psychological journal *Magazin zur Erfahrungsseelenkunde* (1783–93) described as the "ewiger, und ununterbrochener, nothwendiger, wechselseitiger Einfluß der Seele und des Körpers" (eternal, and incessant, necessary, mutual influence of the soul and the body).[24] Manfred Engel contends that Wieland depicts Hippias's materialism in a negative light as radical egoism,[25] but other scholars have drawn attention to the narrative space accorded to Hippias's arguments and to their persuasiveness.[26] When the narrator insists in the preface that he does not endorse Hippias's opinions, he nevertheless concedes that Hippias is not always wrong (*A* 16). Moreover, he repeatedly explains his characters' behavior in physiological terms. When Dionysius begins to embrace Platonic philosophy, for example, he explains that this turn to Platonism is merely the temporary result of an excess of physical pleasure that has weakened his physical fibers (*A* 375). The narrator includes food and climate in a list of influences that have made Agathon the person he is (*A* 516), and describes Agathon's "enthusiasm" as a physical condition: it is a "fever" (*A* 508) that arises from privileging fantasy over reality. In the course of the novel, Agathon modifies his unrealistic belief that the soul and the body are two distinct entities, the former "imprisoned" in the latter. He comes to accept the interdependence of physical and psychological states, agreeing in his debate with Hippias that his view of the world may be determined by the specific configuration of his senses (*A* 58–59 and 62).

This "materialist" aspect would seem to place Wieland's novel at a far remove from the philosophy of "Empfindsamkeit" with its assertion of an innate moral sense, its religious dimension, and its privileging of spiritual over physical love. But in fact sensibility had received decisive impulses from physiology, since the idea that a virtuous person was "moved" by external phenomena drew on the notion of the sensibility of nerves developed by Albrecht von Haller (1708–1777) in 1752. Although the word "empfindsam" which became popular in the late 1760s referred to emotional as well as physical responsiveness, sentimental thinkers were aware of the interrelatedness of the two spheres, and, like Agathon and Hippias, debated the extent to which notions entertained by the "inner self" were influenced by the operations of sensory organs.[27]

Agathon is not an anti-sentimental novel. Experience of the world cures Agathon of what Hippias calls his "romanhaften Schwung" (*A* 64; novelistic fervor), and critics have therefore described the work as a novel of disillusionment.[28] It is clear from the start, however, that Wieland's narrator feels, as he puts it, a "freundschaftliche [. . .] Parteilichkeit" (*A* 125; friendly partiality) for his hero and, to some extent, for his "enthusiastic," sentimental view of the world, equated as it is with faith in human nature and the refusal to use others for his own ends. As the narrator makes clear, Agathon's motives are the right ones; he is "bloß ein mißgeleiteter Wahrheitsforscher" (*A* 118; merely a misguided seeker for the truth). At the end of the novel, the sensitivity and the idealism of Agathon's soul remain intact (*A* 510), even though, with a self-conscious acknowledgement of the novelistic nature of the maneuver, the narrator has to shield him from the "real" world in order to preserve them (*A* 515).[29] The novel is critical of the sensibility's excesses, rather than of sensibility itself, offering a view which has more in common with the diagnoses to be found in the period's psychological journals than in some of its fictional texts.[30]

Feminist scholars have pointed out, however, that the sophistication of Wieland's character analysis does not extend equally to female characters, who are portrayed in comparatively conventional ways. They argue that they represent little more than stages on the hero's path to self-knowledge.[31] Similarly, in his frequent addresses to the novel's female readers, Wieland's narrator reinforces stereotypes of the female sex as vain and concerned solely with matters of the heart (*A* 348–49). His novel paints a somewhat restricted view of women, but in real life Wieland played an instrumental role in the publication of what is recognized as the first German novel written entirely by a woman, *Geschichte des Fräuleins von Sternheim* (1771) by his cousin and one-time fiancée, Sophie von La Roche.

Sophie von La Roche, *Geschichte des Fräuleins von Sternheim*

The rise of sensibility both emancipated women to write and set boundaries on their work.[32] Since they received little academic instruction compared to men, women could seldom have emulated the classical and philosophical learning that abounds in Wieland's *Agathon*. Since its beginnings in the seventeenth century, however, women had been involved in Pietism, a religious movement that rejected the hierarchical structures of the established church and encouraged the narration of personal experience and emotion, and they had long been trained in the "feminine" art of writing letters.[33] The sentimental novels of Richardson, with their female protagonists, epistolary form, and concentration on the private and the domestic, were thus a readily accessible literary form.

On the other hand, according to the late eighteenth-century sentimental conception of gender it was not "ladylike" to enter the public domain through writing or aspire to the status of artist. If women were bold enough to publish their writing, the step had to be inspired by "feminine" altruism rather than "masculine" ambition; their work should be addressed primarily to a female audience; and it could in no way impede their fulfilling of their domestic duties.[34] In his preface to La Roche's *Fräulein von Sternheim*, Wieland anticipated and averted objections to her "unfeminine" authorship by adhering to this strictly gendered view of writing. He emphasizes the "naturalness" and lack of artistry in the anonymous female writer's style, explaining that she only took up her pen after the day's work was done. He insists that he is publishing the novel without her knowledge, and argues that such a step is justified by the value of its moral message.[35]

Like Richardson, La Roche certainly intended her novel to serve a didactic purpose. The heroine, Sophie von Sternheim, is a model of sentimental female virtue who defends her honor and sense of self in the face of multiple trials. When her father dies, she is launched into court society by her worldly aunt, and is coveted by the prince as his mistress. Sophie's virtue is unassailable, but her reputation is not, as is revealed when people read too much into her unguarded behavior at a masked ball. She agrees to marry the English Lord Derby to protect her good name, despite her affection for his countryman, the melancholy Lord Seymour. When she discovers that Derby has tricked her and that their marriage ceremony was a sham, she flees from him and, adopting the name of Madame Leidens, devotes her life to charitable works. During a trip to the baths in Spaa she meets a Lady Summers and goes to live in England with her until Derby reappears and has her abducted to Scotland to ensure she does not stand in the way of his opportunistic marriage to another woman. A prisoner in the Scottish lead hills, Sophie finds solace in educating Derby's illegitimate daughter before being rescued by Seymour and his brother. Derby dies a miserable death; Sophie and Seymour are married and embark upon a happy life together.

Although La Roche's novel, which consists predominantly of letters and extracts from the heroine's diary, is above all a novel about a character — Goethe called it "eine Menschenseele" (a human soul) rather than a book[36] — it is not without adventure elements, as the above summary makes clear. It also contains long passages in which characters expound on their view of the world in abstract, moralizing terms, as, for example, when Sophie's father outlines the principles on which he bases the management of his estate to his new wife. It could be argued that characterization of the work's figures is simplistic; they tend to be either wholly good or bad. In an essay tracing the relationship between "Empfindsamkeit" and the rise of middle-class consciousness in the eighteenth century, Peter Uwe von Hohendahl argues, moreover, that La Roche's social agenda is less ambitious than it at first appears.[37] Sophie may criticize the urban aristocracy and demonstrate an active sympathy for the lower classes, and it may be emphasized, as in the

Schwedische Gräfin, that a person's soul determines his or her true worth, but at the same time Sophie insists that accepting one's position in the social hierarchy is a prerequisite to Christian virtue and, following Rousseau, casts the lives of the rural poor in an idealized, romanticized light.

Fräulein von Sternheim is not as unsophisticated in its form, however, nor is the image of women it portrays as conventional as Wieland's preface might suggest. Other German authors, such as Gellert, had written epistolary novels, but La Roche was the first to follow the model of Richardson's *Clarissa* in including letters from several characters. This technique allows her to present the same event from various different perspectives and thereby to create narrative tension, such as when the reader learns what happens at Graf F*'s party from Derby and Seymour's letters before hearing Sophie's own account. In Schnabel's *Insel Felsenburg* and Gellert's *Schwedische Gräfin,* the voices of the different narrators are barely distinguishable from one another, but La Roche adapts her style to reflect the different personalities of her correspondents.

Unlike Rousseau, she does not advocate marriage and motherhood as the only desirable fate for women. The "beautiful widow" describes marriage as a "yoke" which would deprive her of her freedom,[38] and although Sophie disagrees with her, La Roche formulates the widow's argument in persuasive terms. Like Gellert's Countess, and like the heroines of many women's novels to come, Sophie receives an enlightened education from a man, her father, who encourages her to develop the "masculine" faculty of her reason as well as womanly skills. As Madam Leidens, Sophie sets up a school to train poor girls for various occupations. Sophie may possess sentimental qualities such as sympathy for others, chasteness, and an unquestioning faith in God which are in keeping with the period's ideal of femininity, and may be rewarded in the end with a happy marriage, but the novel's focus is on the active life she leads as a single woman, and it is her sensibility that emancipates her to do so.

Feminist critics have argued that women, long objectified by men in patriarchal society, themselves internalize their object status. Sophie is repeatedly described as the object of the male gaze.[39] Unlike the other women at court, however, who demonstrate an obsession with their appearance, Sophie is uncomfortable with this observation; she feels "de[n] bitterste[n] Schmerz" (the most bitter pain) at being "de[nr] Gegenstand so häßlicher Blicke" (the object of such odious looks) and is glad when, later in the novel, a deterioration in her health means that she no longer needs to fear male attention.[40] If she rejects the love of finery (*Putzsucht*) manifested by other women, neither does she embody that other restrictive female stereotype, the "undivided," natural, unselfconscious woman. On the contrary, her sensibility involves a constant examination and subsequent fashioning of the self in her letters and her journal, not as an object of male desire, but as an example of virtue. Her reliance on the inner voice of conscience rather than on external approbation lends Sophie independence and ensures her happiness even under the most difficult of circumstances.

Novels of Sensibility

La Roche's novel was not only immensely popular with readers,[41] it was also a significant influence on authors, though the novels that followed in its wake were not always characterized by the happy, healthy balance between heart and head that La Roche's heroine displays. Critics argue that Goethe's famous novel *Die Leiden des jungen Werther* (The Sorrows of Young Werther, 1774) owes a debt to *Fräulein von Sternheim,* although in its analysis of the solipsistic and self-destructive nature of the hero's passion Goethe's novel exceeds the boundaries of the sentimental. A more typical example of the type of novel that came to dominate the expanding literary market of the late eighteenth century is Johann Martin Miller's *Siegwart: Eine Klostergeschichte* (Siegwart: A Monastic Tale, 1776), a popular work in which unhappy love, death-bed scenes, and accompanying expressions of emotion mingle to create a lachrymose sense of pathos. The vogue for excessively sentimental works such as Miller's elicited comment from cultural critics, who saw them as issuing a dangerous call to self-indulgence. Joachim Heinrich Campe (1746–1818), for example, published an essay titled "Ueber Empfindsamkeit und Empfindelei in pädogogischer Hinsicht" (On Sensibility and Pseudo-Sensibility in a Pedagogical Regard, 1779) in which he sets up an opposition between "Empfindsamkeit," which engages reason as well as the emotions and is conducive to action, and "Empfindelei" (sentimentalism), which encourages resignation and distance from reality.

Certain fiction writers also warned of the dangers of excessive sentimentality, as did Johann Karl Wezel (1747–1819) in his novel *Wilhelmine Arend, oder die Gefahren der Empfindsamkeit* (Wilhelmine Arend, or the Dangers of Sensibility, 1782). Some novelists, inspired by the English author Laurence Sterne's (1713–1768) *Sentimental Journey through France and Italy* (1768, German 1768–69), adopted a humorous approach to the trend. Sterne's novel is a travel journal, but one in which the narrator's thoughts and emotions are more important than the description of external sights or landscapes. Several German authors wrote fictional accounts of journeys in which they tried to copy Sterne's digressive, often parodic narrative style.[42]

Thümmel, *Reise in die mittäglichen Provinzen*

Moritz August von Thümmel's (1738–1817) *Reise in die mittäglichen Provinzen von Frankreich im Jahr 1785 bis 1786* (Journey to the Southern

Provinces of France in the Years 1785 to 1786), published in ten volumes from 1791–1805, is generally considered the most successful of these travel accounts. Here, the sentimental self-examination La Roche portrays in a positive light is revealed as a potential threat to physical and psychological equilibrium.

Thümmel's novel, highly successful with readers when it was published,[43] is in the form of a diary written by a hypochondriac from Berlin called Wilhelm who undertakes a journey through the South of France for the sake of his health, records his experiences, encounters, and reflections along the way, and believes himself cured by the conclusion of the novel. What this novel, like Sterne's, lacks in terms of a unified plot is compensated for by its wide variety of narrative events and approaches: Wilhelm is socially critical when he writes of the hypocrisies of the Catholic church or the court or describes the state of prisons or lunatic asylums; he is rational and enlightened when he exposes the practitioners of medical trends like magnetism as frauds; sentimental when he praises the virtues of rural life or nature or is intensely moved by reunions with old friends. In addition to an abundance of learned references, there are erotic passages, and the diary's prose is interspersed with passages in verse. The novel also contains episodes borrowed from the adventure tradition, but these do not preclude disparaging references to novelistic convention, accompanied by an insistence that this work by contrast deals with "real life." Wilhelm's frequent, intimate apostrophes to his friend Eduard, to whom the diary is addressed, and the fact that he often mentions what is going on around him as he writes further reinforce the sense that the diary is authentic.

The distinguishing feature of the novel's style, however, is the irony to which readers, characters, and the narrator himself are subjected. In his account of the "Klärchen" episode, for example, Wilhelm sets up the expectation of a sexual dénouement by issuing a warning to any potential female readers that the following pages could endanger their virtue, and heightens the sense of tension by repeatedly postponing the story's conclusion, only to frustrate the reader by revealing, in the end, that the promised seduction never took place. When he leaves the village of Caverac, he takes an ironic view of his own romantic pretensions: only an hour into the journey he realizes that the idealized love he had entertained for Margot is wilting as quickly as the rose she has given him.[44] Beyond individual episodes such as these, the notion of the hypochondriac and his "cure" on which the novel as a whole is based can be read as an ironic statement about "Empfindsamkeit" and the sentimental novel.

Hypochondria was a much debated disease in this period. It was characterized by a variety of physical and psychological symptoms, including depression and lack of appetite, and was believed to afflict individuals who had distanced themselves from nature — people such as scholars, who thought too much and acted too little. It was also seen as the consequence of excessive sensibility and the focus on the self this tendency encouraged, hence the prescription of travel, which diverted the sufferer's attention onto the outside world, as a cure. If the pathologizing of sensibility as hypochondria served to criticize the solipsism of the over-sentimental person, it also brought into focus the physical origin of sensibility its exponents sometimes overlooked. As the novelist Christian Friedrich Timme wrote in 1781–1782: "Empfindsamkeit ist Seelenhipochondrie" (sensibility is hypochondria of the soul).[45] In the sentimental individual, hypochondria translates emotional sensitivity back into a hypersensitivity to physical surroundings, an aversion, for example, to cool draughts, loud noises, or particular kinds of food, and the sentimental emphasis on the "higher" workings of soul becomes a prosaic concern with digestive habits and sleeping patterns.

Wilhelm, a scholar lost in his books and grown pale, thin, depressed, and oversensitive as a result, subscribes to a common stereotype of the period when he associates his poor physical condition with refinement and the red-faced health and hearty appetite of the doctor he meets at Frankfurt with ignorance.[46] But on this occasion, as on many others, the last laugh is on the narrator himself. His anxiety when the doctor leaves without diagnosing his condition betrays his obsession with his physical state. In the course of the novel, Wilhelm's sentimental self-image is repeatedly deflated by an awareness of the dependence of his emotional state on physical factors. On his journey out of Berlin, for example, he notices an improvement in his health and makes the "humiliating" observation that the reason for it must be physical: the vibrations of the carriage in which he is traveling.[47] He realizes too that far from being "die natürliche Sprache des Herzens" (the natural language of the heart), his sentimental outbursts are due to a weakness of the nerves.[48] As Gerhard Sauder observes, Wilhelm's appetite for food also brings him back down to earth.[49]

Toward the end of the novel Wilhelm visits the famous medical center, Montpellier, where he displays a robust acceptance of the materiality of existence that suggests he has been cured of his hypochondria. After an entertaining dinner at the house of a local physician, Wilhelm is informed in horrified tones by a fellow guest, a hypochondriac from England who has been unable to swallow a mouthful all evening, that the men and women with whom he has spent the evening conversing have sold their bodies to their host for dissection after death. The skeletons of their deceased relatives, he explains, are hanging in an adjoining room. After an initial shock, Wilhelm comes to view this arrangement as a positive one, dismissing the excessive sentimental delicacy that dictates that the bodies of the dead are sacred and that grief over the deceased should inhibit the physical pleasures of this life.[50]

Even this apparent statement of Wilhelm's health, however, can be viewed in an ironic light. The deceased, he reflects, might claim that they were not loved enough in life, or that, though the living would give half their lives for the chance to admit their remorse, it is too late, for the hearts they wounded are now decaying and the proffered hands they refused to shake are now devoid of strength. Wilhelm may dismiss such imagined reproaches as not worth heeding, but the fervor and poignancy with which he describes them calls into question his supposed detachment. Several scholars have expressed doubts about Wilhelm's "recovery," pointing out that the writing of a diary is an unlikely cure for excessive inwardness.[51] Such a view suggests that sentimental self-analysis is portrayed in Thümmel's novel as a sterile, self-defeating process. Other critics take the hero at his word when he asserts that he has regained his health, arguing that the ironic approach he adopts in his diary allows him to gain a salutary perspective on his emotions. Whether the novel's irony aids Wilhelm's cure or is directed at the notion of the cure itself, it seems that authors like Thümmel can no longer portray self-fashioning of the kind practiced by La Roche's Sophie von Sternheim without distance or humor. By the 1790s, the excesses of sensibility are difficult to take seriously.

At least, that is, for "serious" writers. Authors such as August Lafontaine (1758–1831) were still writing sentimental, didactic novels of amusement in the early nineteenth century with no ironic intent. It was women writers, however, who were mainly responsible for continuing the sentimental trend in love stories or tales of the trials of irreproachably virtuous female protagonists. In their novels, the heroine's "Empfindsamkeit" is all too often equated with a disposition to masochism, as, for example, in Caroline von Wobeser's *Elisa, oder das Weib wie es seyn sollte* (Elisa, or Woman As She Should Be, 1795), but a few female authors understood the emancipatory potential of a heroine's faith in her "inner" self depicted by La Roche. Friederike Helene Unger (1741–1813) was among them.

Unger's novel *Bekenntnisse einer schönen Seele: Von ihr selbst geschrieben* (Confessions of a Beautiful Soul Written by that Person Herself, 1806) contains many traditionally "sentimental" elements. The heroine Mirabella's "beautiful soul," as manifested in her freedom from physical passions, her sympathy for others, and her close bonds of friendship, is independent of social standing, and she is most at home not in the "worldly" environment of the court, but in rural settings or among a small community of like-minded friends. Although Mirabella reiterates many of the stereotypes about gender roles which had come by this time to characterize the philosophy of "Empfindsamkeit,"[52] feminist critics[53] have read Unger's novel as a feminist revision of Goethe's "Bekenntnisse einer schönen Seele" in the novel *Wilhelm Meisters Lehrjahre* from which Unger's takes its name.[54]

Unaware of who her parents are, Mirabella is encouraged by the pastor who raises her to think for herself and develop "eine achtunggebietende Individualität" (an individuality which commands respect). In the course of the novel, she makes frequent reference and ascribes great importance both to this quality and to her "Eigenthümlichkeit" (peculiarity), though she is aware that it is not considered proper for a woman to do so.[55] She is furthermore "unwomanly" in her refusal to devote her life to the opposite sex. Early in the novel, she writes that other people's appreciative comments about her appearance lead her to the looking glass, where she observes herself with pleasure. But Mirabella rejects the accusation of vanity and insists that her mirror-gazing simply reinforces her sense of self.[56] She does fall in love, but when her beloved Moritz dies in battle, her story does not come to an end, as many women's novels of the period would have done. Mirabella does not even grieve in the manner expected of her. On the contrary, she explains, she feels little loss, since during his life Moritz represented above all a spiritual ideal and will continue to do so after death. Her love for him, in other words, serves to strengthen her own identity. Unlike Goethe's "schöne Seele," Mirabella soon launches into an active, independent life in the outside world, working first as companion to a princess and then traveling extensively through Europe, where she comes into contact with different groups of people and engages in lively debates on art and literature before returning to live with a female friend in Germany. Unger has eschews both conventional conclusions to the women's novel: her heroine is neither married nor dead.

Mirabella takes her self and its fashioning seriously, both in the course of her life and in the process of its narration. In doing so, she conveys a sense of self-importance and self-satisfaction which, to the modern reader, may appear less sympathetic and less sophisticated than the ironic self-image entertained by Thümmel's hero Wilhelm. But irony and humor are more easily self-directed by those whose identity is secure. For women of this period, the analysis of one's soul which sentimentality encouraged still acted as an important tool in the development of an emerging, but fragile self-confidence. In part for this reason, perhaps, but also because it represented an accessible and suitably "feminine" genre, women writers continued to favor the sentimental novel well into the nineteenth century.

As the works examined in this essay illustrate, there was no one kind of sentimental novel published in eighteenth-century Germany. Nevertheless, the best sentimental novels of the period share a character analysis which, far from merely illustrating generalized moral lessons or encouraging inwardness antipathetic to action, is characterized by an emphasis on individual experience and the promotion of psychological health, in step with the development of psychology at this period. None of the novels discussed here endorses the excessive, unrealistic, or sterile indulgence of feelings that would be described as "sentimental" today; the figures in these novels are guided by reason as well as emotion. They are brought back down to earth by the needs of the body. In fact, plot development in later novels often relies on the failure of any over-sentimental or novelistic elements in the protagonist's personality: Agathon learns to be less of a "Schwärmer"; Sophie's sentimental education must be complemented by an experience of the world; the purpose of Wilhelm's journey is to divest himself of his excessive inwardness. The extent to which "Empfindsamkeit" contributed specifically to the emancipation of women and women writers is difficult to determine. But in its redirection of narrative attention from outward adventures to inner states of mind, the sentimental novel of self-fashioning prepared the way for psychological realism and thus for one of the most important tools to be employed by modern novelists both male and female.

Notes

[1] "Self-fashioning" is a term coined by New Historicist scholars to refer to a conscious shaping of individual identity that dates from the Early Modern period. See for example Stephen Greenblatt, *Renaissance Self-Fashioning: From More to Shakespeare* (Chicago: U of Chicago Press, 1980).

[2] As a period designation for German literature "Empfindsamkeit" corresponds most closely with "sensibility" as used for English literature, cf. Janet Todd, *Sensibility: An Introduction* (London: Methuen, 1986). The terms "sentimentality" or "sentimentalism," used in some quarters as translations of German "Empfindsamkeit," connote a devaluation of the period. The word "empfindsam" became popular with Johann Joachim Christoph Bode's German translation of Laurence Sterne's *Sentimental Journey* (1768) as *Empfindsame Reise* (1768–69).

[3] See e.g. Ph. Fr. Walther, *Physiologie des Menschen mit durchgängiger Rücksicht auf die comparative Physiologie der Thiere*, 2 vols. (Landshut: Krüll, 1807/1808), vol. 2, 393–94; Joachim Heinrich Campe, *Väterlicher Rath für meine Tochter. Ein Gegenstück zum Theophron. Der erwachsenern weiblichen Tugend gewidmet* [1789] (Braunschweig, 1809), 71; Wilhelm von Humboldt, "Über den Geschlechtsunterschied und dessen Einfluß auf die organische Natur" [1795], in *Werke*, ed. Andreas Flittner and Klaus Giel, 5 vols. (Stuttgart: Cotta, 1960–1981), vol. 1.

[4] Twenty-six editions of the novel were published between 1731 and 1772. See Rolf Allerdissen, *Die Reise als Flucht: Zu Schnabels "Insel Felsenburg" und Thümmels "Reise in die mittäglichen Provinzen von Frankreich"* (Bern: Herbert Lang, 1975), 80.

[5] Allerdissen, *Die Reise als Flucht*, 32.

[6] Rolf Grimminger, "Roman," in *Deutsche Aufklärung bis zur französischen Revolution 1680–1789*, ed. Grimminger, *Hansers Sozialgeschichte der deutschen Literatur*, vol. 3 (Munich: Hanser, 1908), 676.

[7] Christian Fürchtegott Gellert, *Leben der schwedischen Gräfin von G****, in *Gesammelte Schriften: Kritische, kommentierte Ausgabe,* ed. Bernd Witte (Berlin: De Gruyter, 1989), 4:3 and 30.

[8] Ingeborg Arndt, *Die seelische Welt im Roman des achtzehnten Jahrhunderts* (Giessen: Bölzle, 1940), 10; John van Cleve, "A Countess in Name Only: Gellert's *Schwedische Gräfin*," *The Germanic Review* 55 (1980): 152; Eva D. Becker, *Der deutsche Roman um 1800* (Stuttgart: Metzler, 1964), 28.

[9] D. M. van Abbé, "Some Unspoken Assumptions in Gellert's *Schwedische Gräfin*," *Orbis Litterarum,* 28 (1973): 113–23, here 116.

[10] David Hill, "*Die schwedische Gräfin:* Notes on Early Bourgeois Realism," *Neophilologus* 65 (1981): 574–88, here 578.

[11] Jörg Steitz, *Unter dem Absolutismus* (Opladen: Westdeutscher Verlag, 1983), 114.

[12] *Schwedische Gräfin,* 69–70.

[13] *Schwedische Gräfin,* 65.

[14] *Schwedische Gräfin,* 29.

[15] *Schwedische Gräfin,* 30.

[16] Bernd Witte, "Der Roman als moralische Anstalt: Gellerts *Leben der schwedischen Gräfin von G**** und die Literatur des achtzehnten Jahrhunderts," *Germanisch-Romanische Monatsschrift* 30 (1980): 150–68, here 150 and 153.

[17] The novel was translated into Dutch, English, French, Hungarian, and Italian.

[18] Volker Meid, "Zum Roman der Aufklärung," in *Aufklärung: Ein literaturwissenschaftliches Studienbuch,* ed. Hans-Friedrich Wessels (Königstein/Ts: Athenäum Taschenbücher, 1984), 107.

[19] For a discussion of the differences between editions see Klaus Schaefer, *Christoph Martin Wieland* (Stuttgart: Metzler, 1996), 57–61.

[20] Norbert Miller, *Der empfindsame Erzähler: Untersuchungen an Romananfängen des achtzehnten Jahrhunderts* (Munich: Hanser, 1968), 128.

[21] Christoph Martin Wieland, *Geschichte des Agathon,* in *Werke in zwölf Bänden* (Frankfurt a. M.: Deutscher Klassiker Verlag, 1986), 4:13. Subsequent references cited parenthetically as *A* and page number.

[22] Schaefer writes that the novel came under criticism for its Greek setting; for its imitation of foreign authors; for the new demands it placed on the reader; and for its supposed "immorality" — it was even banned by censors in Zurich and Vienna. See Schaefer, *Christoph Martin Wieland,* 62–63.

[23] Jürgen Jacobs, "Die Theorie und ihr Exempel: Zur Deutung von Wielands *Agathon* in Blanckenburgs 'Versuch über den Roman,'" *Germanisch-Romanische Monatsschrift* 31 (1981): 32–42 and 39–40.

[24] L. A. Schlichting, in *Gnothi Sauton: oder, Magazin zur Erfahrungsseelenkunde* (Berlin: Mylius, 1783–93), 7, 2: 93.

[25] Manfred Engel, *Der Roman der Goethezeit* (Stuttgart: Metzler, 1993), 1:143.

[26] Jürgen Jacobs, *Wielands Romane* (Bern: Francke, 1969), 102.

[27] For a discussion of the impact of empiricist and sensualist theories on the philosophy of sensibility, see Gerhard Sauder, *Empfindsamkeit,* 3 vols. (Stuttgart: Metzler, 1974), 1: 65–72.

[28] See for example Fritz Martini, "Nachwort" to *Geschichte des Agathon* (Stuttgart: Reclam, 1996), 657–58.

[30] The diagnosis of "Schwärmerei" offered in the *Magazin zur Erfahrungsseelenkunde,* for example, is similar to Wieland's. Salomon Maimon, co-editor of the tenth volume, summarizes the view of "enthusiasm" put forward by the contributor "K.St" in an earlier volume and adds observations of his own. K. St., Maimon writes, argues that this "disease of the soul" results from an excessive concentration on inner feelings and a lack of "sich ausbreiten wollende Kraft" (expansive energy). Maimon rejects the criticism of the enthusiast implied in this diagnosis, and compares enthusiasm with philosophy, arguing that both arise from a drive to expand one's knowledge. The enthusiast's failing, he argues, lies not in a shortage of expansive energy, but rather in the fact that he/she seeks knowledge exclusively in his/her own soul, and resorts to "all sorts of fictions" when, because of a lack of experience of the world, this inner source proves lacking. Like Agathon, the enthusiast is depicted sympathetically as a person acting in good faith who compensates for his/her lack of experience with an overactive imagination. See Salomon Maimon, *Gnothi Sauton: oder, Magazin zur Erfahrungsseelenkunde,* 10, 3. This volume was edited by Moritz and Salomon Maimon.

[31] See e.g. Elke Kiltz and Heidrun Harlander, in Gisbert Lepper, Jörg Steitz, Wolfgang Brenn etal., *Einführung in die deutsche Literatur des achtzehnten Jahrhunderts* (Opladen: Westdeutscher Verlag, 1983), I: 201.

[32] Ruth P. Dawson, *The Contested Quill: Literature by Women in Germany, 1770–1800* (Newark, NJ: U of Delaware P, 2002), 100.

[33] See Jeannine Blackwell, "Herzensgespräche mit Gott: Bekenntnisse deutscher Pietistinnen im 17. und 18. Jahrhundert," in Gisela Brinker-Gabler, ed., *Deutsche Literatur von Frauen,* 2 vols. (Munich: Beck, 1988), I: 265–89.

[34] See Magdalene Heuser, "'Ich wollte dieß und das von meinem Buche sagen, und gerieth in ein Vernünfteln': Poetologische Reflexionen in den Romanvorreden," in *Untersuchungen zum Roman von Frauen um 1800,* ed. Helga Gallas and Heuser (Tübingen: Niemeyer, 1990). See also Wieland's preface to *Sternheim.*

[35] Despite this preface, some people first assumed that Wieland himself was the novel's author.

[36] *Frankfurter Gelehrte Anzeigen,* 4 February 1772; cited in Sophie von La Roche, *Geschichte des Fräuleins von Sternheim* [1771], ed. Barbara Becker-Cantarino (Stuttgart: Reclam, 1997), 367.

[37] Hohendahl, "Empfindsamkeit und gesellschafliches Bewusstsein: Zur Soziologie des empfindsamen Romans am Beispiel von *La Vie de Marianne, Clarissa, Fräulein von Sternheim* und *Werther,*" *Jahrbuch der deutschen Schillergesellschaft* 16 (1972): 176–207, here 195–98.

[38] *Sternheim,* 258, 254.

[39] See, for example, Ursula Naumann, "Das Fräulein und die Blicke: Eine Betrachtung über Sophie von La Roche," *Zeitschrift für deutsche Philologie* 107 (1988): 488–516.

[40] *Sternheim*, 98 and 274.

[41] See Barbara Becker-Cantarino, "Nachwort" to *Sternheim*, 399.

[42] Johann Gottlieb Schummel, *Empfindsame Reisen durch Deutschland* (Wittenberg: Zimmermann, 1771–1772); Johann Georg Jacobi, *Die Winterreise* (Düsseldorf, 1769), *Die Sommerreise* (Halberstadt: Gros, 1770).

[43] Allerdissen, *Die Reise als Flucht*, 142–43.

[44] Moritz August von Thümmel, *Reise in die mittäglichen Provinzen von Frankreich*, vols. 2–6, *Sämmtliche Werke* (Stuttgart: Macklot, 1820), 3:11.

[45] Christian Friedrich Timme, *Der Empfindsame Maurus Pankrazius Ziprianus Kurt, auch Selmar genannt. Ein Moderoman*, 4 vols. (Erfurt 1781–82), 3: 43, quoted by Sauder, *Empfindsamkeit* 1:151.

[46] *Reise in die mittäglichen Provinzen*, 1:8.

[47] *Reise in die mittäglichen Provinzen*, 1:5.

[48] *Reise in die mittäglichen Provinzen*, 1:62.

[49] Gerhard Sauder, *Der reisende Epikureer: Studien zu Moritz August von Thümmels "Reise in die mittäglichen Provinzen von Frankreich"* (Heidelberg: Carl Winter, 1968), 35.

[50] *Reise in die mittäglichen Provinzen*, 6:102–105.

[51] Dieter Kimpel, *Der Roman der Aufklärung* (Stuttgart: Metzler, 1967), 111.

[52] See for example *Bekenntnisse*, 80, 152.

[53] E.g. Sigrid Schmid, *Der "selbstverschuldeten Unmündigkeit" entkommen: Perspektiven bürgerlicher Frauenliteratur* (Würzburg: Königshausen & Neumann, 1999), 95; see also Susanne Zantopp, "The Beautiful Soul Writes Herself: Friederike Helene Unger and the 'grosse Goethe,'" in *In the Shadow of Olympus: German Women Writers Around 1800*, ed. Katherine R. Goodman and Edith Waldstein (Albany, NY: State U of New York P, 1992), 29–52.

[54] In his review of Unger's anonymously published novel, Goethe assumed its author was a man and criticized him for portraying "eine Männin" (an Amazon) who did not engage in the relationships — filial, romantic, conjugal and maternal — that should make up the center of a woman's life. Johann Wolfgang von Goethe, "Bekenntnisse einer schönen Seele. Melanie das Findelkind. Wilhelm Dumont," Rezension [1806], in vol. 6.2, *Sämtliche Werke* (Munich: Hanser, 1988), 631.

[55] Friederike Helene Unger, *Bekenntnisse einer schönen Seele von ihr selbst geschrieben* (1806; rpt. Hildesheim: Olms, 1991), 18 and 128.

[56] *Bekenntnisse*, 6.

Josef Anton Stranitzky (1676–1726) as Hanswurst with the hero of a state tragedy in the popular theater at the Kärntnertor, ca. 1720.

Enlightenment in Austria: Cultural Identity and a National Literature

Franz M. Eybl

The "Catholic Enlightenment" and the Emergence of Austrian Literature

WHILE REGIONAL LITERATURES VIED FOR PROMINENCE in the larger cultural setting of German-speaking territories, two trends shaped the development of German-language literature in the eighteenth century. One the one hand there was a trend toward linguistic standardization. On this level the exchange of books, opinions, and literary criticism formed a common ground for German-language literature. It meant that literary texts from Schleswig-Holstein could also be discussed by Swiss readers, and someone (like the enlightened reformer and writer Joseph von Sonnenfels [1733/34–1817]) polemicizing in Vienna could be severely criticized at Wolfenbüttel (by Gotthold Ephraim Lessing). The second trend manifested itself in a divergence of literary tastes in various regions and in the rise of regional literatures. As the major German-speaking territories — above all Switzerland, Austria, Prussia, Saxony, Bavaria with the Palatinate, and Brunswick with Lüneburg)[1] — moved toward political independence, they developed their own cultural identities, and by the late eighteenth century we can speak of two new national literatures in the German language: Swiss and Austrian.[2] This essay outlines the development of an Austrian national literature in the eighteenth century.

Within the Habsburg Empire, the literary culture of Enlightenment and Sensibility took on a form different from that of the German Protestant territories with their cultural centers in Hamburg, Frankfurt, Leipzig, and Berlin.[3] Because both German Enlightenment and "sensibility" were shaped largely by Protestantism and Pietism, considerations of the Enlightenment are often — erroneously—restricted to the Protestant territories.[4] But such a narrow focus overlooks the Catholic south of Germany where French, Italian, and German influences converged, allowing a special form of "Catholic Enlightenment" to develop.[5] The Catholic Enlightenment reached its peak under Emperor Joseph II (1780–1790) and was dubbed "Josephinismus," a hotly debated, seemingly liberal phase in Austrian political and literary culture.

The major opponent of Enlightenment and Josephinism was the conservative faction of the Catholic Church, represented in particular by the majority of Jesuits. The Church had not only acquired immense material possessions within the countries ruled by the Habsburgs, but was also involved in a multiplicity of public and private affairs. The Church provided the symbolic trappings of everyday life and of festivals, as is evidenced by the pilgrimage churches, mount Calvaries (open-air representations of Christ's crucifixion), and wayside chapels still present in the southern German cultural landscape today. The concept of *Pietas Austriaca* — a devout, reverent attitude toward the Church and the Habsburg Imperial House throughout Austria — aptly captures the close link between Habsburg rule and ecclesiasticism.[6] In Austria, according to the major Josephinist poet Aloys Blumauer, religious prejudices ate away at the roots of the Enlightenment.[7]

For Austria the age of Enlightenment signaled a century of intellectual changes, transformations, reforms coupled with administrative and economic modernization.[8] It was a conflict-ridden epoch. During the brilliant reign of Emperor Karl VI (1711–1740) a distinct imperial style (*Kaiserstil*) evolved in the visual arts,[9] but afterward, the House of Habsburg had to conduct a series of Wars of Succession in order to establish Maria Theresia as the first female ruler to ascend to the throne in the hereditary territories. She was denied the rank of Empress of the Holy Roman Empire of the German Nation. This crown passed to her husband, Franz Stephan I of Lorraine (1745–1764), and in 1764 to her son, Emperor Joseph II. Maria Theresia ruled from 1740 to 1780, and under her reign literary life began to flourish during a period of modernization. Joseph II succeeded as ruler of Austria from 1780 to 1790, a decade that to most contemporaries seemed a shining model of enlightened government whose end coincided with the French Revolution. Indeed, from a historical as well as cultural point of view, Josephinism represented the climax of eighteenth-century Austrian developments. However, a reactionary period soon began — Joseph II himself tightened censorship, and conservative forces regained the upper hand both politically and culturally under his successors Leopold II (1790–1792) and Franz II/I (1792–1835).[10]

Austrian literature comprises a system of cultural symbols within the context of an emerging national identity.[11] Its focus on the imperial family, the state, and the authorities can be considered a constant. In this regard, literary developments reflect the political conflict, because political power was Janus-faced in Austria. On the one hand, the sovereign represented the House of Habsburg's territorial rule in the same way the Hohenzollerns represented Prussia. On the other hand, beginning in the Middle Ages, the

Habsburgs had been German emperors as well: Vienna was not only the capital of a multinational state with several national languages, it was also the capital of the German Empire. Likewise, Austrian literature on the one hand related to Habsburg cultural identity and competed with the other Habsburg territories, but on the other it related to German-language literature as a whole and constituted part of it.

A number of accounts (each citing different reasons) stress the autonomy of Austria's literary development and the separate identity of Austrian literature,[12] while others underscore the close relationship to Germany.[13] In describing its literary development, I regard the dialectics between autonomy and connectivity, that is, the constant instability, as a valid constant.[14] It is the driving force behind Austria's cultural and literary evolution.

The Era of Maria Theresia: The Popular Theater and Sonnenfels's Reforms (1740–1760)

Beginning with Maria Theresia's reign, literary developments in Austria can be seen as roughly paralleling important political events. In the 1740s the long tradition of splendid opera performances and lavish spectacles at court continued. Just as the court in Vienna maintained close religious ties to the Catholic Church, it was similarly tied to musical and literary culture, especially Italian opera and French drama. While the court chaplains were Jesuits, the court poets were Italians (Apostolo Zeno 1668–1750, Pietro Metastasio, 1698–1782). The court theater's chief purpose was a dignified representation of the court. Likewise, Latin School dramas and the theater of religious orders were also continuing their baroque tradition and persisted well into the eighteenth century. While the Latin dramatic performances were mainly intended to educate students in Latin and to promote the faith, burlesque German-language or dialect interludes featuring peasants and other uneducated people also gave rise to dramatic literature in dialect. In the 1740s the Latin, French, and Italian culture of representation of the elites inherited from the baroque era was being confronted by a thriving German-language popular culture, with sermons, almanacs, and fiction as its literary genres. Because it was then considered the crude culture of the lower classes, this popular culture did not enter literary history.

In the area of the popular theater, the earliest most lasting expression of Austrian cultural independence evolved from the European tradition of strolling players who settled down at the Vienna Theater am Kärntnertor around 1700. Joseph Anton Stranitzky (1676–1726), the actor-director and playwright, turned the traditional buffoon of the Italian *commedia dell'arte* tradition into the comical character of *Hanswurst*, whose costume and dialect lent him an unmistakable identity.[15] Stranitzky integrated *Hanswurst* into baroque tragedies and into the libretti of Italian Opera as a servant figure who comments on the action and at the same time makes it seem ridiculous through his insistence on gratification of his physical appetites. This character made theater history in Vienna. From 1725 to the end of his life, the actor Gottfried Prehauser (1699–1769) presented a refined version in competition with the actor-playwright Joseph Felix von Kurz (1715–1784), who invented the character of *Bernadon* and performed it at the same theater until 1760. The popular comedy (*Volkskomödie*) became a successful "sideshow" to the court theater and to religious drama.[16] These were the conditions at the beginning of the era of Maria Theresia that propelled the development of Austrian literature in two ways. For one, local authors and readers readily accepted Gottsched's efforts on behalf of linguistic and literary reform led by reason. Second, because of their defeat at the hands of Prussia as well as their need for internal modernization, the Habsburg territories rushed into a reform phase that gradually transformed the institutions of literary life as well — from school reform to changes in the publishing business, from new import restrictions (on books) to the reorganization of censorship.

Johann Christoph Gottsched's enlightened literary program met with interest from disparate groups: the German (Protestant) colony of ambassadors and merchants in Vienna, an enlightened class of civil servants and lower nobility, and most important, theater professionals and progressive clergy. Gottsched seemed to show everyone involved with German language and culture the path of reason. And although an imperial academy for language and literature on the model of the French *Académie française* never materialized, with Gottsched's participation the *Societas Eruditorum Incognitorum* (Society of Anonymous Scholars) was established at Olmütz in 1746. Joseph von Petrasch (1714–1772), who wrote plays and poems according to Gottsched's rules, was able to recruit members from throughout central Europe, eager to spread Enlightenment ideas through a magazine of their own. On this basis Gottsched hoped to establish a *Deutsche Gesellschaft* in Vienna as a first step toward an academy. He visited Vienna in 1749 and discussed the project during an audience with Maria Theresia, but he did not succeed in convincing the Court. Gottsched recognized that transforming literary life would not be possible without changing the prevailing conditions for publishing and marketing, such as the strict censorship, which is why he sought contact with the Court.

Franz Christoph von Scheyb (1704–1777), a civil servant who pursued *belles lettres* in his spare time, was a typical representative of secular Austrian literature of his day.[17] In his *Theresiade: Ein Ehrengedicht* (Theresiade: A Poem of Veneration, 1746), he combined Gottsched's neoclassicist program with the traditional literary function of glorifying the ruler. The twelve-part epic consisting of 7,653 alexandrines is an allegory of Empress Maria Theresia's virtues. What appears to us extremely boring today, at that time filled readers and authors with enthusiasm.

Putting Gottsched's program into practice implied above all adopting a common standard for German grammar and spelling throughout Austria as well as stage reforms. In the theater, showy performance had to yield to the actual text of the drama, preferably one written according to strictly neoclassicist principles.[18] This program did away with the impromptu forms of *commedia dell'arte* and with the *Hanswurst* character, again in accordance with Gottschedian principles. The authorities stepped in as well. As of 1750, administrative reforms had created new local authorities for the theaters and established new standards for censorship: theater censorship was instituted in 1751, and in 1753, its regulation was placed in the hands of the Book Censorship Commission (*Bücher-Zensur-Commission*).

Joseph von Sonnenfels (1733/34–1817) played an important role in the reforms carried out during enlightened absolutism.[19] He advocated pragmatic, patriotic ideas for improving the administration and strengthening the monarch's rule; he also strove to curb the influence of the Church and of the nobility. As a member of both the commission for higher education and commission for censorship, his influence on theater and literature was extensive. He believed that the theater should defend virtue and attack vice, thus safeguarding public order.[20] Censorship was designed to serve this goal. Censorship required a written text for a performance and therefore would not tolerate improvised interludes such as extemporaneous acting. The then common practice of extemporization associated with the *Hanswurst* character sparked the so-called *Hanswurst* controversy during the 1750s and 1760s.[21] In 1751 an ordinance limited extemporaneous acting and by 1770 it was entirely prohibited.[22] There was no *Hanswurst* opponent more vehement than Sonnenfels. In his periodical, *Der Mann ohne Vorurteil* (Man without Prejudice, 1765–66), and subsequently in his *Briefe über die wienerische Schaubühne* (Letters Concerning the Viennese Stage, 1767–69) he advocated the enlightened use of a "vernünftige" (reasonable) theater. Others, such as Christian Gottlob Klemm, in his weekly *Die Welt* (1762–63) and through the drama *Der auf den Parnass versetzte grüne Hut* (The Green Hat Placed on Parnassus, 1767) — a play satirizing Sonnenfels — expressed the view that the *Hanswurst* character only needed to be "cleaned up" and refined in accordance with Enlightenment principles. *Hanswurst* was driven from the urban stage, but the character survived in the suburban theaters and influenced nineteenth-century Austrian drama, the comedies of Ferdinand Raimund (1790–1836) and Johann Nepomuk Nestroy (1801–1862) — perhaps even up to Thomas Bernhard (1931–1989).[23]

After The Seven Year's War: Patriotism and Bardic Poetry (1760–1780)

The development of Austrian literature is also linked to a decisive event that brought political and cultural reorientation: the Seven Year's War (1756–1763). Austria's defeat at the end of the Austrian-Prussian conflict ushered in more stability and initiated a decade of rapid expansion of the literary public: in theater, poetry, and in the form the new magazines. Indeed, a lasting forum for discussion was provided by the many Vienna moral weeklies launched after 1762.[24] They provided relatively affordable material for reading and literary criticism. The reading public was created by a newly flourishing publishing industry, in particular the business of Johann Thomas von Trattner (1717–1798). Trattner received subventions and special dispensations from the government to establish an Austrian book market independent of Prussia and Leipzig. Since 1750 he had worked on expanding his publishing empire by producing textbooks and a plethora of (unauthorized) reprints ("Raubdrucke") of mostly German and French literary and philosophical works. He sold these not merely in his bookstores within the Austrian monarchy, but found ways to peddle them throughout Germany after the end of the Silesian wars — "ein Strom, der alles überschwemmt"[25] (a torrent flooding everything) as one German competitor complained. With the Austrian government's new support for such business ventures, reading materials and publishing opportunities became plentiful.

At about that time Klopstock, whose epic poem *Messias* went into print in 1748, made a sentimental, enthusiastic writing style fashionable; it inspired the younger generation of readers and authors and suddenly made Gottsched's rationalism appear dry and outdated. During that time Michael Denis (1729–1800), author of religious poems, occasional lyrics, hymns, and Latin school plays became the most important poet active in Vienna.[26] Denis corresponded with Klopstock, whom he admired, and published his letters under the title *Poetisches Sendschreiben an den Herrn Klopstock* (A Poetic Epistle to Mr. Klopstock, 1764), *Schreiben an einen Freund über Herrn Klopstocks Messiade* (Letter to a Friend Concerning Mr. Klopstock's Messiah, 1766), and *An den obersten der Barden Teuts* (To the Greatest of Teutonic Bards, 1766). When "Ossian's" *Ballads* appeared in 1762, they were also immediately imitated in Austria and Denis provided the first German translation as *Gedichte Ossians, eines alten celtischen Dichters* (The Poems of Ossian, an Ancient Celtic Poet, 1768–69). He also wrote his most acclaimed work *Lieder Sined des Barden* (Songs of Sined [=Denis] the Bard, 1772) in Ossian's style.

The war between Prussia and Austria that polarized the culture of the two countries and bardic fashion were two factors that transformed poetry into an issue of national loyalty. Austrian poetry stood out by its patriotic orientation and its deference to the ruling dynasty, as is evident in Denis's *Poetische Bilder der meisten kriegerischen Vorgänge in Europa seit dem Jahre 1756* (Poetic Pictures of Most of the Warfare in Europe since 1756, 1760–61). The traditional genre of occasional poetry, the predominance of classical rhetoric, and his conservative religious ideology made Denis's poetry seem very conservative. But although his work did not belong to the literary avant garde, it still was in touch with new literary developments.[27] In his 1775 review of *Lieder Sined des Barden*, the young Goethe assured "Mr. Denis" somewhat condescendingly, "daß wir seine Lieder mit vielem Vergnügen gelesen haben. / Nun wird nächstens Hr. Mastalier auch eine Sammlung seiner Gedichte veranstalten, welcher wir mit Freuden entgegensehen. Endlich gewinnt doch vielleicht die gute Sache des Geschmacks durch die Bemühungen so vieler wackern Männer die Oberhand"[28] (that we have read his songs with much pleasure. Soon Mr. Mastalier will also organize a collection of his poetry, to which we joyfully look forward. Perhaps finally, the worthy cause of good taste shall win out thanks to the efforts of so many good men). The category of good taste was the common bond that united writers of the Enlightenment period throughout the different regions.

The Vienna theaters that offered plays all year round needed German dramas, and increasingly managed to find original plays. The playwright Philipp Hafner (1735–1764), considered the "father" of the Viennese popular theater, transformed the *Hanswurst* drama by blending elements of the improvisational stage with the conventional drama and the required "naturalness" of the actors.[29] Hafner's *Hanswurst* appeared as a representative of Enlightenment utilitarian morals, as in *Die bürgerliche Dame* (The Bourgeois Lady, 1763), where he helped punish the extravagant housewife.[30] The Viennese official (Vice-Chancellor of the Court Chancery) Tobias Philipp Freiherr von Gebler (1720–1786) made a name for himself as a dramatist.[31] Wieland thought highly of his plays, while Lessing had only contempt for them.[32] Cornelius von Ayrenhoff (1733–1819), a prolific dramatist in the classical mode and a disciple of Gottsched's program, was active somewhat later. His tragedy *Hermann's Tod* (Hermann's Death, 1768) on the mythic Germanic hero Hermann the Cheruscan played to the taste for patriotic literature.

Prose writing could hardly keep up with the new developments in other German-speaking lands. Readership in Austria was still comparatively small and the number of authors and journalists even smaller. The essay was a genre that combined utility with pleasantry and thus became popular as can be seen in the prolific work of Joseph von Sonnenfels, who combined political activity and writing using the essay form. Sonnenfels opposed serfdom and torture in *Über die Abschaffung der Tortur* (Concerning the Abolishment of Torture, 1775) and promoted compulsory education and the establishment of public schools.[33] His efforts were closely linked with his German language reform, as documented in his treatise *Über den Geschäftsstyl* (Concerning Business Style, 1784). His own prose was clear and supple. According to his contemporaries, "wenige unsrer Schriftsteller [wussten] das Glänzende und Körnigste mit Natur und Simplicität so zu vereinigen, wie Sonnenfels; auch seine neueste Vorlesung *Über die Bescheidenheit im Vortrage* hat diese Tugenden,"[34] (few of our writers knew how to combine the brilliant and pithy with naturalness and simplicity quite like *Sonnenfels;* even his newest lecture, *On Discretion While Lecturing* exhibits these virtues). Maria Theresia enjoyed listening to him (he had much less influence under Joseph II), and it is not surprising that he had a polarizing effect on Austrian-German culture: the northern Germans, Nicolai and Lessing in particular, about whom Sonnenfels had made disrespectful remarks in private letters that were subsequently published, were put off by his vanity. There was fierce competition between the northern German and Austrian enlightened literati, especially between Berlin and Vienna.

"Josephinism" (1780–1790) and the Rise of Viennese Genres

Enlightenment reforms climaxed in Austria during the decade of Emperor Joseph II's reign from 1780 to 1790. Beginning in 1781, Joseph II, who considered himself an enlightened ruler, relaxed some of the strict laws and opened up areas of unprecedented civil liberties to the extent that some have called this decade a "Tauwetter" (thaw). At the heart of *Josephinism,* which has been assessed differently depending on one's political views,[35] were numerous reforms that reduced the power of the Church in the areas of religious orders (monastery closings), of education, marriage and inheritance law, ecclesiastical administration, indeed, in all areas of Catholic practices. The reforms included the observance of holidays, the organization of brotherhoods, and the collection of alms; even funerary customs were either regulated by new laws or abolished altogether. Thus, Mozart's famous burial in a so-called pauper's grave was completely in line with the new regulations banning pompous funerals — unpopular regulations that were later repealed. Of great importance was the Edict of Tolerance (1781) that permitted for the first time in Austria the free exercise of religion for Protestants. Likewise, several edicts in 1781 gave Jews the right to pursue a socially accepted profession, whereas formerly their only choice (as in the case of Sonnenfels's father) had been between a restricted ghetto life or conversion to Christianity. There was also wide-ranging liberation of peasants from serfdom and numerous additional reforms. As to literature, the floodgates were opened when Joseph II greatly relaxed censorship and declared a so-called "freedom of the press" (Erweiterte Preßfreyheit, 1781). This new freedom of speech and publication suddenly permitted open discussion among readers as well as authors.

During the eighteenth century visual art and literature changed from an art of courtly splendor to one of bourgeois artistic expression. While enlightened despotism gradually relinquished pomp and circumstance, new cultural practices could evolve among the lower nobility and middle class. Just as the palace hall had been the place of art and patronage, so the salon now became its middle-class counterpart. An interesting example of this eighteenth-century transition is the salon at privy councilor Greiner's home. Greiner's daughter Caroline (married name Pichler; 1769–1843), later distinguished herself as a writer and extended the salon tradition into the Biedermeier period. Not only were politics and culture discussed in the salon, but culture was also produced in the form of Haydn's and Mozart's typically Viennese chamber music, as well as readings and discussions of French, and increasingly, German literature.

The Freemasons constituted by far the most important group in the development of Austrian literary culture.[36] A lodge had existed in Vienna since 1742, and by 1780 six different lodges included around 200 Freemasons, among them the Austrian artistic and cultural elite: W. A. Mozart, Aloys Blumauer, Michael Denis, Joseph Haydn, and Emanuel Schikaneder. The lodge *Zur wahren Eintracht* (True Harmony) led by Ignaz von Born contributed academic and journalistic efforts toward the goals of the Enlightenment in its *Journal für Freymäurer*.

Around 1780 poetry and prose experienced a structural change analogous to that which journals and the theater had undergone during the 1760s: there was a sudden proliferation of authors, texts, and readers. By 1777, with the *Wiener Musenalmanach*, a new generation of lyric poets had emerged, most of them Freemasons. Shortly after the accession of Joseph II, the relaxation of censorship led to a "Broschürenflut," a flood of inexpensive, slender polemical tracts that marked a new phase of literary and political development.[37]

Events, characters, and problems pertaining exclusively to daily life in Vienna were the subjects of the leaflets on such mundane topics as chambermaids and pharmacists, church fires and suicides, but also criticism of the pope, and emperor worship (the Papal visit to Austria in 1782 brought an intensification of anti-clerical writings). The pamphlets exposed and criticized current events and daily practices and dared to attack Church and State. Their style included travesty, parody, and above all, satire. Pamphlets might appear as treatises, letters, conversations, or dream visions, that is, in satiric forms that would disappear from the canon of literary genres by the beginning of the more restrictive nineteenth century. Aided by the reading revolution in the eighteenth century that had extended literacy throughout the middle class, the flood of pamphlets signaled a need for communication and showed a new experimentation with journalistic possibilities.[38] The clergy's rhetorical monopoly on opinion formation was now confronted with a reading public's eagerness for discussion.[39]

While the *Hanswurst* controversy was a matter of involving all of German literature, and therefore was carried out within a common framework, Viennese pamphlet journalism was perceived as distinctly independent. The most important review periodicals in Germany, Friedrich Nicolai's *Allgemeine Deutsche Bibliothek* and the *Göttingische Gelehrten Anzeigen,* kept up with the Viennese pamphlets in their own special, separate section on *Wiener Schriften.* On the other hand, the Vienna pamphleteers and newspaper writers debated which of the two promoted the Enlightenment more effectively: the *Allgemeine Deutsche Bibliothek* or the Viennese Review of Sermons. The competition between Prussia and Austria now involved cultural structures, for the cultural systems had evolved differently in analogy with the political and national identity of the two leading powers. When for instance in a Viennese newspaper of 1766 a "Viennese taste" was contrasted with a Berlin one, this demonstrated an insistence on cultural independence.[40]

Austrian lyrical poets found an important publication venue in the *Wienerischer Musenalmanach* (as of 1786, the *Wiener Musenalmanach*), founded in 1777 and published until 1796. An annual publication, the *Musenalmanach* was something between an anthology and a magazine that included only original contributions in order to provide a forum for local poets: Joseph Franz Ratschky (1757–1810), and later, co-editor Aloys Blumauer (1755–1798) promoted an editorial policy of cultural independence from Germany. The *Musenalmanach* favored patriotism and loyalty toward the Habsburgs, while its contributions reflected a carefree, cheerful, and not overly serious view of the Enlightenment.[41] The inaugural volume offered a surprisingly broad selection of lyrical, epic and even dramatic forms (for instance, a *Singspiel*). The authors included young Josephinites, many Freemasons, and numerous clergymen. Besides Ratschky, Blumauer, and Mastalier, the poets Joseph Friedrich von Retzer (1754–1824) and Johann Baptist von Alxinger (1755–1797) are worth mentioning.

Vienna became a magnet for authors from southern Germany during the period of Josephinism. The Bavarian Johann Pezzl (1756–1822) attacked superstition, fanaticism, clerical deception, despotism and persecution in his satirical novel *Faustin oder das philosophische Jahrhundert* (Faustin or the Philosophical Century, 1783–85).[42] On the model of Voltaire's novel *Candide* (1759) and in the tradition of Menippeian satire, Pezzl sends his Faustin on a trip through the civilized world. An enlightened optimism that is constantly disillusioned provides the continuing motivation. The characters remain rather colorless and serve mostly as a mouthpiece for ideas; the novel's satirical traits derive from its function as a key novel and the mentioning of historical figures. Anti-clericalism predominates in Pezzl's attacks on "die Schwarzröcke und Kapuzenköpfe, die geweihten Füchse," "katholischen Idioten"[43] (the black gowns and hooded heads, the consecrated foxes, the Catholic idiots). A review of current events provides an opportunity for satirical commentary. Pezzl pleads for a pact with the powers that be, for intellectuals to align themselves with the ruler. Thus, at the conclusion, the heroes reach Vienna, where in 1780 the true philosophical century is said to have begun, with an "allgemeiner Sieg der Vernunft und Menschheit"[44] (a sweeping victory of reason and humanity) expected from Emperor Joseph. The novel continuously projects the utopian expectations of the Enlightenment onto the absolute monarch. Its many editions and imitations attest to the book's lasting impact.

Verse epic flourished in Vienna in the wake of Wieland and Klopstock.[45] With his *Doolin von Mainz, ein Rittergedicht in zehn Gesängen* (Doolin of Mainz, a Knightly Romance in Ten Cantos, 1787), Johann Baptist von Alxinger succeeded in blending chivalric romance and the tale of enchantment in a heroic epic with a baroque structure and marked elements of fantasy (magic, alchemy and fairy power), but also with a national theme similar to Klopstock's *Hermannsschlacht*, from which Alxinger borrowed certain names and details. *Bliomberis, ein Rittergedicht in zwölf Gesängen* (Bliomberis, a Chivalric Romance in Twelve Cantos, 1791) is conceived as a story of honor redeemed. Bliomberis is an illegitimate son and has to overcome this stigma before he can marry his beloved. The suicide theme is presented in great detail: Lyonel, the hero's faithful uncle, a melancholy Hamlet figure, poisons himself once he sees his life's work accomplished. The "province of the chosen" into which Bliomberis is accepted in the end is a blend of the mystery of the Masonic lodge (as in Mozart's *Die Zauberflöte*) and the Tower Society (in Goethe's novel *Wilhelm Meister*). Fairy machinery so popular on the Viennese stage has been replaced here by a mystical Masonic element.

Joseph Ratschky's comical epic on the French Revolution, *Melchior Striegel: Ein heroisch-episches Gedicht* (Melchior Striegel: A Heroic-Epic Poem, 1793–94) is a parody in the tradition of Wieland's mock-heroic epic.[46] Ratschky takes aim at the authors of idylls, the Storm and Stress poets, and several contemporary literati. While at the university together with his stable boy, Melchior develops a plan to bring the revolution to his native village of Schöpsenheim. They create a National Assembly consisting of staunch craftsmen and enact a storm on the Bastille until the village priest intervenes. The "government" emigrates, while the priest declares that Melchior deserves to enter the Pantheon during his lifetime. In the end the fictitious poet is transported to Parnassus, received by Homer and crowned with poetic laurels. The poets approve his comical epic, regardless of how the reviewers may treat it: "Lasst sie koaxen / Die kritischen Frösch in Preußen und Sachsen" (Never mind the croaking of the critical frogs in Prussia and

Saxony). With this comic finale, the text reflects on its own genre and its context, the literary competition between Germany and Austria.

Aloys Blumauer's *Die Abentheuer des frommen Helden Aeneas oder Virgils Aeneis travestiert* (The Adventures of the Pious Hero Aeneas, or Travesty of Virgil's Aeneid, 1782–88), a comic travesty of the Virgilian epic, was the most popular work of the period.[47] Blumauer used seven-line stanzas with iambic lines of three or four stresses each, some of which resemble doggerel. Blumauer's pleasant meter and rhyme scheme allowed for comical effects. An example is the description of ferryman Charon on the occasion of Aeneas's visit in the underworld (as with Virgil):

> Unzählbar, gleich den Heringen,
>   Die in gedrängten Scharen
> Ins Fischnetz der holländischen
>   Großheringskrämer fahren,
> So drängten sich hier haufenweis
> Die armen Seelen um den Greis
> Und schrieen: Überfahren![48]

[Like countless herrings which in jam-packed swarms dart into the fishing nets of Dutch merchant trawlers, the poor souls crowded in a mass around the ancient ferryman and shouted, "Take us across!"]

The uneven versification proves an effective device for travesty, and the distorted view adds to the parodistic effect: here the lofty scene with the souls at the ancient river Styx, on whose banks the Gods swear their oaths, mutates into a swarm of fish. Top and bottom are reversed: the image has those who want to cross over the water appear as fish *in* the water. The parody turns the world upside down. At the same time it relates to the readers' time and employs the classical material for satirical effect. In this scene the river Styx becomes a "höllische Kloake" (an infernal sewer) smelling as bad "wie zu Berlin die Spree" (as the river Spree at Berlin), and the venerable Stygian ferryman Charon, a son of darkness with a cruel face in classical literature, is changed into an unkempt figure with a rough beard "wie unsre Kapuziner" (like our Capuchins).

In the manner of his day, Blumauer's satirized common daily foibles and fashions and he criticized religion and the Church with its superstitions and monastic orders (Blumauer had himself been a Jesuit!) as well as contemporary literature. This work, too, considered itself a piece of German literature — but not just German literature. In a heavenly Elysium all literary figures of the world unite:

> Hier singt beim frohen Dichtermahl
>   Anakreon Gleims Lieder,

> Und dort umarmen Juvenal
>   Und Swift sich als zween Brüder,
> Da stimmt man Klopstocks Hymnen an,
> Dort trinkt Horaz und Lucian
>   Auf Wielands Wohlergehen.[49]

[At a banquet for all the poets, Anacreon sings Gleim's verses, and there Swift and Juvenal are embracing like two brothers, here Klopstock's hymns are sung, and there Horace and Lucan are drinking a toast to Wieland.]

The conflict between classical and modern literature (*querelle des anciens et des modernes*) has been resolved, as has the one between national literatures. The classical models sing in tune with contemporary authors: Anacreon with the German patriotic poet Johann Wilhelm Ludwig Gleim, and his model Juvenal with the satirist Jonathan Swift. Horace and the satirist Lucian accompany Christian Martin Wieland, the idol of Austrian literature. Blumauer's *Aeneid* travesty went through new editions until far into the nineteenth century. Yet the Aeneid travesty called for a readership not only equipped with knowledge of Virgil's original as well as of contemporary literature, but also with a belief in the benefit of the Enlightenment. When both of these disappeared, the work was dropped from the literary canon.

One work of the Austrian Enlightenment that transcends literature has survived: Mozart's *Die Zauberflöte* (Magic Flute, 1791). Like a reflector of cultural developments, the libretto combined many of Austria's important literary traditions. It was written by a multitalented actor, singer, and poet who was born in Bavaria: Emanuel Schikaneder (1751–1812). An expert theater practitioner, Schikaneder managed to create a brilliant amalgamation of disparate traditions.[50] The exposition alone combines the tradition of the *locus terribilis* and eighteenth-century exoticism resulting in immediate stage magic as Prince Tamino is pursued by a theatrical monster. The prince's language is heroic and elevated from the beginning, but he himself is in a tight spot. The plot begins with an inversion of gender roles: a man is in trouble and women are the rescuers. We also find the sudden shift from the heroic to the comical that was characteristic of the popular stage, for the sphere of noble desire immediately provides a comical effect (the quarrel of the three ladies-in-waiting).

The libretto itself, read without Mozart's music, has severe literary flaws. Schikaneder employed the most ordinary phrases and idioms, an abundance of hyperboles, superlatives, and undifferentiated clichés, particularly with regard to male-female roles. The characters are flat and rigid, and even the kindest interpretation cannot overlook many inconsistencies and credibility gaps. Schikaneder's text does not follow Gottsched's or Lessing's rules of drama, but those of the operatic genre, more specifically, of baroque opera.

Its basic principle, the representation of the public sphere (the plot involves kingdoms, power and legitimacy) is just as evident as the feudal principle:

> Dich schützt der Prinz, trau ihm allein!
> Dafür sollst du sein Diener sein.[51]
>
> [The prince protects you, trust him alone!
> You are his servant in return.]

And yet Tamino's actions and goals are bourgeois, and so are the many maxims.

Schikaneder's literary model was the fairy tale *Lulu, oder die Zauberflöte*, published in a collection by Wieland (*Dschinnistan oder auserlesene Feen- und Geistermärchen*, Djinnistan or Selected Tales of Fairies and Ghosts, 1789) that also provided additional motifs for *Die Zauberflöte*. The opera also drew on the "Zauberspiel" (magic play) and the popular *Singspiel* and demonstrates strong ties to the local theater tradition. Thus the libretto still exhibits the baroque concept of two worlds (heaven and earth) whose agents appear in the images of day (Sarastro) and night (the Queen). A *Singspiel* by Joachim Perinet, *Kasperl der Fagotist oder die Zauberzither* (Kasperl the Bassoonist and the Magic Zither, 1791) used a very similar plot at almost the same time, and in order to compete Schikaneder had to write for the masses to ensure a full house. However, apart from the Vienna theater tradition, the program of bourgeois tragedy shines through, and affinities to classical drama, particularly to Shakespeare's *Tempest*, are also present.

Another important contemporary context is freemasonry, whose goals are reflected in the struggle of light against darkness and of enlightenment against superstition.[52] Sarastro's words at the beginning of the second act underscore the text's Masonic dimension. Freemasonry acted "in the name of Humanity," according to its self-professed ideals. Formal Masonic elements appear in the brothers' preparations, the veiling of the candidate, in the numerology involving the number three, the ritual ordeal, the organization of men and their insistence on Enlightenment goals and in several details of the plot. The first essay in Von Born's *Journal für Freymäurer* (Journal for Freemasons, 1784) dealt with "Die Mysterien der alten Ägypter" (The Mysteries of the Ancient Egyptians) and described initiation rituals in the form of ordeals by fire and water. As participants in this lodge, Mozart and Schikaneder paid homage to their important patrons by including Masonic ritual and mysticism in their opera.

Schikaneder's libretto embraced the trends and moods of Austrian Enlightenment literature, their strengths as well as weaknesses. A combination of these elements comprised the material that Mozart's music then dealt with, either through ironic reflection or rich embellishment, thus transforming the paradoxical text into a lasting work of art.

The development of Austrian literature as a national literature began with the changes during the late phase of absolutism when around 1750 modernization processes strengthened the Habsburg territories as an independent state. This trend toward national independence accelerated the development of a national identity through "disentanglement" from the Holy Roman Empire,[53] and simultaneously fostered independent cultural developments through administrative reforms, new censorship laws, and trade regulations affecting the publishing business. On the one hand, Gottsched's literary reforms initiated a movement of literary standards that required Austrian authors to join an overarching Enlightenment program. On the other hand, the Seven Years' War (1756–1763), the armed conflict between Austria and Prussia during which the issue of the German nation was hotly debated, forced the two primary German states to map out and define their own cultural territory in comparison and competition with one another. This competition produced a patriotic, Austrian phase in the German-speaking Habsburg lands. Yet literary trends such as the reception of Klopstock and bardic poetry linked Austrian developments once more with those in German literature elsewhere. It was only then that Josephinism, whose influence extended into the middle of nineteenth-century Austria, followed as a third phase. As a result of this phase of Josephinism, Austrian literature became largely autonomous and a new national literature came into being.

— Translated by Barbara Becker-Cantarino

Notes

[1] It should be noted that Switzerland was an independent confederation and had ceased to be part of the Holy Roman Empire of German Nation since the Peace of Westphalia in 1648. Austria within the Empire consisted of the Austrian Circle and Swabian possessions, Bohemia, and the Burgundian Circle where the dominant language was German (except for Burgundia), estimated at approx. 9 million in the eighteenth century (before the Napoleonic Wars). Its capital Vienna had about 105,000 inhabitants in 1700 and 247,000 around 1800 (Berlin had 24,000 in 1700; 172,000 in 1800). The Austrian (Habsburg ruled) Territory outside of the Empire consisted of Hungary, Illyria, Transylvania, Bukovina, East and West Galicia, and Lombardy with an estimated 11 million inhabitants. Here most of the nobility spoke French and German besides their native tongue; see Helmuth Kiesel and Paul Münch, *Gesellschaft und Literatur im 18. Jahrhundert: Voraussetzungen und Entstehung des literarischen Markts in Deutschland* (Munich: Beck, 1977), 14–18; and Walter Bruford, *Germany in the Eighteenth Century: The Social Background of the Literary Revival* (Cambridge: Cambridge UP, 1965), 333–35.

[2] See also the essay on Swiss literature by Rosmarie Zeller in this volume.

[3] Leslie Bodi, *Tauwetter in Wien: Zur Prosa der österreichischen Aufklärung*. 2nd ed. (Vienna: Böhlau, 1995), 109.

[4] See Martin Gierl, *Pietismus und Aufklärung: Theologische Polemik und die Kommunikationsreform der Wissenschaft am Ende des 17. Jahrhunderts* (Göttingen: Vandenhoeck & Ruprecht, 1997).

[5] Harm Klueting, ed., *Katholische Aufklärung — Aufklärung im katholischen Deutschland* (Hamburg: Meiner, 1993).

[6] Anna Coreth, *Pietas Austriaca: Österreichische Frömmigkeit im Barock*. 2nd ed. (Vienna: Verlag für Geschichte und Politik, 1982).

[7] Roger Bauer, "Quelques ancêtres d'Ulrich et d'Arnheim: Aux origenes du débat littérature autrichienne et/ou littérature allemande," in *Literatur im Kontext Robert Musil: Littérature dans le contexte de Robert Musil*, ed. Marie-Louise Roth and Pierre Béhar (Berlin: Lang, 1999), 54.

[8] Karl Vocelka, *Glanz und Untergang der höfischen Welt: Repräsentation, Reform und Reaktion im habsburgischen Vielvölkerstaat. Österreichische Geschichte 1699–1815* (Vienna: Ueberreuter, 2001).

[9] Franz Matsche, *Die Kunst im Dienst der Staatsidee Kaiser Karls VI. Ikonographie, Ikonologie und Programmatik des "Kaiserstils"* (Berlin: de Gruyter, 1981).

[10] As Holy Roman Emperor he was Franz II (1792–1806), as Austrian Emperor he was Franz I (1792–1835). Napoleon abolished the Holy Roman Empire in 1806.

[11] By 1984, already more than 400 papers on the identity of Austrian literature were in existence, see Donald G. Daviau, "Österreichische Identität in historischer Perspektive," in *Literatur im Kontext*, 63. See also Wendelin Schmidt-Dengler et al., eds., *Literaturgeschichte: Österreich. Prolegomena und Fallstudien* (Berlin: E. Schmidt, 1995); and Ruth Wodak et al., *The Discursive Construction of National Identity*, trans. Angelika Hirsch and Richard Mitten (Edinburgh: Edinburgh UP, 1999).

[12] Roger Bauer, "Die österreichische Literatur des Josephinischen Zeitalters: Eine werdende Literatur auf der Suche nach neuen Ausdrucksformen," *Das achtzehnte Jahrhundert als Epoche*, ed. Bernhard Fabian and Wilhelm Schmidt-Biggemann (Nendeln: KTO Press, 1978), 25–37; Herbert Zeman, "Die österreichische Literatur — Begriff, Bedeutung und literarhistorische Entfaltung in der Neuzeit," in *Die österreichische Literatur: Ihr Profil von den Anfängen im Mittelalter bis ins 18. Jahrhundert (1050–1750)*, ed. Herbert Zeman (Graz: Akademische Verlagsanstalt, 1986), 640; Bodi, *Tauwetter*, 22.

[13] Herbert Seidler, *Österreichischer Vormärz und Goethezeit: Geschichte einer literarischen Auseinandersetzung* (Vienna: Verlag der Österreichischen Akademie der Wissenschaften, 1982), 31.

[14] Franz M. Eybl, "Probleme einer österreichischen Literaturgeschichte des 18. Jahrhunderts," in *Literaturgeschichte: Österreich*, ed. Wendelin Schmidt-Dengler et al., Philologische Studien und Quellen, vol. 132 (Berlin: E. Schmidt, 1995), 146–57.

[15] Other names for the buffoon in the eighteenth century were: *arleccino, Pickelhäring, Jean Potage*. See also Johann Sonnleitner, "Hanswurst, Bernardon, Kasperl und Staberl," in *Joseph Anton Stranitzky, Joseph Felix Kurz, Philipp Hafner, Joachim*

Perinet, Adolf Bäuerle: Hanswurstiaden: Ein Jahrhundert Wiener Komödie (Salzburg: Residenz, 1996), 340.

[16] Herbert Zeman, "Die Alt-Wiener Volkskomödie des 18. und frühen 19. Jahrhunderts — ein gattungsgeschichtlicher Versuch," in *Die österreichische Literatur*, 1301.

[17] Hilde Haider-Pregler, *Des sittlichen Bürgers Abendschule: Bildungsanspruch und Bildungsauftrag des Berufstheaters im 18. Jahrhundert* (Vienna: Jugend & Volk, 1980), 278.

[18] Bernhard Greiner, *Die Komödie: Eine theatralische Sendung: Grundlagen und Interpretationen* (Tübingen: Francke, 1992), 144.

[19] Robert A. Kann, *Kanzel und Katheder: Studien zur österreichischen Geistesgeschichte vom Spätbarock zur Frühromantik* (Vienna: Herder, 1962), 149; Helmut Reinalter, ed., *Joseph von Sonnenfels* (Vienna: Verlag der Österreichischen Akademie der Wissenschaften, 1988); Vocelka, *Glanz und Untergang*, 55.

[20] Kann, *Kanzel und Katheder*, 214.

[21] Kann, *Kanzel und Katheder*, 209–24; Haider-Pregler, *Des sittlichen Bürgers*, 267–350; Franz M. Eybl, "Hanswurststreit und Broschürenflut. Die Struktur der Kontroversen in der österreichischen Literatur des 18. Jahrhunderts," in *Konflikte — Skandale — Dichterfehden in der österreichischen Literatur*, ed. Wendelin Schmidt-Dengler et al. (Berlin: E. Schmidt, 1995), 24–35.

[22] Franz Hadamowsky, "Ein Jahrhundert Literatur- und Theaterzensur in Österreich (1751–1830)," in *Die österreichische Literatur*, 291–92.

[23] Gerhard Scheit, *Hanswurst und der Staat: Eine kleine Geschichte der Komik: Von Mozart bis Thomas Bernhard* (Vienna: Deuticke, 1995).

[24] Wolfram Seidler, *Buchmarkt und Zeitschriften in Wien 1760–1785: Studie zur Herausbildung einer literarischen Öffentlichkeit im Österreich des 18. Jahrhunderts* (Szeged: Scriptum, 1994), 65–75. See also the essay by Helga Brandes in this volume.

[25] Norbert Bachleitner et al., *Geschichte des österreichischen Buchhandels* (Wiesbaden: Harrassowitz, 2000), 140.

[26] Paul von Hofmann-Wellenhof, *Michael Denis. Ein Beitrag zur deutsch-oesterreichischen Literaturgeschichte des XVIII. Jahrhunderts* (Innsbruck: Wagner, 1881).

[27] Bodi, *Tauwetter*, 101.

[28] Johann Wolfgang von Goethe, *Werke. Weimarer Ausgabe*. Section I, vol. 37 (Weimar: Böhlau, 1919), 246.

[29] Johann Sonnleitner, "Die Wiener Komödie am Scheideweg: Zu Philipp Hafners Possen," in *Philipp Hafner: Komödien*, ed. Johann Sonnleitner (Vienna: Lehner, 2001), 428.

[30] Scheit, *Hanswurst*, 65.

[31] Wolfgang Martens, *Der patriotische Minister: Fürstendiener in der Literatur der Aufklärungszeit* (Weimar: Böhlau, 1996), 198–207.

[32] Gotthold Ephraim Lessing and Eva König, *Briefe aus der Brautzeit 1770–1776*, ed. Wolfgang Albrecht (Weimar: Böhlau, 2000), 57, 68.

[33] Sonnenfels also produced pioneering work in the areas of administrative reform, legislation and education: *Grundsätze aus der Polizey-, Handlungs- und Finanz-Wissenschaft* (3 vols. 1765–69) and the *Handbuch der inneren Staatsverwaltung* (1798). These manuals went through several editions and were the official texts for teaching law in Austria until 1845.

[34] Christian Heinrich Schmid, *Über den gegenwärtigen Zustand des deutschen Parnasses* [1773]. With additions by Christoph Martin Wieland, ed. Robert Seidel (St. Ingbert: Röhrig, 1998), 33.

[35] Vocelka, *Glanz und Untergang*, 368.

[36] Edith Rosenstrauch-Königsberg, *Freimaurerei im Josephinischen Wien: Aloys Blumauers Weg vom Jesuiten zum Jakobiner* (Vienna: Braumüller, 1974); Stephan Tull, *Die politischen Zielvorstellungen der Wiener Freimaurer und Wiener Jakobiner im 18. Jahrhundert* (Frankfurt a. M.: Lang, 1993).

[37] Cf. Aloys Blumauer, *Beobachtungen über Oesterreichs Aufklärung und Litteratur* (1782, rpt. Vienna: Antiquariat H. Geyer, 1970).

[38] Bachleitner et al., *Geschichte des Buchhandels*, 154–57; Bodi, *Tauwetter*, 167.

[39] Some periodicals were even published for the sole purpose of reviewing the Sunday sermonizers in Vienna week after week; see Eybl, "Hanswurststreit" 34.

[40] Robert Haas, "Von dem Wienerischen Geschmack in der Musik," in *Festschrift Johannes Biehle zum 60. Geburtstage*, ed. Erich H. Müller (Leipzig: Kistner & Siegel 1930), 59–65.

[41] Matti Schüsseler, *Unbeschwert aufgeklärt: Scherzhafte Literatur im 18. Jahrhundert* (Tübingen: Niemeyer, 1990).

[42] Johann Pezzl, *Faustin oder das philosophische Jahrhundert* (1783, rpt. Hildesheim: Gerstenberg, 1982); Bodi, *Tauwetter* 184–90.

[43] Pezzl, *Faustin*, 121, 370.

[44] Pezzl, *Faustin*, 381.

[45] With their verse epics the Josephinites represent a literary tradition that was subsequently displaced and obscured by German Classicism.

[46] Joseph F. Ratschky, *Melchior Striegel*, ed. Wynfrid Kriegleder (Graz: Akademische Verlagsanstalt, 1991).

[47] See Barbara Becker-Cantarino, *Aloys Blumauer and the Literature of Austrian Enlightenment* (Bern: Lang, 1973), 63–77.

[48] G. Chr. Lichtenberg, Th. G. v. Hippel und Al. Blumauer, ed. Felix Bobertag. Deutsche Nationalliteratur, vol. 141 (Berlin and Stuttgart: W. Speman, n.d.), 405 (v. 3214–3220).

[49] G. Chr. Lichtenberg, Th. G. v. Hippel und Al. Blumauer, 423 (v. 3816–3822).

[50] Anke Sonnek, *Emanuel Schikaneder. Theaterprinzipal, Schauspieler und Stückeschreiber* (Kassel: Bärenreiter, 1999); Günter Meinhold, *Zauberflöte und Zauber-*

flöten-Rezeption: Studien zu Emanuel Schikaneders Libretto "Die Zauberflöte" und seiner literarischen Rezeption (Frankfurt a. M.: Lang, 2001).

[51] All quotes from Wolfgang Amadeus Mozart, *Die Zauberflöte: Oper in zwei Aufzügen* (Stuttgart: Reclam, 1974), 22 (I: 8).

[52] See Jacques Chailly, *The Magic Flute, Masonic Opera: An Interpretation of the Libretto and the Music,* trans. from the French by Herbert Weinstock (New York: Knopf, 1971).

[53] Harm Klueting, "Zwischen wittelsbachischem Kaisertum und josephinischer Diözesanregulierung (1742/45–1783): Faktoren österreichischer Identitätsbildung im 18. Jahrhundert," in *Strukturwandel kultureller Praxis: Beiträge zu einer kulturwissenschaftlichen Sicht des Theresianischen Zeitalters,* ed. Franz M. Eybl (Vienna: Wiener Universitätsverlag, 2002), 15–44.

"Tolerance." Allegorical engraving by Daniel Chodowiecki. Minerva takes the devotees of all religions under her protection.

Eighteenth-Century Germany in its Historical Context

W. Daniel Wilson

A Multitude of Sovereign States

THE END OF THE THIRTY YEARS' WAR in 1648 was almost as disastrous for Germany as the war itself, which had devastated huge parts of the country.[1] The Treaty of Westphalia cemented the division of German-speaking lands into hundreds of sovereign states, ranging from large ones like Saxony and Bavaria to smaller and even miniscule ones that consisted of little more than a sovereign lord, his castle, and a few villages. The sovereigns of these territories were sometimes kings, but more often dukes, counts, and bishops or archbishops. The territories were loosely bound together in the Holy Roman Empire, which, as the joke went, was neither holy nor Roman nor an empire. Mainly coextensive with the German-speaking lands, with the exception of Switzerland, it was a legal umbrella centered on the emperor in Vienna (by tradition, the Habsburg king of Austria served as emperor), his court, and various institutions. Most important among these were the Imperial Diet (*Reichstag*) in Regensburg and the Imperial courts in Wetzlar and Vienna (*Reichskammergericht* and *Reichshofrat*).

These courts settled disputes among the various territories and even between local authorities and their sovereign. Because a small village could take its local prince to court in Wetzlar or Vienna, the Empire had the reputation of being less autocratic and the power of "absolutist" monarchs of being less absolute than later ages would have it, and in any case less than in countries like France with its centralist government. This arrangement was called the "German constitution," though of course it was not a constitution in the modern sense. Contemporaries and modern historians of the Empire alike have sometimes tended to exaggerate the liberties under this system and the courts' capacity to resolve conflicts peacefully,[2] but this was true only for the powerful and the wealthy. Lowly subjects most often lost their cases against their princes, and often did not have the financial means to see the case through. Added to this were the notorious decades-long delays in trials, so that the Imperial courts were a remedy more in name than in substance. Nevertheless, German princes ruled with a keen awareness of possible sanctions from Vienna or from the Reichstag in Regensburg, and for some, though not all of them, this consciousness bridled their self-interest.

Another reason that the term "absolutism" — suggesting absolute princely authority — has been questioned recently is that sovereigns were inhibited by the remnants of aristocratic power. In each principality, the non-ruling nobles (gentry) formed an assembly of estates, the *Landstände* or *Ständeversammlung*, which they convened together with representatives of towns and clergy. In this arrangement, the nobility clearly dominated. The prince relied on taxes granted by the estates to finance the growing bureaucracy. They met at irregular intervals, usually at the prince's initiative, to consider his requests for funds. Thus, they had a certain measure of power to refuse such levies. However, the prince was usually able to convince the nobles in his realm to do his bidding, primarily by offering them sinecures at his court and other signs of his favor. Since many nobles were unable to eke a living from their impoverished estates, they were increasingly tempted to accept such courtly positions and were thus drawn into the prince's sphere of influence. The estates, no less than the Empire, thus became mere shadows of a countervailing weight to princely power and sovereignty.

There were, to be sure, non-princely polities, mainly Free Imperial Cities like Frankfurt and Hamburg that were ruled by a sort of oligarchy, a few patrician families. These "free cities" prided themselves on not being subject to aristocratic or absolutist whims. They cultivated a certain republican consciousness — although the structures were hardly democratic in the modern sense. The cities were ruled by selected male members of patrician families, a narrow, privileged class of citizens who could demonstrate a certain level of wealth and property. Observers often remarked that the class distinctions in these cities were hardly less marked than in the principalities.

The Social Classes

Most territories, however, were ruled by a prince. Their economies were agrarian and feudal. The nobility was free of the myriad taxes levied on town and village dwellers and benefited from various other privileges. The peasants, often at the brink of subsistence, labored not only for their own benefit, but had to carry out unpaid or minimally paid feudal duties (*Frondienste*) for their lords; they often were forbidden to move, leave their residence, or marry without the permission of their landlord. To be sure, in the Habsburg lands Joseph II ended personal serfdom in 1781 (so that peasants were allowed to marry and to move), but it was only his radical land reform of 1784–1789 that might have fundamentally lessened the crushing burden on peasants — and this reform was postponed and eventually revoked. The peasants had to wait until 1848 for the final abolition of seigneurial dues.[3]

The peasants did not suffer as patiently or happily under this regime as older historiography would have it. Since the 1960s, German historians have increasingly unraveled the lasting tradition of peasant revolts and disturbances that continued throughout the eighteenth century.[4] German peasants knew of the Peasants' War of the sixteenth century, and so did their lords. Their grievances proved a constant threat to noble and state authority (very often, the prince himself was the largest landowning noble in the realm). In 1752, there was a revolt of unified peasants and townspeople — a relatively rare occurrence — in Anhalt-Bernburg; the peasants were suffering under feudal dues, the townspeople under taxes. This revolt had to be put down by military force, but in 1766–67 violence flared again. Silesia was a particular hot spot for revolts beginning in 1765; in 1785, a local newspaper said that "ein beständiger, wirklicher Krieg" (a constant, genuine war) existed between peasants and their lords.[5] The years 1774–75 saw extended revolts in Bohemia — events that were entirely ignored in literature, as was a massive famine in many German lands in the early 1770s.[6]

Feudal duties were regulated by age-old contracts between the villages and the lord. The authorities exploited every opportunity to expand the duties that peasants were required to perform, and the peasants resisted these encroachments. Even when an individual peasant was abused, the entire village showed remarkable solidarity in standing behind him. Because of the contracts and the legal status of their collective rights, the peasants were the only group in a position effectively to resist princely power in eighteenth-century Germany. In general, however, their narrow horizon — the lack of mobility, resources, and education — barred the peasants from developing any kind of revolutionary consciousness. They were concerned mainly with protecting their ancient rights within the existing system, and these rights were defined almost entirely with respect to their feudal duties, not to modern notions like freedom of speech or assembly. When they did challenge violations of their rights with violent protests and resistance, they were easily brought in line by police or military suppression. Despite the predominance of conflicts between peasants and their authorities in political culture of the eighteenth century, writers of belles-lettres almost never treated these struggles in their works. Nor were the peasants themselves usually literate and thus had only scant knowledge of literary culture.

The focus of cultural and political life in the typical small to medium-sized principalities was the city in which the prince resided, the *Residenz*. Here life revolved around the prince and his court, modest though the latter may have been. A strict hierarchy in the population was evident even in the clothing proscribed for each estate. The lower classes, consisting of day laborers, servants, and petty craftsmen, subsisted sometimes relatively well, but often on the verge of starvation. The nobles jostled for the prince's favor, which was reflected in the seating order at the noon dinners at court, and in the dizzying array of — largely useless — courtly positions and titles that were coveted because they were richly endowed.[7] The nobles also dominated the state bureaucracy; normally, all higher positions were reserved for the aristocracy. However, middle-class men, who were increasingly well educated, were beginning to contest this system of privilege. Princes chafed under it too, because untrained aristocratic administrators proved disastrous for a well-run polity. Under this pressure, nobles began seeing higher education as a prerequisite to retaining their privilege, and many of them served illustriously as statesmen and administrators. Conversely, many of the best middle-class bureaucrats were given patents of nobility so that they could advance and represent the court on an equal footing when on diplomatic missions.

The middle classes (*Bürgertum*) were the real motor of culture and change in the eighteenth century.[8] However, it is important to differentiate sociologically. The older, established city-dwellers were fundamentally conservative. They consisted mostly of small merchants and craftsmen organized in guilds that were as stagnant as any ancient institution. In the capital cities, they were largely dependent on the court economically since they provided it with goods and services. Thus, their loyalties were usually to the prince rather than to any vision of a new order. Often, in smaller towns, they owned land and pursued limited agriculture in addition to their town occupation (*Ackerbürger*). What later became known as the bourgeoisie, that is, merchants with considerably more wealth who often dealt in commerce that extended beyond local borders or who owned proto-industrial factories, were exceedingly rare in eighteenth-century Germany. However, there was indeed a new middle class in Germany, defined primarily by education and culture—values not generally cherished by the traditional middle classes. This dynamic new class was marked by upward mobility, openness to liberal ideas, and an ambivalent attitude toward traditional values. However, old and new *Bürgertum* were united in their valorization of the central notion of virtue. Christian morality and "virtue" became the rallying point for this class to establish itself as the vanguard of culture and progress. The literature discussed in this volume had as its audience largely members of this class (along with some nobility, as well as older middle classes and even lower classes in the case of certain literature with religious content such as Gellert's). This newer middle class is the underpinning of Enlightenment culture in Germany. In contrast to the traditional middle classes, they were marked by many of the traits of the modern world: restlessness, mobility, and a critical attitude. In his verse epic *Herrmann und Dorothea* (1796), Johann Wolfgang von Goethe depicted in succinct form the gulf between these two types of middle-class burghers.

Authorship and Publishing

Many sons of this new, educated class entered administrative service to the state, and it is within the bureaucracies of cities and principalities that we find many of the leading writers and intellectuals of the day. Particularism, the splintering of Germany into so many territories, meant that authors could not live from their writing alone as modern authors do. If a novel were published, say, in Leipzig (in the Electorate of Saxony), it could immediately be printed in a legal "pirated" edition in Mannheim or Vienna. The author would be paid for the first edition sold by his Saxon publisher, but additional print runs were usually thwarted by competition from unauthorized editions.

Only late in the century did the first attempts at copyright laws beyond territorial boundaries take place. Because of these relatively small, fragmented book markets, no writer lived as a freelancer in Germany for more than a few years before the 1790s.[9] It was especially difficult for a woman author without income from a profession or family support, as was the case with Anna Louisa Karsch (1722–1791), who with considerable business acumen managed to eke out an existence, first by reciting her poetry as entertainment and then publishing occasional poetry dedicated to wealthy clients; later she managed to publish her lyrics (with Gleim collecting subscribers for the volume) and established herself as poet in Berlin. Later, other women were forced to live from their writings when they were widowed or unmarried, and many writers could make a modest living by translating newly published and popular books from other languages, mostly French and English. But for most of the eighteenth century, gaining a livelihood only from publishing literature was impossible.

Eighteenth-century Germany saw the emergence of authorship as a profession. Men aspiring to dedicate all their time and efforts to writing met the economic challenge with various schemes to allow them to pursue writing as their calling. One of these ideas was the notion that princes should magnanimously support academies of writers — but of course no sovereigns saw any benefit to such an institution, though it seemed for a time that they were interested.[10] Some managed to receive a lifelong pension from a prince, as did Klopstock from the king of Denmark. Other authors tried financing their own publications, but this venture was only minimally successful. So writers had to earn their living from other occupations: some as tutors to nobles, others as pastors, teachers, professors; some found work at the theater. Many served in the new, rationalized, and expanding bureaucracies of princely territories. The vast majority of German writers — regardless of their wage-earning occupation — thus remained dependent on the church, the governing body of a city or a principality, or a noble for their livelihood. Loyalty to the respective employer was mandated, and this meant that truly oppositional thinking was, by and large, inaccessible to them. The splintering of cultural centers — the lack of a single metropolis like London or Paris, where intellectuals could gather and share ideas — exacerbated this political paralysis. Germany was a land of courts, and the courts absorbed educated young men like sponges. As servants of the state, the main, narrow focus of their discontent lay in the privilege of nobles within the bureaucracy. When Goethe's young bureaucrat Werther complains about this aristocratic privilege, he is expressing the limited agenda of a whole generation of young German men. They felt that their education and their middle-class values had given them an inner superiority, a nobility of the mind and accomplishments, that was superior to the inherited nobility given precedence in state service and practically every other sphere of life. While their enmeshment with state interests prevented this consciousness from developing into a principled critique of the feudal and absolutist status quo, resentment of noble privilege remained a constant irritant in eighteenth-century political affairs and found many points of entry into literature.

"Enlightened Absolutism"

Such thinking clearly grew out of the Enlightenment. Enlightened ideas affected political culture in several ways. First, the state administration benefited from rationalized thought, which provided impulses for modernization. Particularly in the area of agriculture, many reform-minded princes introduced measures that sought to rationalize tradition-bound farming and — not coincidentally — increased princely and aristocratic revenues. Second, several progressive sovereigns expanded the rights of their subjects. In Prussia, for example, torture — which was essentially useless for obtaining accurate confessions — was banned under Friedrich II (r. 1740–86); in Austria, Emperor Joseph II (r. 1780–90) diminished the power of the Catholic Church and introduced various legal reforms. Finally, several princes associated themselves with Enlightenment thinkers, most famously when Friederich II invited the quintessential French *lumière* Voltaire to his court.

The alliance of the princely sovereign with Enlightenment goes under the term — coined in the nineteenth century — "enlightened absolutism" (or, primarily in the English-speaking world, "enlightened despotism"). The term is riddled with problems. In the first place, we have seen that "absolutism" is a somewhat inaccurate description of eighteenth-century principalities, since the sovereign's power was limited by that of the various estates, and very few subjects in eighteenth-century Germany considered their prince despotic. More important, "enlightened absolutism" can be seen as a contradiction in terms. Whenever Enlightenment allies itself with autocratic government, it sacrifices some of its central tenets. The logical consequence of Enlightenment is democratic government, as it developed (in vastly differing forms) in the United States and France toward the end of the century. Inherited privilege and power are anathema to rationalist thought — and princes were well aware of this. Their flirtation with Enlightenment rarely crossed their own interests. On the contrary, the alliance of Enlightenment with princely power strengthened the latter, not the former. Rationalist reforms usually benefited the prince economically or otherwise, and the rights of his subjects were never substantially expanded.

Historians have sometimes interpreted "enlightened absolutism" as an attempt on the part of economically backward states in Central Europe to "catch up" with Western Europe through forced modernization. But it could also be seen as a defensive measure against the perceived threat of revolutionary or democratic ideals borne of Enlightenment thinking. In any case, "enlightened absolutism" did successfully help block democracy in Germany, whether this was the intent of its adherents or not. German thinkers generally approved of the Revolution of 1789 in France, but rejected revolutionary change for Germany, because they argued that their reformist princes made revolution unnecessary. Even in the long term, this stabilizing effect of "enlightened absolutism" is evident. Historians have pointed out that almost all the countries which favored "enlightened absolutism" in the eighteenth century developed totalitarian regimes in the twentieth: not only Germany and Austria, but Italy, Spain, and Russia had important monarchs who claimed to govern according to Enlightenment principles (in Russia, it was a German-born tsarina, Catherine II).[11] While it would be wrong to construct a linear causal connection between "enlightened absolutism" and twentieth-century totalitarianism with its myriad causes, the legitimizing strategy that Enlightenment provided for autocratic, but supposedly benevolent government, was certainly part of the equation, even if other, more direct causes were more decisive.

The predominance of "enlightened absolutism" as a political model and writers' dependence on the state meant that few intellectuals of the German eighteenth century conceived the kind of radical political critique seen in England or France. Nevertheless, by the 1770s and 1780s, the authority of monarchs and the reputation of courtly life were increasingly called into question. The easiest target was courtly culture. In the eyes of its critics, the court was the locus of all that was evil and anathema to middle-class virtues (though of course many writers felt the contradiction inherent in their critique, since they hoped for support from precisely these courts). The court was supposedly rife with sexual license, intrigue, and deception, all of which corrupted the monarch and led to a decline in the common weal. The courts were thus the target of critiques that were essentially moralistic in origin but became eminently political in their anti-aristocratic and anti-monarchist thrust.[12] Still, the moralist tone remained characteristic of German political life. In plays such as *Emilia Galotti* (1772) by Gotthold Ephraim Lessing

(1729–81), *Der Hofmeister* (1774; The Tutor) by J. M. R. Lenz (1751–92) or *Kabale und Liebe* (1784; Intrigue and Love) by Friedrich Schiller (1759–1805), or in poems by writers like Gottfried August Bürger (1747–94) and Christian Friedrich Daniel Schubart (1739–1791), middle-class outrage at courtly vice and aristocratic privilege was forcefully articulated. In theoretical books and articles, too, Enlightenment thinkers questioned myriad aspects of the feudal and absolutist regime.[13] Practically none of these writers, however, called for an end to monarchies, though certainly most of them favored restrictions on princely power and noble privilege. Instead, the positive model driving most of these writings is that of the honest, moral middle-class intellectual who works in the service of a monarch for the common good. He helps surround the prince with like-minded men who — in a variant of the ancient mentor ideal — have a beneficial, enlightening influence on the sovereign.[14] This influence translates ultimately into social and economic reforms, in which the prince becomes the advocate of the commoners against the unjust advantages of the aristocracy. Thus, "enlightened absolutism" was fed by moralistic middle-class impulses and came in many different forms.

One of the most unique of these was the mentor as mistress, a model found in Schiller's *Kabale und Liebe* and the quintessential novel of sensibility *Die Geschichte des Fräuleins von Sternheim* (1771; The History of Lady Sternheim) by Sophie von La Roche (1731–1807). Here we find the notion (in La Roche's novel only a possibility) of a woman who uses her female charms in order to influence a prince and instill a "higher," political virtue in him. However, the writers were aware of the futility of the mentor ideal and imbued their portrayals with considerable irony and distance.

Secret Societies

A unique and intriguing variant of enlightened mentoring of absolutist princes can be found among the many secret societies that flourished in the eighteenth century. Of course, these societies were more than just a form of "enlightened absolutism." They provided men (women were generally excluded, as were Jews) with a venue for developing middle-class morality and for beginning to articulate its social and political implications. Contemporaries and later scholars alike have puzzled over this widespread phenomenon: how could an age that defined itself as the paradigm of light and clarity favor organizations that operated in the dark, behind a veil of secrecy? Some have suggested that secret societies filled a void left by religion's demise in an enlightened age, providing an outlet for mystical and spiritual needs. The secret societies also seem to have met a need for traditionalism, for they based their legitimacy on supposedly ancient compacts and foundations. Whatever the impulse, secret societies were an obsession of the eighteenth century. Practically all major thinkers were Freemasons, a fact that had more immediate political implications than in later centuries. A variant of Masonry, the Strict Observance (Strikte Observanz), dominated German lands up to the 1780s. This society envisioned a colony outside of Europe and harbored large-scale plans for dubious financial transactions, and its members swore obedience to unidentified leaders--factors which discredited the Strict Observance in the eyes of its many critics and especially of suspicious governments.[15] At the same time, Masonry was not a genuine secret society, since a Mason could inform anyone of his membership.

Potentially — but only potentially — more radical were true secret societies, especially the Order of Illuminati.[16] Known today chiefly in science fiction as the instigators of sinister plots, the historical Illuminati were a group of no more than 1,500 mainly German intellectuals formed in 1776 by a Bavarian professor, Adam Weishaupt (1748–1830). Ultimately, quasi-political goals were formulated: princes and states were to disappear from the earth. However, this quasi-anarchist aim was never part of any clear political program, but rather the vague end-point of a long historical process. In this unique twist on "enlightened absolutism," Illuminati were to infiltrate the highest echelons of state service, surrounding the prince and influencing him morally. And in fact, the membership rolls of the Illuminati contain a disproportionate number of high-ranking administrators and statesmen.[17] Ultimately, some princes were accepted as members, though not without resistance from within the organization. In 1783–84, the locus of power in the order shifted from Weishaupt's Bavaria to Weimar, where Goethe and even Duke Carl August became members — though probably only to find out more about this suspicious-sounding group and to keep an eye on it.[18] Finally, in 1784–85, renegades betrayed the organization to Bavarian authorities, and it was suppressed. In 1787, the Bavarian government published a large collection of Illuminati documents that severely compromised the order. More disturbing to most contemporaries than the quasi-political designs were breaches of contemporary morality such as Weishaupt's advocacy of abortion. But recipes for poison and in particular the use of internal informants deeply shocked Germany and indeed all of Europe.

The scandal surrounding the Illuminati and a more radical secret society, the German Union (Deutsche Union) of the renegade theologian Carl Friedrich Bahrdt (1741–92), sparked imaginative conspiracy theories and radicalized the political atmosphere. Police actions against the Illuminati and the discourse aimed at them are counted as the beginnings of modern conservatism in Germany.[19] After the French Revolution began in 1789, German Illuminati who had visited Parisian Masonic lodges two years earlier were suspected of instigating the revolt. This notion developed into the grand conspiracy theory that in later centuries accrued Jews and Communists into a massive Masonic-Jewish-Bolshevist plot that became an obsession of National Socialists and other reactionaries. Already in the era of the French Revolution, however, it provided fuel for increasing repression, especially in Austria, Prussia, and Saxony. The French Revolution caused an intellectual upheaval in German-speaking lands.[20] For some, it rendered the notion of "enlightened absolutism" obsolete and in any case focused critical attention on those rulers who made no attempt to assimilate Enlightenment into their governing practices. This small minority demanded a revolution in Germany, too. But most thinkers clung to the model of benevolent autocratic government. They saw the revolution in France as a warning to German princes that they could only avoid revolt if they introduced real reforms and even shared power. As the revolution spiraled into an orgy of violence, almost all of its German champions turned against the French cause. At the same time, they rejected the harsh repression employed by some governments in Germany to meet the perceived danger of revolt and unrest in their own lands. The Revolution heightened awareness of backward German conditions, but critics of absolutism and feudalism were immediately suspected of being revolutionaries. Caught in this dilemma, many German intellectuals learned to stay silent on political and social issues. Even some of the most liberal principalities intimidated their writers.

Religious Life

Political and cultural developments in eighteenth-century Germany were deeply enmeshed in religious life. The Treaty of Westphalia had cemented the existing division of Protestant and Catholic lands according to the confession of their ruler (*cujus regio ejus religio*). Catholicism dominated in Austria, Bavaria, the Rhineland, Saxony, and in smaller pockets throughout the German-speaking lands. The Lutheran confession, the established state religion in most remaining territories, soon found itself challenged by unorthodox sects and in particular by Pietism. This dynamic movement — ably lampooned by Luise Adelgunde Viktorie Gottsched (1730–1762) in her comedy *Die Pietisterey im Fischbein-Rocke; Oder die Doctormäßige Frau* (Pietism in Petticoats, or: The Learned Woman, 1736) — proceeded from a profoundly mystical inward bond of the individual with God.[21] Characteristic of Pietism was the patient waiting for the *Durchbruch* (breakthrough) of the spirit and grace in the individual soul. This passivity translated into a keen awareness of feelings and inner stirrings. Since many writers were influenced in one way or another by Pietism (Lessing, Sophie La Roche, Karl Philip Moritz, and Immanuel Kant in their childhoods; Friedrich Gottlieb Klopstock and Johann Caspar Lavater later in life), this religious movement is considered crucial in the development of a culture of feeling and subjectivism in German literature later in the century. In particular, various scholars have argued that Pietism was instrumental in the genesis of sensibility (*Empfindsamkeit*) with its close attention to emotions and its cult of friendship.[22] Pietists were persecuted in certain Lutheran lands, and they returned the favor in those areas where they dominated (in Königsberg and Halle, for example). Although Enlightenment thinkers generally ridiculed it, they sometimes found themselves allied with Pietism in their critique of Lutheran orthodoxy. Furthermore, the social and practical side of Pietism — its concrete charitable activities — earned the respect of many Enlightenment thinkers.

The Catholic lands were not as backward as subsequent scholarly neglect might indicate; Austria experienced a spirited Enlightenment culture[23] and was home to one of the few genuine revolutionary movements in Germany during the French Revolution, the group around Andreas Riedel.[24] However, most culture that we associate with Enlightenment Germany emerged from Protestant lands in the north, especially Hamburg, Prussia, Saxony, and Saxe-Weimar, and in Switzerland. Protestantism was generally more liberal in its attitude toward culture and especially fictional literature. The tradition of the individual's relation to the divine and the cultivation of scriptural heritage easily accommodated a more positive approach to fictional literature and reading. Accordingly, censorship was much less severe in Protestant territories than in Catholic lands. The index of forbidden books in Catholic Austria soon became such a cherished source of titles worth reading that it had to be banned itself.

In other political matters, however, Protestant lands were hardly more liberal than Catholic ones. We have already seen that Joseph's Austria provided fertile ground for enlightened reforms, though none, of course, that really subverted the prevailing absolutist and feudal system. In the 1760s, Lessing considered moving to Vienna because he expected greater support for writers there. His friend Friedrich Nicolai (1733–1811), a staunch supporter of the Prussian monarchy, warned him of the illiberal power of the Austrian Catholic Church. Lessing responded by pointing out that Protestant Prussia was no better when it came to substantial political issues: "Lassen Sie einen auftreten in Berlin, der für die Rechte der Untertanen und gegen die Aussaugung und den Despotismus seine Stimme erhebt, und Sie werden bald die Erfahrung haben, welches Land bis auf den heutigen Tag das sklavischste Land in Europa ist"[25] (Let someone in Berlin raise his voice for the rights of ordinary people and against exploitation and despotism, and you will soon see which land is the most slavish land in Europe right up to today). And in fact, Friederich the Great's acclaimed enlightened rule was in many respects the polar opposite, even in the area of religion. An avowed freethinker, Friederich nevertheless made sure that village pastors, and especially military chaplains, kept the lower classes pious and in particular obedient. Luther had, after all, proclaimed that state authority proceeded from

God, and had rebuffed the peasants who attempted to enlist his aid in their struggle against feudal abuses — and this was a powerful tradition both in popular memory and in sermons to peasants in the eighteenth century. Friederich's celebrated policy of tolerance — for example, his welcoming of persecuted French Huguenots into his lands — suited contemporary mercantilist policy as much as it flowed from Enlightenment ideas. In the case of Jews, they received favored treatment in Prussia only when they were useful as merchants or financiers.

Jews still lived without full rights in German lands.[26] They were tolerated in a given territory at the whim of the prince, and his policy could — and sometimes did — change overnight to their disadvantage. Jews were also subject to special taxes and restrictions. They were excluded from all professions and limited to certain occupations such as merchant or banker, in some cases providing major financing for the small territories. In cities like Frankfurt (which was especially notorious), they lived in ghettos and were allowed to leave them only at certain times. The century of Enlightenment took modest steps toward changing this situation by arguing for religious tolerance and for the civic rights of Jews, but little was achieved in practice. The few champions of their cause, such as Lessing, did not achieve many concrete advances despite shining examples of cultivated Jews like his philosopher friend Moses Mendelssohn (1729–1786), whose appointment to teach at the Royal Academy in Berlin was blocked by Friederich the Great. Emancipation of Germany's Jews had to wait until the reforms under French occupation in the early nineteenth century.

Women

Jews were not the only second-class residents of Enlightenment Germany. In traditional European society, the head of the household ruled over his (usually extended) family as well as other residents such as servants or renters. Women were entirely subject to the authority of their fathers or husbands. Their only moment of potential free choice — moving from the father's tutelage to that of a new husband — was normally determined without their participation, though in the eighteenth century more attention was given to the couples' desires than in previous times (and the conflicts around this transition into a new family were fertile ground for the new domestic tragedies of the time, the *bürgerliches Trauerspiel*).[27] Women could not own property or carry out any kind of transactions, much less pursue a career or study at a Latin school or university. Female education was markedly inferior to that of boys and young men. Unless they were widowed, women were essentially not citizens and technically were not even allowed to travel without male companionship (though later in the century some women began to travel for pleasure or education).[28] However, in the middle and lower classes, women played an important role in the economic life of the family. Most work was usually still carried out in the home, which functioned as a sort of economic collective. The wife supplied important labor for the household, and this participation gave her status and influence in family affairs. Although some scholars have exaggerated women's power in this early modern extended family type (the *ganzes Haus* or *große Haushaltsfamilie*), wives certainly assumed a vital role in the household.[29]

In the course of the eighteenth century, the household changed, at least for most of the middle classes. With increasing specialization, rationalization, and beginning industrialization came the separation of the husband's workplace from the home; in addition, there were many more bureaucrats for the expanding modern state, and they, too, worked outside the home. This shift meant, on the one hand, that far fewer women were involved in the primary economic activity of the family, and, on the other, that some of the laborious production of household necessities (weaving, spinning, preserving foods, washing and so on) were made easier. Upper middle-class women gained leisure time (for instance for reading) and devoted more time to childbearing and childrearing, supervising servants, and to early childhood education and religious instruction. Although they had always been generally responsible for these tasks, now women were focused more on them. They remained isolated from the men's world of work and public life, and were entirely responsible for the home. At the same time, the emotional bonds within the family received more attention. The older model of the "household" with its various members was replaced by the smaller family unit, in which children began to be appreciated in their own right rather than being regarded as small adults. Breastfeeding, which had been shunned for some time as the upper-middle classes — in imitation of the nobility — farmed out their children to wet-nurses, was again viewed approvingly. The emotional demands on mothers as caregivers increased.

The sociologist Karin Hausen, in a pioneering article, describes the "secondary patriarchy" that arose in this situation and the attending dichotomous gender characteristics (*Geschlechtscharaktere*) that accompanied it.[30] She argues that the new situation required altered gender definitions for women to justify their house-bound existence. Whereas earlier gender characteristics had focused on the virtues emanating from estate-specific functions, the newer literature spoke simply of the *nature* of man and woman. The characteristics assigned to each of them corresponded to their new roles in economic life. The man possessed traits that equipped him to function in the world of commerce and bureaucracy; his *innate nature* was considered to be rational, active, dignified, and so forth. The woman's characteristics corresponded to her role as housewife and mother: emotional, passive, charming. These gendered characteristics — and a host of others — had been expressed for centuries in the Judeo-Christian tradition in various forms, something that Hausen overlooks. But she is correct to point out that the definitions became an obsession in the late eighteenth century and were codified once again rigidly and widely. In the 1790s a wide array of treatises and essays in Germany attempted to define the nature of women and men along these lines.[31] The family became the domain of woman and defined her existence; for men, it was a refuge from the stress and burdens of the work world and no longer a central part of his life. This, at least, was the theory, which legitimized the now crassly unequal work spheres of men and women — of course, women's work was now not recognized as work, but was simply called "love."

Complementing the analyses of Hausen and others, largely based on economics, an intellectual historian would stress the role of cultural developments, particularly the rise of sentimentalism (whatever its cause), in the development of gender stereotypes. Central here is the role of the cultural theories of Jean-Jacques Rousseau, particularly his conservative gender perspectives. Rousseau was immensely influential in Germany,[32] and Book 5 of his pedagogical novel *Émile ou de l'Éducation* (1760) reads like a compendium of the newly retrenched gender ideology. Rousseau's ideas — and those of his epigones and other sentimentalist thinkers — worked in tandem with the division of work and family to produce a powerful regression in gender affairs.

Literary Women

The effect on those women who dared to consider writing and publishing was profound.[33] In the early part of the eighteenth century, writing women were championed by Germany's self-proclaimed literary arbiter, Johann Christoph Gottsched (1700–1766). His efforts on behalf of female writers have been interpreted as part of the Enlightenment's project of expanding self-realization and fulfillment to include women, but Gottsched was driven less by truly enlightened emancipatory motives than by a desire to enlist women in his plan to prove that Germany's literature could compete with other national literatures; after all, both Italy and the Netherlands boasted of celebrated learned women (Laura Bassi and Anna Maria van Schurman).[34] Gottsched also notoriously used his own wife to write under his name.[35] In any case, there were several important women writers in this period, especially "the two Z's," Sidonia Hedwig Zäunemann (1714–40) and Christiana Mariana von Ziegler (1695–1760), as well as Luise Gottsched herself. Their works display an often brazen feminist consciousness. Later in the century, the situation had changed dramatically. One need only compare two celebrated Dorotheas. In 1741, Dorothea Christiane Leporin (1715–62) succeeded (at the intervention of the Prussian king) in becoming the first woman to study in Germany when she enrolled at the University of Halle as a student of medicine. After she had completed her studies and in 1754 became the first woman in Germany to receive a medical doctorate, she was given exceptional permission to pursue her career. Much later in the century Dorothea Schlözer (1770–1825) was trained by her father as a sort of *Wunderkind* whom he used to demonstrate his pedagogical theories.[36] Since he was a professor at the University of Göttingen, his daughter was allowed to hear lectures — but only from behind a curtain, hidden from the regular male students. She completed her examinations and was awarded a doctorate in 1787, celebrating the fiftieth anniversary of Göttingen's university. But in contrast to Leporin, Dorothea Schlözer was not allowed to pursue a career. Her energies found an outlet in an unorthodox *ménage à trois* (which has been interpreted as a perhaps unconscious protest against her contradictory situation), and she died frustrated by her inability to apply her talents and training.[37] The gender ideology of the later eighteenth century did not permit women to view themselves as professionals.

But women pursued writing careers nonetheless. Because of the gender rigidity, they had to develop various defensive strategies, chief among them the oft-repeated claim in forewords to their works that they were not professionals, but only wrote in their spare time and considered housework and childrearing their "true" calling. Many of these women were anything but housewives: some were widows or otherwise single women who were forced to live from their writing. Others wrote under a male pseudonym in order to find a willing publisher. In their works, they often resorted to the same clichés of the docile, passive, emotional woman that were instrumental in excluding women from conventional participation in culture. Still, these female writers seemed to challenge the established male authors, especially Goethe and Schiller, who feared losing a sizable segment of their audience to them. The Weimar luminaries tried to stay in control of the literary market and begrudgingly expressed respect for some of these women and ridiculed others.[38]

The culture and society surrounding the development of German Enlightenment and sensibility can hardly be called anything but backward in a European context. Germany lacked the glorious and sparkling culture of London or Paris, indeed, it lacked any single major metropolis where cultural life could flourish. Writers could not yet live from their writing alone and thus had to make accommodations with their employers — princes, municipalities, the church — on whom they usually depended. Economic conditions were only slowly improving since the disastrous Thirty Years' War, a situation exacerbated by particularism.

The new middle classes vied for respect with the more traditional ones, and religion held a firm sway over most Germans. Cultural life centered around the bewildering array of courts, to which most middle-class people harbored an extremely ambivalent, if not outright hostile attitude. German letters was plagued by a certain sense of abstractness: though sociability and the cult of friendship were important factors in literary life, many writers were able to cultivate this sociability only in letters and felt isolated from one another. Rococo culture, which in other countries was a courtly trend, was practiced in Germany by a group of middle-class writers in far-flung towns, who themselves remarked on the artificiality of their enterprise. And yet some would see this abstractness, the isolation and "backwardness" as a boon to the rise of a literature that was perhaps most clearly characterized by its inwardness, its valorization of feeling and morality — not to mention a philosophical culture that was marked by dizzying heights of abstraction.

Notes

[1] The best English-language history of the later part of the eighteenth century — with relevant information for the first part — is James J. Sheehan, *German History, 1770–1866* (New York: Oxford UP, 1989). For a comprehensive social history of this period, see Hans-Ulrich Wehler, *Deutsche Gesellschaftsgeschichte,* vol. 1: *Vom Feudalismus des alten Reiches bis zur defensiven Modernisierung der Reformära, 1700–1815* (Munich: Beck, 1987).

[2] See for example Georg Schmidt, *Geschichte des alten Reiches: Staat und Nation in der Frühen Neuzeit 1495–1806* (Munich: Beck, 1999).

[3] As a useful introduction, see T. C. W. Blanning, *Joseph II and Enlightened Despotism* (New York: Harper & Row, 1970).

[4] See especially the various works by Peter Blickle, including *Unruhen in der ständischen Gesellschaft, 1300–1800* (Munich: Oldenbourg, 1988) and *Deutsche Untertanen: Ein Widerspruch* (Munich: Beck, 1981), trans. Thomas A. Brady, Jr., as *Obedient Germans? A Rebuttal: A New View of German History* (Charlottesville: UP of Virginia, 1997).

[5] Quoted by Gerhard Schilfert, *Deutschland von 1648 bis 1789,* 3rd ed. (Berlin: Deutscher Verlag der Wissenschaften, 1975), 145 (for the other revolts mentioned here, see 144, and for earlier examples, 25–30, 85–91).

[6] See Wilhelm Abel, *Massenarmut und Hungerkrisen im vorindustriellen Deutschland,* 3rd ed. (Göttingen: Vandenhoeck & Ruprecht, 1986), 46–54.

[7] See Jürgen Freiherr von Kruedener, *Die Rolle des Hofes im Absolutismus* (Stuttgart: Fischer, 1973).

[8] Some historians writing in English use the term "bourgeois" as an equivalent of the German *bürgerlich*. However, since German historians reserve *Bourgeoisie* for upper-middle-class newer capitalist strata, I have used the term "middle-class" to avoid confusion.

[9] The classic study of the development of the freelance writer in Germany — marred somewhat by antiquated literary concepts — is Hans Jürgen Haferkorn, "Zur Entstehung der bürgerlich-literarischen Intelligenz und des Schriftstellers in Deutschland zwischen 1750 und 1800," in *Deutsches Bürgertum und literarische Intelligenz 1750–1800,* ed. Bernd Lutz (Stuttgart: Metzler, 1974), 113–275.

[10] See *Der Akademiegedanke im 17. und 18. Jahrhundert: Vorträge gehalten anläßlich des 2. Wolfenbütteler Symposions vom 9. bis 12. Dezember 1975 in der Herzog August Bibliothek,* ed. Fritz Hartmann and Rudolf Vierhaus (Bremen: Jacobi, 1977).

[11] See the introduction to, and, for different views on "enlightened absolutism," the various essays in *Der Aufgeklärte Absolutismus,* ed. Karl Otmar Freiherr von Aretin (Cologne: Kiepenheuer & Witsch, 1974).

[12] On the relation between middle-class morality and political critique, see the now classic work by Reinhard Koselleck, *Critique and Crisis: Enlightenment and the Pathogenesis of Modern Society* [1959] (Cambridge, MA: MIT P, 1988). However, Koselleck's study, which essentially blames the Enlightenment for the supposed return of seventeenth-century religious strife in the French Revolution, must be viewed with critical distance; on his distorted interpretation of secret societies as subversive, see W. Daniel Wilson, "Shades of the Illuminati Conspiracy: Koselleck on Enlightenment and Revolution," in *The Enlightenment and Its Legacy: Studies in German Literature in Honor of Helga Slessarev,* ed. Sara Friedrichsmeyer and Barbara Becker-Cantarino (Bonn: Bouvier, 1991), 15–25.

[13] For the first assessment of pre-revolutionary Germany as a sophisticated political culture, see Fritz Valjavec, *Die Entstehung der politischen Strömungen in Deutschland, 1770–1815* (Munich: Oldenbourg, 1951).

[14] For a seminal study of the reflection of this ideal in fictional literature, see Wolfgang Martens, *Der patriotische Minister: Fürstendiener in der Literatur der Aufklärungszeit* (Weimar: Böhlau, 1996).

[15] See Hermann Schüttler, "Geschichte, Organisation und Ideologie der Strikten Observanz," *Quatuor Coronati Jahrbuch* 25 (1988): 159–75.

[16] The seminal modern work — outdated in some respects — is Richard van Dülmen, *Der Geheimbund der Illuminaten: Darstellung, Analyse, Dokumentation* (Stuttgart: Frommann, 1975); still very useful is René Le Forestier, *Les illuminés de Bavière et la Franc-Maçonnerie allemande* (Paris: Hachette, 1914).

[17] See W. Daniel Wilson, "Zur Politik und Sozialstruktur des Illuminatenordens, anläßlich einer Neuerscheinung von Hermann Schüttler," *Internationales Archiv für Sozialgeschichte der deutschen Literatur* 19 (1994): 141–75.

[18] See W. Daniel Wilson, *Geheimräte gegen Geheimbünde: Ein unbekanntes Kapitel der klassisch-romantischen Geschichte Weimars* (Stuttgart: Metzler, 1991).

[19] See Klaus Epstein, *The Genesis of German Conservatism* (Princeton: Princeton UP, 1966).

[20] See the essays in *Deutschland und die französische Revolution 1789–1806,* ed. Theo Stammen and Friedrich Eberle (Darmstadt: Wissenschaftliche Buchgesellschaft, 1988), and, despite its conservative bias, Thomas P. Saine, *Black Bread, White Bread:*

German Intellectuals and the French Revolution (Columbia, SC: Camden House, 1988).

[21] See the monumental *Geschichte des Pietismus,* ed. Martin Brecht for the Historische Kommission zur Erforschung des Pietismus, 4 vols. (Göttingen: Vandenhoeck & Ruprecht, 1993–2000).

[22] See the discussion of this debate by Gerhard Sauder, *Empfindsamkeit,* vol. 1 (Stuttgart: Metzler, 1974).

[23] See Franz Eybl's essay in this volume, and Leslie Bodi, *Tauwetter in Wien: Zur Prosa der österreichischen Aufklärung, 1781–1795* (Frankfurt: Fischer, 1977).

[24] See Helmut Reinalter, *Österreich und die Französische Revolution* (Vienna: Österreichischer Bundesverlag, 1988), and Ernst Wangermann, *From Joseph II to the Jacobin Trials: Government Policy and Public Opinion in the Habsburg Dominions in the Period of the French Revolution,* 2nd ed. (London: Oxford UP, 1969).

[25] Letter of 25 August 1769, Gotthold Ephraim Lessing, *Gesammelte Werke,* ed. Paul Rilla, 2nd ed., 10 vols. (Berlin & Weimar: Aufbau, 1968), 9: 327.

[26] See Alfred D. Low, *Jews in the Eyes of the Germans: From the Enlightenment to Imperial Germany* (Philadelphia: Institute for the Study of Human Issues, 1979); and Klaus L. Berghahn, *Grenzen der Toleranz: Juden und Christen im Zeitalter der Aufklärung* (Cologne: Böhlau, 2000).

[27] From the burgeoning scholarship on family issues in eighteenth-century literature, see especially Günter Sasse, *Die aufgeklärte Familie: Untersuchungen zur Genese, Funktion und Realitätsbezogenheit des familialen Wertsystems im Drama der Aufklärung* (Tübingen: Niemeyer, 1988) and Bengt Algot Sørensen, *Herrschaft und Zärtlichkeit: Der Patriarchalismus und das Drama im 18. Jahrhundert* (Munich: Beck, 1984).

[28] See the pioneering study of early travel fiction by women: Annegret Pelz, *Reisen durch die eigene Fremde: Reiseliteratur von Frauen als autobiographische Schriften* (Cologne: Böhlau, 1993); and of actual travel by Irmgard Scheitler, *Gattung und Geschlecht: Reisebeschreibungen deutscher Frauen 1780–1850* (Tübingen: Niemeyer, 1999).

[29] Barbara Duden, "Das schöne Eigentum: Zur Herausbildung des bürgerlichen Frauenbildes an der Wende vom 18. zum 19. Jahrhundert," *Kursbuch* 47.3 (1977): 125–42.

[30] Karin Hausen, "Die Polarisierung der 'Geschlechtscharaktere' — Eine Spiegelung der Dissoziation von Erwerbs- und Familienleben," *Sozialgeschichte der Familie in der Neuzeit Europas: Neue Forschungen,* ed. Werner Conze (Stuttgart: Klett, 1976), 363–93, translated (with substantial errors) as "Family and Role-Division: The Polarization of Sexual Stereotypes in the Nineteenth Century: An Aspect of the Dissociation of Work and Family Life," in *The German Family,* ed. Richard J. Evans and W. Robert Lee (Towota, NJ: Barnes & Noble, 1981); Volker Hoffmann, "Elisa und Robert oder das Weib und der Mann, wie sie sein sollten. Anmerkungen zur Geschlechtercharakteristik der Goethezeit," in *Klassik und Moderne: Die Weimarer Klassik als historisches Ereignis. Walter Müller-Seidel zum 65. Geburtstag,* ed. Karl Richter and Jörg Schönert (Stuttgart: Metzler, 1983), 80–97.

[31] See the anthology *Ob die Weiber Menschen sind: Geschlechterdebatten um 1800*, ed. Sigrid Lange (Leipzig: Reclam, 1992); and especially Claudia Honegger, *Die Ordnung der Geschlechter: Die Wissenschaften vom Menschen und das Weib 1750–1850* (Frankfurt a. M.: Campus, 1991).

[32] See *Rousseau in Deutschland: Neue Beiträge zur Erforschung seiner Rezeption*, ed. Herbert Jaumann (Berlin: de Gruyter, 1995).

[33] For general background on the social situation of women and of female writers, see Barbara Becker-Cantarino, *Der lange Weg zur Mündigkeit: Frau und Literatur in Deutschland von 1500 bis 1800* (Stuttgart: Metzler, 1987).

[34] Susanne Kord, "Die Gelehrte als Zwitterwesen in Schriften von Autorinnen des 18. und 19. Jahrhunderts," *Querelles* 1 (1996): 158–89.

[35] See Katherine Goodman's essay in this volume, and Susanne Kord, *Little Detours: The Letters and Plays of Luise Gottsched (1713–1762)* (Rochester, NY: Camden House, 2000).

[36] See Bärbel Kern and Horst Kern, *Madame Doctorin Schlözer: Ein Frauenleben in den Widersprüchen der Aufklärung* (Munich: Beck, 1998).

[37] Bärbel Kern and Horst Kern, *Madame Doctorin Schlözer*.

[38] See Barbara Becker-Cantarino, "Goethe as a Critic of Literary Women," in *Goethe as a Critic of Literature*, ed. Karl J. Fink and Max L. Baeumer (Lanham, MD: UP of America, 1984), 160–81.

Johann Gottfried Herder (1744–1803).
Painting by Anton Graff, 1785.

The Legacy of the Enlightenment: Critique from Hamann and Herder to the Frankfurt School

Robert C. Holub

CRITIQUE OF THE ENLIGHTENMENT is almost as old as the Enlightenment itself. Since Enlightenment thinkers promulgated a worldview that undermined traditional values and doctrines, it was inevitable that they would provoke rejoinders and objections from those who felt threatened. Many of the most heralded figures in the Enlightenment engaged in debates with representatives of the *ancien régime* whose ideas and ideals in politics, religion, aesthetics, and philosophy were suddenly called into question. Indeed, the history of the Enlightenment can be written as a series of conflicts between a new approach to nature and human endeavors, on the one hand, and retrograde and futile attempts to counter this approach, on the other. Reactionary critique, however, is ultimately barren, leading only backward to positions that were already known, and that were surpassed and discarded with the advent of the Enlightenment. Reactions to enlightened propositions from the establishment that felt itself under attack were mired in the dogma and superstitions of a bygone era. Much more interesting and productive was criticism that took issue with aspects of the Enlightenment, but developed a line of thought that would be productive for subsequent centuries. In some instances this sort of anti-Enlightenment critique sought to recognize dimensions of human activity left unilluminated by enlightened thought, thus demonstrating that light has been shed on only a portion of human existence, and that the human being in his entirety has been ignored. Using critique in its Kantian sense, detractors pointed to the limitations inherent in Enlightenment itself. At other times, those engaged in critique have considered themselves continuators of the Enlightenment, employing the very weapons of Enlightenment against it. Indeed, the fact that Enlightenment propagated "Kritik" as a central tenet inevitably encourages intellectuals dissatisfied with a perceived timidity of the Enlightenment or seeking to expand its scope to employ this notion of critique against particular aspects of enlightened thought. Unlike their retrograde and sterile counterparts, these productive critiques of Enlightenment thus partook in a necessary and constructive ambivalence: simultaneously opposing Enlightenment and carrying it further, critics of Enlightenment opened up possibilities and defined new terrain for thought.

A central difficulty in understanding this sort of anti-Enlightenment critique is identifying exactly what is being criticized. It has become increasingly apparent in recent scholarship that the European Enlightenment of the eighteenth century is not a unified movement. It consists of many different tendencies in several countries, and it covers a variety of disciplines and practices. Although the Enlightenment rejects orthodoxy in religion, eschewing doctrinaire traditions and teachings, it counts among its advocates deists, theists, pantheists, agnostics, and atheists. The Enlightenment is often identified with republican politics and even revolutionary movements, but there was no consensus among its supporters regarding political systems or worldviews: monarchists and democrats, nationalists and cosmopolitans, all could lay claim to enlightened opinions. There was an array of preferences voiced among enlightened thinkers in the realm of art and aesthetics: from the strict adherence to neo-classical style and universal rules, to the advocacy of the subjective expression of human emotions. Some Enlightenment thinkers' primary concern was science; others focused on theology and philosophy; still others believed in the supreme importance of the human, psychological, and social sciences. In view of this disparity of concerns, it is no wonder that Johann Friedrich Zöllner, late in the Enlightenment in 1783, expressed confusion and dismay about the very identity of the movement everyone seemed to know and acknowledge, but no one seemed able to define. The consequences of his simple query, "what is enlightenment?" led to a seminal essay on the topic by the foremost philosophical mind of the century, Immanuel Kant, although the debate about the definition of Enlightenment continued for the next decade in the pages of the *Berlinische Monatsschrift*, where Kant's essay appeared. Kant's celebrated answer, that Enlightenment is "der Ausgang des Menschen aus seiner selbst verschuldeten Unmündigkeit"[1] (the emergence of man from his self-inflicted immaturity), focused primarily on one aspect of the Enlightenment: the public, political dimension. Still, it is representative for the way in which enlightened thinkers approached issues. Indeed, the Enlightenment is perhaps better understood as a method of dealing with intellectual matters rather than as a specific view on a particular topic. For critics of Enlightenment the Kantian answer is less significant for its content or its precise definition than for its framework of progress, pedagogy, and universality.

Hamann, Herder, and the "Metacritique" of Enlightenment

Johann Georg Hamann (1730–88) felt that Kant's response to Zöllner's query evidenced traits typical of a perspective he disdained. Like Kant a citizen of Königsberg, Hamann was well acquainted with the philosopher, and although he remained on friendly terms with him throughout his life, the two men stood on opposite sides of questions concerning the Enlightenment. Hamann's reaction to "Plato's" (that is, Kant's) essay in the December issue of the *Berlinische Monatschrift* (which he dubbed the *"Berlinschen Christmonath"*) is contained in his customarily cryptic and obscure form in a letter to Christian Jacob Kraus, who had forwarded him a copy of the journal.[2] In the first instance we note Hamann's tendency to play with the key words in Kant's text: *Aufklärung, verschuldet, Mündigkeit,* frequently punning on them and in the process twisting their meaning and import. But Hamann also refers to deficiencies in Kant's reasoning, calling the *proton pseudos* of the definition the notion that immaturity is self-inflicted. An inability, Hamann writes, concurring for the moment with Kant, cannot be a fault except insofar as it results from a lack of resolution or courage.[3] Hamann would appear to take issue with this clarification, but at this point he pursues it no further, and turns instead to the mysterious "other" of the first paragraph in Kant's essay. Immaturity is defined by Kant as the inability to use one's understanding without the guidance of "another," and Hamann objects that this other is not named properly, and that, in fact, if blame is to be assigned, it rightly belongs to this "other," who is ultimately responsible for the self-inflicted immaturity of his ward. Hamann's point is less convoluted than his manner of expression: Kant sets himself up in the essay as a sort of guardian, one who is able to guide the immature to enlightenment, while he criticizes unnamed others and their immature followers for precluding enlightened thought. But Kant has thereby only substituted himself for those he refuses to name and in the process remains aloof from those he is labeling immature. He offers only abstract reasoning and speculation, and no solutions to the problem he has identified as self-inflicted immaturity: "Die Aufklärung unsers Jahrhunderts ist also ein bloßes Nordlicht, aus dem sich kein kosmopolitischer Chiliasmus als in der Schlafmütze u. hinter dem Ofen wahrsagen läßt" (Hamann, *Briefwechsel* 5: 291; The enlightenment of our century is therefore a mere northern light, from which can be prophesied no cosmopolitan chiliasm except in a nightcap & by the stove[4]). Kant's essay is tantamount to "eine blinde Illumination für jeden unmündigen, der im Mittag wandelt" (5: 291; a blind illumination for every immature one who walks at *noon*). Hamann's counterdefinition calls upon religious beliefs to supply the guidance that Kant obviously abjures. "[W]ahre Aufklärung," he writes in his postscript to Kraus,

> [bestehe] in einem Ausgang des unmündigen Menschen aus einer allerhöchst *selbst verschuldeten Vormundschaft*. Die Furcht des Herrn ist der Weisheit Anfang — und diese Weisheit macht uns *feig* zu lügen und *faul* zu dichten — desto muthiger gegen Vormünder, die höchstens den Leib tödten und den Beutel aussaugen können — desto barmherziger gegen unsere unmündige Mitbrüder und fruchtbarer an guten Werken der Unsterblichkeit. (*Briefwechsel* 5: 291)

> [True enlightenment consists in an emergence of the immature person from a supremely self-inflicted guardianship. The fear of the Lord is the beginning of wisdom and this wisdom makes us *cowardly* at lying and *lazy* at inventing — but all the more courageous against guardians who at most can kill the body and suck the purse dry — all the more merciful to our immature brethren and more fruitful in good works of immortality.[5]]

These views do not represent a mere return to a religiously based value system and to conventional piety, although Hamann advocated belief as the central element in his writings. What is important about Hamann's criticism of Kant is his refusal to validate the movement toward abstractions as progress, his recognition that reasoning is perhaps less likely to produce courageous actions in the face of the taskmaster or the tax official, and his compassion for those who seek and need guidance in concrete ways.

Hamann's more encompassing anti-Enlightenment views are better captured in his objections to Kant's critical writings. Although he never published his "metacritique" of Kant's *Kritik der reinen Vernunft* (Critique of Pure Reason, 1781), the draft he composed in 1784, which was circulated and published posthumously, contains several principled objections to Kant's philosophical outlook and, with it, to the general tendencies of the Enlightenment. Initially Hamann takes on reason itself, at least as it is presented in Kant's seminal work. At issue is the possibility of a priori knowledge, that is, pre-experiential knowledge. Hamann clearly indicates that for him such knowledge, and therefore Kant's entire critical enterprise, is an impossibility. "Zu den *verborgenen Geheimnissen,* deren Aufgabe geschweige ihre Auflösung noch in keines Philosophen Herz gekommen seyn soll, gehöret die Möglichkeit menschlicher Erkenntnis von Gegenständen der Erfahrung ohne und vor aller Erfahrung und hiernächst die Möglichkeit einer sinnlichen Anschauung vor aller Empfindung eines Gegenstandes"[6] (To the *hidden mysteries,* the task of which [let alone their solution] has yet to come into a philosopher's heart, belongs the possibility of human knowledge of objects *without* and *before* any experience and thus the possibility of a sensible intuition *before* any sensation of an object).

Hamann cannot countenance the distinction between empirical and a priori knowledge that is a basic tenet of Kant's thought; for him all knowledge is empirical, and to speak of knowledge prior to the sensation or the experience of an object is absurd.

Neither does Hamann approve of the separation of judgments into analytic and synthetic, and his spirited objection recalls Nietzsche's later quip about Kant's invention of a faculty to deal with the category of synthetic a priori judgments:

> Wie sind synthetische Urtheile a priori *möglich*? fragte sich Kant, — und was antwortete er eigentlich? *Vermöge eines Vermögens:* leider aber nicht mit drei Worten, sondern so umständlich, ehrwürdig und mit einem solchen Aufwande von deutschem Tief- und Schnörkelsinne, dass man die lustige niaiserie allemande überhörte, welche in einer solchen Antwort steckt.[7]

> [How are synthetic a priori judgments *possible*? wondered Kant, and what did he answer? They are *facilitated by a faculty:* unfortunately, however, he did not say this in four words, but so cumbersomely, so venerably, and with such an expense of German profundity and ornateness that people failed to hear the comical *niaiserie allemande* in such an answer.]

The foundation of transcendental philosophy, which examines a priori forms of thought, and in particular synthetic a priori judgments, is an object of ridicule for Nietzsche and Hamann. The tasks that critical philosophy sets for itself are based on assumptions and distinctions that themselves go against "reason."

Hamann proceeds by enumerating the steps taken by Kant in purifying reason. Quite obviously the entire notion of pure reason is anathema to Hamann's thinking: reason is always concrete, sensual, and empirical, so that any idealism purporting to elucidate reason disengaged from practical interaction with the world is immediately suspect. Hamann first points to the necessity for divorcing pure reason from tradition, custom, and belief; only when reason is thus removed from its historical context does it become an object for philosophical reflection. Second, Hamann notes that pure reason is always reason independent from experience and from the everyday reality in which human beings actually exist and think. The purification process here necessarily neglects the world of objects and encounters, abstracting instead a realm of thoughts unaffected by mundane concerns. Finally, the third and highest stage in purifying reason entails an endeavor to escape language, an impossibility, Hamann contends, for any discourse, even one concerning pure reason. In fact, critical philosophy depends heavily on language, and one might even contend that it is marked exclusively by linguistic practices, since it has disavowed any connection with the world of objects and experience.

Receptivität der *Sprache* und *Spontaneität* der *Begriffe*! — Aus dieser doppelten Quelle der Zweideutigkeit schöpft die reine Vernunft alle Elemente ihrer Rechthaberey, Zweifelsucht und Kunstrichterschaft, erzeugt durch eine eben so willkührliche Analysin als Synthesin des dreimal alten Sauerteigs neue Phänomene und Meteoren des wandelbaren Horizonts, schafft Zeichen und Wunder mit dem Allhervorbinger und zerstörenden mercurialischen Zauberstabe ihres Mundes oder dem gespaltenen Gänsekiel zwischen den drei syllogistischen Schreibefingern ihrer herkulischen Faust. (*Sämtliche Werke* 3: 284)

[*Receptivity* of *language* and *spontaneity* of *concepts*! From this double source of ambiguity pure reason draws all the elements of its doctrinairism, doubt, and appraisal. Through an analysis just as arbitrary as the synthesis of the thrice old leaven, it brings forth new phenomena and meteors on the inconstant horizon, creates signs and wonders with its all-creating and destroying mercurial caduceus of a mouth or with the split goose quill between the three syllogistic writing fingers of its herculean fist.[8]]

Hamann adds to this scathing condemnation of abstract idealism his criticism of the exact sciences on which critical philosophy is based. Especially worthy of censure is the "kaltes Vorurtheil" (cold prejudice)[9] for mathematics that informs Kant's method. Indeed, the most general of Hamann's objections to Kant and the crux of his invective against the Enlightenment is the flight from the concrete, the empirical, and the sensual for the abstract, the metaphysical, and the intellectual. Hamann's philosophy, if he can be said to have one, is based on particulars, on traditions, on direct experience, and he is deeply distrustful of an Enlightenment project that pretends to ignore these fundamental aspects of human existence.

To a large degree, Hamann's disciple, Johann Gottfried Herder (1744–1803), inherited the same sort of distrust. Herder's metacritique of Kant's *Kritik der reinen Vernunft,* written in the winter of 1798–99, over a decade after Hamann's death, is a more elaborate and less elusive response to Kant's seminal work.[10] It consists of a paragraph by paragraph commentary that uses frequent citation from Kant's original text and runs over 300 pages in length. In its general conception and many of its details its objections are very similar to Hamann's. Herder, for example, also disputes the notion of a priori knowledge, contending that even mathematics, Kant's primary example for knowledge independent of experience, is actually "aufs innigste mit der Erfahrung verbunden"[11] (most intimately connected with experience). Herder's most incisive criticisms are listed briefly in his comments on the title and introduction to Kant's text. In the first instance he calls into question the efficacy of having reason sit in judgment on reason. Kant's critique purports to examine *Vernunft* (reason), but the only faculty he has at his disposal to complete this examination is reason itself. In order to accomplish a critique of reason, however, one would have to call upon a higher faculty that can oversee reason's purview. Thus Kant, according to Herder, is positing that reason transcend itself in order to carry out its critical task.

Herder's second misgiving has to do with the exclusivity implied in Kant's project. For analytical purposes he can separate reason from other powers in the human being, he contends, but we must not forget that reason is only one of many faculties, and that they all work in close consort. The soul is a unity, whether it is feeling, imagining, or thinking, and Kant appears to forget or ignore or exclude the multi-faceted nature of human existence. Herder repudiates Kant's methodical and exclusionary approach to reason by concluding that "Mit Namen zimmern wir keine Fächer in unsrer Seele" (*W* 21:19; With names we do not construct compartments in our soul). Finally, Herder, like his mentor, notes Kant's insensitivity to the connection between language and thought. Since human beings think with words, language must be a central concern for anyone examining reason. Although Herder does not specifically take Kant to task for his neglect of language, he suggests that his procedures do not account for the centrality of language for philosophical inquiry. Citing authorities from Aristotle to Locke, Herder demonstrates that previous analyses of our reasoning faculties have accounted for the proximity or identity of words and thought, and he implicitly criticizes Kant for failing to account for words in his dealings with concepts. A critique of reason, whether pure or impure, is a wayward enterprise in danger of erroneous conclusions if it does not include an account of language: "Ein grosser Theil der Misverständnisse, Widersprüche und Ungereimtheiten also, die man der Vernunft zuschreibt, wird wahrscheinlich nicht an ihr, sondern an dem mangelhaften oder von ihr schlecht gerbrauchten Werkzeuge der Sprache liegen, wie das Wort *Widersprüche* selbst saget" (*W*, 21: 19–20; A large part of the misunderstandings, contradictions and inconsistencies attributed to reason are thus probably not attributable to reason, but to the deficient or poorly employed tool of language, as the word contra*diction* itself indicates). Logos, after all, is the Greek expression for both reason and speech (*W*, 21: 21).

Herder's late remarks against Kant's first critique are a continuation of ideas he had developed over decades and represent only one dimension of his anti-Enlightenment position. In the early text *Auch eine Philosophie der Geschichte* (Another Philosophy of History, 1774), he voices more general objections to the Age of Reason. Above all, Herder accuses the Enlightenment of hubris. It imagines that it has increased virtue, but it has only brought an impoverishment in human existence (*W*, 5: 554–55). Thought may have become refined and reason may have flourished, but the price we have paid is a loss of other essential qualities: "Herz! Wärme! Blut!

Menschheit! Leben!" (*W*, 5: 538; Heart! Warmth! Blood! Humanity! Life!). Enlightenment aspires to be a worldly discourse, at least insofar as it seeks to encompass all worldly concerns, but it remains for Herder an academic, anemic undertaking that never connects with real life. The philosophers dancing on the academic tightrope to the admiration and joy of others are actually divorced from all praxis; whereas philosophy formerly grew out of the concrete needs, contributed to daily activities and served a purpose in the affairs of men, it has now become dry and mechanical, the work of scholarly artisans(*W*, 5: 535). Enlightenment, however, fails to recognize its own limitations. Although it has gained currency on only a small portion of the earth (*W*, 5: 564), it considers itself superior to everything that has ever existed on the globe. Herder was one of the first thinkers to regard Enlightenment as an imperialist strategy used to level cultural differences and to enslave other parts of the world under European hegemony. The English, for example, are reproached for their imperialist attitudes toward the Irish and Scottish populations — attitudes that eliminated customs and traditions that enriched the lives of these minorities in Great Britain (*W*, 5: 547). Enlightenment may have contributed to the formal abolition of slavery, but it has not prevented the economic enslavement of significant portions of the world (*W*, 5: 550). And in Europe itself it has not necessarily been a boon to the people, but has served to enhance the "ewigen Nachruhm" (eternal fame) of princes (*W*, 5: 539). The Enlightenment prides itself on fostering progress in human affairs, but Herder repeatedly emphasizes the trade-off for our reliance on a mechanistic and one-sided application of reason. We may have enlightenment, thriftiness, philosophy, and freedom of thought, but we have also suffered an exhaustion of genuine feeling, a poverty of spirit, a myopic lack of conviction, and a slavery of action (*W*, 5: 582). The benefits of an enlightened age are overstated, according to Herder, and its implicit claim to superiority is an injustice to the heterogeneity of human activity on other parts of the globe and in other epochs.

Romanticism and the Limitations of Enlightenment

That the Romantic movement inherited its critique of the Enlightenment from Hamann and Herder is evident. Indeed, the subtitle to Rudolf Ungar's magisterial study of Hamann refers to the "prehistory of the Romantic spirit in the eighteenth century."[12] The Romantics, however, especially if one examines the movement as a whole, were less interested in opposing the philosophical tradition that culminated in Kant's critical works than in viewing the reliance on reason as a one-sided endeavor that does not capture the totality of the human spirit. One important form of Romantic criticism therefore targets the philistine, whose smug dependence on reason and reasonableness is contrasted with the artistic, the poetic, the imaginative. E. T. A. Hoffmann (1776–1822) provides one of the best contrasts of this sort in his novel *Lebensansichten des Kater Murr* (The Life and Opinions of the Tomcat Murr, 1820–22), in which the autobiographical musings of a pretentious feline spouting wisdom about himself and the world are juxtaposed with the travails of the composer Johannes Kreisler. The fiction Hoffmann perpetrates is that the Murr autobiography has mistakenly been confounded with the Romantic Kreisler story in a printing error, so that one alternates with the other, further emphasizing their differences in outlook. In the Romantic period the representative of reason often becomes a self-satisfied member of the bourgeoisie, marked by egotism, conformity, and sham morality. A variant on this satire of Enlightenment can be found in Heinrich Heine's (1797–1856) *Harzreise* (The Harz Journey, 1824). After recalling a particularly fearful night spent in Goslar, the narrator recounts conversations he had with Saul Ascher, a Berlin bookseller and philosopher who had embraced Kantian rationalism. In Heine's caricature Ascher insists that only reason is a power, not emotions or spirit, and Ascher's statement, "Die Vernunft ist das höchste Prinzip!" (reason is the highest principle) becomes a leitmotif in the narration of Heine's Goslar nightmare. Heine describes Ascher as someone who could not appreciate nature, art, or beauty, and whose insistence on rationality became itself irrational:

> Dieser Mann, tief in den Funfzigern, war eine personifizirte grade Linie. In seinem Streben nach dem Positiven hatte der arme Mann sich alles Herrliche aus dem Leben heraus philosophirt, alle Sonnenstrahlen, allen Glauben und alle Blumen, und es blieb ihm nichts übrig, als das kalte, positive Grab.... Er hat überhaupt eine ganze Menge Bücher geschrieben, worin immer die Vernunft vor ihrer eigenen Vortrefflichkeit renommirt, und wobey es der arme Doctor gewiß ernsthaft genug meinte, und also in dieser Hinsicht alle Achtung verdiente.[13]

> [This man, well into his fifties, was a personified straight line. In his strivings for the positive, the poor fellow had philosophized everything glorious out of life, all sunbeams, all faith, and all flowers, and nothing remained for him but the cold, positive grave.... He wrote, indeed, a great many books, in which reason always boasts of its own excellence. The poor doctor certainly had serious intentions and accordingly deserved all respect.[14]]

Heine's portrayal is in part sympathetic and appreciative of Ascher's accomplishments. But Heine, like other Romantics, believes that the overly rational world view of Enlightenment thinkers has led to a pernicious neglect of other aspects of human existence, and the Romantic themes of nature, poetry, love, and sensuality can be understood as correctives to the one-dimensionality they believe is the legacy of the Age of Reason.

The overriding sentiment that the Enlightenment was a rational, even a critical, period that contributed to human progress, but that it was lacking in poetry and imagination is captured well in Friedrich Schlegel's early essay on the chief German literary representative of the Enlightenment, Gotthold Ephraim Lessing. Composed in the mid-1790s, "Über Lessing" (1797) is ostensibly an encomium to a German genius.[15] It begins by extolling Lessing as a revolutionary spirit who managed to secure praise from almost all parties. Indeed, Schlegel proceeds in his exposition by relating various opinions about Lessing, initiating his critique at times by citing others' views and, in other instances, by disagreeing with previous judgments. In this manner he can also repeat complimentary views that he does not necessarily share. Thus, Schlegel writes that everyone views Lessing as a great poet and a superior judge of poetry (*KA* 103–04). But he also alludes to a common perception that Lessing lacks "Gemüt" (soul) because he does not exude love. Schlegel pretends to defend Lessing against this charge: "Ist denn Lessings Haß der Unvernunft nicht so göttlich wie die echteste, die geistigste Liebe? Kann man so hassen ohne Gemüt?" (*KA* 106; Is Lessing's hatred of unreason not as divine as the most authentic, the most spiritual love? Can one hate in this fashion without soul?). The negative appraisal is presented as broadly disseminated, although not often voiced, and Schlegel notes with feigned indignation that some even deny his geniality because of this fault. Schlegel also employs the technique of citing flattering opinions held by others, while maligning their ability to evaluate the matters on which they are commenting. That "the mediocre" (*Mediocristen*) have focused on his dramaturgical and poetic works and raised them to the status of holy texts (*KA* 107) reflects poorly on them perhaps, but it also calls into question the value of Lessing's writings on these topics. Schlegel's review of the general judgments on Lessing is therefore in no way an innocent undertaking, but prefigures the criticism that he will later, and cautiously, articulate.

After rehearsing the views of anonymous others, Schlegel turns to his own judgments, and again he remains apparently appreciative of Lessing's accomplishments. At one point he seems to recruit Lessing as a Romantic, stating that his most interesting and most accomplished works contain suggestions and hints, while his most mature and perfected writings are Romantic in form, fragments of fragments (*KA* 112). But the criticism indirectly administered through his overview of opinions now comes into the open when he takes exception to the *sensus communis:* "Man meint zum Beispiel nicht nur, sondern man glaubt sogar entschieden zu wissen, daß Lessing einer der größten Dichter war; und ich zweifle sogar, ob er überall ein Dichter gewesen sei, ja ob er poetischen Sinn und Kunstgefühl gehabt habe" (*KA* 113; People not only believe, for example, but they think they know for a fact that Lessing was one of the greatest poets; and I doubt whether he was really a poet in every instance, indeed, whether he had poetic sense and an appreciation for art). Schlegel supports his view by citing Lessing himself: in various remarks made over the years Lessing recognized his shortcomings as a creative artist. Schlegel also follows Lessing's lead in discussing his dramatic works. *Emilia Galotti* (1772), which for Schlegel indicates how much or how little Lessing achieved in poetic refinement, is "unstreitig ein großes Exempel der dramatischen Algebra" (*KA* 116; unquestionably a prime example of dramatic algebra). Schlegel continues: "Man muß es bewundern dieses in Schweiß und Pein produzierte Meisterstück des reinen Verstandes; man muß es frierend bewundern, und bewundernd frieren; denn ins Gemüt dringts nicht und kanns nicht dringen, weil es nicht aus dem Gemüt gekommen ist" (*KA* 116; It has to be admired, this masterpiece of pure understanding produced in sweat and blood; one has to admire it coldly and while admiring it remain cold; for it does not and cannot penetrate the soul since it does not come from the soul). Similarly, *Nathan der Weise* (1779), although lauded because it does originate in Lessing's soul, is a product of the enthusiasm of pure reason (*KA* 119). By the end of Schlegel's essay we gain the impression that Lessing was a great man and a courageous critic, but that he lacked the creativity and imagination that are part of the Romantic spirit. Schlegel, like his fellow Romantics, appreciates Lessing, but cautions his reader against making him into something he was not:

> Hört doch endlich auf, an Lessing nur das zu rühmen, was er nicht hatte und nicht konnte, und immer wieder seine falsche Tendenz zur Poesie und Kritik der Poesie, statt sie mit Schonung zu erklären und durch die Erklärung zu rechtfertigen, sie nur von neuem in das grellste Licht zu stellen. Und wenn ihr denn einmal nur bei dem stehenbleiben wollt, was wirklich in ihm zur Reife gekommen und ganz sichtbar geworden ist, so laßt ihn doch wie er ist, und nehmt sie, wie ihr sie findet, diese *Mischung von Literatur, Polemik, Witz und Philosophie*. (*KA* 398)

[It's finally time to stop appraising Lessing according to what he did not have and could not do, always simply placing his false tendency to poetry and the criticism of poetry anew in the most glaring light instead of explaining it with forbearance and justifying it with the explanation. And then, if for once you wish to dwell on what really matured in him and came clearly into view, then let him be what he is, and take it however you will, this mixture of literature, polemics, wit and philosophy.]

Lessing thus represents for Schlegel the best of the Enlightenment, its most progressive and worthwhile tendency. In the worst of cases the Enlightenment produced a new dogmatism of reason that lent itself to satire or ridicule; in its best representatives it is a valiant expression of the critical spirit. But in either case it remains a narrow, shallow perspective on an infinitely richer and more creative human existence.

Nietzsche's "New Enlightenment"

The writings of Friedrich Nietzsche mark a turning point in the criticism of Enlightenment. Like Hamann and Herder, Nietzsche was profoundly interested in philosophical issues, and he often commented on Kantian philosophy. In almost all cases, and especially in his later works, Nietzsche denounced Kant's first critique with arguments similar to those articulated by his detractors in the eighteenth century. The moral philosophy embodied in the categorical imperative was especially troubling to Nietzsche, who believed it was an idealistic remnant of a pernicious, life-negating Christian value system. Echoing his illustrious predecessors in the eighteenth and nineteenth centuries, he castigated the Enlightenment for neglecting instincts and relying instead on a shallow rationality.[16] Like the Romantics, Nietzsche did not necessarily disparage the Enlightenment project, and he exhibits a good deal of respect for individual thinkers. *Menschliches, Allzumenschliches* (Human All Too Human, 1878), for example, inspired by and dedicated to Voltaire, was published on the centenary of his death, and at various times during the 1880s Nietzsche himself contemplated composing a book entitled "Die neue Aufklärung" (The New Enlightenment). Thus although he could not countenance the rationalist mode of thought associated with much of the philosophical Enlightenment, he considered himself to be working in some sense as a continuator of the broader Enlightenment tradition. However, Nietzsche's seminal contribution to anti-Enlightenment thought consists in his relentless questioning of notions accepted as truths by Enlightenment thinkers and their nineteenth-century disciples. The Enlightenment had taken the first steps toward eradicating dogma, especially in the realm of religion, that had dominated Europe for centuries. But according to Nietzsche it had stopped short of questioning its own presuppositions and thereby either instituted new dogmas or retained the very dogmas it was combating under a secular guise. Nietzsche's "new enlightenment" thus entails a more radical critique that ultimately calls into question the values the Enlightenment meant to uphold.

Nietzsche began his university and professorial career as a classical philologist, and although his scholarly writings are rather traditional in scope, his philosophical works reevaluated the prevailing view of ancient Greece. For much of the Enlightenment Greece was the cradle of Western Civilization and propagated values that were foundational for modern Europe. In art and literature the Greeks produced the most noble and beautiful works; in politics and social thought they were credited with a love of freedom and an incipient democratic attitude; in philosophy they were the first to articulate standard concepts that retain eternal validity. Although not without predecessors, Nietzsche was the most important subverter of the Grecophilic tradition. He appreciated the art and literature of the ancients, but only insofar as they partook of a Dionysian spirit of revelry and instinctual abandon. Nietzsche regarded the philosophical tradition most prized by modern thinkers, in particular the writings of Plato, as the initial sign for the demise of a preferred, aristocratic value system: for him Plato's idealism segues neatly into Christianity, producing a debilitating effect on humanity. The democratic impulse that emanates from Greece is for Nietzsche an unfortunate and late development that canceled a superior, hierarchical order he endorsed. In Nietzsche's view Greece was not built on harmony and beauty, but on struggle and conflict.

> In den Griechen "schöne Seelen," "goldene Mitten" und andre Vollkommenheiten auszuwittern, etwa an ihnen die Ruhe in der Grösse, die ideale Gesinnung, die hohe Einfalt bewundern — vor dieser "hohen Einfalt," einer niaiserie allemande zuguterletzt, war ich durch den Psychologen behütet, den ich in mir trug. Ich sah ihren stärksten Instinkt, den Willen zur Macht, ich sah sie zittern vor der unbändigen Gewalt dieses Triebs, — ich sah alle ihre Institutionen wachsen aus Schutzmaassregeln, um sich vor einander gegen ihren inwendigen Explosivstoff sicher zu stellen. Die ungeheure Spannung im Innern entlud sich dann in furchtbarer und rücksichtsloser Feindschaft nach Aussen: die Stadtgemeinden zerfleischten sich unter einander, damit die Stadtbürger jeder einzelnen vor sich selber Ruhe fänden.[17]

> [From scenting out "beautiful souls," "golden means," and other perfections in the Greeks, from admiring in them such things as their repose in grandeur, their ideal disposition, their sublime simplicity — from this "sublime simplicity," a *niaiserie allemande* when all is said and done, I was preserved by the psychologist in me. I saw their strongest instinct, the will to power, I saw them trembling at the intractable force of this drive — I saw all their institutions evolve out of protective measures designed for mutual security against the *explosive material* within them. The tremendous internal tension then discharged itself in fearful and ruthless external hostility; the city states tore one another to pieces so that the citizens of each of them might find peace within himself.]

The Enlightenment was not wrong to celebrate Greece as an ideal, but its evaluation of the meaning of Greece was distorted by its liberal and aesthetic biases. Nietzsche's Greece is also a model, but it is one that challenges the Enlightenment values that eighteenth-century figures erroneously attributed to the ancient world.

Nietzsche's most virulent assault on the Enlightenment occurs in connection with his consideration of ethics. The Enlightenment had questioned the religious foundation for traditional moral precepts, but it retained a system of ethical values that, for Nietzsche, was tantamount to a secularized version of what formerly existed. Much of Nietzsche's writing in the 1880s is devoted to a critical examination of utilitarian and idealist ethics, which continued to evidence a quasi-religious structure of good and evil. Nietzsche's method of critiquing Enlightenment thought and its continuation in the nineteenth century was to challenge universalist presumptions by introducing a historical dimension to morality. Kant's ethics, for example, assume unchanging, formal laws to which all human beings in all societies and epochs must adhere. Utilitarians propose an accepted notion of moral behavior that is beneficial to the community. Previous reflections on the history of moral thought, Nietzsche contends, have produced results that are contrary to human psychology since they propose that we have forgotten our original association of altruistic action and morality. Nietzsche advances an alternative that questions the very notions of good and evil so readily accepted by all of the foremost ethical theorists. "Good," he contends, relying on etymological clues and psychological intuition, was originally a designation that affirmed the status and values of an aristocratic order, and it must be contrasted with, although not necessarily opposed by, the notion of "bad," which refers to the actions of those situated outside noble circles, those who are subjected to them, their vassals or slaves or serfs. This noble value system was gradually replaced by the herd or slave values we currently accept, whereby "good" is not the original, affirmative term, but a reactive afterthought to the notion of "evil." Nietzsche postulates a socio-historical revolt in ethics by means of which a lower strata of society, directed by clever priests, reversed the noble value system. Fueled by weakness, a pernicious intelligence, and *ressentiment*, the "herd" labeled "evil" everything connected with those to whom they were subjected, and introduced in opposition to "evil" the notion of "good" to designate their own actions. Thus the weak and powerless, the sickly and deformed, and the actions they performed, were labeled "good," while the powerful and "noble," who formerly called themselves "good," were transformed into "evil" beings effecting "evil" deeds.[18] With this explanation of the origin of the dominating value system Nietzsche maintains that the Enlightenment has not gone far enough in its critique: although it set in motion a train of thought that would eventually culminate in the "death of God," it did not understand that with the demise of the divinity, religiously informed value systems would have to be abolished as well.

The Enlightenment was similarly inconsequential in its handling of truth, which it continued to regard as the ultimate philosophical value. In contrast to a theoretical tradition that asked "What is truth?" or "How can we attain the truth?" Nietzsche poses the more fundamental questions, "*Was in uns will eigentlich 'zur Wahrheit'?*" (*What* is it in us that really wants to 'get at the truth'?) or "*warum nicht lieber* Unwahrheit? Und Ungewissheit? Selbst Unwissenheit?"[19] (*why do we not prefer* untruth? And uncertainty?

Even ignorance?). In connection with these unusual queries Nietzsche refers to the riddle of the Sphinx and the myth of Oedipus, intimating that the search for the truth, as it is incorporated in this ancient tale, may result in disastrous consequences for the seeker, and that truth is intimately connected with blindness. Nietzsche does not solve the conundrum regarding the value of truth, although he does suggest at various points that our way of thinking, as well as our mode of existence, is based on error, deception, and illusion. He continues by maintaining that our habit of setting up terms in opposition, truth versus error, is a deception of language that leads us to a false manner of dealing with the world. In reality the world may be more aptly conceived as a continuum than a series of antitheses, and the fact that we conceive of antithetical values and ideals may be a sign that we are covering something more fundamental.[20] Important here is not Nietzsche's answer to conventional Enlightenment propositions about truth, but his radically new way of approaching these traditional issues. Nietzsche's "new enlightenment" consists only in part in an anti-Enlightenment stance; it is also, and more important, an extension of Enlightenment critique that does not refrain from questioning even the most cherished inherited values. Although the results of Nietzsche's procedure often lead to values antagonistic to those of the Enlightenment — an ancient Greece dominated by *agon* and inequality, an ethical system based on strength and domination, an indifference to truth — he arrives at those conclusions not by recourse to the dogmas of the past, but by a resolute criticism of Enlightenment itself.

The Frankfurt School's "Dialectic of Enlightenment"

One possible conclusion we can draw from Nietzsche's writings is that the enlightenment of the Enlightenment does not necessarily result in an increase or perfection of enlightened values as much as an overturning of these values. Perhaps the most eloquent statement of the necessary reversal of Enlightenment from its progressive trajectory is contained in the book *Dialektik der Aufklärung* (Dialectic of Enlightenment, 1947) by Max Horkheimer (1895–1973) and Theodor Adorno (1903–1969). Written in exile in the United States during the final years of the Second World War, it consists of a series of essays on various topics: a general theoretical chapter is followed by two excurses that take up Odysseus as the prototypical enlightener and de Sade's Juliette, whose activities are used to demonstrate how enlightened release from moral strictures turns into something rather less than morality. A severe censure of the "culture industry" in the United States, which performs a function similar to political oppression in other parts of the world; a discussion of anti-Semitism as a multi-faceted phenomenon related not only to National Socialism, but to psychological factors based in our anthropological, as well as our socio-historical constitution; and some fifty pages of fragmentary notes and sketches complete this unusual and heterogeneous discussion of enlightenment. Despite the wide variety of topics and the occasional obscurity in argument, the main thesis is easily discernible: enlightenment, the authors argue, has turned upon itself, producing something contrary to its original impulses. Conceiving enlightenment in its broadest sense as human domination over nature or instrumental rationality, Adorno and Horkheimer postulate that this domination, which was originally emancipatory and beneficial to humankind, eventually evolves into coercion and repression in various spheres of human existence. Hegemony over nature ultimately becomes suppression of human nature and oppression of human beings; and emancipation from social, historical, and religious constraints becomes enslavement in a despotic social order in which individuality is crushed and uniformity is ruthlessly enforced. The negation of enlightenment is the dialectical product of its extension into human affairs.

The dark vision advanced by Adorno and Horkheimer emerged from a particularly bleak period in world affairs. In the mid 1940s they believed they were confronted with a totally administered world. In Germany and much of Europe fascism reigned; the Soviet Union was ruled by an oppressive state socialism; and, as they argued, in the United States, which pretended to be the democratic alternative, the culture industry held sway. Despite differences, the effect of each regime was to eliminate autonomous subjectivity, to restrict individual freedom and responsibility, and to inculcate pernicious ideologemes in a nationalist, socialist, or pseudo-democratic myopia. In a postwar essay Adorno poses an alternative to the wayward development of enlightenment in the twentieth century in a pedagogy that would strengthen the ego, enabling it to resist the political slogans and cultural trivia that constantly bombard it.[21] In *Dialektik der Aufklärung*, however, the authors supply a glimmer of hope in their discussion of "mimesis." The term, borrowed from ancient Greek, usually means imitation and is obviously related to mimicry and mime. But Adorno and Horkheimer have something slightly different in mind. They associate it on the one hand with the individual, relating it to the "idiosyncratic," a term that means literally an "individual mixture." Mimesis is also related to the natural, to responses to the environment that precede or predate the generalizing and leveling effects of social and conceptual orders. Adorno and Horkheimer detect remnants of mimesis even in the rationalized environment around them, and their description gives us a clue to what it entails.

> Es ist die ansteckende Gestik der von Zivilisation unterdrückten Unmittelbarkeit: Berühren, Anschmiegen, Beschwichtigen, Zureden. Anstößig heute ist das Unzeitgemäße jener Regungen. Sie scheinen die

längst verdinglichten menschlichen Beziehungen wieder in persönliche Machtverhältnisse zurückzuübersetzen, indem sie den Käufer durch Schmeicheln, den Schuldner durch Drohen, den Gläubiger durch Flehen zu erweichen suchen. Peinlich wirkt schließlich jede Regung überhaupt, Aufregung ist minder. *Aller nicht-manipulierte Ausdruck erscheint als die Grimasse, die der manipulierte* — im Kino, bei der Lynch-Justiz, in der Führer-Rede — immer war. (3: 206)

[It is the infectious gestures of direct contacts, suppressed by civilization, for instance, touch, soothing, snuggling up, coaxing. We are put off by the old-fashioned nature of these impulses. They seem to translate long verified human relations back into individual power relations: in trying to influence the purchaser by flattery, the debtor by threats and the creditor by entreaty. Every impulse is finally embarrassing; mere excitement is preferable. Every non-manipulated expression seems to be the grimace which the manipulated expression always was — in the movies, in lynch law, or in speeches by Hitler.[22]]

Adorno and Horkheimer argue that modern society has outlawed all forms of mimesis that it cannot categorize and control. "Zivilisation hat anstelle der organischen Anschmeigung ans andere, anstelle des eigentlich mimetischen Verhaltens, zunächst in der magischen Phase, die organisierte Handhabung der Mimesis und schließlich, in der historischen, die rationale Praxis, die Arbeit, gesetzt. Unbeherrschte Mimesis wird verfemt" (3:205; Civilization has replaced the organic adaptation to others and mimetic behavior proper, by organized control of mimesis, in the magical phase; and finally, by rational practice, by work in the historical phase. Uncontrolled mimesis is outlawed, *DE* 180). This broad and encompassing thesis extends to all aspects of human endeavor, since any attempt to assimilate phenomena to each other and to reduce the individuality of response to a single pattern destroys mimesis: thus the very act of linguistic conceptualization is anti-mimetic, as is all of science: "Wissenschaft ist Wiederholung, verfeinert zu beobachteter Regelmäßigkeit, aufbewahrt in Stereotypen" (3:206; Science is repetition, refined into observed regularity, and preserved in stereotypes, *DE* 181). In a sense Adorno and Horkheimer have refurbished in an anthropological and psychological guise Hamann's opposition to the natural sciences and Herder's polemics against philosophical abstractions. Like their eighteenth-century predecessors, they accuse the Enlightenment of a hegemony that entails a linguistic leveling and a disregard for individual and cultural differences. Uncorrupted and authentic mimesis provides the antipode not only to the excesses of enlightenment, but to its very essence.

The second generation of the Frankfurt School, as represented in the writings of Jürgen Habermas (b. 1929), took a much different view with regard to the dialectic of enlightenment. In essence Habermas's worldview in the postwar era differed significantly from Adorno's and Horkheimer's in the mid 1940s. In his early work Habermas implicitly opposed the leveling of fascism, state socialism, and parliamentary democracy when he suggested the possibility of reinvigorating a public sphere of open and free communication and decision-making. Habermas's more philosophical objections to Adorno and Horkheimer remained tacit until the publication of *Der philosophische Diskurs der Moderne* (1985), which devoted a chapter to *Dialektik der Aufklärung*. The inadequacies of Adorno and Horkheimer are due not so much to their analysis of instrumental reason as to their adherence to a Hegelian model in which changes are perceived as the production of antagonisms. Habermas's discussion of *Dialektik der Aufklärung* in his *Philosophische Diskurs der Moderne* emphasizes the aporia reached when the critique of enlightenment turns back on itself. He contends that Enlightenment's original opposition to myth, its critique of unfounded knowledge as superstition, at one point boomerangs. "Allerdings erreicht das Aufklärungsdrama erst seine Peripetie, wenn die Ideologiekritik selbst in Verdacht gerät, keine Wahrheiten (mehr) zu produzieren"[23] (Yet the drama of enlightenment first arrives at its climax when ideology critique itself comes under suspicion of not producing (any more) truths). This "second-order reflectiveness" calls into question the foundations of reason itself and, in the process, undermines the basis for all critique. Only two choices remain for the would-be critic: one can have recourse to an all-pervasive explanatory principle, such as Nietzsche did in his reduction of all knowledge and values to power; or one can refuse to resolve the inherent self-contradiction (or performative contradiction) of critique and undertake occasional and unreinforced forays against the enemy in a sort of guerrilla warfare against totalizing systems. The latter alternative, chosen by Adorno and Horkheimer, is as unsatisfactory for Habermas as the former, although it can be conceived as the dialectical alternative to a Nietzschean essentialism. In keeping with his skepticism regarding this totalized application of the dialectic, Habermas implies that this solution only covers a portion of the problems associated with modernity. Neither the *Dialektik der Aufklärung* nor Adorno's subsequent work does justice to a realm of problems and experiences that define our contemporary world.

> Ich meine die theoretische Eigendynamik, die die Wissenschaften, auch die Selbstreflexion der Wissenschaften, über die Erzeugung technisch verwertbaren Wissens immer wieder *hinaus*treibt; ich meine ferner die universalistischen Grundlagen von Recht und Moral, die in den Institutionen der Verfassungsstaaten, in Formen demokratischer Willensbildung, in individualistischen Mustern der Identitätsbildung *auch* eine (wie immer verzerrte und unvollkommene) Verkörperung gefunden haben; ich meine schließlich die Produktivität und die sprengende Kraft ästhetischer Grunderfahrungen, die eine von

Imperativen der Zwecktätigkeit und von Konventionen der alltäglichen Wahrnehmung freigesetzte Subjektivität ihrer eigenen Dezentrierung abgewinnt.[24]

[I am thinking here of the specific theoretical dynamic that continually pushes the sciences, and even the self-reflection of the sciences, beyond merely engendering technically useful knowledge; I am referring, further, to the universalistic foundations of law and morality that have also been incorporated (in however distorted and incomplete a fashion) into the institutions of constitutional government, into the forms of democratic will formation, and into individualist patters of identity formation; I have in mind, finally, the productivity and explosive power of basic aesthetic experiences that a subjectivity liberated from the imperatives of purposive activity and from conventions of quotidian perception gains from its own decentering.]

In a neat reversal of traditional anti-Enlightenment critique, Habermas suggests that the dialectic of enlightenment is not wrong, but simply partial, one-sided, and incomplete. The dialectic that Adorno and Horkheimer regard as determinative for the course of history is cast as one segment in a broader development.

Habermas's alternative to his first-generation mentors is derived from a more differentiated view of what the Enlightenment accomplished. In contrast to Adorno and Horkheimer, Habermas does not conceive of the seminal achievement of the eighteenth century solely in terms of epistemological, technical, or scientific progress, but rather in terms of social and political forms of interaction as well. Expressed in the vocabulary of *Erkenntnis und Interesse* (Knowledge and Human Interest, 1968), the achievements Habermas values would be labeled "practical" and "critical." In the language of *Theorie des kommunikativen Handelns* (The Theory of Communicative Action, 1981) Habermas finds a communicative rationality alongside its instrumental counterpart. The Enlightenment is thus not simply a cipher for hegemony over nature or a period of bourgeois ideals and obfuscations, but an age that develops concrete, albeit incomplete, because insufficiently realized, modes for democratic decision-making. Power is asserted not only to control the external world of nature and to tame the inner world of desires, as it is conceived in the *Dialektik der Aufklärung*, but against those forces that exclude individual and collective participation in activities that affect people's livelihoods and lives. When extended into the twentieth century, these achievements may become tarnished, but in general Habermas is still unwilling to relinquish their viability or desirability for the modern era. We can never return to the liberal public sphere of bourgeois society, but the conceptual underpinnings of that ideal entity possess validity for the contemporary world. Habermas does not share the pessimism of the mid 1940s with regard to liberal democracy. As pernicious as the American culture industry may be, the direct and violent coercion of fascism is still qualitatively different from the manipulative tactics of American culture. As inadequate as Western parliamentary democracies may be as genuine participatory structures, they nonetheless retain an original ideal and an unrealized potential that is not available under repressive forms of government. Habermas's more favorable, though critical views on the eighteenth-century sources of the Western heritage and their inherent possibilities lead him to a more sanguine view of the Enlightenment's contribution to human emancipation.

Anti-Enlightenment Critique or Higher Enlightenment?

Critiques of the Enlightenment always confront a strange predicament. Unlike dogmatic rejections of the Enlightenment, they do not depend on blind subservience to unfounded convictions, superstitions, or subjective fantasies, but rely instead on argument, reasoning, and persuasion. The tools they employ are thus nearly identical to those found in the Enlightenment writings they criticize. Indeed, critique itself, whether conceived as setting limits to the competence of a faculty or as an act of trenchant criticism of a commonly held belief, is a vital part of Enlightenment thought. To a large extent any reasonable critique of Enlightenment involves itself in a contraction simply because it must accept basic tenets of the Enlightenment as part of its own presuppositions. On a more specific level critiques raise other, related problems, leading to aporetic entanglements. Herder, for example, opposes the cultural hegemony of abstract enlightenment, but it is not clear how far he can press for equality of cultures. If any social order advocates a lack of tolerance for otherness, or if it insists on one true belief to which all of humankind must be converted in order to achieve redemption, then it becomes more difficult to accord this order an equal status with others. It is, in fact, a threat to the community of nations that Herder postulates. Furthermore, as anthropologists have discovered, the very fact of interpreting a foreign culture may be the result of, and may result in, domination; it is difficult to know how an outside observer can hope to comprehend observed alterity without the assumption of some common, overriding humanity. Adorno and Horkheimer have to confront similarly intricate difficulties in their radical advocacy of mimesis. Like Nietzsche, they at times suggest that language itself, as well as our linguistically informed consciousness, partakes in an exclusion of individuality and authenticity that is related to oppressive dimensions of the Enlightenment. Individual perceptions and impressions are necessarily leveled by the conventions that control us, thus thwarting any chance at genuine expression of autonomous subjectivity. But they too are compelled to articulate these objections in traditional language and concepts, although the unusual syntax often employed in Adorno's texts — and the hermetic art he extols — is a sign of rebellion against this necessary and seemingly unavoidable conformity. Ultimately, as he himself recognized, Adorno too is caught in and beholden to the very features of Enlightenment he seeks to castigate, and it may be that anti-Enlightenment critique, although a recurring activity for over two centuries, can never avoid its paradoxical underpinnings.

Perhaps the paradoxical nature of anti-Enlightenment critique explains why critics repeatedly either adopt the vocabulary of enlightenment or claim that they are merely trying to correct a perceived imbalance of reason. Nietzsche, as we have seen, was captivated by the notion of a "new Enlightenment" that would presumably extend the insights of the original Enlightenment, while both Hamann and Herder adopted the language of "critique" in order to settle their differences with Kant. The motif of a different sort of enlightenment, one that builds upon and augments the foundations of the Age of Reason is implicit in the Romantic reaction as well, and even when reason is caricatured and belittled, the Romantics do not advocate jettisoning rational thought altogether. In this connection Friedrich Hölderlin captured well the divided spirit of critique when he postulated a "höhere Aufklärung" (higher Enlightenment),[25] which, to be sure, we have not yet completely attained, but which is more encompassing and less restrictive than the Enlightenment that was bequeathed to subsequent thinkers by the *siècle de lumières*. Hölderlin's thoughts resonate with many features of Romantic criticism in that they suggest that a simplistic or dogmatic reliance on reason is an imbalance that needs correction. We must recognize the limitations of human understanding, in particular that human affairs cannot always be adequately described by the rigid concepts of thought. In harmony with his aesthetic proclivities Hölderlin proposes at times that a harmony between the antithetical tendencies of understanding and sensuality can be achieved in literature, a suggestion that accords well with the contemporaneous theoretical work of Schiller. But like Hamann and Herder, Hölderlin also attributes a certain religiosity to this harmonious reconciliation. In other texts, Hölderlin, anticipating the first generation of the Frankfurt School, excoriates Enlightenment's hegemony toward nature, noting that it thereby ignores human feelings and emotions, as well as nature's beneficence toward us.[26] "Higher enlightenment" for Hölderlin, and perhaps for other constructive critics of Enlightenment thought, is thus simply another — and a more productive — expression of their putatively antithetical critique. Herder's frequent appeals to progress and the lofty notions of humanity; the Romantic theme of universal poetry and fulfilled subjectivity; Nietzsche's search for truth, even if it means calling truth itself into question; Adorno's and Horkheimer's social commitment in the face of an administered world — demonstrate the fundamental allegiance of presumably anti-Enlightenment thinkers to the very movement they criticize. The ultimate lesson the Age of Reason has to offer — even in the harshest critiques from the most inveterate adversaries — may be that it is impossible to escape the legacy of the Enlightenment.

Notes

[1] Immanuel Kant, *Werke*, Akademie Textausgabe (Berlin: Walter de Gruyter, 1968), 8: 35.

[2] Johann Georg Hamann, *Briefwechsel*, ed. Arthur Henkel (Frankfurt a. M.: Insel, 1965), 5: 289.

[3] The German word for "fault" in this context is "Schuld"; thus Hamann is also punning here on the notion of self-inflicted (selbst verschuldet).

[4] English translations of this and the following quotation from Hamann are from Garrett Green's translation of "Letter to Christian Jacob Kraus," in *What is Enlightenment: Eighteenth-Century Answers and Twentieth-Century Questions,* ed. James Schmidt (Berkeley: U of California P, 1996), 147.

[5] Johann Georg Hamann, "Letter to Christian Jacob Kraus," trans. Garrett Green, in *What is Enlightenment,* ed. James Schmidt, 147–48.

[6] Johann Georg Hamann, *Sämtliche Werke,* ed. Josef Nadler (Vienna: Verlag Herder, 1951), 3: 283. English translation by Kenneth Haynes, "Metacritique on the Purism of Reason," in *What is Enlightenment,* ed. James Schmidt, 154.

[7] Friedrich Nietzsche, *Kritische Gesamtausgabe,* ed. Giorgio Colli and Mazzino Montinari (Berlin: de Gruyter, 1969), 6.2: 18. English translation: Friedrich Nietzsche, *Beyond Good and Evil,* trans. Marion Faber (New York: Oxford, 1998), 12.

[8] English translation of Hamann's "Metacritique on the Purism of Reason" by Kenneth Haynes, in *What is Enlightenment,* ed. James Schmidt, 155.

[9] Hamann, *Sämtliche Werke,* 3: 285.

[10] Hamann had sent Herder his "metacritique" on 15 September 1784. See Hamann, *Briefwechsel,* 5: 210–16.

[11] Johann Gottfried Herder, *Sämtliche Werke,* ed. Bernhard Suphan (rpt. Hildesheim: Georg Olms, 1967), 21: 37. Subsequent references to this edition are cited parenthetically in the text using the abbreviation *W,* volume and page number.

[12] Rudolf Ungar, *Hamann und die Aufklärung: Studien zur Vorgeschichte des romantischen Geistes im 18. Jahrhundert,* 2 vols. (Tübingen: Max Niemeyer, 1963).

[13] Heinrich Heine, *Sämtliche Werke,* ed. Manfred Windfuhr (Hamburg: Hoffmann und Campe, 1973), 6: 103.

[14] English translation by Frederic T. Wood from Heinrich Heine, *Poetry and Prose,* ed. Jost Hermand and Robert C. Holub (New York: Continuum, 1982), 138.

[15] Friedrich Schlegel, *Kritische Ausgabe*, vol. 2, ed. Ernst Behler (Munich: Schöningh, 1975), 100. Subsequent references to this work are cited parenthetically in the text using the abbreviation *KA* and page number.

[16] Nietzsche *Kritische Gesamtausgabe*, 6.3: 151.

[17] Nietzsche, *Kritische Gesamtausgabe*, 6.3: 151. English translation: Friedrich Nietzsche, *Twilight of the Idols / The Anti-Christ*, trans. R. J. Hollingdale (London: Penguin, 1990), 118.

[18] See the first essay in *Zur Genealogie der Moral*, 6.2: 269–303.

[19] Nietzsche 6.2: 9; English translation: Nietzsche, *Beyond Good and Evil*, trans. Marion Faber, 5.

[20] Nietzsche 6.2: 10.

[21] "Was bedeutet: Aufarbeitung der Vergangenheit" in Theodor W. Adorno, *Gesammelte Schriften* (Frankfurt a. M.: Suhrkamp, 1977), 10.2: 555–72.

[22] English translation, with slight alteration, from Max Horkheimer and Theodor W. Adorno, *Dialectic of Enlightenment*, trans. John Cumming (New York: Continuum, 1999), 182. Subsequent references to this translation will be indicated by *DE* and page number.

[23] Jürgen Habermas, *Der philosophische Diskurs der Moderne: Zwölf Vorlesungen* (Frankfurt a. M.: Suhrkamp, 1985), 141. English translation from Jürgen Habermas, *The Philosophical Discourse of Modernity: Twelve Lectures*, trans. Frederick Lawrence (Cambridge, MA: MIT Press, 1987), 116.

[24] Habermas, *Philosophische Diskurs der Moderne*, 138. English translation: Habermas, *The Philosophical Discourse of Modernity*, trans. Lawrence, 113.

[25] Friedrich Hölderlin, *Sämtliche Werke*, ed. Friedrich Beissner (Stuttgart: W. Kohlhammer, 1961), 4: 275–79.

[26] Hölderlin 3: 187.

Bibliography

Primary Literature

Alxinger, Johann Baptist von. *Doolin von Maynz: Ein Rittergedicht*, 1787

———. *Bliomberis: Ein Rittergedicht*, 1791

Bach, C. P. E. *Versuch über die wahre Art das Clavier zu spielen*, 1753–62.

Blanckenburg, Christian Friedrich von. *Versuch über den Roman*, 1774.

Blumauer, Aloys. *Beobachtungen über Oesterreichs Aufklärung und Litteratur*, 1782.

———. *Vergils Aeneis travestirt*, 1785–88.

Bodmer, Johann Jakob. *Von dem Einfluss und Gebrauche der Einbildungskraft*, 1727.

———. *Critische Abhandlung von dem Wunderbaren in der Poesie und dessen Verbindung mit dem Wahrscheinlichen*, 1740.

Bodmer, Johann Jakob and Breitinger, Johann Jakob, eds. *Die Discourse der Mahlern*, 1721–23.

———. *Der Mahler der Sitten*, 1746.

Bräker, Ulrich. *Lebensgeschichte und natürliche Ebentheuer des armen Mannes im Tockenburg*, 1789. Translated by Derek Bowman as *The Life and Story and Real Adventures of the Poor Man of Toggenburg*. Edinburgh: Edinburgh UP, 1970.

Breitinger, Johann Jakob. *Von dem Einfluß und Gebrauche der Einbildungskraft*, 1727

———. *Critische Dichtkunst*, 1740.

Brockes, Barthold Heinrich. *Irdisches Vergnügen in Gott, bestehend in Physicalisch- und Moralischen Gedichten*, 1724–46 (8 vols.).

Campe, Joachim Heinrich. *Väterlicher Rath für meine Tochter*, 1789.

Claudius, Matthias. *Tändeleyen und Erzählungen* (anon.), 1763.

———, ed. *Der Wandsbecker Bothe*, 1771–75. Translated anonymously as *Claudius, or The Messenger of Wandsbeck, and His Message*. London: Ward, 1859.

Denis, Michael. *Die Lieder Sined des Barden,* 1772.

Gellert, Christian Fürchtegott. *Lieder* (anon.), 1743.

———. *Die Betschwester: Ein Lustspiel in drei Aufzügen,* 1745. Translated and ed. by Johann Setzer and Elaine Gottesman as *Christian Fuerchtegott Gellert's The Prayer Sister.* Flushing, NY: International Council on the Arts, 1980.

———. *Fabeln und Erzählungen,* 1746–48. Translated by Joseph A. Nuske as *Fables, a Free Translation from the German of Gellert and other Poets.* London: Whitacker, 1850.

———. *Das Leben der schwedischen Gräfin von G**** (anon.), 1746–48.

Translated anonymously as *History of the Swedish Countess of Guildenstern.* London: Dodsley, 1752.

———. *Lustspiele* including *Die zärtlichen Schwestern,* 1747.

Translated by Thomas Holcroft as *The Tender Sisters* in *The Theatrical Recorder* edited by Holcroft. London: Symonds, 1805, 1:1–50.

———. *Briefe, nebst einer Abhandlung von dem guten Geschmacke in Briefen,* 1751.

———. *Lehrgedichte und Erzählungen,* 1754.

Gessner, Salomon. *Daphnis* (anon.), 1754. Translated anonymously as *Daphnis: a Poetical Pastoral Novel. Translated from the German of Mr. Gessner, the Celebrated Author of The Death of Abel.* London: Sold by J. Dodsley, 1768.

———. *Idyllen,* 1762. Translated anonymously as *Rural Poem.* London: Printed for T. Becket, 1762

———. *Der Tod Abels* (anon.), 1758. Translated by Mary Collyer as *The Death of Abel.* London: Printed for R & J Dodsley, 1761.

———. *Neue Idyllen,* 1772. Translated by William Hooper as *New Idylles.* London: S. Hooper, 1776.

Gleim, Johann Wilhelm Ludewig. *Versuch in scherzhaften Liedern* (anon.), 1744–45.

———. *Romanzen,* 1756.

———. *Kriegs- und Siegeslieder von einem preußischen Grenadier* (anon.), 1758.

———. *Sieben kleine Gedichte nach Anacreons Manier* (anon.), 1764.

———. *Lieder nach dem Anakreon* (anon.), 1766.

———. *Briefe von den Herren Gleim und Jacobi,* 1768.

Gottsched, Johann Christoph. *Grundriß zu einer Vernunfftmäßigen Redekunst,* 1729.

———. *Versuch einer critischen Dichtkunst vor die Deutschen,* 1730.

———. *Erste Gründe der Weltweisheit,* 1730.

---. *Sterbender Cato: Ein Trauerspiel*, 1732.

---. *Beyträge Zur Critischen Historie der Deutschen Sprache, Poesie und Beredsamkeit*, 1732–44.

---. *Ausführliche Redekunst, Nach Anleitung der alten Griechen und Römer, wie auch der neueren Ausländer*, 1736.

---. *Grundlegung einer Deutschen Sprachkunst*, 1748, rev. and enl. 1749, 1752.

---, trans. *Die vernünftigen Tadlerinnen*, 1725–26.

---. ed. *Der Biedermann*, 1728–29.

---, ed. *Neuer Büchersaal*, 1745–50.

---, ed. *Das Neueste aus der anmuthigen Gelehrsamkeit*, 1751–62.

---, ed. *Nöthiger Vorrat zur Geschichte der deutschen Dramatischen Dichtkunst*, 1757–65.

Gottsched, Luise Adelgunde Victorie Kulmus. *Die Pietisterey im Fischbeinrocke* (anon.), 1736. Translated and with an introduction by Thomas Kerth and John R. Russell as Luise Gottsched. *Pietism in Petticoats and Other Comedies*. Columbia, SC: Camden House, 1994.

---, trans. *Der Zuschauer. Aus dem Englischen übersetzt*, 1739–51.

---. *Die ungleiche Heirat*, 1743.

---. *Die Hausfranzösin, oder die Mamsell*, 1744.

---. *Der Witzling*, 1745.

---. *Das Testament*, 1745.

---, trans. *Der engländische Guardian, oder, Aufseher*, 1749.

Hagedorn, *Versuch einiger Gedichte, oder erlesene Proben Poetischer Neben-Stunden*, 1729.

---. *Oden und Lieder*, 1747.

---. *Moralische Gedichte*, 1750.

Haller, Albrecht von. *Versuch schweizerischer Gedichte*, 1732. Translated by Stanley Mason as *The Alps*. Dübendorf: Amstutz de Clivo, 1987

---. *Usong: Eine morgenländische Geschichte*, 1771.

---. *Alfred, König der Angelsachsen*, 1773.

---. *Fabius und Cato: Ein Stück römischer Geschichte*, 1774.

Hamann, Johann Georg. *Sokratische Denkwürdigkeiten*, 1759. Translated by James C. O'Flaherty as *Hamann's Socratic Memorabilia: A Translation and Commentary*. Baltimore: Johns Hopkins UP, 1967.

Heinse, Wilhelm. *Ardinghello und die glückseligen Inseln*, 1787.

Hermes, Johann Timotheus. *Sophiens Reise von Memel nach Sachsen,* 1766–70 (5 vols.).

Hippel, Theodor von. *Lebensläufe nach aufsteigender Linie,* 1778–81.

———. *Über die bürgerliche Verbesserung der Weiber,* 1792. Translated by Timothy F. Sellner as *On Improving the Status of Women.* Detroit: Wayne State UP, 1979

Jacobi, Friedrich Heinrich. *Woldemar,* 1779.

———. *Ueber die Lehre des Spinoza in Briefen an den Herrn Moses Mendelssohn,* 1785

———. *Eduard Allwills Briefsammlung,* 1792.

Jacobi, Georg Johann. *Briefe von den Herren Gleim und Jacobi,* 1768.

———. *Die Winterreise,* 1769.

———. *Die Sommerreise,* 1770.

———, ed. *Iris: Vierteljahresschrift für Frauenzimmer,* 1774–77.

Jung-Stilling, Johann Heinrich. *Henrich Stillings Jugend. Eine wahrhafte Geschichte,* 1777. Translated by Robert Oswald Moon as *Jung Stilling; His Biography.* London: Foulis, 1938.

Kant, Immanuel. *Beobachtungen über das Gefühl des Schönen und Erhabenen,* 1764. Translated by John T. Goldthwait as *Oberservations on the Feeling of the Beautiful and the Sublime.* Berkeley: U of California P, 1960.

———. *Beantwortung der Frage: Was ist Aufklärung?,* 1784. Translated by James Schmidt as *An Answer to the Question: What is Enlightenment?* in *What is Enlightenment? Eighteenth-Century Answers and Twentieth-Century Questions,* ed. Schmidt. Berkeley: U of California P, 1996, 58–65.

———. *Kritik der reinen Vernunft,* 1781, rev. 1787. Translated by Norman Kemp as *Immanuel Kant's Critique of Pure Reason.* London: Macmillan, 1929

———. *Kritik der praktischen Vernunft,* 1788. Translated by Lewis White Beck as *Critique of Practical Reason.* New York: Liberal Arts Press, 1956

———. *Kritik der Urteilskraft,* 1790. Translated by James C. Meredith as *Critique of Judgement* (1911). Rpt. Oxford: Clarendon P, 1957.

———. *Zum ewigen Frieden,* 1795–96. Translated by Ted Humphrey in *Perpetual Peace and Other Essays on Politics, History, and Morals.* Indianapolis: Hackett, 1983.

Karsch, Anna Louisa. *Auserlesene Gedichte,* 1764.

———. *Neue Gedichte,* 1772.

———. *Gedichte von Anna Louisa Karschin geb. Dürbach, nach der Dichterin Tode nebst ihrem Lebenslauf herausgegeben von ihrer Tochter,* 1792.

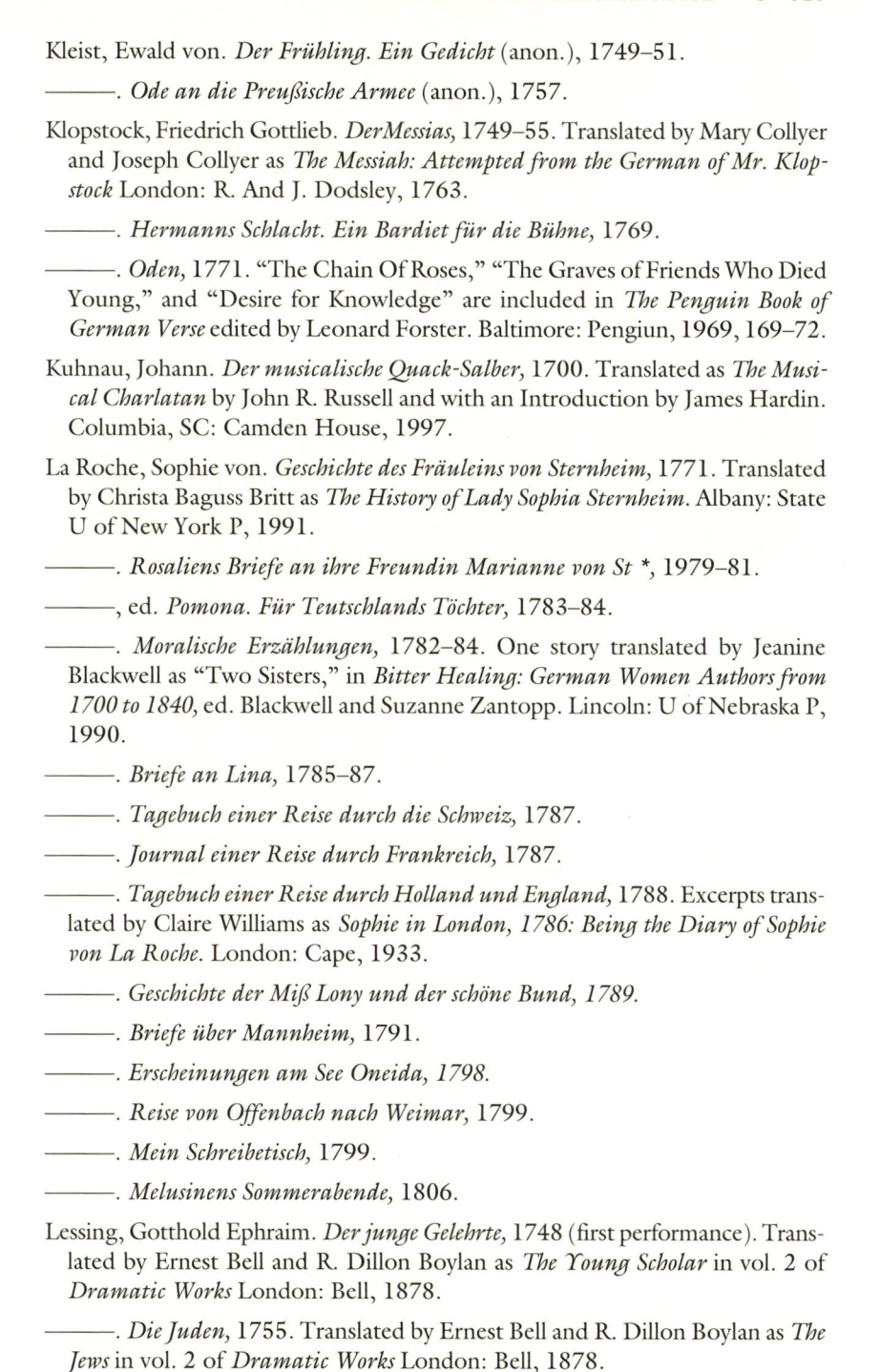

Kleist, Ewald von. *Der Frühling. Ein Gedicht* (anon.), 1749–51.

———. *Ode an die Preußische Armee* (anon.), 1757.

Klopstock, Friedrich Gottlieb. *DerMessias,* 1749–55. Translated by Mary Collyer and Joseph Collyer as *The Messiah: Attempted from the German of Mr. Klopstock* London: R. And J. Dodsley, 1763.

———. *Hermanns Schlacht. Ein Bardiet für die Bühne,* 1769.

———. *Oden,* 1771. "The Chain Of Roses," "The Graves of Friends Who Died Young," and "Desire for Knowledge" are included in *The Penguin Book of German Verse* edited by Leonard Forster. Baltimore: Pengiun, 1969, 169–72.

Kuhnau, Johann. *Der musicalische Quack-Salber,* 1700. Translated as *The Musical Charlatan* by John R. Russell and with an Introduction by James Hardin. Columbia, SC: Camden House, 1997.

La Roche, Sophie von. *Geschichte des Fräuleins von Sternheim,* 1771. Translated by Christa Baguss Britt as *The History of Lady Sophia Sternheim.* Albany: State U of New York P, 1991.

———. *Rosaliens Briefe an ihre Freundin Marianne von St*,* 1979–81.

———, ed. *Pomona. Für Teutschlands Töchter,* 1783–84.

———. *Moralische Erzählungen,* 1782–84. One story translated by Jeanine Blackwell as "Two Sisters," in *Bitter Healing: German Women Authors from 1700 to 1840,* ed. Blackwell and Suzanne Zantopp. Lincoln: U of Nebraska P, 1990.

———. *Briefe an Lina,* 1785–87.

———. *Tagebuch einer Reise durch die Schweiz,* 1787.

———. *Journal einer Reise durch Frankreich,* 1787.

———. *Tagebuch einer Reise durch Holland und England,* 1788. Excerpts translated by Claire Williams as *Sophie in London, 1786: Being the Diary of Sophie von La Roche.* London: Cape, 1933.

———. *Geschichte der Miß Lony und der schöne Bund,* 1789.

———. *Briefe über Mannheim,* 1791.

———. *Erscheinungen am See Oneida,* 1798.

———. *Reise von Offenbach nach Weimar,* 1799.

———. *Mein Schreibetisch,* 1799.

———. *Melusinens Sommerabende,* 1806.

Lessing, Gotthold Ephraim. *Der junge Gelehrte,* 1748 (first performance). Translated by Ernest Bell and R. Dillon Boylan as *The Young Scholar* in vol. 2 of *Dramatic Works* London: Bell, 1878.

———. *Die Juden,* 1755. Translated by Ernest Bell and R. Dillon Boylan as *The Jews* in vol. 2 of *Dramatic Works* London: Bell, 1878.

———. *Miß Sara Sampson*, 1755. Translated by G. Hoern Schlage as *Miss Sara Sampson: A Tragedy in Five Acts.* Stuttgart: Heinz, 1977.

———. *Philotas*, 1759. Translated by Ernest Bell and R. Dillon Boylan as *Philotas* in vol. 1 of Lessing, *Dramatic Works.* London: Bell, 1878.

———. *Laokoon: Oder über die Grenzen der Mahlerey und Poesie*, 1766. Translated by Edward Ellen McCormick as *Laocoon; or, The Limits of Painting and Poetry.* Indianapolis: Bobbs-Merrill and New York: Noonday Press, 1957.

———. *Minna von Barnhelm, oder das Soldatenglück*, 1767. Translated by Kenneth Northcott as *Minna von Barnhelm: A Comedy in Five Acts.* Chicago: U of Chicago P, 1972.

———. *Hamburgische Dramaturgie*, 1767–69. Translated by Helen Zimmern as *Hamburg Dramaturgy.* New York: Dover, 1962.

———. *Emilia Galotti*, 1772. Translated by Edward Dvoretzky as *Emilia Galotti: A Tragedy in Five Acts.* New York: Ungar, 1962.

———. *Ernst und Falk: Gespräche für Freymäurer*, 1778. Translated by A. Cohn as *Masonic Dialogues.* London: Baskerville Press, 1927.

———. *Nathan der Weise*, 1779. Translated by Walter Frank Charles Ade as *Nathan the Wise.* Woodbury, NY: Barron's, 1972.

———. *Die Erziehung des Menschengeschlechts*, 1780. Translated by Frederick William Robertson as *The Education of the Human Race.* New York: Collier, 1909.

———, ed. (with Mendelssohn and Nicolai). *Briefe die neueste Literatur betreffend*, 1759–65.

Lichtenberg, Georg Christoph. *Timorus, das ist Vertheidigung zweyer Isrealiten, die durch die Kräftigkeit der Lavaterischen Beweisgründe und der Göttingischen Mettwürste bewogen den wahren Glauben angenommen haben*, 1773.

———. *Über Physiognomik wider die Physiognomen*, 1778.

———. *Ausführliche Erklärung der Hogarthischen Kupferstiche*, 1794–99. Selections translated by Innes and Gustav Herdan as *The World of Hogarth: Lichtenberg's Commentaries on Hogarth's Engravings.* Boston: Houghton Mifflin, 1966. Excerpts translated and ed. by Franz H. Mautner and Henry Hatfield as *The Lichtenberg Reader: Selected Writings of Georg Christoph Lichtenberg*, Boston: Beacon, 1959.

Marpurg, Friedrich Wilhelm. *Anleitung zur Musik überhaupt, und zur Singkunst besonders*, 1763.

Mattheson, Johann. *Grundlage einer Ehren-Pforte, woran der tüchtigsten Capellmeister, Componisten, Musikgelehrten, Tonkünstler &c. Leben, Werke, Verdienste &c. erscheinen sollen*, 1740

Mendelssohn, Moses. *Ueber die Empfindungen*, 1755.

———. *Phaedon oder Über die Unsterblichkeit der Seele in drey Gesprächen*, 1767. Translated by Charles Cullen as *Phaedon; or, The Death of Socrates*, 1789. Rpt. New York: Arno Press, 1973.

———. *Jerusalem oder Über religiöse Macht und Judentum*, 1783. Translated by Allan Arkush as *Jerusalem: Or on Religious Power and Judaism*. Hanover, NH: UP of New England, 1983.

Miller, Johann Martin. *Siegwart. Eine Klostergeschichte*, 1776–77.

Moritz, Karl Philipp. *Anton Reiser: Ein psychologischer Roman*, 1785–90. Translated by Percy Ewing Matheson as *Anton Reiser. A Psychological Novel*. 1926. Rpt. Westport, CT: Hyperion, 1978. Translated by John R. Russell as *Anton Reiser: A Psychological Novel*. Columbia SC: Camden House, 1996.

———. *Gnothi Sauton: oder, Magazin zur Erfahrungsseelenkunde als ein Lesebuch für Gelehrte und Ungelehrte*, 1783–93.

Mozart, Leopold. *Versuch einer gründlichen Violinschule*, 1756.

Mozart, Wolfgang Amadeus and Emanuel Schikaneder. *Die Zauberflöte*, 1791.

Müller, Johann Gottwerth ("von Itzehoe"). *Gedichte der Freundschaft, der Liebe, und dem Scherze gesungen*, 1771.

Musäus, Karl August. *Volksmährchen der Deutschen*, 1782–86 (5 vols.). Translated anonymously as *Select Popular Tales, from the German of Musäus*. London: Lumley, 1845. Selected translations by Thomas Carlyle in his *German Romance: Specimens of Its Chief Authors*. Vol. 1. Edinburgh: Tait, 1827, 1–215.

Nicolai, Friedrich. *Das Leben und die Meinungen des Herrn Magister Sebaldus Nothanker*, 1773–76.

———. *Eyn feyner kleyner Almanach Vol. Schoenerr echterr liblicher Volkslieder, lustiger Reyen, unndt kleglicherr Mordgeschichte*, 1777–78.

———. *Freuden des jungen Werthers; Leiden und Freuden Werthers des Mannes*, 1775.

———. *Vertraute Briefe von Adelheid B** an ihre Freundinn Julie S***, 1799.

———, ed. *Allgemeine deutsche Bibliothek*, 1765–1796.

Pestalozzi, Johann Heinrich. *Lienhard und Gertrud*, 1781–1787. Translated by Eliza Shepherd as *Leonard and Gertrude: A Book for the Poor*. Geneva: W. Fick 1824.

Pezzl, Johann. *Faustin oder Das philosophische Jahrhundert*, 1783.

Quantz, Johann Joachim. *Versuch einer Anweisung die Flöte traversière zu spielen*, 1752.

Schlegel, Johann Elias. *Hermann*, 1743.

———. *Canut*, 1746.

———. *Die stumme Schönheit*, 1747.

———. *Gedanken zur Aufnahme des dänischen Theaters*, 1747.

Schnabel, Johann Gottfried. *Wunderliche FATA einiger Seefahrer* (*Die Insel Felsenburg*), 1731–43.

Schummel, Johann Gottlieb. *Empfindsame Reisen durch Deutschland*, 1771/72.

Thomasius, Christian. *Monats-Gespräche*, 1690.

———. *Vernunfft-Lehre*, 1691.

———. *Sitten-Lehre*, 1692.

———. *Das Recht Evangelischer Fürsten in theologischen Streitigkeiten*, 1697

———. *Theses de Crimine Magiae*, 1701.

———. *De Tortura ex foris Christanorum proscribenda*, 1705.

Teuber, Anna Barbara. *Vermischte Gedichte*, 1735.

Thümmel, Moritz August von. *Reise in die mittäglichen Provinzen von Frankreich im Jahr 1785 bis 1786*, 1791–1805 (10 vols.).

Unger, Friederike Helene. *Julchen Grünthal. Eine Pensionsgeschichte*, 1784.

———. *Gräfin Pauline*, 1800.

———. *Albert und Albertine*, 1804.

———. *Bekenntnisse einer schönen Seele. Von ihr selbst geschrieben*, 1806.

Uz, Johann Peter. *Lyrische Gedichte*, 1749, 1756, 1767.

Weiße, Christian Felix. *Die Matrone von Ephesus*, 1748.

———, ed. *Bibliothek der schönen Wissenschaften und der freyen Künste*, 1759–89.

———, ed. *Der Kinderfreund*, 1775–82.

Wezel, Karl Johann. *Lebensgeschichte Tobias Knauts des Weisen*, 1773–76.

———. *Belphegor*, 1776.

———. *Hermann und Ulrike*, 1780.

———. *Wilhelmine Arend, oder, Die Gefahren der Empfindsamkeit*, 1782.

Wieland, Christoph Martin. *Lady Johanna Gray, oder Der Triumph der Religion: Ein Trauerspiel*, 1758.

———. *Der Sieg der Natur über die Schwärmerey oder die Abentheuer des Don Sylvio von Rosalva*, 1764.

———. *Comische Erzählungen*, 1765.

———. *Die Geschichte des Agathon*, 1766–67. Translated by Samuel Richardson as *The History of Agathon*. London: Cadell, 1773.

———. *Musarion, oder die Philosophie der Grazien*, 1768.

———. *Der goldene Spiegel, oder die Könige von Scheschian,* 1772.

———. *Die Abderiten, eine sehr wahrscheinliche Geschichte,* 1774.

———. *Oberon, eine Gedicht in vierzehn Gesängen,* 1780.

———. *Dschinnistan oder Auserlesene Feen- und Geister-Mährchen,* 1786–89.

———, ed. *Der teutsche Merkur,* 1773–1796.

Winckelmann, Johann Joachim. *Gedancken über die Nachahmung der griechischen Wercke in der Mahlerey und Bildhauerkunst,* 1755. Translated by Henry Fusseli as *Reflections on the Painting and Sculpture of the Greeks.* London: Millar, 1765.

Wobeser, Wilhelmine Caroline von [pseud.]. *Elisa, oder das Weib wie es seyn sollte,* 1795.

Zachariae, Friedrich Just. *Der Renommiste,* 1744.

Zäunemann, Sidonia Hedwig. *Poetische Rosen in Knospen,* 1738.

———. *Die von denen Faunen gepeitschte Laster,* 1739.

Ziegler, Christiane Mariane von. *Versuch in gebundener Schreib-Art,* 1728–29

———. *Moralische und vermischte Send-Schreiben,* 1731.

Zinzendorf, Graf Ludwig von. *Teutsche Gedichte,* 1735.

Select Secondary Literature

(This bibliography presents only a selection of the scholarly works cited in the individual essays. Beyond these, preference has been given to book publications in English, standard works, and recent scholarship in German.)

General, Philosophical, Cultural, and Historical Studies

Bachleitner, Norbert, Franz M. Eybl, and Ernst Fischer. *Geschichte des österreichischen Buchhandels.* Wiesbaden: Harrassowitz, 2000.

Berlin, Isaiah. *Three Critics of the Enlightenment: Vico, Hamann, Herder.* Ed. Thomas Hardy. Princeton: Princeton UP, 1997.

Berghahn, Klaus L. *Grenzen der Toleranz: Juden und Christen im Zeitalter der Aufklärung.* Cologne: Böhlau, 2000.

Bovenschen, Silvia. *Die imaginierte Weiblichkeit: Exemplarische Untersuchungen zu kulturgeschichtlichen und literarischen Präsentationsformen des Weiblichen.* Frankfurt a. M.: Suhrkamp, 1979.

Braunbehrens, Volkmar. *Mozart in Vienna, 1781–1791.* New York: Grove, 1990.

Burrows, Donald. *Handel.* The Master Musicians. Oxford: Oxford UP, 1994.

Bruford, Walter. *Germany in the Eighteenth Century: The Social Background of the Literary Revival*. Cambridge: Cambridge UP, 1965.

Brunner, Otto, Werner Conze, and Reinhart Koselleck, eds. *Geschichtliche Grundbegriffe: Historisches Lexikon zur politisch-sozialen Sprache in Deutschland*. 8 vols. Stuttgart: Klett-Cotta, 1972–97.

Cassirer, Ernst. *The Philosophy of Enlightenment*, trans. Fritz C. A. Koelln and James Pettegrove. Princeton: Princeton UP, 1951.

Dülmen, Richard van. *The Society of the Enlightenment: The Rise and Fall of the Middle Class and Enlightenment Culture in Germany*, trans. Anthony Williams. New York: St. Martin's, 1992.

Eybl, Franz M., ed. *Strukturwandel kultureller Praxis: Beiträge zu einer kulturwissenschaftlichen Sicht des theresianischen Zeitalters*. Vienna: Wiener Universitäts-Verlag, 2002.

Flaherty, Gloria. *Opera in the Development of German Critical Thought*. Princeton: Princeton UP, 1978.

Gawthrop, Richard L. *Pietism and the Making of Eighteenth-Century Prussia*. Cambridge: Cambridge UP, 1993.

Gay, Peter. *The Enlightenment: An Interpretation*. Vol. 1: *The Rise of Modern Paganism*. Vol. 2: *The Science of Freedom*. New York: Knopf, 1966, 1969.

Habermas, Jürgen. *Strukturwandel der Öffentlichkeit: Untersuchungen zu einer Kategorie der bürgerlichen Gesellschaft*. Neuwied: Luchterhand, 1962. Translated by Thomas Burger with the assistance of Frederick Lawrence as *The Structural Transformation of the Public Sphere: An Inquiry into a Category of Bourgeois Society*. Cambridge, MA: MIT P, 1989.

Hardin, James, and Christoph E. Schweitzer, eds. *German Writers in the Age of Goethe: Sturm und Drang to Classicism*. Dictionary of Literary Biography, vol. 89. Detroit: Gale, 1990.

Helm, Ernst Eugene. *Music at the Court of Frederick the Great*. Norman, OK: U of Oklahoma P, 1960.

Hess, Jonathan M. *Germans, Jews and the Claims of Modernity*. New Haven: Yale UP, 2002.

———. *Reconstituting the Body Politic: Enlightenment, Public Culture and the Invention of Aesthetic Autonomy* Detroit: Wayne State UP, 1999

Holub, Robert, and Daniel Wilson, eds. *Impure Reason: Dialectic of Enlightenment in Germany*. Detroit: Wayne State UP, 1993.

Honegger, Claudia. *Die Ordnung der Geschlechter: Die Wissenschaften vom Mensch und das Weib 1750–1850*. Frankfurt a. M.: Campus, 1991.

Howard, Patricia. *Gluck and the Birth of Modern Opera*. London: Barrie & Rockliff 1963.

Im Hof, Ulrich. *Das gesellige Jahrhundert: Gesellschaft und Gesellschaften im Zeitalter der Aufklärung.* Munich: Beck, 1982.

———. *Die Entstehung einer politischen Öffentlichkeit in der Schweiz: Struktur und Tätigkeit der Helvetischen Gesellschaft.* Frauenfeld & Stuttgart: Huber, 1983

Kiesel, Helmuth and Paul Münch. *Gesellschaft und Literatur im 18. Jahrhundert. Voraussetzungen und Entstehung des literarischen Markts in Deutschland.* Munich: Beck, 1977.

Klueting, Harm, ed. *Katholische Aufklärung — Aufklärung im katholischen Deutschland.* Studien zum achtzehnten Jahrhundert, vol. 15. Hamburg: Meiner, 1993.

Kondylis, Panjotis. *Die Aufklärung im Rahmen des neuzeitlichen Rationalismus.* Munich: dtv, 1986.

Koselleck, Reinhart. *Kritik und Krise* (1959), *Critique and Crisis: Enlightenment and the Pathogenesis of Modern Society.* Cambridge, MA: MIT P, 1988

Martens, Wolfgang, ed. *Leipzig: Aufklärung und Bürgerlichkeit.* Heidelberg: Lambert Schneider, 1990.

Maurer, Michael. *Aufklärung und Anglophilie in Deutschland.* Veröffentlichungen des Deutschen Historischen Instituts in London, vol. 19. Göttingen: Vandenhoeck & Ruprecht, 1987.

Plachta, Bodo. *Damnatur – Toleratur – Admittitur: Studien und Dokumente zur literarischen Zensur im 18. Jahrhundert.* Studien und Texte zur Sozialgeschichte der Literatur, vol. 43, Tübingen: Niemeyer, 1994.

Ratner, Leonard G. *Classic Music: Expression, Form and Style.* London: Schirmer, 1980.

Redekop, Benjamin. *Enlightenment and Community: Lessing, Abbt, Herder, and the Quest for a German Public.* Montreal: McGill-Queen's UP, 2000.

Saine, Thomas P. *The Problem of Being Modern, or, The German Pursuit of Enlightenment from Leibniz to the French Revolution.* Detroit: Wayne State UP, 1997.

Schmidt, James, ed. *What is Enlightenment? Eighteenth-Century Answers and Twentieth-Century Questions.* Berkeley: U of California P, 1996.

Schmidt, Jochen, ed. *Aufklärung und Gegenaufklärung in der europäischen Literatur, Philosophie und Politik von der Antike bis zur Gegenwart.* Darmstadt: Wissenschaftliche Buchgesellschaft, 1989.

Schmidt-Biggemann, Wilhelm. *Theodizee und Tatsachen: Das philosophische Profil der deutschen Aufklärung.* Frankfurt a. M.: Suhrkamp, 1988.

Schleuning, Peter. *Der Bürger erhebt sich: Geschichte der deutschen Musik im 18. Jahrhundert.* 2nd revised ed. Stuttgart: Metzler, 2000.

Schneiders, Werner, ed. *Lexikon der Aufklärung: Deutschland und Europa.* Munich: Beck, 1995

Schröder, Dorothea. *Zeitgeschichte auf der Opernbühne: Barockes Musiktheater in Hamburg im Dienst von Politik und Diplomatie (1690–1745).* Göttingen: Vandenhoeck & Ruprecht, 1998.

Smeed, J. W. *German Song and its Poetry, 1740–1900.* London: Croom Helm, 1987.

Vierhaus, Rudolf. *Germany in the Age of Absolutism,* trans. by Jonathan B. Knudsen. Cambridge: Cambridge UP, 1988.

Wiora, Walter. *Das deutsche Lied: Zur Geschichte und Ästhetik einer musikalischen Gattung.* Wolfenbüttel: Möseler, 1971.

Literary Genres, Schools, Periods, Music, and the Visual Arts

Alt, Peter-André. *Aufklärung.* Stuttgart: Metzler 1996.

Bauer, Werner M. *Fiktion und Polemik. Studien zum Roman der österreichischen Aufklärung 1781–1795.* Schriftenreihe der Österreichischen Gesellschaft zur Erforschung des 18. Jahrhunderts, vol. 6. 2nd ed. Vienna: Böhlau, 1995.

Blackall, Eric A. *The Emergence of German as a Literary Language 1700–1775.* 2nd edition. Ithaca and London: Cornell UP, 1978.

Bodi, Leslie. *Tauwetter in Wien: Zur Prosa der österreichischen Aufklärung.* 2nd expanded ed. Schriftenreihe der Österreichischen Gesellschaft zur Erforschung des 18. Jahrhunderts, vol. 6. Vienna: Böhlau, 1995.

Boor, Helmut de, and Richard Newald, eds. *Geschichte der deutschen Literatur.* Vol. 5: Richard Newald, *Vom Späthumanismus zur Empfindsamkeit. 1570–1750.* 6th edition. Munich: Beck, 1967. Vol. 6,1: Jorgensen, Sven-Aage, Bohnen, Klaus and Per Ohrgaard. *Aufklärung, Sturm und Drang, frühe Klassik. 1740–89.* Munich: Beck, 1990.

Böckmann, Paul. "Das Formprinzip des Witzes in der Frühzeit der deutschen Aufklärung" and "Die Entwicklung der literarischen Ausdruckshaltung durch Klopstock und den Sturm und Drang," in Böckmann, *Formgeschichte der deutschen Dichtung, vol. 1: Von der Sinnbildsprache zur Ausdruckssprache. Der Wandel der literarischen Formensprache vom Mittelalter zur Neuzeit.* Hamburg: Hoffmann und Campe, 1949, 471–552 and 553–694.

Brandes, Helga. *Die "Gesellschaft der Maler" und ihr literarischer Beitrag zur Aufklärung: Eine Untersuchung zur Publizistik des 18. Jahrhunderts.* Studien zur Publizistik, vol. 21. Bremen: Schünemann, 1974.

Browning, Robert M. *German Poetry in the Age of Enlightenment from Brockes to Klopstock.* The Penn State Series in German Literature. University Park: Pennsylvania State UP, 1978.

Colvin, Sarah. *The Rhetorical Feminine: Gender and Orient on the German Stage, 1647–1742*. Oxford: Clarendon, 1999

Dawson, Ruth P. *The Contested Quill: Literature by Women in Germany, 1770–1800*. Newark, NJ: U of Delaware P, 2002.

Engel, Manfred. *Der Roman der Goethezeit*. Germanistische Abhandlungen, vol. 71. Stuttgart: Metzler, 1993.

Friedrichsmeyer, Sara, and Barbara Becker-Cantarino, eds. *The Enlightenment and Its Legacy: Studies in German Literature in Honor of Helga Slessarev*. Modern German Studies, vol. 17. Bonn: Bouvier, 1991.

Gallas, Helga, and Magdalene Heuser, eds. *Untersuchungen zum Roman von Frauen um 1800*. Tübingen: Niemeyer, 1990.

Goodman, Katherine, and Edith Waldstein, eds. *In the Shadow of Olympus: German Women Writers Around 1800*. Albany, NY: State U of New York P, 1992.

Goepfert, Herbert G., ed. *"Unmoralisch an sich..." Zensur im 18. und 19. Jahrhundert*. Wiesbaden: Harrassowitz, 1988.

Grimminger, Rolf, ed. *Deutsche Aufklärung bis zur Französischen Revolution*. Vol. 3.1 of *Hansers Sozialgeschichte der deutschen Literatur vom 16. Jahrhundert bis zur Gegenwart*. Munich: Hanser, 1984.

Greis, Jutta. *Drama Liebe: Zur Entwicklungsgeschichte der modernen Liebe im Drama des 18. Jahrhunderts*. Stuttgart: Metzler: 1991.

Guthke, Karl S. *Literarisches Leben im achtzehnten Jahrhundert in Deutschland und in der Schweiz*. Bern: Francke, 1975.

Haider-Pregler, Hilde. *Des sittlichen Bürgers Abendschule. Bildungsanspruch und Bildungsauftrag des Beruftheaters im 18. Jahrhundert*. Vienna: Jugend und Volk, 1980.

Hart, Gail. *Tragedy in Paradise: Family and Gender Politics in German Bourgeois Tragedy 1750–1850*. Columbia, SC: Camden House, 1996.

Heinz, Jutta. *Wissen vom Menschen und Erzählen vom Einzelfall. Untersuchungen zum anthropologischen Roman der Spätaufklärung*. Berlin: de Gruyter, 1996.

Heitner, Robert R. *German Tragedy in the Age of Enlightenment: A Study in the Development of Original Tragedies 1724–1768*. Berkeley: U of California P, 1963.

Herrmann, Hans Peter. *Nachahmung und Einbildungskraft: Zur Entwicklung der deutschen Poetik von 1670–1740*. Bad Homburg: Gehlen, 1970.

Jäger, Georg. *Empfindsamkeit und Roman*. Stuttgart: Kohlhammer, 1969.

Jirku, Brigitte. *"Wollen Sie mit Nichts...Ihre Zeit versplittern?" Ich-Erzählerin und Erzählstruktur in von Frauen verfaßten Romanen des 18. Jahrhunderts*. Fankfurt a. M.: Lang, 1994.

Kaiser, Gerhard. *Pietismus und Patriotismus im literarischen Deutschland: Ein Beitrag zum Problem der Säkularisation.* 2nd ed. Frankfurt a. M.: Athenäum, 1973.

Kann, Robert A. *Kanzel und Katheder: Studien zur österreichischen Geistesgeschichte vom Spätbarock zur Frühromantik* (1962). *A Study in Austrian Intellectual History: From Late Baroque to Romanticism.* New York: Octagon Books, 1973.

Kemper, Hans-Georg. *Deutsche Lyrik der frühen Neuzeit,* vol. 5/1: *Aufklärung und Pietismus.* Tübingen: Niemeyer, 1991.

———. *Deutsche Lyrik der frühen Neuzeit,* vol. 5/2: *Frühaufklärung.* Tübingen: Niemeyer, 1991.

———. *Deutsche Lyrik der frühen Neuzeit,* vol. 6/1: *Empfindsamkeit.* Tübingen: Niemeyer, 1997.

Knudsen, Jonathan B. *Justus Möser and the German Enlightenment.* Cambridge: Cambridge UP, 1986.

Lange, Siegrid. *Spiegelgeschichten: Geschlechter und Poetiken in der Frauenliteratur um 1800.* Frankfurt a. M.: U. Helmer Verlag, 1995.

Martens, Wolfgang. *Die Botschaft der Tugend: Die Aufklärung im Spiegel der deutschen Moralischen Wochenschriften.* Stuttgart: Metzler, 1968.

Mauser, Wolfram. *Konzepte aufgeklärter Lebensführung. Literarische Kultur im frühmodernen Deutschland.* Würzburg: Königshausen & Neumann, 2000.

Mauser, Wolfram, and Barbara Becker-Cantarino, eds. *Frauenfreundschaft — Männerfreundschaft: Literarische Diskurse im 18. Jahrhundert.* Tübingen: Niemeyer, 1991.

McCarthy, John A. *Crossing Boundaries: A Theory and History of Essay Writing in German 1680–1815.* Philadelphia: U of Pennsylvania P, 1989.

Meinhold, Günter. *Zauberflöte und Zauberflöten-Rezeption: Studien zu Emanuel Schikaneders Libretto "Die Zauberflöte" und seiner literarischen Rezeption.* Hamburger Beiträge zur Germanistik, vol. 34. Frankfurt a. M.: Lang, 2001.

Meise, Helga. *Die Unschuld und die Schrift: Deutsche Frauenromane im achtzehnten Jahrhundert.* Berlin: Guttandin & Hoppe, 1983.

Mücke, Dorothea E. von. *Virtue and the Veil of Illusion: Generic Innovation and the Pedagogical Project in Eighteenth-Century Literature.* Stanford: Stanford UP, 1991.

Osinski, Jutta. *Über Vernunft und Wahnsinn: Studien zur literarischen Aufklärung in der Gegenwart und im 18. Jahrhundert.* Bonn: Bouvier, 1983.

Pütz, Peter. *Die deutsche Aufklärung.* Darmstadt: Wissenschaftliche Buchgesellschaft, 1978.

———, ed. *Erforschung der deutschen Aufklärung*. Neue Wissenschaftliche Bibliothek Literaturwissenschaft, vol. 94. Königstein/Ts.: Verlagsgruppe Athenäum, 1980.

Radandt, Friedhelm. *From Baroque to Storm and Stress*. New York: Barnes & Noble 1977.

Rigby, Catherine. *Transgressions of the Feminine: Tragedy, Enlightenment and the Figure of Woman in German Classic Drama*. Heidelberg: Winter, 1996.

Sauder, Gerhard. *Empfindsamkeit*. Vol. 1: *Voraussetzungen und Elemente*. Stuttgart: Metzler, 1974; vol. 3: *Quellen und Dokumente*. Stuttgart: Metzler, 1980.

Schieth, Lydia. *Die Entwicklung des deutschen Frauenromans im ausgehenden 18. Jahrhundert: Ein Beitrag zur Gattungsgeschichte*. Helicon, vol. 5. Frankfurt: Lang 1987.

Schmid, Sigrun. *Der "selbstverschuldeten Unmündigkeit" entkommen: Perspektiven bürgerlicher Frauenliteratur*. Würzburg: Königshausen & Neumann, 1999.

Schroeder, David P. *Mozart in Revolt: Strategies of Resistance, Mischief, and Deception*. New Haven: Yale UP, 1999.

Scott-Prelorentzos, Alison. *The Servant in German Enlightenment Comedy*. Edmonton: U of Alberta P, 1982.

Segebrecht, Wulf. *Das Gelegenheitsgedicht: Ein Beitrag zur Geschichte und Poetik der deutschen Lyrik*. Stuttgart: Metzler, 1977.

Thomke, Hellmut, Martin Bircher, and Wolfgang Pross, eds. *Helvetien und Deutschland: Kulturelle Beziehungen zwischen der Schweiz und Deutschland in der Zeit von 1770–1830*. Amsterdamer Publikationen zur Sprache und Literatur, vol. 109. Amsterdam: Rodopi, 1994.

Wagenknecht, Christian. *Deutsche Metrik: Eine historische Einführung*. Munich: C. H. Beck, 1981.

Wilke, Jürgen. *Literarische Zeitschriften des 18. Jahrhunderts (1688–1789)*. Sammlung Metzler, vol. 174–75. Stuttgart: Metzler, 1978.

Zeman, Herbert. *Die deutsche anakreontische Dichtung: Ein Versuch zur Erfassung ihrer ästhetischen und literarhistorischen Erscheinungsformen im 18. Jahrhundert*. Stuttgart: Metzler, 1972.

———, ed. *Die österreichische Literatur: Ihr Profil an der Wende vom 18. zum 19. Jahrhundert (1750–1830)*. Die österreichische Literatur. Eine Dokumentation ihrer literarhistorischen Entwicklung. Graz: Akademische Verlagsanstalt, 1979, 1: 289–305.

Authors and Works

Blumauer, Aloys

Becker-Cantarino, Bärbel. *Aloys Blumauer and the Literature of Austrian Enlightenment*. Bern: Lang, 1973.

Bodmer, Johann Jakob

Bender, Wolfgang. *J. J. Bodmer und J. J. Breitinger*. Sammlung Metzler, vol. 113. Stuttgart: Metzler, 1983.

Claudius, Matthias

Fechner, Jörg Ulrich, ed. *Matthias Claudius (1740–1815). Leben, Zeit, Werk*. Tübingen: Niemeyer, 1996.

Kranefuss, Annele. *Die Gedichte des Wandsbeker Boten*. Göttingen: Vandenhoeck & Ruprecht, 1983.

Rowland, Robert. *Matthias Claudius*. Boston: Twayne, 1983.

Gellert, Christian Fürchtegott

Engbers, Jan. *Der "moral sense" Gellert, Lessing und Wieland: Zur Rezeption von Shaftesbury and Hutcheson in Deutschland*. Heidelberg: Winter, 2001.

Meyer-Krentler, Eckhardt. *Der andere Roman: Gellerts Schwedische Gräfin*. Göppingen: Kümmerle, 1974.

Gessner, Salomon

Hibberd, John L. *Salomon Gessner: His Creative Achievement and Influence*. Cambridge: Cambridge UP, 1976.

Gleim, Johann Wilhelm Ludewig

Riedel, Volker, ed. *Der Aufklärer Gleim heute*. Stendal: Winckelmann-Gesellschaft, 1987.

Gottsched, Johann Christoph

Ball, Gabriele. *Moralische Küsse. Gottsched als Zeitschriftenherausgeber und literarischer Vermittler*. Göttingen: Wallstein, 2000.

Lehmann, Ulf. *Der Gottschedkreis und Rußland: Deutsch-russische Literaturbeziehungen im Zeitalter der Aufklärung*. Berlin: Akademie-Verlag, 1966.

Lerchner, Gotthard, ed. *Johann Christoph Gottsched zum 300. Geburtstag: Gelehrter, Theaterreformer und Schriftsteller der Aufklärung*. Leipzig: Sächsische Akademie der Wissenschaften, 2000.

Mitchell, Philipp Marshall. *Johann Christoph Gottsched (1700–1766): Harbinger of German Classicism*. Columbia, SC: Camden House, 1995.

Niefanger, Susanne. *Schreibstrategien in Moralischen Wochenschriften: Formalistische, pragmatische und rhetorische Untersuchungen am Beispiel von Gottscheds "Vernünftigen Tadlerinnen."* Tübingen: Niemeyer, 1997.

Rieck, Werner. *Johann Christoph Gottsched: Eine kritische Würdigung seines Werkes*. Berlin: Akademie-Verlag, 1972.

Gottsched, Luise Adelgunde Victorie Kulmus

Kord, Susanne. *Little Detours: The Letters and Plays of Luise Gottsched (1713–1762)*. Rochester, NY: Camden House, 2000.

Haller, Albrecht von

Guthke, Karl S. *Haller und die Literatur*. Göttingen: Vandenhoeck & Ruprecht, 1962

Siegrist, Christoph. *Albrecht von Haller*. Sammlung Metzler, vol. 57. Stuttgart: Metzler, 1967.

Wiswall, Dorothy R. *A Comparison of Selected Poetic and Scientific Works by Albrecht von Haller*. Bern: Lang, 1981.

Hamann, Johann Georg.

German, Terence J. *Hamann on Language and Religion*. Oxford: Oxford UP, 1981.

O'Flaherty, James C. *Johann Georg Hamann*. Boston: Hall, 1979.

Jung-Stilling, Johann Heinrich

Willert, Albrecht. *Religiöse Existenz und literarische Produktion: Jung-Stillings Autobiographie und seine frühen Romane*. Frankfurt a. M.: Lang, 1982.

Klopstock, Friedrich Gottlob

Hebeisen, Dagmar. *Die Cidli-Oden: Zu Klopstocks Lyrik um 1750*. Giessener Arbeiten zur neueren deutschen Literatur und Literaturwissenschaft, vol. 18. Frankfurt a. M.: Lang, 1998.

Hilliard, Kevin. *Philosophy, Letters, and the Fine Arts in Klopstock's Thought*. London: Institute of Germanic Studies, London, 1987.

Kaiser, Gerhard. *Klopstock: Religion und Dichtung*. Gütersloh: Gerd Mohn, 1963.

Kohl, Katrin M. *Friedrich Gottlieb Klopstock*. Sammlung Metzler, vol. 325. Stuttgart: Metzler, 2000.

———. *Rhetoric, the Bible, and the Origins of Free Verse: The Early Hymns of Friedrich Gottlob Klopstock*. Berlin: de Gruyter, 1990.

Pape, Helmut. *Klopstock: Die "Sprache des Herzens" neu entdeckt: Die Befreiung des Lesers aus seiner emotionalen Unmündigkeit*. Frankfurt a. M.: Lang, 1998.

La Roche, Sophie von

Langner, Margrit. *Sophie von La Roche: Die empfindsame Realistin*. Heidelberg: Winter, 1995.

Loster-Schneider, Gudrun. *Sophie La Roche: Paradoxien weiblichen Schreibens*. Tübingen: Narr, 1995

Nenon Monika. *Autorschaft und Frauenbildung: Das Beispiel Sophie von La Roche*. Epistemata. Reihe Literaturwissenschaft, vol. 31. Würzburg: Königshausen & Neumann, 1988.

Wiede-Behrend, Ingrid. *Lehrerin des Schönen, Wahren, Guten: Literatur und Frauenbildung im ausgehenden 18. Jahrhundert am Beispiel von Sophie von La Roche*. Frankfurt a. M.: Lang, 1987

Lessing, Gotthold Ephraim

Albrecht, Wolfgang. *Gotthold Ephraim Lessing*. Sammlung Metzler, vol. 297. Stuttgart: Metzler, 1995.

Barner, Wilfried et al., eds. *Lessing: Epoche — Werk — Wirkung*. 5th ed. Munich: Beck, 1987.

Fick, Monika. *Lessing-Handbuch: Leben — Werk — Wirkung*. Stuttgart: Metzler, 2000.

Gustafson, Susan E. *Absent Mothers and Orphaned Fathers: Narcissism and Abjection in Lessing's Aesthetic and Dramatic ProductionDramas*. Detroit: Wayne State UP, 1996.

Lamport, F. J. *Lessing and the Drama*. Oxford: Clarendon, 1981.

Wellbery, David E. *Lessing's Laokoon: Semiotics and Aesthetics in the Age of Reason*. New York: Cambridge, 1984.

Lichtenberg, Georg Christoph

Brinitzer, Carl. *A Reasonable Rebel: Georg Christoph Lichtenberg*. London: Allen & Unwin, 1960.

Stern, Peter Joseph. *Lichtenberg: A Doctrine of Scattered Occasions. Reconstructed from His Aphorisms and Reflections*. Bloomington: Indiana UP, 1959.

Mendelssohn, Moses

Altmann, Alexander. *Moses Mendelssohn: A Biographical Study*. U of Alabama P, 1973.

Arkush, Allan. *Moses Mendelssohn and the Enlightenment*. Albany, NY: State U of New York P, 1994.

Sorkin, David Jan. *Moses Mendelssohn and the Religious Enlightenment*. Berkeley: U of California P, 1996.

Segreff, Klaus Werner. *Moses Mendelssohn und die Aufklärungsästhetik im 18. Jahrhundert*. Bonn: Bouvier, 1984.

Moritz, Karl Philipp

Boulby, Mark. *Karl Philipp Moritz: At the Fringe of Genius*. Toronto: U of Toronto P, 1979.

Minder, Robert. *Glaube, Skepsis und Rationalismus*. Frankfurt a. M.: Suhrkamp, 1974.

Saine, Thomas P. *Die ästhetische Theodizee; Karl Philipp Moritz und die Philosophie des 18. Jahrhunderts.* Munich: Fink, 1971.

Kestenholz, Claudia. *Die Sicht der Dinge: Metaphorische Visualität und Subjektivitätswandel im Werk von Karl Philipp Moritz.* Munich: Fink, 1987.

Müller, Lothar. *Die kranke Seele und das Licht der Erkenntnis: Karl Philipp Moritz' Anton Reiser.* Frankfurt a. M.: Athenäum, 1987.

Nicolai, Friedrich

Möller Horst. *Aufklärung in Preußen: Der Verleger, Publizist und Geschichtsschreiber Friedrich Nicolai.* Berlin: Colloquium, 1974.

Parthey, Gustav C. F. *Die Mitarbeiter an Friedrich Nicolai's Allgemeiner Deutscher Bibliothek (1842).* Rpt. Hildesheim: Olms, 1973

Selwyn, Pamela. *Everyday Life in the German Book Trade: Friedrich Nicolai as Bookseller and Publisher in the Age of Enlightenment, 1750–1810.* University Park: Pennsylvania State UP, 2000.

Schneider, Ute. *Friedrich Nicolais Allgemeine Deutsche Bibliothek als Integrationsmedium der Gelehrtenrepublik.* Wiesbaden: 1995.

Schnabel, Johann Gottfried

Vosskamp, Wilhelm. "Theorie und Praxis der literarischen Fiktion in Johann Gottfried Schnabels Roman *Die Insel Felsenburg.*" *Germanisch-Romanische Monatsschrift* 28 (1968): 131–52.

Thümmel, Moritz August von

Allerdissen, Rolf. *Die Reise als Flucht: Zu Schnabels "Insel Felsenburg" und Thümmels "Reise in die mittäglichen Provinzen von Frankreich."* Bern: Herbert Lang, 1975.

Sauder, Gerhard. *Der reisende Epikureer: Studien zu August von Thümmels Roman "Reise in die mittäglichen Provinzen von Frankreich."* Heidelberg: Winter, 1968.

Unger, Friederike Helene

Giesler, Birte. *Literatursprünge: Das erzählerische Werk von Friederike Helene Unger.* Göttingen: Wallstein, 2003.

Wezel, Johann Carl

Klingenberg, Anneliese, ed. *Johann Carl Wezel und die Aufklärung.* Weimar: Kulturbund, 1989.

Kremer, Detlef. *Wezel. Über die Nachtseite der Aufklärung: Skeptische Lebensphilosophie zwischen Spätaufklärung und Frühromantik.* Munich: Fink, 1984.

McNight, Philip S. *The Novels of Karl Wezel: Satire, Realism, and Social Criticism in Late 18th Century Literature.* Bern: Lang, 1981.

Wieland, Christoph Martin

Jacobs, Jürgen. *Wielands Romane*. Bern: Francke, 1969.

McCarthy, John. *Christoph Martin Wieland*. Boston: Twayne, 1979.

Oettinger, Klaus. *Phantasie und Erfahrung: Studien zur Erzählpoetik Christoph Martin Wielands*. Munich: Fink, 1970.

Schaefer, Klaus. *Christoph Martin Wieland*. Stuttgart: Metzler, 1996.

Wilson, Dan. *The Narrative Strategy of Wieland's "Don Sylvio von Rosalva."* Bern: Lang, 1981.

Contributors

BARBARA BECKER-CANTARINO is Research Professor in German at the Ohio State University. Her publications focus on German literature and culture of the seventeenth and eighteenth century, Romanticism, gender studies, and women writers. Among her book publications are *Der lange Weg zur Mündigkeit: Frau und Literatur in Deutschland 1500–1750, Schriftstellerinnen der Romantik,* and *Pietism and Autobiography* (forthcoming).

HELGA BRANDES is Professor of Modern German Literature at the University of Oldenburg. She has published on reading and readership, literature and the public sphere, journals and moral weeklies, and women writers. Her books include *Die Gesellschaft der Maler und ihr literarischer Beitrag zur Aufklärung* and *Die Zeitschriften des Jungen Deutschland.*

SARAH COLVIN is Eudo C. Mason Professor at the University of Edinburgh, UK. She is the author of books and articles on early German-language opera and drama, and on drama by women writers. Her current project looks at the language used by Ulrike Marie Meinhof and the terrorist organization Red Army Faction in Germany in the 1970s.

FRANZ M. EYBL is Professor of Modern German Literature at the University of Vienna. He has published widely on Austrian literature, cultural studies, and literary theory. His publications include *Abraham a Santa Clara: Vom Prediger zum Schriftsteller* and *Geschichte des österreichischen Buchhandels.*

KATHERINE R. GOODMAN is Professor of German Studies at Brown University. She is the author of *Dis/Closures: Women's Autobiography in Germany 1790–1914* and *Amazons and Apprentices: Women and the German Parnassus in the Early Enlightenment.* She has edited a number of books on German women writers.

KAI HAMMERMEISTER is Associate Professor of German at the Ohio State University. He focuses on philosophy and literature, aesthetics, hermeneutics, German idealism, and intellectual history. His books include *Hans-Georg Gadamer* and *The German Aesthetic Tradition.*

KEVIN HILLIARD is Fellow and Tutor in German at St. Peter's College, Oxford. He works mainly on the eighteenth century and has published on Klopstock, Günderrode, and Goethe.

ROBERT C. HOLUB is Professor of German and Dean of the Undergraduate Division in the College of Letters and Science at the University of California at Berkeley. He has written extensively on topics in German literature and intellectual history from the eighteenth to the twentieth century, in particular on Heinrich Heine, Friedrich Nietzsche, and Jürgen Habermas.

FRANCIS LAMPORT has recently retired as a lecturer in German at Oxford University and a Fellow of Worcester College. His publications include *Lessing and the Drama, German Classical Drama: Theatre, Humanity and Nation,* and translations and articles on German literature and drama of the classical period (Lessing, Goethe, Schiller, Kleist etc.).

ANNA RICHARDS is Lecturer in German at Birkbeck College, University of London. She has published articles on German women writers and a book, *The Wasting Heroine in German Fiction by Women 1770–1914.* She is currently researching the theme of mourning in late eighteenth-century German culture.

W. DANIEL WILSON is Professor of German at the University of California, Berkeley. He has written on Wieland, Lessing, Lenz, and other writers of the late eighteenth century, but in recent years has worked particularly on the political role played by Goethe in Weimar society. Publications include *Geheimräte gegen Geheimbünde: Ein unbekanntes Kapitel der klassisch-romantischen Geschichte Weimars* and *Das Goethe-Tabu: Protest und Menschenrechte im klassischen Weimar.*

ROSMARIE ZELLER is Professor of Modern German Literature at the University of Basel. She specializes in Swiss literature, narratology, poetics, and literary history. Her publications include *Der neue Roman in der Schweiz: Die Unerzählbarkeit der modernen Welt* and *Conrad Ferdinand Meyer im Kontext.*

Index

Abbt, Thomas, 27, 96
absolutism, 1, 38, 266; enlightened, 249, 270–72, 273, 274, 281
Académie Française, 62, 73, 248
Ackermann, Konrad, 170, 171, 192
Acta Eruditorum, 57, 91, 94
Addison, John, 75; work by: *Cato*, 68, 75; *Dream of Religion and Liberty*, 138; editor (with Steele) of: *Guardian*, 81; *Spectator*, 81, 108, 126, 132; *Tatler*, 81
Adorno, Theodor, 304, 305, 307; work by: (with Horkheimer), *Dialektik der Aufklärung*, 299–304
Aesop, 67
aesthetics, 10, 37, 46–49, 71, 96, 156, 285, 286; aesthetic effect, 135
Age of Goethe, 2, 8, 9
Albrecht, Sophie von, 87
Albrecht, Wolfgang, 101, 180
Alewyn, Richard, 30
Allerdissen, Rolf, 225
Alexandrine verse, 69, 138, 158, 249
almanac, 10, 112; literary (*Musenalmanach*) 91–94, 124; *Wiener Musenalmanach*, 253
Alps, 88, 138, 139, 140, 141, 145
Alt, Peter André, 24, 25, 180
Altdorf, 63
Alxinger, Johann Baptist von, 254; work by: *Doolin von Mainz*, 255; *Bliomberis*, 255
Anacreon, 57, 72, 257; Anacreotic poetry, 114, 115, 116, 210; poets, 115; tradition, style, 58, 221
Ancien régime, 285
Anger, Alfred, 123

Anna Amalia, Duchess of Sachsen-Weimar, 4, 203, 204, 206
Ansbach, court at, 186
anthropology, 9, 15, 38
Anton Ulrich of Braunschweig-Lüneburg, Duke of, works by: *Aramena* 30
anti-clericalism, 6, 10, 40, 253
antiquity, 21, 38, 48, 49, 59, 142
Aquinas, Thomas, 36, 38
Arcadia, 131, 139, 146
Aristotle, 13, 38, 66, 67, 172; work by: *Poetics*, 166, 167
Ariosto, 109; work by: *Orlando Furioso*, 107
Arndt, Johann, 45
Arnold, Gottfried, *Unpartheyische Kirchen- und Ketzer-Historie*, 3
Athens, 57
Aufklärung, see Enlightenment
August the Strong, Elector of Saxony and August II of Poland, 58, 187
Austria, 167, 204, 208, 211, 216, 245–63
Austrian literature, 245–63; reforms in, 248–49
autobiography, 31, 146–48, 153, 228, 293
authorship, 16, 80, 269–70
Ayrenhoff, Cornelius von, 251; work by: *Hermanns Tod*, 251

Bach, Johann Sebastian, 58, 185, 186, 193, 216, 218; cantatas and oratorios, 212–13
Bach, Christian Philipp Emanuel, 184, 189, 193; work by: *Versuch über die wahre Art das Klavier zu spielen*, 209

Baden, Grand Duchy of, 26
Bahr, Erhard, 25, 50
Bahrdt, Karl Friedrich, 273
Baker, Keith Michael, 23
Baldinger, Friderika, 18–19, 31; works by: *Versuch über meine Verstandeserziehung,* 18
Ball, Gabriele, 74
ballad opera, English, 204
balladeer (*Bänkelsänger*), 115
Bardoni, Faustina, 187, 189
Barner, Wilfried, 182
baroque era (*Barock*), 3, 24, 25, 67, 131, 247; figure poems, 110; opera, 257; style, 46, 60–61, 63, 67, 134, 255, 258; tradition, 47, 247; tragedy 248
Basel, 63, 161
Basic Law (*Grundgesetz*), 38
Baumann, Gerhart, 26
Baumgarten, Alexander Gottlieb, 47–48, 71
Bavaria, 190, 265, 273, 274
Bayle, Pierre, 41, 57; work by: *Dictionnaire historique et critique,* 34, 95
Bayreuth, court at, 186
Beaugeant, Guillaume-Hyacinthe, work by: *Le Femme docteur,* 68
"beautiful soul," 20, 237–38
beauty, 47–48
Beccaria, Cesare, work by: *Dei delitti e delle penne,* 35
Becker-Cantarino, Barbara, 30, 98, 99, 100, 127, 150, 242, 245, 259, 262, 283
Beethoven, Ludwig van, 185, 191
Béhar, Pierre, 25
Belles Lettres, 16, 21–23, 30, 79, 80, 94, 96
Bender, John, 24
Berghahn, Klaus L., 102
Berlin, 4, 25, 28, 95, 102, 131, 143, 168, 170, 187, 206, 236, 237, 252; enlighteners, 13; musical culture in, 187, 188–89, 207, 210–11; Royal Library, 4

Berlin, Isaiah, 51
Berlinische Monatsschrift, 34, 39, 286, 287
Bern, 63, 138
Bertuch, Friedrich Justin, 100; founder (with Schütz and Wieland) of *Allgemeine Literatur-Zeitung,* 97
Besser, Johann von, 65, 85
Beutin, Wolfgang, 29
Biberach, 12
Bible, 19, 27, 28, 42, 112
Bildung, see education
Bildungsroman, 229
Bismarck, 8, 26
Blackall, Eric A., 73, 74, 123
Blanckenburg, Christian Friedrich von, work by: *Versuch über den Roman,* 230
blank verse, 163, 160, 174, 179
Blumauer, Aloys, 246, 254, 262; work by: *Aeneis travestiert,* 256–57
Blumenberg, Hans, 49,
Boccacio, work by: *Decamerone,* 177
Bode, Johann Joachim Christoph, 11, 240
Bodi, Leslie, 260, 261
Bodmer, Johann Jakob, 5, 12, 74, 82, 84, 85, 88, 95, 107, 113, 125, 126, 142, 143, 149, 150, 152; works by: *Anklagung des verderbten Geschmackes,* 134, 151; *Critische Abhandlung von dem Wunderbaren in der Posie,* 134–36; "Lob der Mundart," 151; editor (with Breitinger) of: *Die Discourse der Mahlern,* 132–33, 151; *Sammlung critischer, poetischer und anderer geistvollen Schriften,* 95
Bohemia, 215
Boie, Heinrich Christian, editor (with Gotter) of *Göttinger Musenalmanach,* 92
Boileau, 65, 57, 110

Bokemeier, Heinrich, 197
book market, 1, 16, 97, 250, 269
book production, 1, 80, 94
Bonds, Mark Evan, 220
bourgeois drama or tragedy, 5, 10, 15–16, 155, 160–68, 173, 174, 175, 176, 179, 258
bourgeoisie, 15, 80, 83, 84, 131, 137, 185, 268, 293
Bovenschen, Silvia, 27, 31
Bräker, Ulrich, 153; work by: *Arme Mann im Tockenburg*, 146–49
Brandes, Helga, 5, 30, 74, 98, 99, 100, 101, 123, 150, 261
Braunschweig, 25, 28, 69, 174, 188, 192
Braunschweig-Wolfenbüttel, court of, 186; Duchess of, 5, 174; Duke of, 173, 174
Brawe, Johann Wilhelm von, work by: *Der Freigeist*, 161, 163, 164
Bremen, 63
Brecht, Martin, 29
Breitinger, Jakob, 82, 84, 85, 107, 136, 137, 141–42, 143, 149, 150; *Critische Dichtkunst*, 10, 74, 134–35, 151; editor (with Bodmer) of: *Die Discourse der Mahlern*, 132–33, 151; *Sammlung critischer, poetischer und anderer geistvollen Schriften*, 95
Briefe die neueste Literatur betreffend, 95–96
Breslau (Wroclaw), 96, 168
Brinker-Gabler, Gisela, 99
broadsheet, 59, 60
Brockes, Barthold Heinrich, 72, 118, 212, 213; work by: *Irdisches Vergnügen in GOTT*, 71, 113, 114, 117, 118, 125
Browning, Robert M., 123
Bruford, W. H., 180
Brüdergemeinde, see Moravian Brethren
Bürger, Bürgertum, see bourgeoisie
Bürger, Gottfried Heinrich, 93, 115
Burgtheater, 173, 201, 205

Buxtehude, Dietrich, 185

calendar, 91–92, 101
Calderon, work by: *La vida is sueño*, 70
Calvinists, 212
Camden House History of German Literature, 2, 25
Campe, Joachim Heinrich, 93, 97, 109; works by: *Väterlicher Rath für meine Tochter*, 240; *Ueber Empfindsamkeit und Empfindelei in pädagogischer Hinsicht*, 12, 235
Canitz, Freiherr Rudolf von, 65, 85; work by: *Neben-Stunden unterschiedener Gedichte*, 126
Carpzov, Benedict, 56
Cassirer, Ernst, 49
Catholics 69; Catholic Church, 41, 68, 164, 236, 246, 247, 252, 256; court, 190, 213, 214; Habsburg; 212; lands, 275; practices, 252; south, 245
Catholicism, 274
Catholy, Eckehart, 180
censorship, 68, 96, 102, 144, 177, 241, 246, 248–49, 252, 253, 259, 275
chancery style (*Kanzleistil*), 61
Christ, Johann Friedrich, 72
Christian Ludwig II, Duke of Mecklenburg-Schwerin, 170
Christian VI, King of Denmark, 170
Christianity, 42, 105, 178, 252, 297
Church, 1, 7, 9; Christian, 177; history, 3; of Brethren, see Moravian Brethren (*Brüdergemeinde*); music, 211–14
Cicero, 64, 73
class, 266–68; aristocracy, 5, 10, 59; clause (*Ständeklausel*), 160; nobility, 266; peasants, 267; structure, 89; urban, bourgeois middle, 1, 4, 10, 14, 23, 24–25,

58, 69, 83, 110–11, 269; upper middle, 18, 59
classicism, German 2, 6, 8, 9, 25, 26, 110, 179; French; 46
Claudius, Matthias, 93, 115, 127; "Abendlied," 115; "Wandsbecker Bote," 115
Code Civil (1804), 38
coffeehouse, 109, 111, 117
Coffey, Charles, work by: *The Devil to Pay*, 203
Collegium musicum, 193, 215
commedia dell'arte, 199, 200, 203, 247, 249
Colvin, Sarah, 109, 181, 218, 219
comedy, 10, 16, 67, 85, 158–60, 168–69; moving ("rührend," *larmoyante*, Saxon tradition), 12, 68, 159; popular, 248
Common Code of Civil Law (*Allgemeines Bürgerliches Gesetzbuch*), 38
Congreve, William, 162
Corneille, Pierre, 200; works by: *Cid*, 68, 74, 173; *Cinna*, 69; *Horace*, 68; *Le mort de Pompée*, 188; *Rodigune*, 172
Corse, Sandra, 219
Cortez, 188
Corvinus, Gottlieb Siegmund, 61–62; work by: *Frauenzimmerlexikon*, 72, 73
Cotta, 90
Cramer, Carl Friedrich, work by: *Magazin der Musik*, 185
Cronegk, Johann Friedrich von, 82, 181; works by: *Codrus*, 163, 166, 168; *Olint und Sophronia*, 163, 171, 177
criticism, 8, 23, 40, 82, 94, 136, 140, 171, 179, 285, 290, 294; literary, 81, 85, 95, 110; Romantic, 292–95; *see also:* Enlightenment, critique of
culture: court, 4, 5, 24, 44; bourgeois literary 4; domestic, 10; musical, 185–216; non-Western, 33

Dacier, Anne, 72
Dainat, Holger, 26
d'Alembert, 35
Damrosch, Leo, 23
Dante, 150
Da Ponte, Lorenzo, 200
Daviau, Donald G., 260
Dawson, Ruth P., 100, 242
drama, 18, 23; reform, 67–68; secular, 69
Declaration of Independence, 38
Defoe, Daniel, 224
Deism, 10, 28, 41, 51
Democritus, 37
Denis, Michael, 250–51; works by: *An den obersten Barden Teuts*, 250; *Gedichte Ossians*, 250; *Lieder Sined des Barden*, 250–51; *Poetische Bilder der meisten kriegerischen Vorgänge*, 251; *Poetisches Sendschreiben an den Herrn Klopstock*, 250
Denmark, 157, 269
Descartes, 35, 36, 37, 42
Deschamp, 75; work by: *Cato d'Utique*, 68
Deutsche (teutsch-übende) Gesellschaft, 59, 62, 63–64, 74, 198, 199
d'Holbach, 34
Diderot, 35, 167, 173, 177, 179, 182; works by: *Contes Morales*, 144; *Le Père de Famille*, 173
Dilthey, Wilhelm, 8
Ditters von Dittersdorf, Karl, 192, operetta by: *Doktor und Apotheker*, 205
Döring, Detlev, 74
Doktor, Wolfgang, 29
Dresden, 4, 25, 56, 61, 69, 71, 213, 214; Zwinger, 186; music in, 187; opera in, 186
Dülmen, Richard van, 27, 281

Dubos, Jean Baptiste, 71, 141; *Réflexions critiques,* 152

early modern period, 3, 24
East Prussia, 4
Ebert, Johann Arnold, 174
education (*Bildung*), 9, 10, 18, 19, 39, 82, 90, 149; German women's, 20, 21, 59
Ehrmann, Marianne, 100; editor of: *Amaliens Erholungsstunden,* 88–89; *Die Einsiedlerin aus den Alpen,* 88–89
Eichendorff, Joseph von, work by: *Geschichte der poetischen Literatur der Deutschen,* 26
Ekhof, Konrad, 170
Elias, Norbert, 99
Elenson, Sophie 69
Eliot, T. S., 28
Elisabeth Christine of Braunschweig-Wolfenbüttel, 188
emancipation, 15, 16, 23, 29; emancipatory aspects, 82, 88, 91, 224, 238, 278, 300
emotions, feelings, 10, 12, 13, 14–15, 20, 22, 107, 120, 227, 239–40; in music (*Affekte*), 196
Empfindsamkeit, see Sensibility
empiricism, 9, 71
Engelhard, Philipine, 87
Engelsing, Rolf, 27, 98
England, 1, 9, 22, 27, 33, 72, 157, 215, 237
Enlightenment, 1, 2, 11, 12, 14, 15, 18, 23, 39–40, 80, 94, 146, 299–304; anti-Enlightenment position, 291–92; as a cultural and literary period, 5–10; Catholic, 5, 245–46; critique of, 285–86, 304–5; culture, 12, 268; journals as medium of, 94–98; in Europe: 33–35, 286; limitations of, 292–95; literary history of, 131; "metacritique" of, 287–92; philosophy, 83, 138; Nietzsche's "New Enlightenment," 296–99;

satire of, 293; values and ideals, 84, 144, 176, 179, 209
enthusiasm (*Schwärmerei*), 229, 240, 242
epic, 17, 28, 116; comic 10; mock-epic, 122; religious, sacred, 10, 13, 105–7; verse, 255
Epicurus, 37
Epicureanism, 108
epigram, 10
Erfurt, 12, 92
Erlangen, 63
essay, 10, 17
ethics, 8, 41, 84, 297, 298
Euripides, 199, 202; work by: *Iphigenia in Tauris,* 156
Europe, 300
Eybl, Franz M., 5, 218, 260, 261, 263, 282

Fabian, Bernhard, 30
family, 19, 176, 282; household, 277
Farinelli, 191
Faulstich, Werner, 98, 99
Fauser, Markus, 123
Federal Republic of Germany, 38
Feind, Barthold, 197, 217, 218; work by: *Simson,* 196
Feuilleton, 94
Fichte, Johann Gottlieb, 20, 30, 37
Fielding, Henry, 230
figures (musical analogies), 196
Flachsland, Caroline, 20, 22, 31
Fontenelle, 56
Forkel, Johann Nikolaus, 217; works by: *Allgemeine Geschichte der Musik,* 195; *Musikalischer Almanach für Deutschland,* 194
Forster, Georg, 90
Foucault, Michel, 12; work by: *Madness and Civilization,* 28
Franck, Wolfgang, opera by: *Cara Mustapha,* 208–9
France, 1, 9, 34, 35, 72, 73, 114, 157, 190, 215, 236
Francke, August Hermann, 14, 45

Frank, Manfred, 50
Frankfurt, 70, 206; book fair, 79
Frankfurt School, 299–304
Franklin, Benjamin, 34, 35
Franz II/I of Austria, Emperor, 246, 260
freedom of the will, 41; of artistic expression, 46
Freemasons, 273; in Vienna, 253
Freemasonry, 258
French Revolution, 5, 14, 25, 80, 89, 100, 176, 255, 271, 274
French literature, 133
Frederik V of Denmark, 157, 170
Friedrich August II of Saxony (August III of Poland), 187
Friedrich Wilhelm I of Prussia (the "Soldier King"), 3, 65, 188
Friedrich II of Prussia ("the Great"), 5, 25, 34, 41, 167, 184, 188, 270, 275; and music: 186, 187–88, 216; work by: *De la Littérature Allemande*, 4
friendship, 14, 21, 22, 118, 121
Füssli, Johann Heinrich, 132, 152
Fux, Johann Joseph, 185, composer of *Constanza e Fortezza*, 191; work by: *Gradus ad Parnassum*, 191–91

Gallas, Helga, 30
Gallant poets, 56
Galli-Bibiena, Alessandro, 190
Galli-Bibiena, Guiseppe, 191
Garber, Klaus, 3, 24
Gatterer, Philippine, 116, 127
Gaus, Detlev, 27
Gay, John, work by: *Beggar's Opera*, 203
Gay, Peter, 25, 50, 52, 122
Gebler, Tobias Philipp Freiherr von, 251
Gellert, Christian Fürchtegott, 10, 12, 15, 24, 27, 71, 110, 112, 115, 123, 177, 181; works by: *Das Leben der schwedischen Gräfin*, 21, 159, 226, 234; *Das Los in der Lotterie*, 159, 169; *Die Betschwester*, 159; *Die zärtlichen Schwestern*, 21, 159–60; *Fabeln und Erzählungen*, 112; *Pro comoedia commovente*, 160–61
gender, 9, 10, 20, 94, 232, 277; dichotomy, 89; roles, 84, 89, 223
gendering of genres, 115
Geneva, 74
Genlis, Madame de, 93
George I of England, 192
Gerhard, Paul, 5
German idealism, 8
German language, 56–57, 61, 62–63
German-speaking areas (countries, lands, territories), 3, 97, 142, 186, 199, 214, 245, 251, 259, 265, 274
Gerstenberg, Heinrich Wilhelm von, 82, 96
Gervinus, Georg Gottfried, 7, 26
Geselligkeit, see sociability
Gessner, Salomon, 112, 131, 138, 144, 146, 152; works by: *Der Tod Abels*, 13; *Idyllen*, 142–45, 152
Gilson, Etienne, 50
Giseke, Nikolaus Dietrich, 82
Gleim, Johann Wilhelm Ludwig, 12, 71, 72, 82, 96, 113, 114, 144, 165, 257; works by: "Aufmunterung zum Spazierengehn," 115; *Preußische Kriegslieder*, 126; *Versuch in scherzhaften Liedern*, 126
Gluck, Christoph Willibald, 200–203, 208; operas by: *Alceste*, 202; *Ataserse*, 201; *Iphigénie en Aulide*, 202; *Iphigénie en Tauride*, 202; *Orfeo ed Euridice*, 202; *Paride ed Helene*, 202; (with Metastasio) *Semiramide riconosciuta*, 201
Goepfert, Herbert, 180
Goslar, 293

INDEX 337

Goethe, Johann Wolfgang von, 5, 6, 8, 24, 26, 28, 37, 47, 48, 86, 87, 109, 138, 174, 182, 270; *Singspiele*, 206–7, 219, 243; poetry, 9; works by: *Claudine von Villa Bella*, 206; *Clavigo*, 179; *Der Triumph der Empfindsamkeit*, 13; *Die Fischerin*, 204; *Die Leiden des jungen Werther*, 12, 28, 111, 145, 235; *Erwin und Elmire*, 206; *Götter, Helden und Wieland*, 204; *Götz von Berlichingen*, 158, 179; *Iphigenie auf Tauris*, 156, 179; *Jery und Bätely*, 206; *Wilhelm Meisters theatralische Sendung*, 180; *Wilhelm Meisters Lehrjahre*, 238
Göttingen, 18, 63, 92, 138
Göttingische Zeitungen von Gelehrten Sachen, 94
Götz, Johann Nikolaus, 114
Goeze, Pastor, 177
Goldoni, Carlo, work by: *La Finta semplice*, 200
Goldsmith, Oliver, work by: *The Vicar of Wakefield*, 206
Goodman, Katherine, 4, 30, 71, 73, 75, 180, 243, 283
Gotter, Wilhelm, editor of *Göttinger Musenalmanach*, 93
Gottsched, Johann Christoph, 3, 4, 10, 13, 21, 28, 34, 54, 55–76, 82, 155, 158, 218; literary feud, 96, 133–35; literary program, 248; theater reform, 167; works by: *Agis, König zu Sparta*, 74; "Akademische Rede...," 74; *Critische Dichtkunst*, 7, 65–67, 74, 134, 181, 201; *Deutsche Sprachkunst*, 62–63; *Die parisische Bluthochzeit*, 75; *Erste Gründe der Weltweisheit*, 63; *Grundriß zu einer vernünftigen Redekunst*, 63–65; *Sterbender Cato*, 68, 69, 74, 161, 167; editor of: *Critische Beyträge*, 63, 64, 74, 95; *Die deutsche Schaubühne*, 10, 67–68, 155, 159; *Das Neueste aus der anmuthigen Gelehrsamkeit*, 64, 74, 125; *Der Biedermann*, 64; *Die vernünftigen Tadlerinnen*, 64; *Neuer Büchersaal*, 64, 74
Gottsched, Luise Adelgunde Victorie, 10, 11, 18, 20, 27, 28, 54, 56, 63–64, 68, 70, 71, 74, 82, 155; works by: *Das Testament*, 68; *Der kleine Prophet von Böhmisch-Broda*, 64; *Der Witzling*, 68; *Die Horatier*, 64, 74; *Die Pietisterey im Fischbeinrocke*, 68, 74; *Die ungleiche Heirat*, 68; *Die Hausfranzösin*, 68; *Panthea*, 74; translations by, 74
Graff, Anton, 284
Graffigny, Françoise de, 68
Graun, Karl Heinrich, 184, 188; operas by: *Cesare e Cleopatra*, 188; *Montezuma*, 188, 216
Greece, 297
Greenblatt, Stephen, 240
Greifswald, 63
Greiner, Caroline (married name Pichler), 253
Grimmelshausen, 91
Grimmiger, Rolf, 14, 29, 98, 123, 225, 240
Grosse, Siegfried, 26
Grotius, Hugo, 38
Grunert, Frank, 24
Günther, Johann Christian, 2, 57–58, 72, 109, 123
Guthke, Karl S., 152

Habermas, Jürgen, 27, 301–4, 307; works by: *Der philosophische Diskurs der Moderne*, 302–3; *Erkenntnis und Interesse*, 303; *Theorie des kommunikativen Handelns*, 303–4
Habermas, Rebecca, 27
Habsburg court, 186, 200
Habsburg Empire, 245, 246–47, 259

338 · INDEX

Hafner, Philipp, 251, work by: *Die bürgerliche Dame*, 251
Hagedorn, Friedrich von, 72, 110, 113, 114, 115; works by: "Die Alster," 117; "Horaz," 126; *Oden und Lieder,* 1126; "Schreiben an einen Freund," 125; *Versuch einiger Gedichte*, 123, 126
Hahn, Karl-Heinz, 21
Halberstadt, 12
Halle, 14, 45, 65, 131; circle of poets, 114, 126
Haller, Albrecht von, 5, 10, 145, 146, 152, 153, 231; works by: *Alfred*, 152; *Die Alpen*, 138–40; *Fabius und Cato*, 152; *Usong*, 152; *Versuch schweizerischer Gedichte*, 71, 137–42
Hamann, Johann Georg, 30, 40, 51, 82, 287–90, 305, 306; works by: *Aesthetica in nuce*, 45; "Brief an Christian Jacob Kraus," 51; *Sokratische Denkwürdigkeiten*, 51–52
Hamburg, 12, 70, 71, 82, 108, 170, 174, 177; music in, 185, 186, 195; musical civic activity, 192–93; Nationaltheater, 5, 163, 169–74; Theater am Gänsemarkt, 192
Hammermeister, Kai, 3, 76
Händel, Georg Friedrich, 185, 192, oratorios, 214; composition by: *Almira, Königin von Castilien*, 192
Hanover, 69, 186, 192
Hanswurst, 70, 201, 244, 247–48, 249; controversy in Austria, 254
happiness, 139, 146
Hart, Gail K., 182
Hasse, Johann Adolf, 187
Hausen, Karin, 277, 282
Haydn, Josef, 185, 192, 208; oratorios, 214; opera by: *Lo Speciale*, 200
Hegel, 7, 25, 48

Heine, Heinrich, 7, 306; work by: *Die Harzreise*, 293
Heinse, Wilhelm, editor (with Jacobi) of *Iris*, 85
Helmstedt, 63
Helvetische Gesellschaft, 150, 153
Helvétius, 35
Hensel, Sophie, 171, 173
Herder, Johann Gottfried, 5, 17, 20, 22, 27, 30, 31, 36, 44, 48, 93, 97, 109, 115, 210, 211, 219, 284, 290–99, 305, 306; works by: *Auch eine Philosophie der Geschichte*, 51, 291–92; *Briefwechsel mit Caroline Flachsland*, 31; *Kalligone*, 198; *Volkslieder*, 115; "Vom Erkennen und Empfinden der menschlichen Seele," 37; "Über die neuere deutsche Literatur," 101
Herman (Arminius) the Cheruskan, 157, 251
Herrnhag, 14
Herrnhut, 14, 45
Herzog, Reinhart, 24
Hess, Jonathan M., 26
Hessen-Darmstadt, 30
Hettner, Hermann, 8
Heuser, Magdalene, 30, 31
hexameter verse, 105
Hezel, Charlotte Henriete von, *Wochenblatt für's Schöne Geschlecht*, 85
Hill, David, 25, 241
Hiller, Johann Adam, 189, 195, 203
Hilliard, Kevin, 5, 76
Hirzel, Caspar, work by: *Die Wirtschaft eines philosophischen Bauern*, 146
history: philosophy of, 43–44; of salvation (*Heilsgeschichte*), 106–7
Hobbes, 38
Hochstrasser, T. J., 24
Hölderlin, 26, 305, 307
Hoffmannswaldau, Christian Hoffmann von, 61, 85

Hofmann, Ernestine, editor of *Für Hamburgs Töchter*, 85
Hoffman, E. T. A., work by: *Lebensansichten des Kater Murr*, 293
Hohendahl, Peter Uwe, 31, 232
Hohenzollern, 187
Holub, Robert, 6, 306
Holy Roman Empire of German Nation, 6, 34, 136, 208, 215, 265
Homer, 66, 105, 109
Horace, 66, 74, 119, *prodesse et delectare*, 121; *ut pictura poesis*, 141; work by: *Odes*, 106
Horkheimer, Max, 304, 305; work by (with Adorno): *Dialektik der Aufklärung*, 299–94
household literature (*Hausväterliteratur*), 92
Hüon of Bordeaux (*Oberon*), 107
Humanism, 3, 24
Humboldt, Wilhelm von, 47, 48
Hume, David, 34
Hungary, 56
Hurlebusch, Klaus, 30
Hutcheson, Francis, works by: *A System of Moral Philosophy*, 13
hymn, 211; free verse, 114, 123; Pietist, 14, 15

idyll, 10, 131, 145
Iffland, Wilhelm 90
Illuminati, 273
imagination, 134–35
Im Hof, Ulrich, 152, 153
imitation, 134–36; of nature, 141
Imperial Diet, 265
intermezzo, 200
Islam, 178
Italian Marinism, 61
Italy, 47, 72, 161, 164, 174, 185, 188, 190, 192, 198, 200, 215, 235, 271, 278

Jacobi, Friedrich Heinrich, 36, 45–46, 97; works by: *Eduard Allwills Papiere*, 45; *Woldemar*, 45
Jacobi, Johann Georg, works by: *Die Winterreise*, 243; *Die Sommerreise*, 243; editor (with Heinse) of *Iris*, 85, 87
Jacobin journals, 100
Jäger, Ernst, 28
Jefferson, Thomas, 34, 35, 37
Jena, 53, 97
Jerusalem, 180
Jerusalem, Friedrich Wilhelm, 28
Jews, 252, 272, 273, 276, 282
Joseph I of Austria, Emperor, 191
Joseph II of Austria, Emperor, 5, 41, 205, 246, 242, 266, 270; reforms by, 252–53
Josephinism, 5, 246, 252–53, 259
journals, 10, 18, 23, 70; Jacobin, 100; medium of the Enlightenment, 79–102; women's, 85–91; review, 98–98
Judaism, 178
Jung, Johann Heinrich (Jung-Stilling), 148, 153; work by: *Heinrich Stillings Jugend*, 153
Juvenal, 257

Kästner, Abraham Gotthelf, work by: "Anakreontische Ode," 126
Kaiser, Gerhard, 125
Kaiser, Gerhard R., 102
Kann, Robert A., 261
Kant, 1, 3, 8, 10, 21, 27, 42, 43, 44, 48, 65, 94, 286, 287–89, 305, 306; works by: *Beobachtungen über das Gefühl des Schönen und Erhabenen*, 30; *Gesammelte Schriften*, 25; "Idee zu einer allgemeinen Geschichte in weltbürgerlicher Absicht," 51; *Kritik der reinen Vernunft*, 41, 51, 288, 290; *Kritik der praktischen Vernunft*, 51; *Kritik der Urteilskraft*, 47; *Was ist Aufklärung?*, 2, 25, 39–40, 51

Karl I of Austria, Emperor, 191
Karl VI of Austria, Emperor, 246, 260
Karl Albrecht, Elector of Bavaria, 190
Karl Philipp, Elector of the Palatinate, 190
Karl Theodor, Elector of the Palatinate, 190, 215
Karsch, Anna Luisa, 2, 104, 112–13, 115, 125, 127, 269
katharsis, 13, 166, 173
Kaufmann, Doris, 28
Keiser, Reinhart, composition by: *Der blutige und sterbende Jesu*, 212; *Fredegunda*, 198–99
Kemper, Hans Georg, 15, 29, 123, 125
Kindermann, Heinz, 9, 26
Kirchgässer, Marianne, 194
Kleist, Ewald von, 96, 112, 128, 143
Kleist, Heinrich von, works by: *Die Hermannsschlacht*, 157; *Über die Aufklärung des Weibes*, 34
Klemm, Christian Gottlob, work by: *Der auf dem Parnass versetzte grüne Hut*, 249
Klinger, work by: *Die Zwillinge*, 158
Klopstock, 10, 12, 17, 21, 22, 27, 30, 45, 71, 108, 110, 112, 113, 125, 143, 250, 270; works by: "An Gleim," 115; bardic dramas, 157; "Das Rosenband," 115; "Die frühen Gräber," 115; "Die Frühlingsfeier," 118; "Die Sommernacht," 115; *Der Messias*, 2, 5, 17, 105–7, 113, 122, 136, 151; "Elegie," 115; *Geistliche Lieder*, 15; *Hermanns Schlacht*, 202; "Kriegslied," 126; *Oden und Elegien*, 17, 115, 122; "Ode von der Fahrt auf der Zürcher See," 118–21
König, Eva, 25

König, Johann Ulrich, 71, 198, 218; libretto by: *Fredegunda*, 198–99
Königsberg, 4, 40, 74
Köster, Albert, 121
Kord, Susanne, 74, 283
Kording, Inka, 28
Korff, August Hermann, 9, 26
Koschorke, Albrecht, 15
Koselleck, Reinhart, 24, 27, 281
Kraus, Christian Jacob, 287
Krause, Christian Gottfried, 197, 218
Krummacher, Hans-Henrik, 123
Kuhnau, Johann, 188–89; work by: *Der musikalische Quacksalber*, 188–89, 195, 216
Kurz, Felix von, 248

Lake Geneva, 145
Lamettrie, 35
Lamport, Francis, 5
Lange, Samuel Gotthold, 82; work by (with Pyra): *Thirsis und Damons freundschaftliche Lieder*, 15
Langen, August, 29
Langensalza, 18
La Roche, Sophie von, 6, 18, 31, 222; social agenda, 233; *Geschichte des Fräuleins von Sternheim*, 12, 22, 232–35, 238; *Pomona*, 18, 30, 86–87, 100; "Ueber das Lesen," 18
Latin, 56, 80, 111, 160, 247
Lavater, Johann Caspar, 17, 97, 177
Le Clerc, 74
Lehms, Georg Christian, work by: *Deutschland galante Poetinnen*, 73
Leibniz, 1, 28, 35, 37, 38, 41, 42, 47, 50, 132, 134, 150; works by: *Ermahnung an die Teutschen, ihren Verstand und Sprache besser zu üben*, 3; *Von der Glückseligkeit*, 50

Leipzig, 56–57, 62, 65, 70, 72, 82, 123, 131, 133, 185, 186, 213, 215; book fair, 4, 79; *Collegium musicum* in, 193; opera house in, 192; Thomasschule, 188; university, 4, 159; university library, 28
Leipziger Taschenbuch für Frauenzimmer, 93–94
leisure, 110–11, 114
Leopold I of Austria, Emperor, 191
Leopold II of Austria, Emperor, 201, 246
Leporin, Dorothea Christiane, 279
Lessing, Gotthold Ephraim, 1, 4, 10, 13, 18, 25, 26, 27, 28, 34, 36, 41, 42, 46, 72, 82, 95–96, 155–65, 271; experiment and theory, 165–68; theater criticism, 168–74; works by: *Das Theater des Herrn Diderot*, 167, 181; *Der junge Gelehrte*, 10, 168; *Die Erziehung des Menschengeschlechts*, 51; *Emilia Galotti*, 5, 173, 174–77, 179, 180, 295; *Hamburgische Dramaturgie*, 13, 165–68, 177, 179; *Laokoon*, 48–49; 141; *Literaturbrief* (seventeenth), 155, 167, 172; *Minna von Barnhelm*, 154, 168–69, 171, 177, 179, 180; *Miß Sara Sampson*, 12, 155, 161–63, 165, 166, 167, 173, 174, 175, 179; *Nathan der Weise*, 41, 52, 174, 177–80, 295; *Philotas*, 167, 174, 176; editor of *Theatralische Bibliothek*, 161
Lessing, Justina Salome, 18
Lichtenberg, Johann Christoph, 27, 93
Lieder (songs), 209–11, 216
Lillo, George, work by: *History of George Barnwell, or The London Merchant*, 161
Lipkin, Lawrence, 23
literacy, 16, 17, 18, 55, 80, 111
literary canon, German, 3
literary history, German, 13–14

literary language, German, 60–63; Swiss, 136–37
literary market, 79–81, 110, 112, 115
literary review, 95–96
literature, 49; autobiographical, 14; classical, 20; devotional 14, 24; didactic, 10; early modern German, 24; English, 23; German eighteenth-century, 3, 5–6; German-language, 4; German Enlightenment 10; imaginative, 110; religious, 10, 18, 19; trivial, 20
Linden Opera (Berlin), 188
Livy, 191 work by: *History of Rome*, 175
Locke, John, 41; work by: *Letters on Toleration*, 34
locus amoenus, 143
Lohenstein, Daniel Caspar von, 61, 85, 134, 138
Lohmeier, Dieter, 122
Löwen, 170–71; work by: *Geschichte des deutschen Theaters*, 170
London, 133, 214
Louis XIV, 73
Lutheranism, orthodox, 56
Luther, Martin, 211, 212
Luther's New Testament, 120

Madland, Helga Stipa, 100
Magdeburg, 17
Mahoney, Dennis, 25
Mannheim, 63, 173, 186, 215; Catholic Court at, 190; School, 190
Marburg, 18
Marpurg, Friedrich Wilhelm, work by: *Anleitung zur Musik*, 210, 219
Maria Antonia Walpurgis, Electress of Saxony, 190–91, composer of *Talestri, regina delle Amazzoni*, 191
Maria Theresia, Archduchess of Austria, 191, 246; era of, 247–49

Martens, Wolfgang, 29, 71, 81, 99, 124
marvelous, the, 134–35
materialism, 35, 41
Mattheson, Johann, 193, 194, 217; works by: *Critica Musica,* 191, 197; *Das neu-eröffnete Orchester,* 196; *Der vollkommene Kapellmeister,* 196–97; composer of *Die Plejades,* 191
Maurer, Michael, 28
Maximilian II Emanuel, Elector of Bavaria, 190
Maximilian III, Elector of Bavaria, 190
McCarthy, John, 99
Medea, 199
Meier, Friedrich Georg, 126
Meise, Helga, 30
Meissen dialect, 63
melancholy, 115, 176
men: young, 10, 22; intellectual, 40; the nation's great, 93
Mencke, Johann Burkhard, 56, 58, 59, 62, 72; editor of *Acta Eruditorum,* 57, 81
Mendelssohn, Moses, 13, 27, 36, 39, 47, 95–96, 97, 101, 165, 177, 182; works by: *Briefe über die Empfindungen,* 15; "Über die Frage: Was heißt aufklären?," 50; editor (with Lessing and Nicolai) of *Briefe die neueste Literatur betreffend,* 165
Metastasio, Pietro, 200, 201, 247; opera by: *La clemenza di Tito,* 200
Mettrie, Julian Offray de la, 231
Meyer, Reinhart, 25
Mexico, 188
Michaelis, Johann David, 101; editor (with Schmidt) of *Almanach der deutschen Musen,* 93
Michelsen, Peter, 28
Middle Ages, 38

Miller, Johann Martin, 93; work by: *Siegwart: eine Klostergeschichte,* 235
Milton, 67, 109, 133–34; work by: *Paradise Lost,* 133
mimesis, 48–49
Mitchell, P. M., 74
Mix, York-Gotthart, 101, 124
modernity, 71
Molière, work by: *Le Misanthrope,* 68
Montesquieu, work by: *Lettres Persanes,* 34
moral-sense philosophy, 13, 14, 35
moral tales, 10, 93, 98, 144
moral weekly, 10, 64, 81–85, 112; *Der Patriot,* 18, 82; *Die vernünftigen Tadlerinnen,* 78, 81, 82, 85, 86; *Der Biedermann,* 81; *Der Gesellige,* 124; *Die Matrone,* 81, 85
morality, 1, 5, 10, 11, 21, 34, 36, 39, 48, 55, 60, 66, 69, 82, 83, 135, 138, 145, 166, 268, 272, 273, 280, 281, 293, 298, 299, 303
Moravian Brethren (Church of), 14, 45
Moore, Edward, work by: *The Gamester,* 161
Moorhof, Daniel Georg, work by: *Unterricht von der Teutschen Sprache,* 63
Moritz, Karl Philipp, 6, 27, 47, 148; works by: *Anton Reiser,* 10; *Magazin der Erfahrungsseelenkunde,* 13
Mozart, Maria Anna "Nannerl," 194
Mozart, Leopold, 198, 217; *Versuch zu einer gründlichen Violinschule,* 196
Mozart, Wolfgang Amadeus, 185, 192, 194, 197–98; church music, 214; compositions by: *Die Zauberflöte,* 205, 206, 257–59; *Entführung aus dem Serail,* 205,

207–9; *La clemenza di Tito*, 200–201
Müller, Johann Gottwerth ("von Itzehoe"), 112; work by: *Gedichte der Freundschaft*, 124
Munck, Thomas, 49
Munich, 4, 215; musical culture in, 190–91; Residenztheater, 190
Muralt, Béat Louis de, work by: *Lettres sur les Anglois et François*, 138
music: a European culture, 214–16; centers of, 186–93; church music, 211–14; in Germany and Austria, 185; review journals of, 195; score versus libretto, 197–98; theory of, 195–97

Naples, 214
Napoleon, 6, 34, 157
Nasse, Peter, 99
National Socialism, 300
National Socialist ideology, 9
nature, 1, 36
natural law, 1, 3, 24, 27, 37–39
Neology, 10, 27
neoclassicism, 10, 60–61
neo-Romantic movement, 8
Nestroy, Johann Nepomuk, 249
Netherlands, the, 44, 56, 74
Neuber, Caroline Friderike, 69–70, 155, 168; "Das Schäferfest oder die Herbstfreude," 70; *Der allerkostbarste Schatz*, 70
Neuber, Johann, 69
Neumeister, Erdmann, 65; work by: *Madrigalische Cantaten*, 212
Newald, Richard, 24
Nicolai, Friedrich, 13, 27, 95–96, 102, 157, 166; works by: *Freuden des jungen Werthers*, 13; editor of: *Allgemeine Deutsche Bibliothek*, 96–97, 101, 150; *Bibliothek der schönen Wissenschaften und der freyen Künste*, 95, 163

Nietzsche, 8, 304, 305, 306, 307; work by: *Menschliches, Allzumenschliches*, 296–99
nobility, 15, 17
Nohl, Hermann, 9, 26
North America, 33, 37
Novalis, 26, 45; works by: "Die Christenheit oder Europa," 52
novel, 10, 17, 18, 23, 59, 87; epistolary, 21–22, 234; of adventure, 227

ode, religious, 114, 116
Öffentlichkeit, see public sphere
opera buffa, 198
opéra comique, 202, 203
opera seria, 190, 198, 200
opera, German and Italian, 198–200; German-language, 201; reform of, 200–202
Opitz, Martin, 47, 85; work by: *Buch von der deutschen Poeterey*, 72
orientalism, 207–9
Ottoman Empire, 208
Ovid, work by: *Amores*, 57

Paine, Thomas, 35
Palatine National Theater, 173
Palestrina, Giovanni Perluigi, 192
Pantheism, 10, 36
Pape, Helmut, 3
Paradis, Maria Theresia von, 194
Paris, 57, 80, 202, 214
Peace of Baden, 190
Pelagius, 41
Perinet, Joachim, work by: *Kasperl, der Fagotist*, 258
Pestalozzi, Johann Heinrich, 131; work by: *Lienhard und Gertrud*, 149–50
Petrasch, Joseph von, 248
Pezzl, Johann, 254–55, 262; works by: *Faustin* 25, 254
Pfeffel, Konrad Gottlieb, 90, 93

Pfeil, Johann Gottlieb Benjamin, work by: *Lucie Woodvil*, 161, 162, 181
Physico-Theology, 10, 27
Pietism, 8, 10, 13–14, 29, 45, 147, 223, 274
Pietists, 19, 65, 68, 212; Pietist circles 1, 18,
Pietsch, Johann Valentin, 66, 74
Pikulik, Lothar, 14–15, 29
Plato, 38
poetics, 133–36; academic, 110; normative, 136
poetry, 10, 16, 17, 23, 29, 49, 59, 67; aesthetic and social determinants, 109–14; anonymous "street," 57; bardic, 250, 259; devotional 18, 112; didactic, 138; erotic, 10, 25, 57; gallant, 134; lyric, 15, 114–15; occasional, 10, 57, 58, 73, 112, 251; of pleasure, 117–21; patriotic, 10; secular 18, 30; religious, 10, 73; theory of, 66–67
Poland, 56, 168, 215
Pope, Alexander, 110, 138; work by: *Essay on Criticism*, 95
Postel, Christian Heinrich, 199
Potsdam, 189
Pott, Martin, 27
Pradon, Nicolas, works by: *Regulus, Brutus, Alexander*, 74
Prague, 191, 201
Prehauser, Gottfried, 248
print medium, 55, 79
Promies, Wolfgang, 123, 125
Protestant church, 45, 214; city, 132, 144; ethics, 84; lands, 6, 14, 167, 212, 257, 274–75
Protestantism, 7, 44, 257
Protestants, 69, 212
Prussia, 102, 167–68, 187, 245, 246, 259, 270, 275, 276
Prussian-Austrian conflict, 5, 250, 254, 259
Prussian General Code, 34
précieuses, 59

public sphere (*Öffentlichkeit*), 10, 27, 79; woman in, 90
Pütz, Peter, 25, 182
Pufendorf, Samuel, 3, 38
Pyra, Jacob, 82; works by (with Lange): *Thirsis und Damons freundschaftliche Lieder*, 15

Quantz, Johann Joachim, 184; works by: *Neue Kirchenmelodien*, 211; *Versuch einer Anweisung die Flöte traversière zu spielen*, 189, 216
Quintilian, 64; work by: *Institutio oratoria*, 125
querelle des femmes, 85

Rabener, Gottlieb Wilhelm, 82
Racine, 200, 202; works by: *Berenice*, 69; *Iphigenie*, 68, 69
Raimund, Ferdinand, 249
Rammler, Karl Wilhelm, 161, 210
rationalism, 7, 9, 35, 55, 56; anti-rationalist tendencies, 44–46
Ratner, G. Leonard, 217
Ratschky, Joseph Franz, 254, 262; work by: *Melchior Striegel*, 255
readership, 142, 146
reading, 1, 9, 30, 80, 85, 98, 121; debate about, 16; reading mania ("Lesewut"), 80 public, 16, 22–23, 59, 105, 112, 113; reading societies, 17, 98, 108, 111, 147
reason, 1, 3, 10, 20, 22, 33, 36, 40, 42, 44, 49, 55, 66, 67, 82, 288, 289, 290–91; 293
Recke, Elisa von, 87
Redekop, Benjamin W., 27
Reformation, 24
Regensburg, 265
Reill, Hans Peter, 23
religion, 105–7, 178; philosophy of 40–43
religious life, 274–76
Reichardt, Friedrich, 206; compositions by: *Wiegenlieder für gute deutsche Mütter*, 210

Renaissance, 24, 25, 91
Reimarus, Hermann Samuel, 42
Reitz, Johann Heinrich, works by: *Historie der Wiedergebohrnen,* 14, 28
Restoration period, 34
Retzer, Friedrich von, 254
Revolution of 1848, 26
Richards, Anna, 6
Richardson, Samuel, 11, 22; *Clarissa,* 13, 22, 162, 226; *Pamela,* 13, 226; *Sir Charles Grandison,* 13, 161
rococo, 45, 114
Richelieu, 73
Robertson, J. G., 182
Rochlitz, Johann Friedrich, editor of *Allgemeine Musikalische Zeitung,* 215
Romanticism, German, 2, 6, 8, 9, 25, 28, 292–93
Romantics, 305
Rorty, Richard, 1, 23
Rosenberg, Rainer, 26
Rost, Johann Christoph, work by: *Das Vorspiel,* 70
Rousseau, Jean-Jacques, 12, 35, 43, 88, 89, 131; works by: *Confessions,* 147; *Contrat sociale,* 149; *Discours sur l'inégalité,* 13; *Emile,* 278; *Julie ou La Nouvelle Heloïse,* 16, 145
Rousseau, Jean-Baptiste, 116, 223
Rowe, Nicholas, work by: *Lady Jane Gray,* 163
Runckel, Dorothea Henriette von, 11
Russia, 56, 70

Sachsen-Weimar-Eisenach, Duchy of, 4
Salieri, Antonio, 192
Salzburg, 214
Sasse, Günter, 182
Sauder, Gerhard, 14, 29, 153, 237, 241, 282
Sanssouci, 184
Saxony, 4, 45, 63, 136, 168, 265
Scaliger, Julius Caesar, work by: *Poetices,* 72
Scheffner, Johann George, works by: "Einladung auf das Feld," 18; "Ermunterung zum Vergnügen," 118; *Gedichte im Geschmack des Grecourt,* 128
Scheibe, Johann Adolph, 217; work by: *Compendium Musices,* 196
Scheibel, Gottfried Ephraim, work by: *Die unerkannten Sünden der Poeten,* 72, 122; "Von der Poeten Bettelei," 125
Schelling, 46, 48, 49
Schenda, Rudolf, 98
Schenk, Friederike Marie Charlotte von, work by: *Versuche in Gedichten,* 127
Scherer, Wilhelm, 8, 26
Scheyb, Franz Christoph von, work by: *Theresiade: Ein Ehrengedicht,* 248–49
Schikaneder, 204–5, 257; libretto by: *Die Zauberflöte,* 204, 257–59
Schiller, Friedrich, 7, 8, 47; works by: *Die Räuber,* 158, 179; *Kabale und Liebe,* 179; *Über die ästhetische Erziehung des Menschen,* 40, 51, 48; *Über naive und sentimentalische Dichtung,* 107; *Wilhelm Tell,* 131, 140
Schings, Hans-Jürgen, 27, 28
Schlegel, Friedrich, works by: *Athenäum,* 6, 307; "Über Lessing," 294–95
Schlegel, Johann Elias, 82, 156–59, 179, 181; works by: *Canut,* 157–58, 167, 177; *Der geschäftige Müßiggänger,* 158–59; *Der Triumph der guten Frauen,* 158; *Dido,* 157; *Die Trojanerinnen,* 156; *Die stumme Schönheit,* 158–59; *Gedanken zur Aufnahme des dänischen Theaters,* 170; *Hermann,* 157; *Orest und Pylades,* 156, 158, 163, 179;

"Von der Würde und Majestät des Ausdrucks im Trauerspiel," 181; *Von Errichtung eines Theaters in Kopenhagen,* 170
Schleiermacher, Friedrich, 46
Schlözer, Dorothea, 279
Schmähling, Gertud Elisabeth ("die Mara"), 189
Schmid, Christian Heinrich: editor (with Michaelis) of *Almanach der deutschen Musen,* 93; editor of *Anthologie der Deutschen,* 123
Schmidt, James, 23, 306
Schnabel, Johann Gottfried, 24, 223; work by: *Wunderliche Fata einiger Seefahrer (Insel Felsenburg),* 224–25, 234
Schneider, Karl Ludwig, 121, 128
Schön, Erich, 27, 30, 101
Schöne Literatur, see *Belles Lettres*
Schönemann, J. F., 170
schöne Seele, see "beautiful soul"
Scholasticism, 36, 56
Scholze, Johan Sigismund, work by: *Sperontes Singende Muse an der Pleisse,* 210
Schrader, Hans-Jürgen, 29
Schröter, Corona, 189, 206
Schubart, Christian Friedrich Daniel, 219; work by: *Ideen zu einer Ästhetik der Tonkunst,* 207
Schulpforta, 156
Schulz, Gerhard M., 181
Schulz, Johann Abraham Peter, work by: *Lieder im Volkston,* 211
Schummel, Johann Gottlieb, work by: *Empfindsame Reisen durch Deutschland,* 243
Schwarz, Sibylle, work by: *Deutsche Poetische Gedichte,* 30
Schwerin, 170
Scudéry, Madelaine, 58, 70; works by: *Conversations,* 59, 73; *Les Bains de Thermopylae,* 59, 73
Second Silesian School, 61
secret societies, 272–74
secular, secularization, 9, 80, 105

Secundus, Johannes, 58
Seifert, Siegfried, 102
Selwyn, Pamela E., 102
Seneca, 156
Sensibility (*Empfindsamkeit*), 2, 5, 6, 10, 18–23, 28, 29, 40, 86, 115, 173, 176, 211, 226, 227, 229, 231, 232, 234; as a literary period, 11–16, 46, 88, 97, 159, 223–24, 240, 246; 275, 279; pathologized as hypochondria, 236–37; values of, 223
sentimentality, 14, 235
Seven Years' War, 96, 147, 167, 168, 187, 250
Shaftesbury, Earl of, 13, 35, 138
Shakespeare, 67, 133, 150, 172; work by: *Richard III,* 165
Sheehan, James J., 280
Sibylle Ursula of Braunschweig-Lüneburg, 30
Silesia, 63, 187
Simons, Olaf, 24
Singspiel, 174, 192, 203, 204–7, 215, 216, 254
Smart, Sara, 217
Smeed, J. W., 219
Smith, Adam, 35, work by: *Lectures on Rhetoric and Belles-Lettres,* 127
sociability, 10, 14, 16, 18, 23, 59, 61, 114, 118, 143, 178, 280
Sonnenfels, Joseph von, 82, 262; reforms, 247–49, 251–52; works by: *Briefe über die wienerische Schaubühne,* 249, *Über den Geschäftsstyl,* 251; *Über die Abschaffung der Tortur,* 251; editor of *Der Mann ohne Vorurteil,* 249
Spalding, Johann Joachim, 17, 28
Spener, Johann Jakob, 14, 45
Spee, Friedrich von, 38
Spinoza, 35, 36, 41, 45, 50; works by: *Ethica,* 36, 37
St. Petersburg, 155
Stamitz, Johann, 190
Ständeklausel, see "class clause"

Steele, Richard, work by: *The Conscious Lover*, 159; editor (with Addison) of: *Tatler*, 81; *Spectator*, 81, 132; *Guardian*, 81
Steinmetz, Horst, 180, 181
Stenzel, Jürgen, 123
Sterne, Laurence, 112; work by: *Sentimental Journey*, 11, 235, 240
Stockfleth, Margarethe, work by: *Die Kunst- und Tugendgezierte Macarie*, 30
Storm and Stress (*Sturm und Drang*), 2, 6, 8, 9, 14, 158
Stranitzky, Joseph Anton, 244, 247–48
Sturz, Peter Helfrich, 124
Stuttgart, 4, 214
Sulzer, Johann Georg, 96
Swift, Jonathan, 257
Switzerland, 63, 71, 131–50

Taylor, William, of Norwich, work by: *Historic Survey of German Poetry*, 106, 108, 122
Telemann, Georg Philipp, 193; composition by: *Die ungleiche Heirath (Pimpinone)*, 198, 200
Tersteegen, Gerhard, 123
Teuber, Anna Barbara, 112, 116, 127; work by: *Vermischte Gedichte*, 124
theater, 25, 69; court, 247; national (German-language), 1, 155; of religious orders, 247; popular, 6, 247–49; reform, 69
Theocritus, 145
Thirty Years' War, 265
Thomasius, Christian, 1, 3, 34, 38, 50; works by: *Das Recht Evangelischer Fürsten in theologischen Streitigkeiten*, 3; *De crimine magiae*, 56; editor of *Monatsgespräche*, 81
Thomson, 110, 112

Thümmel, Moritz August von, work by: *Reise in die mittäglichen Provinzen*, 235–38
Timme, Christian Friedrich, 237
Todd, Janet, 28, 181, 240
tolerance, 82, 264
tragedy, 10, 13, 28, 67, 85; bourgeois, 160–68, 176; Christian martyr, 163; heroic, neoclassical, 156, 163; unities, 164, 180
Trattner, Johann Thomas von, 250
travel narrative, 10
traveling acting company, 69
Treaty of Westphalia, 265, 274
Triller, Daniel Wilhelm, 72

Ungar, Rolf, 292, 306
Unger, Friederike Helene, 6; works by: *Julchen Grünthal*, 10; *Bekenntnisse einer schönen Seele*, 238–40, 243
Ungern-Sternberg, Wolfgang von, 98, 124
Unzer, Ludwig August, work by: "Der Winter," 123, 124
urbanity, 114, 125
utopia, 149
Uz, Johann Peter, 82, 114; *Lyrische Gedichte*, 126

Venice, 198, 199, 200, 214
Vienna, 4, 61, 63, 100, 170, 173, 202, 205, 206, 207, 208, 213, 214, 247, 248, 252, 265; musical culture in, 186, 191–92; Theater am Kärntnertor, 247
Vienna Congress, 34
Viennese genres, 253–59
Virgil, 66, 105, 109
Voltaire, 35, 41, 46, 164, 172, 173; works by: *Alzire*, 68, 188; *Candide*, 42, 254; *Zaire*, 68; *Siècle de Louis XIV*, 25
Vorderstemann, Jürgen, 100
Voss, Johann Heinrich, 17, 93
Vosskamp, Wilhelm, 26

Waldstein, Edith, 243
wandering minstrels, 69
War of the Austrian Succession, 187, 190, 246
War of the Spanish Succession, 187
Ward, Albert, 98
Watanabe O'Kelly, Helen, 24, 25
Weckel, Ulrike, 27, 86, 99, 100
Wegmann, Nikolaus, 29
Wekhrlin, Ludwig, 80
Wehler, Hans-Ulrich, 280
Weimar, 203, 204, 205
Weishaupt, Adam, 273
Weisse, Christian Felix, 101, 164–65; works by: *Atreus und Thyest*, 164; *Die Befreiung von Theben*, 164; *Die verschmähten Weiber oder Der Teufel ist los*, 181, 203; *Die verwandelten Weiber*, 202; *Jean Calas*, 164; *Richard III*, 164–65, 173, 182, 183; *Romeo und Julie*, 164; *Rosamunde*, 164
Weißenfels, 69; court at, 186
Wetzlar, 265
Wezel, Johann Carl, work by: *Belphegor*, 42, 51; *Wilhelmine Arend*, 235
Wieland, 5, 6, 10, 12, 15, 17, 27, 46, 71, 96, 143, 218, 232; and the *Singspiel*, 204–5; works by: *Agathon*, 229–32, 241; *Alceste*, 204; *Aurora*, 204; "Briefe an einen jungen Dichter," 122; *Clementina von Porretta*, 161; *Comische Erzählungen*, 126; *Dschinnistan*, 258; *Lady Johanna Gray*, 163, 165; *Musarion*, 126; *Oberon*, 107–9, 111, 122; *Rosamunde*, 204; "Versuch über das deutsche Singspiel," 204; editor of *Teutsche Merkur*, 7, 101, 125; founder (with Bertuch and Schütz) of *Allgemeine Literatur-Zeitung Jena*, 97
Wilke, Jürgen, 99
Wilkinson, E. M, 181
Wilson, Dan, 6, 281

Winckelmann, Johann Joachim, 34; work by: *Gedanken über die Nachahmung der griechischen Werke in der Malerey und Bildhauerkunst*, 48
Wirtz, Thomas, 181
Wittman, Reinhard, 80, 98, 99
Wobeser, Elisa, work by: *Elisa oder das Weib wie es seyn sollte*, 238
Wolfenbüttel, 25, 197; opera, 199
Wolff, Christian, 1, 35, 42, 47, 56, 64, 65, 66, 70, 72, 134
Wolzogen, Caroline von, 87
women, 111, 113, 276–78; and music, 194–95; aristocratic, 30; authors, 10; bourgeois 1; "destiny" (*Bestimmung*), 88, 90; education, 84; learned, 11, 20; library for, 84; literary, 278; poetry by, 127; reading, 16, 17–18, 20–21, 22, 30, 80, 85, 89; upper-middle class, 4; writing by, 115–17

Zachariae, Friedrich Just, works by: *Der Renommiste*, 122; *Das Schnupftuch*, 122
Zammito, John H., 27
Zäunemann, Sidonia, 92, 127, 278; works by: *Die von den Faunen gepeitschte Laster*, 123; "Landtag...," 116; *Poetische Rosen in Knospen*, 124
Zarlino, Gioseffo, work by: *Le istitutioni harmoniche*, 197
Zeller, Rosmarie, 5, 75, 99, 107
Zemann, Herbert, 72, 260
Zeno, Apostolo, 200, 247
Ziegler, Christiane Mariane von, 4, 57, 58–60, 70, 75, 212–13, 278; *Versuch in gebundener Schreibart*, 59, 72, 220; *Moralische und Vermischte Sendschreiben*, 59, 72; "Verteidigung des P. Cerceau...," 73; translations by: 73

Zinzendorf, Nikolaus Ludwig von, 14, 45, 123, 125; works by: *Teutsche Gedichte,* 15, 122

Zurich, 12, 82, 131, 144; poets, 132–36